AF839314

Metaphor

Embodied Cognition and Discourse

Metaphor theory has shifted from asking whether metaphor is "conceptual" or "linguistic" to debating whether it is "embodied" or "discursive." Although recent work in the social and cognitive sciences has yielded clear opportunities to resolve that dispute, the divide between discourse- and cognition-oriented approaches has remained. To unite the field, this book brings together leading metaphor researchers from a number of disciplines. It collects major arguments and presents a wide variety of empirical evidence, placing special emphasis on the embodiment and sociocultural embeddedness of cognition, as well as the multimodal and social-interactive nature of communication. It shows that metaphor theory cannot but profit from an approach that takes multiple perspectives into consideration and tries to account for findings yielded by multiple methodologies. By doing so, it works toward a dynamic, multidimensional, socio-cognitive model of metaphor that goes beyond what research traditions have separately achieved.

BEATE HAMPE received a Ph.D. in English Linguistics from Jena University (Germany) and was appointed Professor of Language and its Structure at the University of Erfurt (Germany) in 2009, where she currently teaches English linguistics, cognitive linguistics, and corpus linguistics. Hampe has worked on various topics in image schema theory, conceptual metaphor theory, and cognitive usage-based construction grammar. She is the author of *Superlative Verbs* (2002) and the editor of *From Perception to Meaning: Image Schemas in Cognitive Linguistics* (2005).

Metaphor

Embodied Cognition and Discourse

Edited by

Beate Hampe

Universität Erfurt, Germany

CAMBRIDGE
UNIVERSITY PRESS

CAMBRIDGE
UNIVERSITY PRESS

University Printing House, Cambridge CB2 8BS, United Kingdom

One Liberty Plaza, 20th Floor, New York, NY 10006, USA

477 Williamstown Road, Port Melbourne, VIC 3207, Australia

4843/24, 2nd Floor, Ansari Road, Daryaganj, Delhi – 110002, India

79 Anson Road, #06–04/06, Singapore 079906

Cambridge University Press is part of the University of Cambridge.

It furthers the University's mission by disseminating knowledge in the pursuit of education, learning, and research at the highest international levels of excellence.

www.cambridge.org
Information on this title: www.cambridge.org/9781107198333
DOI: 10.1017/9781108182324

© Cambridge University Press 2017

This publication is in copyright. Subject to statutory exception and to the provisions of relevant collective licensing agreements, no reproduction of any part may take place without the written permission of Cambridge University Press.

First published 2017

Printed in the United Kingdom by Clays, St Ives plc

A catalogue record for this publication is available from the British Library.

Library of Congress Cataloging-in-Publication Data
Names: Hampe, Beate, editor.
Title: Metaphor : embodied cognition and discourse / edited by Beate Hampe, Universität Erfurt, Germany.
Description: Cambridge : Cambridge University Press, 2017. | Includes bibliographical references and index.
Identifiers: LCCN 2016059378 | ISBN 9781107198333 (hardback : alk. paper)
Subjects: LCSH: Cognitive neuroscience. | Metaphor. | Psycholinguistics.
Classification: LCC QP360.5 .M477 2017 | DDC 612.8/233–dc23
LC record available at https://lccn.loc.gov/2016059378

ISBN 978-1-107-19833-3 Hardback

Cambridge University Press has no responsibility for the persistence or accuracy of URLs for external or third-party internet websites referred to in this publication and does not guarantee that any content on such websites is, or will remain, accurate or appropriate.

Contents

Figures

Tables

Contributors

GIORGIO A. ASCOLI received a Ph.D. in Biochemistry and Neuroscience from the Scuola Normale Superiore of Pisa, Italy, and continued his research at the National Institutes of Health in Bethesda, MD, to investigate protein structure and binding in the nervous system. He moved to George Mason University in 1997, where he is University Professor in the Bioengineering Department and Neuroscience Program. He is also founder and director of the Center for Neural Informatics at the Krasnow Institute for Advanced Study and founding editor-in-chief of the journal *Neuroinformatics*.

DANIEL CASASANTO is Professor of Psychology at the Department of Psychology and director of the Experience & Cognition Laboratory of the University of Chicago. He has worked and published extensively on metaphor in thought. He acts as a general editor of the journal *Language and Cognition* and is the scientific director and co-founder of THE THINK TANK (thinktank.uchicago.edu).

VALENTINA CUCCIO received a Ph.D. in Philosophy of Language and of Mind from the University of Palermo. She has done postdoctoral research at the University of Parma (Dept. of Neuroscience), John Hopkins University (Dept. of Cognitive Science), the University of Amsterdam, Humboldt University (Berlin School of Mind and Brain), as well as the University of Palermo (Dept. of Humanities). Her research interests range from philosophy to neuroscience, psychology, and cognitive linguistics. Cuccio has published on language and embodied cognition, especially embodied simulation (also with Vittorio Gallese), and is currently working on the embodiment of metaphor (with Gerard Steen).

ALICE DEIGNAN is Professor of Applied Linguistics in the School of Education, University of Leeds. She works with corpora to investigate lexical meaning, focusing on metaphor and metonymy. She is interested in cross-register variation and its implications for non-expert language users such as young people and language learners. She is the author of *Metaphor and Corpus Linguistics* (2005) and co-author of *Figurative Language,*

Genre and Register (Cambridge University Press, 2013). Deignan serves as an associate editor of the journal *Metaphor and the Social World* and is on the editorial boards of *Metaphor and Symbol,* the *Review of Cognitive Linguistics*, and *Empirical Language Research.*

ZSÓFIA DEMJÉN is Senior Lecturer in Applied Linguistics at University College London, Institute of Education, specializing in health communication, metaphor, and the intersections of language, mind, and health(care). She is author of *Sylvia Plath and the Language of Affective States: Written Discourse and the Experience of Depression* (2015) and co-editor of *The Routledge Handbook of Metaphor and Language* (2017). She has published in the journals *Journal of Pragmatics*, *Applied Linguistics*, *Metaphor and the Social World*, and the *BMJ's Medical Humanities*, among others.

CHARLES J. FORCEVILLE is Associate Professor in the Media Studies Department at the University of Amsterdam. He has pioneered the study of visual and multimodal metaphor in various genres and media (advertising, documentary, feature film, animation, comics, cartoons). More recently, he has worked on multimodality in argumentation and narrative discourse as well as on the application of relevance theory to mass-communicative visuals. He co-edited *Multimodal Metaphor* (2009) and *The Agile Mind* (2013) and serves on the advisory boards of several journals, including *Metaphor and Symbol*, *Journal of Pragmatics*, *Public Journal of Semiotics*, and the *Review of Cognitive Linguistics.*

RAYMOND W. GIBBS, JR. is Distinguished Professor of Psychology at the Department of Psychology, University of California at Santa Cruz. His extensive and widely influential research on embodied cognition, especially image schemas and metaphor, has been published in major journals of the cognitive and language sciences. Among others, Gibbs is the author of *The Poetics of Mind* (Cambridge University Press, 1994) and *Embodiment and Cognitive Science* (Cambridge University Press, 2006), as well as the editor of the journal *Metaphor and Symbol* and of *The Cambridge Handbook of Metaphor in Language and Thought* (Cambridge University Press, 2008). His most recent work is *Metaphor Wars: Conceptual Metaphor in Human Life* (Cambridge University Press, 2017).

JOSEPH E. GRADY received his Ph.D. in linguistics from the University of California at Berkeley and taught linguistics at the University of Maryland and Georgetown University. He has explored fundamental cognitive and linguistic aspects of metaphor, emphasizing "primary metaphor," an idea proposed in early publications. Grady is the co-founder of Cultural Logic and more recently the Topos Partnership, firms that use cognitive and social science approaches to develop effective ways of communicating about public interest topics.

BEATE HAMPE was appointed Professor of Language and its Structure at the University of Erfurt (Germany) in 2009, where she currently teaches English linguistics, cognitive linguistics, and corpus linguistics. Hampe has published on various topics in cognitive linguistics, especially image schema theory, conceptual metaphor theory, and cognitive usage-based construction grammar. She is the author of *Superlative Verbs* (2002) and the editor of *From Perception to Meaning: Image Schemas in Cognitive Linguistics* (2005).

THOMAS W. JENSEN is Associate Professor at the Department of Language and Communication, Centre for Human Interactivity at the University of Southern Denmark. His research centers on multimodality and metaphor(icity) in social interaction, emphasizing an ecological approach to cognition, emotion, and theory of science. He is the author of *Kognition og Konstruktion* (2011) as well as the editor of the journal *Nydanske Sprogstudier* (NyS) and has published in journals such as *Metaphor and Symbol*, *Frontiers in Psychology*, and *Cognitive Semiotics*.

GINA JOUE is a member of the Department of Neurosciences, Biomedicine and Movement Sciences at the University of Verona. She studied cognitive science with an emphasis on language and mind at the University of California at Berkeley and Ben-Gurion University (Israel), and with a computational twist at the University of Edinburgh and University College Dublin. Joue's research is strongly interdisciplinary, her recent work in cognitive neuroscience focused on abstract cognition in multimodal communication (RWTH Aachen, Germany) and the visual, attentional, and memory processes that have an impact on it.

JEANNETTE LITTLEMORE is Professor of Applied Linguistics in the Department of English Language and Applied Linguistics at the University of Birmingham. Her research focuses on metaphor and metonymy in cross-cultural communication and language learning. Her main publications include: *Figurative Thinking and Foreign Language Learning* (with Graham Low, 2006); *Applying Cognitive Linguistics to Second Language Learning and Teaching* (2009); *Figurative Language, Genre and Register* (with Alice Deignan and Elena Semino, Cambridge University Press, 2013); and *Metonymy: Hidden Shortcuts in Language, Thought and Communication* (Cambridge University Press, 2015).

TEENIE MATLOCK is Professor of Cognitive Science and McClatchy Chair in Communications at the University of California, Merced, where she does research at the intersection of cognitive linguistics and psycholinguistics. Her research examines how people interpret and use everyday language, especially non-literal language, and its relation to everyday thought and reasoning. She is associate editor for the journal *Cognitive Linguistics* and serves on the editorial boards of *Metaphor and Thought* and *Environmental Communication*. She also serves on the Governing Board for the Cognitive Science Society.

IRENE MITTELBERG is Professor of Linguistics and Cognitive Semiotics at the Institute of English, American and Romance Studies at RWTH Aachen University, where she directs the Natural Media Lab and the Center for Sign Language and Gesture (SignGes). Mittelberg received a Ph.D. in Linguistics and Cognitive Studies from Cornell University; her interdisciplinary research on embodied cognition, language, visual art, and gesture has emphasized the role of metonymy and image schemas in multimodal communication. Mittelberg is co-editor of *Empirical Methods in Cognitive Linguistics* (2006) and serves on the advisory board of the journal *Cognitive Semiotics*.

CORNELIA MÜLLER is Professor of Language Use and Multimodal Communication at the European University Viadrina, Frankfurt/Oder, Germany. She has published on multimodal forms of language use, focusing on embodied processes of meaning emergence in co-speech gestures as well as on the experiential dynamics of metaphoric meaning in speech, gestures, and audio-visual media. Müller is the author of *Redebegleitende Gesten* (1998) and of *Metaphors Dead and Alive, Sleeping and Waking* (2008). She is also the editor-in-chief of *Body–Language–Communication: An International Handbook on Multimodality in Human Interaction* (2014).

ROY PORAT works as a researcher and teaching fellow at the School of Cultural Studies as well as the School of Philosophy at Tel Aviv University. He is a Ph.D. candidate in psycholinguistics, his main areas of research being the relation between language and thought, metaphor and conceptual structure, and synesthesia. He is simultaneously a Ph.D. candidate and a teaching fellow at the Department of East Asian Studies in Tel Aviv University, specializing in Early Chinese (Daoist) philosophy. Porat has published on the psycholinguistics of metaphor (with Yeshayahu Shen) and on Chinese philosophy of language.

L. DAVID RITCHIE is Professor of Communication at Portland State University in Portland, Oregon (USA). His primary research focus is metaphor use, storytelling, and humor in naturally occurring discourse including conversation, political speeches, and environmental communication. He is the author of three books on metaphor, *Context and Connection in Metaphor* (2006), *Metaphor* (Cambridge University Press, 2013), and *Metaphorical Stories in Discourse* (Cambridge University Press, 2017).

FRANCISCO J. RUIZ DE MENDOZA IBÁÑEZ is Professor of Linguistics at the University of La Rioja. He works on cognitive linguistics and pragmatics. He has developed the Lexical Constructional Model and is the co-founder of the international research group Lexicom (www.lexicom.es). Ruiz de Mendoza is also the founding editor of the *Review of Cognitive Linguistics* as well as founding co-editor of the series Applications of Cognitive Linguistics.

ELENA SEMINO is Professor of Linguistics and Verbal Art in the Department of Linguistics and English Language at Lancaster University, UK. She holds a Visiting Professorship at the University of Fuzhou in China. She has (co-) authored four monographs, including *Metaphor in Discourse* (Cambridge University Press, 2008) and *Figurative Language, Genre and Register* (with Alice Deignan and Jeannette Littlemore, Cambridge University Press, 2013). She is co-editor of the *Routledge Handbook of Metaphor and Language* (with Zsófia Demjén, 2017).

YESHAYAHU SHEN is a full professor teaching at the Program of Cognitive Studies of Language and its Uses and in the Literature Department at Tel Aviv University. His main areas of research are narrative comprehension, discourse analysis, cognition and figurative language, cognitive poetics, metaphor and conceptual structure, and the relation of language and thought.

GERARD J. STEEN is Professor of Language and Communication at the University of Amsterdam. He previously held chairs in Language and Communication as well as Language Use and Cognition at Vrije Universiteit Amsterdam. He is the director of the Metaphor Lab Amsterdam and has published twenty monographs, edited books and special issues as well as over 120 articles and book chapters on metaphor and discourse analysis.

BODO WINTER is Lecturer in Cognitive Linguistics at the University of Birmingham, UK, where he researches metaphor, gesture, and sensory language. He has received an MA in linguistics from the University of Hawaiʻi at Mānoa and a Ph.D. in Cognitive and Information Sciences from the University of California, Merced. His work combines experimental approaches and corpora with data science and computational modeling.

Editor's Preface and Acknowledgments

This volume is the result of the combined long-term efforts of a large group of scholars representing embodied-cognition and discourse approaches to metaphor. All chapters to this volume were invited and present the specific contributions of their authors to a project intending to unite these two research traditions. I wish to thank all contributors for their long-term commitment and outstanding sense of cooperation. I am especially grateful to Lynne Cameron, Ray Gibbs, Joe Grady, and Gerard Steen, without whose generous amounts of encouragement and support from the earliest stages of this project, I would not have been able to make it happen.

The book would not have been possible either without the financial support of the Fritz Thyssen Foundation (grant no. 20.14.0.021), which enabled the members of the group to come together at a project workshop attached to RaAM-10 on June 24, 2014, in Cagliari (Italy). I thank the organizing committee of RaAM-10 for hosting this additional conference event, and in particular Elisabetta Gola and Maria Grazia Rossi, not only for their enthusiastic help, especially in organizing the live-streaming and recording of the talks, but also for their excellent culinary advice that helped turn this workshop into a wonderful experience for everyone involved.

The edition in its present form is furthermore indebted to the comments and advice of two anonymous reviewers of the book proposal as well as of the following colleagues who shared their expertise by acting as external reviewers, providing the authors and editors with very insightful chapter reviews: Lynne Cameron, Alan Cienki, Seana Coulson, Mark Johnson, and Klaus-Uwe Panther.

Special thanks go to Frank Lorenz at the Linguistics Department of the University of Erfurt for his untiring assistance in the creation of the shared bibliography and the index, as well as to Cambridge University Press's editorial and production team, especially Jane Bowbrick, Emma Collison, Jacqueline French, and Sarah Starkey, for their good advice and assistance in all technical matters.

Finally, I wish to sincerely thank Lynne Cameron a third time, for supporting this project not only as a linguist and metaphor scholar but also as an artist (for her artworks, see http://lynnecameron.com): This book would not be complete without the special contribution made by its cover image, which is taken from an original painting on paper that belongs to her "Dynamic Series" and is entitled *We tried them once; they broke our teeth.*

BEATE HAMPE, ERFURT, JULY 12, 2016

Introduction

1 Embodiment and Discourse: Dimensions and Dynamics of Contemporary Metaphor Theory

*Beate Hampe**

Chapter Preview

Metaphor scholars used to debate over the "conceptual" or "linguistic" nature of metaphor. More recently, they have been considering whether metaphor is "embodied" or "discursive." Despite the shift in focus implied by this terminological change, the divide between communication-oriented and cognition-oriented approaches to metaphor has not disappeared. This introductory chapter surveys how research from the *social-sciences* and the *cognitive-sciences perspectives* on metaphor has been brought together in this volume. It identifies obvious opportunities for real convergence and argues that metaphor theory cannot but profit from an approach that strives to account for findings yielded by multiple methodologies. By showing how contributors to this volume place special emphasis on the multimodal and interactive nature of communication, the chapter assesses the potential of contemporary metaphor research for a *dynamic multidimensional socio-cognitive model of metaphor* that goes beyond what either of the research traditions have separately achieved.

1 The Cognition–Discourse Divide in Metaphor Theory

> Metaphor need not be stored in minds as passively listed entities in memory for metaphor to really be seen as conceptual . . . Examining real-life discourse offers significant insights into the dynamics of metaphor in social life that may also lead to a more social, discursive view of metaphor, one that still sees metaphor as part of thought, but as socially emergent cognition, not just as private concepts buried inside people's heads.
>
> (Gibbs 2014a: 34–38)

Researchers from disciplines devoted to either cognition or communication have approached metaphor from opposing perspectives, employing different methods to answer what appeared to be diverging questions (see also Gibbs, *this volume*). While cognition researchers were perceived as mostly dealing with theoretical issues of what metaphor *is*, communication research were thought to pursue more applied issues of how it is *used* (Zinken & Musolff 2009). Uniting the two approaches may thus require an appreciation of the fact that a deeper understanding of what metaphor *is* depends to a significant extent on understanding what it *does*.

A first strong link between cognition-oriented and discourse-oriented research has been forged in the past two decades by research on gesture and multimodal communication, which has emphasized that communicative events are *by default* constituted by expressions from multiple semiotic channels. Gesture research in particular has always combined the fine-grained qualitative analysis of actual discourse events with a deep concern for cognitive motivations (e.g. McNeill 1992, 2005). Luckily, metaphor studies have greatly profited from both of these research fields (e.g. Cienki 2010; Cienki & Müller 2008a,b; Forceville 2006a; Forceville & Urios-Aparisi 2009; Müller 2008b).

Encouraged by a range of previous attempts to bridge the cognition–discourse divide (e.g. Gibbs 2013a; Gibbs & Tendahl 2008; Koller 2008; Musolff 2004; Ritchie 2010a; Semino 2010; Semino et al. 2013; Zinken 2007), this edition works toward a model capable of reflecting the "socio-cognitive dynamics" of metaphor (e.g. Gibbs 1999, 2012, 2013a; Gibbs & Cameron 2008; Gibbs & Lonergan 2009). Though disagreeing over many specific points, its authors share the commitment that, given the separate insights gained over the past two decades in both cognition-oriented and discourse-based approaches to metaphor, it is high time for metaphor theory to integrate the major insights yielded by these as yet largely separate, but ultimately complementary strands of inquiry.

2 The Influence of Conceptual Metaphor Theory

The story of contemporary metaphor research cannot be told (or understood) without reference to Conceptual Metaphor Theory (CMT), the first widely influential theory that rejected the traditional notion of metaphor as a poetic or rhetorical device, a figure of *language in use* (e.g. Lakoff 1993; Lakoff & Johnson 1980, 1999, 2003). Viewing the latter as something like the mere tip of the metaphorical iceberg, CMT redefined metaphor as a ubiquitous *conceptual* figure, i.e. as part of the shared tacit knowledge of speakers – not just within but to a considerable extent also across speech communities/languages. Large numbers of coherently related and conventionalized linguistic expressions were claimed to reflect cross-domain connections at the conceptual level, allowing targets in abstract domains to be understood and hence also talked about in terms of their (more concrete or accessible) sources. The authentic expressions in (1), gathered from chapters of this edition, reflect conceptualizations of the target domain of LIFE in terms of (aspects of) the source domain of JOURNEYS but leave the metaphorical mapping itself implicit.

(1) a. ... we may not look the same and we may not have *come from the same place*, but we all want to *move in the same direction* – *towards* a better future ... (Obama "A more perfect union," quoted in Ritchie, *this volume*)
b. I've *covered a lot of ground* ... I've *made a lot of progress*, but there are a lot of *ups and downs* on the *journey* I'm on. It isn't easy. (patient with spinal-cord injury, quoted in Deignan, *this volume*)

While strongly influenced by CMT, representatives of both embodied-cognition approaches and discourse-oriented approaches to metaphor have also raised considerable criticism, much of which can be traced back to the fact that the major claims made by CMT about metaphor as a part of human *cognition* were based on results yielded by a traditional *linguistic* methodology, which largely consisted in the introspective analysis of collections of decontextualized examples.

Cognition researchers who welcomed the ideas advanced by CMT as a contribution to research on embodied cognition more generally (for surveys, see Barsalou 2008a; Barsalou & Wiemer-Hastings 2005; Gibbs 2006a; Pecher & Zwaan 2005; Shapiro 2014) viewed its major claims about conceptual metaphors as raw material for a wealth of testable and falsifiable hypotheses about human cognition (e.g. Casasanto 2008b). Gibbs (2005a, 2007b) offered a variety of options defining what it could mean for a *linguistic* metaphor to be " conceptual," or "embodied." From the weakest hypothesis to the strongest, these included (i) the original motivation of sense extensions in the history of a language, or (ii) in individual language acquisition, via (iii) its tacit presence in the minds of speakers motivating, for instance, the creation and understanding of novel expressions, to (iv) the actual activation of relevant source–target mappings in the online comprehension of language containing source-domain lexical material. In its strongest form, the latter is known as the "metaphorical simulation hypothesis" (Bergen 2012: 198). To this array of hypotheses, a stronger version of (iii) has recently been added by research in social and cognitive psychology. It concerns (v) the tacit influence of conceptual/mental metaphor on people's *non-linguistic* cognitive behavior (e.g. Casasanto & Boroditsky 2008; Landau et al. 2014b).

Language researchers, in turn, criticized that the conventional metaphorical mappings postulated by CMT were not (or not fully) able to account for the *linguistic* properties of metaphor as observed in authentic usage data: The macroanalyses of usage tendencies in languages or varieties done by corpus linguists, for instance, drew attention to the fact that the patterns of linguistic metaphors uncovered from usage data did not precisely follow the metaphorical mappings postulated by CMT. Semino (2006), for example, found argument-related expressions in written British English to give rise to a mapping of the sort ANTAGONISTIC COMMUNICATION IS PHYSICAL CONFLICT, rather than ARGUMENT IS WAR. While such an empirically motivated revision by itself does not contradict *basic* CMT claims, corpus studies also showed metaphor in language use to be relatively more messy – or perhaps rather *dramatically enriched* (e.g. Deignan 2006b, 2008a,b; Musolff 2000, 2004; Stefanowitsch & Gries 2006): First, metaphorical expressions in discourse appeared constrained by usage, i.e. characterized by strong collocational preferences and highly specific uses of particular lexical forms in ways not predicted by CMT. Expressions about JOY and HAPPINESS in English and German, for instance, prefer the alternative sources of LIQUIDS IN CONTAINERS and DESIRABLE OBJECTS, respectively (Stefanowitsch 2004, 2006). Similarly, different kinds of sea-journey metaphors involving "boat" vs. "ship," for instance, are related to specific targets (namely, 'people sharing common interests' or 'closed social groups' on the one hand, and 'complex social/economic systems' on the other) (Zinken 2007). Second, parts of source domains supposedly not participating in metaphorical mappings (the "poverty of mapping" problem in CMT) were actually found to do so. Chimneys, fire escapes, rubbish bins, caretakers, or first-floor apartments all appeared in BUILDING metaphors about the European Union as a STATE (Musolff 2000, 2004). Third, the use of metaphorical expressions also appeared to depend on non-linguistic aspects of the respective usage situations. In a study of metaphors about economic systems in a corpus built from the issues of *The Economist* over ten years (Boers 1999), more metaphors from health-related source domains were used during the winter months.[1] Fourth, authentic, contextualized linguistic expressions were found to exhibit varying degrees of "metaphoricity" (Hanks 2006: 31): "The prototypical oasis is in a hot desert, but there are also Antarctic oases ... which may or may not be classified as literal oases; an oasis in a big city is more metaphorical [than that]; an oasis in the mind is more metaphorical than either."

The fine-grained micro-analyses of communicative interactions produced by discourse analysts, finally, showed that "conceptual metaphors" – if understood as static representations in the minds of single speakers – could not explain the emergence of metaphorical expressions from the social interaction of the participants in specific discourse contexts, their intricate patterns of co-occurrence over larger stretches of discourse (including different turns or even related communicative events) as well as the shifts in metaphorical meaning entailed by these, their highly significant social/interactive functions, or their dependence on and variation across genres/registers (e.g. Cameron 2008a,b,

2010c,d; Cameron & Deignan 2006; Deignan et al. 2013; Semino 2008; Semino et al. 2013).

As stressed by a number of researchers (e.g. Gibbs & Lonergan 2009; McArthur & Oncins-Martinez 2012; Zinken & Musolff 2009), these findings about metaphor as an aspect of language *in use* provide insights that any empirically valid theory of metaphor needs to take into account – especially one that views metaphor as an aspect of embodied cognition. Though many of the above-listed findings about metaphor were presented as part of a critical response to a static notion of conceptual metaphor, it is hard to see how any of these findings can constitute counterevidence against the embodiment of metaphor (or of discourse more generally). Although social interaction as well as language systems definitely play a role in the explanation of these results, all of them also bear witness to the fact that the use of metaphor in discourse feeds on rich, situated experiences that may also determine the salience of a given source domain in a particular communicative situation (see also Kövecses 2009: 21).

3 Toward a Multidimensional and Dynamic Socio-Cognitive Model

A variety of suggestions and developments from both research traditions have together inspired the combined efforts of the authors of this volume toward *a multidimensional, dynamic model of metaphor* in which what might be called the "social-science perspective" and the "cognitive-science perspective" can actually meet, or even merge.

3.1 "Primary" vs. "Complex" Metaphors

One of the more recent developments within CMT itself, the discovery of "primary metaphor" (Grady 1997a,b, 1998, 1999, 2008; Lakoff & Johnson 1999: 45–59), provides a major reference point for this project, for two main reasons: First, Primary Metaphor Theory made testable claims about metaphors as conceptual entities, thereby considerably refining embodiment claims. Second, the distinction between "primary" and "complex" metaphor has opened CMT for discourse concerns in ways that only few scholars with a focus on metaphor in discourse have so far fully appreciated (e.g. Musolff 2004, 2006; Semino 2006, 2010).

To elaborate on the first of these, "primary" metaphors (ex 2, for large inventories, see Grady 1997a: 281–299; Lakoff & Johnson 1999: 50–54) are assumed to be *directly embodied*, i.e. constituted by conceptual correspondences that arise from bodily experience.[2] Each of them connects a particular aspect of sensori-motor experience (the source concept) with a specific subjective "response concept" (the target) that it tightly *correlates* with in a basic *experiential* scenario, called a "primary scene." Response concepts are from domains that are "abstract" only in the sense of 'not accessible via any of the perceptual modalities.' Source and target are equally basic, contiguous aspects of *one* experience, hypothesized to be initially "conflated," and only later "dissociated" into two concepts from different domains which remain tightly linked (Grady & Johnson 2002; for discussion, see Grady & Ascoli, *this volume*).

(2) a. The theory is going to have a *huge* influence. (IMPORTANCE IS SIZE)
b. How did we *get into* this situation? (CHANGE IS MOVEMENT, STATES ARE LOCATIONS)
c. That was a very *warm* welcome. (AFFECTION IS WARMTH)
d. They are *distant* acquaintances. (FAMILIARITY IS PROXIMITY)
e. Our positions are still *far apart.* (SIMILARITY IS PROXIMITY)

Rapidly accumulating experimental research in social psychology (Landau et al. 2014b) confirms the psychological reality of cross-domain conceptual associations of the type constituting primary metaphors (hypotheses iii and v) by showing that they influence *non-linguistic* cognitive behavior, i.e. social judgment and decision-making. Tacit manipulations of subjects' source-domain experiences related to DISTANCE or TEMPERATURE, for example, influence cognitive behavior in tasks related to respective target domains, here SIMILARITY or FAMILIARITY and AFFECTION (*this volume*: Casasanto; Shen & Porat; Winter & Matlock). At the same time, experimental findings indicate that, in non-linguistic cognition, target experiences can also influence judgments about their respective source domains. This apparent bidirectionality contrasts sharply with the fact that novel expressions following primary source > target mappings are readily interpretable, while their reversed versions (instantiating target > source mappings) are not only unattested as conventionalized expressions but also very hard to interpret as novel creations (for discussion, see Lakoff 2014; *this volume*: Grady & Ascoli; Shen & Porat).

The distinction between "primary" and "complex" metaphors (Grady 1997a, 1999; Lakoff & Johnson 1999: 45–76) formalizes an important insight that was inherent in CMT from its very beginning, namely, that the analogical comparisons apparently inspiring conventionalized domain analogies like those presented by conceptual metaphors of the LOVE IS A JOURNEY type are made plausible by *experiential correlations* between these domains in the first place (Lakoff & Johnson 1980). Primary metaphors reflect these correlations; they motivate or constrain complex metaphors by providing deeply embodied point-wise connections between domains. Within Blending Theory (Dancygier & Sweetser 2014; Fauconnier & Turner 2002, 2008; Turner & Fauconnier 2009), these are described as a specific subtype of the "vital relations" that link domains. In other words, they provide the counterpart connections which determine the co-alignment of the activated conceptual frames that constitute the two input spaces required for the creation of analogical blends (Grady 2005b; Hampe 2005c; Ruiz de Mendoza, *this volume*, on "metaphoric amalgams").[3]

Despite misinterpretations in the literature (e.g. Zinken et al. 2008), which might be caused by early work on complex metaphors as "compounds" (Grady et al. 1996), CMT does *not* claim that the figurative force of a complex metaphor can be reduced to the combination of the primary metaphors motivating it. Instead, CMT agrees with much recent work stressing the importance of rich frame knowledge and contexts in the interpretation of complex (multimodal) figurative expressions (*this volume*: Deignan; Forceville; Mittelberg & Joue; Ritchie; Ruiz de Mendoza).

Being correlational, primary metaphors differ from complex (analogical) ones in a variety of ways that are relevant to further concerns in cognition and discourse. First, primary metaphors, though clearly domain-crossing, are much *closer to the metonymy pole* of the metonymy–metaphor cline than resemblance-based ones (e.g. Barcelona 2000b; Hampe 2005c; Kövecses 2013; Mittelberg 2014; Mittelberg & Waugh 2009; *this volume*: Littlemore; Mittelberg & Joue). This is not just a terminological issue, as expressions instantiating primary metaphors will often be literally *and* metaphorically true (namely, in all contexts that have the experiential properties of primary scenes):

> The ... motivations [of primary metaphors] sound strikingly like metonymic relationships between aspects of experienced scenes ... While it is clearly metaphoric to cast difficulty as heaviness in cases where no physical burdens or physical weights are relevant, the origins of the conceptual association between the physical assessment of weight and the affective experience of exertion certainly bear comparison to the type of frame-internal relations typical of metonymy. (Grady 1999: 85)

Second, primary metaphors are more *constrained* than resemblance-based ones concerning how cogently they arise from experiential correlations in "recurrent experiential scenarios" across individuals and even cultural communities (Grady 1999; Grady & Johnson 2002: 537). In the form of the question of whether something like "basic metaphor" actually exists, this issue has also been taken up in social psychology (Schnall 2014). The crucial point here is that the conceptual associations characterizing primary metaphors can in principle be acquired (and usually are) *in the absence of any linguistic input* (e.g. Casasanto 2013; Grady & Johnson 2002).

Third, the deeply entrenched conceptual associations between source and target concepts in primary metaphors are regularly reflected at the level of language (systems) by highly conventionalized lexical polysemy or word-formation devices – hence the quasi-literal feel of most instantiations of primary metaphors in actual discourse. Speakers routinely refer to target concepts by making use of deeply entrenched extended uses of terms denoting the respective source, or of terms regularly derived from these source terms. In accordance with DIFFICULTY IS HEAVINESS, for instance, a "*difficult* task" is called "schwer" or "schwierig" in German. The core meaning of the first term is 'heavy,' the second term is transparently derived from the first and can only refer to the target (for a survey of expressions reflecting five primary metaphors across sixteen languages, see Grady, *this volume*). Sometimes, the metaphorical motivations of abstract lexemes are so deeply "buried" in the lexicon of a language that they can only be recovered from their etymology (Sweetser 1990; Goatly 1997). Goatly (1997: 45) makes an important point when saying that transparent metaphors of the type presented by primary metaphors do not die like other lexicalized metaphors because "their original vehicles are . . . so basic and universal to our experience, being concerned with objects, space, movement, orientation and so on, that they have no chance of disappearing."

With this observation, he anticipates the fourth point, which has more recently been made by cognitive and social psychologists about *non-linguistic* metaphorical cognition: Correlation-based "mental" metaphors contrast with complex analogical ones in that they remain "active" *for good* (Casasanto 2013; Landau et al. 2014b). That is to say, their above-mentioned power to influence cognitive behavior (hypothesis v) remains undiminished, no matter how conventional the linguistic expressions they motivate may be.

3.2 Manifestations of Metaphor at Multiple Levels

The project documented in this volume elaborates on a number of (previously unrelated) suggestions from both embodied-cognition and discourse traditions to investigate manifestations of metaphor at or across multiple levels of various kinds. Casasanto (2009b, 2014b) sets apart "mental" metaphors – all cross-domain associations influencing people's non-linguistic cognitive behavior – from "linguistic" metaphors – those that are also "enshrined," i.e. lexicalized in language(s). Steen's (2008) work on the activation of source-domain content in metaphor comprehension is based on a tripartite distinction between metaphor in *thought*, *language (systems)*, and *discourse*. To account for the interplay between bodily and cultural factors motivating conventional metaphorical expressions across languages, Kövecses (2002: 241–245) also assumes a three-level model. Here, the "individual" level is concerned with the use of metaphorical expressions in actual communicative situations (i.e. *discourse*). The bodily/experiential grounding of metaphorical expressions is provided at the "sub-individual" level of individual *cognition*, e.g. in the form of image schemas and primary metaphors. Conventionalized complex metaphors appear at the "supra-individual" level of specific *languages* and *cultures*.

From a wider perspective, namely, that of complex-dynamic systems, Gibbs and Cameron (Cameron 2010b; Gibbs 2012; Gibbs & Cameron 2008; Gibbs & Santa Cruz 2012) suggest that what researchers call metaphor encompasses phenomena occurring at a number of levels defined by vastly different temporal scales ranging from the split-seconds of cognitive processing up to the centuries or millennia of human culture, and even evolutionary time. To these correspond equally wide-ranging scales of a spatial, material, or social nature. Social scales, for instance, range from individual human beings up to the entire species, via successively larger groups – both short-lived ones, such as those constituted by human beings united in spontaneous interactions, and progressively more stable ones, such as those constituted by human beings considering themselves members of the same community of practice, speech community, or cultural group.

Though the levels of cognition, language, discourse, and culture have traditionally attracted the attention of metaphor researchers most, a multidimensional model of metaphor should span a larger array of levels, in principle ranging from the bodily foundations – both substrates and processes – that enable human body-world interactions, i.e. movement, perception, and ultimately also cognition (*this volume*: Cuccio; Grady), all the way up to the evolutionary scale of the development of the human species (including its genome) over temporal scales that go far beyond cultural time:

1. (neuro-)physiology
2. cognition (on/off-line)
3. discourse/communication (especially but not exclusively face-to-face interaction)
4. language (systems)
5. culture
6. evolution

A few clarifying remarks on levels 2 to 5 from the perspective of this volume are in order. Studies of metaphor across the verbal and gestural planes in *spontaneous face-to-face communication* (as the most immediate form of discourse) naturally foreground both the multimodal character and crucial interactive functions of communication. By doing so, they have opened a new "window to the mind," i.e. produced evidence of vital relevance to studies of metaphor in *cognition* (e.g. Cienki 2010; Müller 2008b; Sweetser 2007; *this volume*: Jensen; Mittelberg & Joue; Müller). Outside of metaphor theory, research on the role of gestures in embodied cognition stresses that gestures are not just communicative devices but evidence for "embodied knowledge." The "Gesture as Simulated Action" framework, for instance, holds that gestures "derive from simulated actions" and "are produced as part of the cognitive processes that underlie thinking and speaking" (Alibali et al. 2014: 150–151).

Culture appears as the wider matrix of the relatively more stable socio-historical contexts in which any communicative event is ultimately embedded. These contexts are simultaneously reflected in *and* constituted by speakers' participation in and (shared) knowledge/memory of cultural practices, which include social interaction/discourse, special forms of bodily behavior, and artifact use. This perspective foregrounds the "distributive" nature of cognitive systems (i.e. distributions across the members of a social group, and over time): "culture can be seen as a potent, cumulative reservoir of resources for learning, problem solving, and reasoning, 'ratcheting up' the collective insights of previous generations so individuals do not have to start from scratch" (Theiner 2014: 353–354). Most immediately relevant to the present project is perhaps the question of what it could mean for culture itself to be literally "embodied." Soliman and Glenberg (2014: 207) view culture as "the tuning of sensori-motor systems for situated action," arising from social interactions at the level of small, relatively stable social groups (e.g. families). They argue that the mutual adaption of the (bodily) behaviors of individuals in close, everyday interactions creates "in-group" behavior which maximizes the efficiency of the most frequent social interactions. Culturally "distant" people are perceived as "out-group" to the extent that interaction with them is not "synchronized," thus more effortful and requiring negotiation.

People's knowledge of *language* is assumed to be non-modular. Following cognitively oriented, usage-based models, language (systems) are viewed as structured, dynamic inventories of symbolic units which continually emerge from the myriads of (culturally drenched) usage events that its speakers experience (e.g. Langacker 2000). In this way, language systems lexicalize conceptualizations that are of significance to the members of the respective speech community, i.e. *culturally relevant.* Usage-based models make clear that individual knowledge of language is intertwined with situated usage and that the *shared* knowledge that constitutes (dynamic) language *systems* belongs to speech communities rather than single speakers, because the (dynamic) knowledge that individual speakers possess of their language(s) is neither fully identical nor complete.

3.3 Complex-Dynamic Systems

Given all this, the emphasis on embodied cognition characterizing this volume is not meant to narrow down metaphor research to aspects of individual cognition or bodily experience narrowly defined. On the contrary, embodied-cognition research explicitly acknowledges the sociocultural situatedness of all cognition: "In viewing cognition as embedded or situated, embodied cognitive science emphasizes feedback between an agent and the world" (Dawson 2014: 62; for relevant discussions, see *this volume*: Casasanto; Jensen; Winter & Matlock).

Outside of metaphor research, it was recognized early on that dynamic systems theory provides "a crucial tool for embodied cognitive science" (Richardson & Chemero 2014: 39). In a nutshell, complex-dynamic systems have three major properties (cf. ibid.: 40–48): First, they consist of a number of "interactive components or agents" that need not be homogeneous: "*a brain in a body in an environment* can comprise a heterogeneous, complex dynamic system" (ibid.: 39, emphasis inserted). Second, the collective behavior of the entire system may result in "coherent patterns" that are unpredictable from the behaviors of its components, i.e. not related to them in a linear manner. Third, this "emergent" behavior is "self-organized" in that it does not require any "controlling component agent." The intricate structures of relatively more stable natural configurations like snowflakes or termites' nests have been cited as illustrations of such emerging patterns, as have the fast-changing and context-dependent coordination patterns of living animals like flocks of birds or schools of fish, which are described as "soft-assembled" and "interaction-dominant."

Unsurprisingly, this description also applies to the dynamics of *social interaction*. Studies of metaphorical expressions emerging from social interactions in particular discourse contexts will thus naturally foreground that the synergy emerging from the individuals co-acting as a group under specific contextual conditions "enslaves" the behavior of individual actors so that the group behavior cannot be understood by investigating individual behavior in isolation and so that it becomes difficult or impossible to assign causal roles to any of the individual "components" constituting the situation, including the human actors (cf. ibid.: 41; Jensen, *this volume*). Similar considerations apply to *cognition* as a complex-dynamic system in its own right made up of highly heterogeneous components and depending on the interaction of bodily components way beyond the brain itself, but also on the interaction with further component systems outside the boundaries of the biological body, including aspects of the (natural and man-made) physical environment as well as social-interactive contexts (for relevant discussions, see *this volume*: Cuccio; Littlemore). The opportunities afforded by this for studying metaphor (and metonymy!) as an aspect of cognition *and* discourse, as both embodied *and* socially constituted, are blatantly obvious.

In metaphor theory, the complex-dynamic systems framework has so far served to deepen the insight that a more complete understanding of metaphor requires the appreciation of the tight relations and mutual interdependencies between its various levels of appearance. In discourse-oriented research, it has predictably foregrounded the role of distributed/group cognition in ongoing interactive meaning-making and led to the rejection of a narrow notion of embodiment that is tied to individual minds – or rather to fixed representations like CMT's conventional domain analogies as a property of individual minds (e.g. Cameron 2010b; Gibbs 2012; *this volume*: Deignan; Gibbs; Jensen; Müller; Semino & Demjén).

4 Complex Interrelations between Levels

The preceding section emphasized that the dynamic systems approach fosters an appreciation of the *interrelations* between the various levels at which metaphor can become manifest. However, given the vast differences in the correlated temporal, material, spatial, and social scales that define these levels, partial *dissociations* are also to be expected. This is to say the manifestations of metaphor across levels are unlikely to reduce to mere *reflections* of one another by default. Though both of these points deserve extended discussion, I will point out only a few issues that are of particular concern to this volume.

4.1 Primary Metaphor in a Multidimensional Model

In view of what was said above about language (systems) as inventories of symbolic units, it seems likely, for instance, that not all of the correlational mental metaphors that are active at the conceptual level will also qualify as primary by being lexicalized, i.e. reflected by the conventionalized symbolic units of language (Casasanto 2008b, 2013). Cultural contexts may act as a kind of "filter" (Yu 2008; see also Kövecses 2005: 283–294) letting some but not all of the potentially relevant experiential correlations pass, i.e. making certain aspects of bodily experiences more accessible or salient than others. Relevant cross-linguistic data come from Australian Aboriginal languages that do not exhibit KNOWING IS SEEING, a primary metaphor otherwise extremely widespread across languages, but instead employ KNOWING IS HEARING (cf. Evans & Wilkins 2000). Obviously, the two alternative metaphors belong to a larger group of coherent experiential correspondences all reflecting the fact that the acquisition of knowledge depends on perception. Vice versa, but by the same token, cultural experience such as that provided by communicative practices (including the use of language and artifacts) can be argued to provide "feedback loops" that reach down to the sub-individual level, reinforcing primary metaphors (Winter & Matlock, *this volume*). From this perspective, arguments over whether primary metaphors are embodied or cultural are futile because they ignore vital interactions between the interdependent levels of cognition, language, communication, and culture.

Based on the assumption that associative learning can strengthen preexisting mental correlations that are more frequently activated (e.g. through linguistic experience and other cultural feedback loops) at the expense of less frequently activated ones, Hierarchical Mental Metaphors Theory (Casasanto 2014b, *this volume*) is intended to resolve issues related to the (Whorfian) element of language-specificity in conventionalized linguistic expressions reflecting experiential correlations (i.e. primary metaphors). Crucially, this entails partial divergences between "mental" metaphors and metaphors that are conventionally expressed in language (systems) or other cultural artifacts (such as calendars). Here, the question arises whether the existence of the additional "experiential contexts" provided by such feedback loops can do more than suppress or strengthen preexisting experiential correlations and actually *create* correlational mental metaphors that are not directly embodied but acquired solely on the basis of cultural and/or linguistic experience. According to Casasanto (2014b), this is the case.

It was mentioned in section 3.1 that experimental evidence from cognitive and social psychology not only supports hypotheses (iii) and (v) for correlation-based mental metaphors but has also yielded new findings about their apparent bidirectionality, which seem to contradict CMT claims about the strong unidirectionality (source > target) of *all* conceptual metaphors. For primary metaphors, these claims are based on linguistic evidence relating to (i) known conventional instantiations across many languages, and (ii) the fact that novel expressions exhibiting the directionality (target > source) are not readily interpretable (Grady & Ascoli, *this volume*). While Grady and Ascoli delve deeper into the sub-individual level to search for potential neural correlates of "sourceness" and "targetness," Shen and Porat (*this volume*) go in a different direction and offer a tentative explanation of the directionality of *all* verbal metaphors (i.e. both primary and complex ones) in terms of a multi-dimensional approach that assumes "shared labor" between the levels of cognition and language systems, with conceptual preferences for a given directionality being turned into full-blown unidirectionality only at the level of language.

4.2 *Complex Metaphors in a Multidimensional Model*

A multidimensional model might also help resolve a few misunderstandings about the complex, analogy-based metaphors that have attracted the attention of scholars interested in language and discourse/communication at least since classical antiquity. Concerning the relation between metaphor in language (systems) and communication, usage-based models of language predict that metaphor at the level of language systems will *not* closely mirror metaphor in actual communication, because schematizations over large amounts of usage events arise from the interlocutors' repeated experience of the (formally and conceptually) *invariant* elements of pieces of discourse that are otherwise unique in many respects (see Deignan, *this volume*, for an extensive analysis of the unique aspects of JOURNEY metaphors in authentic contexts). What is varied at the level of actual discourse will thus be reflected at the level of language (systems) by relatively more stable but also much more schematic structures.

Complex conceptual metaphors such as LIFE IS A JOURNEY or THEORIES ARE BUILDINGS were inferred on the basis of *conventional* metaphorical expressions (i.e. figurative idioms). They thus reflect these more stable *inter-individually shared* aspects of the conceptual knowledge of speakers. This is broadly in line with Kövecses' (2002, 2005, 2015) suggestions about complex conceptual metaphors as elements of the "supra-individual" level, with Zinken's (2007) notion of "discourse metaphor," and with Musolff's (2004) notion of "metaphor scenario." Rather than focusing on issues of conceptual complexity (as CMT does), these terms emphasize the importance of *discursive practices* in a cultural community as a valid experiential context. From a dynamic systems perspective, such "enduring" conceptual metaphors present "stabilities" that "emerge" in bigger groups and over larger timescales than that of face-to-face interactive encounters (e.g. Gibbs 2014a). The notion of metaphor scenario anticipates this by actively invoking a conception of public discourse as a "virtual conversation within and between communities" (Musolff 2004: 5). All of these notions also foreground functional issues to do with the "framing" potential of conventionalized domain analogies in public discourse (cf. Zinken 2007; *this volume*: Deignan; Ritchie), which raises important questions about the ways in which metaphors from earlier texts and possibly different genres may be "recontextualized," i.e. put to new uses with shifted meanings and functions by other writers (Semino et al. 2013).

To capture the emergence of metaphorical expressions from particular contexts of face-to-face interaction and their functionality in these contexts, discourse analysts have advanced further notions like "systematic metaphor" (e.g. Cameron 2010b), and "metaphoreme" (Cameron & Deignan 2006). While the former stresses the ways in which the full functionality of a metaphor emerges from repeated occurrences of token expressions over the course of a social interaction, the latter stresses that these occurrences – though varied to some extent – lead to stabilities in the linguistic realizations of the metaphor. Both notions thus foreground the social character of the observed "connected patterns" of metaphor as "important tools in understanding and talking" (Cameron 2010b: 91). Both also emphasize their tight dependence on the original usage context and could thus be said to capture minor or temporary stabilities in metaphorical thought and expression which emerge on the discourse level in very small social groups over the course of only a single communicative event or a sequence of closely related events. That co-participants schematize over very small amounts of usage data does not keep these low-level generalizations from becoming productive in the sense of licensing novel and creative forms of expressions. But this happens both *within* the limits (or: affordances) set by these communicative situations and *for* the purpose of interacting in them (e.g. Cameron 2007b, 2011; *this volume*: Deignan; Jensen; Müller; Semino & Demjén).

Because they capture the dynamics of interactive meaning-making, the notions of systematic metaphor and metaphoreme are not entirely on a par with those relating to more enduring forms of metaphor, such as CMT's complex conceptual metaphors. They should thus be seen as complementing existing work on the latter rather than be used to reject work on embodied metaphor. Discourse analysts may actually overestimate the power of discourse (at the expense of the power of embodiment) when claiming that "conventional metaphorical ways of talking-and-thinking" can evolve without the presence of *any* embodied motivations, "*solely* through the dialogic dynamics of social interaction" (Cameron 2010b: 93): Though it is true that conventionalized forms will always emerge from the more varied expressions of individual speakers in dynamic, usage-based systems, that does not explain the deeply embodied nature of many of the invariant elements found across the original expressions. Primary Metaphor Theory has shown many of these to reflect experiential correlations.

At the same time, discourse analysts were absolutely right to stress that the top-down influences that conceptual metaphors may exert are far from being the sole or even major determinants of speakers' behavior in actual discourse. What is thus perhaps most relevant to the goal of building bridges between embodied-cognition and discourse approaches to metaphor is a better understanding of what precisely it means for "enduring" metaphors to act as framing devices in a number of different usage scenarios and, vice versa, what it means for actual expressions in more spontaneous forms of social interaction, to "actualize" (Gibbs 2014a: 35) some of the metaphorical potential offered by more enduring conceptualizations in highly individual, context-dependent ways (*this volume*: Deignan; Semino & Demjén).

5 More on Metaphor in Real-Time Face-to-Face Interaction

Real-time face-to-face communication has been characterized as the place where the negotiation of meaning is an essential part of the social interactions between human individuals who make use of all the semiotic channels at their disposal. It is thus the place where metaphor – the rare and beautiful multimodal "butterfly" (to borrow the metaphor from Gibbs, *this volume*) – can be observed "in the wild." It is also the place where cognition appears not just as embodied in a narrow sense but most obviously also as discursive, distributed, and strongly contextually situated (Jensen, *this volume*), and where cognitive motivations of the kinds discussed in CMT provide only *one* of an array of factors that determine the appearance of actual expressions.

However, this multiplicity of motivating factors does not by itself present an argument against the embodiment of spontaneous "metaphor performance" (*this volume*: Gibbs; Müller). While this point is most strongly emphasized in research on gestural metaphors (*this volume*: Mittelberg & Joue; Müller), it can also be made about metaphors instantiated verbally: The expressions in (3) are taken from Cameron's (2007b, 2010b, 2011) work on a series of reconciliation talks between Pat Magee, a former IRA activist, and Jo Berry, whose father had been killed by a bomb planted by Pat more than a decade earlier. Example (4) is taken from Jensen's (*this volume*) analysis of a couple-therapy session. Cameron's and Jensen's detailed analyses of these expressions as systematic metaphors show how they emerge from and function within their highly specific contexts, to some extent jointly created by the co-participants in these discourses.

(3) a. ... *in* the er – *the journey*, ... *coming* ... *to a bridge*, / ... you know. ... with *two ends* (Pat taking up a metaphor previously articulated in a poem by Jo, cf. Cameron 2010b: 15)
b. all those *bridges* are there to be *built* (Pat, 6 months later, elaborating the metaphor to refer to a larger process of reconciliation involving other people, cf. ibid.: 16)

(4) it is like (.) *running with the wind at one's back* right from the start without warming up (Ann about her being in a good mood, elaborating a metaphor used by Mike a few minutes before, cf. Jensen, *this volume*)

At the same time, these speakers obviously view their different long-term activities at least partially in terms of preestablished JOURNEY metaphors and perhaps also draw on conventionalized metaphorical expressions to do with social changes or social bonds, such as "bridge the gap/divide" and "build/burn bridges," or "make progress" and "come far," so that at least some aspects of the frames and frame connections provided by conventionalized bridge and journey metaphors are actuated. Vital connections between the source and target of the BRIDGE metaphors for 'reconciliation' in (3) are provided by the primary metaphors SOCIAL BONDS ARE PHYSICAL CONNECTIONS, RELATIONS ARE BOUNDED REGIONS/CONTAINERS, INTIMACY IS CLOSENESS, as well as perhaps CHANGE IS MOTION (since conceptual frames tell us that bridges span opposite sides of river banks to enable us to walk across the divide). Some of the most salient primary metaphors motivating (4) are CHANGE IS MOTION, STATES ARE LOCATIONS and CAUSES ARE FORCES from the "event-structure" complex (cf. Grady 1997a; Lakoff 1993), perhaps in conjunction with a few others that are coherent in this particular context, such as CIRCUMSTANCES ARE WEATHER. It goes without saying that, even taken together, these will not exhaust the meaning of the metaphorical expressions in their contexts (as these invoke rich frame knowledge about bridges, or running), nor will they explain any of the interactional functions of those expressions (see also Gibbs, *this volume*).

At the same time, this is clearly not where the embodiment of situated meaning-making ends. Jensen's (*this volume*) dynamic systems analysis also includes the (increasingly synchronized) whole-body performances which the couple interacting in this dialogue are engaged in. Gibbs (*this volume*) is thus right to emphasize that such performances are quite literally embodied, not least because the bodily "fine-tuning" characterizing the interactive behavior of closely interdependent persons can be viewed as the birthplace of culture itself.

6 Activation of Source-Domain Content in Discourse

To capture the graded potential of metaphorical expressions to activate source-domain content in online cognition or communication, communication researchers have employed a number of metaphorical labels – from "dead," "buried," and "sleeping" to "tired," "awake," and even "walking" (e.g. Goatly 1997; Müller 2008a). Earlier work on "metaphoricity" (cf. Goatly, ibid.) listed a variety of factors interacting in the creation of highly metaphorical expressions: Among these were the distance between the concepts involved in an analogical metaphor (determining the salience of the recategorization, recall Hanks' "oasis" examples cited above), the explicitness of the mapping in the discourse, and the degree to which the expressions reflecting it are conventionalized.

In embodied-cognition research on metaphor, hypothesis (iv) – especially in the form of the *metaphorical-simulation hypothesis* – not only makes the strongest claim about conceptual/embodied metaphor but is also hotly debated.

6.1 Approaching Salient Metaphor in Discourse

Steen's (2008) postulation of the "paradox of metaphor" is probably the most provocative contribution to the ongoing debate about the online activation of source-domain content in the comprehension of language in actual discourse. Referring to the fact that the overwhelming majority of all metaphorical expressions in discourse is highly conventionalized, and inspired by the "career" of (complex) metaphor from active to "retired" analogy (Casasanto 2013, 2014b; Gentner & Bowdle 2008; Glucksberg 2008), the paradox states that most of the verbal metaphors in discourse are not processed *as* metaphors but by categorization. In other words, the claim is that, when processing verbal metaphors, people largely use the shortcuts provided by language systems in the form of preestablished sense extensions. While not denying the embodiment of conceptual metaphor at levels (i) to (iii) sketched out above, the paradox argues against the activation of source-domain knowledge as a *default* in embodied-cognition approaches to metaphor in discourse. The claims it advances about hypothesis (iv) are, first, that the activation of source-domain content in language comprehension is comparatively rare and, second, that it is bound to "deliberate" metaphor use, i.e. to cases in which the speaker *intentionally* chooses a source domain to draw the co-participants' *attention* to the new perspective on the target that this may yield (Steen 2008, 2011b,c, 2013, 2015, *this volume*). Deliberate metaphors are thus conceived of as "vital," "strong," and "creative" in Black's (1993) sense, and hence also as relevant to social interaction. However, the preceding discussion in the literature (e.g. Gibbs 2011b, 2015c; Müller 2011) as well as in this chapter indicate that the problem may be considerably more complex than suggested by the paradox, not least because the interaction of factors in ongoing social interaction makes it difficult to trace back the creation of a particular form to the conscious intention of a single "author" (Jensen, *this volume*).

Work in gesture studies (e.g. Mittelberg 2013b; Mittelberg & Joue, *this volume*; Mittelberg & Waugh 2009; Müller 2008b, 2011, *this volume*; Müller & Cienki 2009), work on metaphor in multiple modalities (e.g. Forceville 2006a, 2008, *this volume*; Forceville & Urios-Aparisi 2009), and experimental work on verbal metaphor (for surveys, see Gibbs 2011c, 2014b; Gibbs & Matlock 2008) over the last two decades have shown that source-domain content which *transparently* motivates conventionalized linguistic metaphors provides at the very least a *potential* for speakers that may become relevant to discourse concerns. In other words, the fact that a speaker uses a conventionalized verbal metaphorical expression does not by itself entail that its source-domain contents remain inactive or inaccessible. Neither is it the case that this content can only influence the cognitive and communicative behavior of speakers/hearers when these are consciously aware of it – for a number of reasons.

First, the preceding discussion in this chapter implies that source-domain activation may partially depend on *metaphor type*: "Even for highly frequent totally conventional metaphors ... source-target mappings continue to be activated automatically when people process the target domains: Correlational metaphors never retire" (Casasanto 2013: 10). Moreover, experiments in social psychology employing the "alternate source strategy" have shown that tacitly exposing subjects to different commonplace linguistic metaphorical framings of the same fact influences their subsequent reasoning about the respective target domain (Landau et al. 2014a).

Second, recent work on the degree of metaphoricity displayed by multimodal expressions in discourse (Jensen, *this volume*; Jensen & Cuffari 2014; Müller 2008a, 2011, 2014, *this volume*) has stressed the "co-experiential" nature of metaphor and focused on foregrounding processes that occur as part of "whole-body communicative-cognitive behavior" in social interactions (Jensen & Cuffari 2014). The notion emphasizes that metaphors can simultaneously "surface" in several semiotic modes and that the gestural mode is to a much lesser degree than the verbal one accessible to/monitored by conscious awareness.

Scholars approaching metaphor in discourse from this interactional perspective do not deny that the amount of *attention* drawn to metaphorical expressions as an aspect of semiotic behavior itself may be one of the factors relevant to the activation of source-domain conceptualizations. Binding it back to the conscious deliberation of the speaker/writer, however, is not generally accepted as a valid criterion (*this volume*: Gibbs; Jensen; Müller; Ritchie). The alternative concept of (foregrounded multimodal) "waking metaphor" (Müller 2008a,b, 2014, *this volume*; Müller & Tag 2010) argues against this over-emphasis on deliberate language use as a single factor.

6.2 *Simulation of Source-Domain Content*

Much recent metaphor research has debated whether metaphor comprehension quite literally involves "re-living" relevant source-domain experiences, i.e. incurs the "embodied simulation" of source-domain content (e.g. Bergen 2012; Gibbs 2005a, 2006b,c, 2012; Gibbs & Matlock 2008; *this volume*: Cuccio; Ritchie). The "metaphorical simulation hypothesis" is the strongest version of hypothesis (iv). At the same time, the notion of embodied simulation is not always clearly defined. Broad definitions of the notion rely to a large extent on behavioral evidence consistent with the assumption of simulation and remain agnostic about whether such simulations activate modality-specific areas of the sensori-motor cortex or functionally independent, multimodal brain areas (e.g. Gibbs 2005a: 89).

Increasing amounts of experimental evidence (both behavioral data and results from the application of neuro-imaging techniques like fMRF and EEG) indicate that the comprehension of concrete, literal language involves detailed simulations of the respective action and perception scenarios – even according to a narrow interpretation of the simulation hypothesis (for surveys, see Bergen 2012, 2015; Kaschak et al. 2014). The evidence for metaphorical language, however, is mixed to date (Bergen 2012: 195–264), with evidence supporting a narrow interpretation being sparse and controversial, even for correlational metaphors (for discussion: see Bergen 2012: 195–264; Casasanto & Gijssels 2015; Ritchie, *this volume*).

One of the tentative conclusions that have been drawn from this is that metaphorical simulations may generally be less detailed and specific than simulations of literal, non-abstract meanings – considering, for instance, that literal (but not metaphorical) grasping covaries with the size and kind of object grasped (e.g. Bergen 2012). Another is that simulation and symbolic modes of processing may coexist (Zwaan 2014, 2016; for discussion, see Kaschak et al. 2014), such that presence and depths of simulations may be determined by the factors discussed in the previous section as well as contextual dimensions. Crucially for the present concerns, usage-based models of language indicate that such symbolic modes need not be entirely disembodied either, as they reflect speakers' experiences of the regularities of situated language use.

Ritchie (2008a,b, 2009, 2010b, *this volume*) explores how (depth of) simulation is related to the capacity of (analogical) verbal and visual metaphors to index rich, contextually driven stories about their targets. Müller's (2014, *this volume*) detailed analyses of extended "waking" multimodal metaphors, finally, serve as a reminder that the gestural, or even full-bodied, "performance" of a novel analogical metaphor literally and visibly simulates its source-domain content.

7 Concluding Remarks

Despite obvious points of disagreement, many open issues, and hosts of new questions, the combined efforts of the authors of this edition make it clear that understanding what metaphor is requires a *thorough* understanding of what it does.

The cognition-oriented chapters of Part I show that an emphasis on the embodiment of cognition in general and metaphor in particular does not amount to a denial of the linguistically/culturally situated, discursive and distributed nature of both, and that the supra-individual levels of language and culture feed back into the sub-individual one by providing further experiential contexts. Vice versa, the discourse-oriented chapters of Parts III and IV provide abundant evidence indicating that discourse data, especially if capturing the multimodal and interactive nature of communication, are directly relevant to a conception of metaphor as embodied.

Part II of this volume widens the scope to "embodied metonymy" and other kinds of "figuration" in thought and expressive behavior (both linguistic and gestural). Its chapters show how basic conceptual operations work on conceptual frames in the creation of a range of figurative (verbal and multimodal) expressions, placing special emphasis on the relation and interactions between metaphor and metonymy.

The editor and authors of this edition hope to have bridged the cognition–discourse divide in a variety of ways and thereby opened new pathways for metaphor scholars from different research traditions – not least by raising awareness of the way in which a number of issues in metaphor research that appear to be either cognition- or communication-related at first sight are in fact so strongly intertwined that they require the joint investigation from the complementary perspectives provided by the two different research traditions.

Notes and Acknowledgments

* I warmly thank Lynne Cameron for her feedback on an early version of this chapter. The chapter has also profited enormously from discussions of selected issues with Daniel Casasanto, Alice Deignan, Charles Forceville, Ray Gibbs, Joe Grady, Thomas

Jensen, Teenie Matlock, Dave Ritchie, and Bodo Winter. It goes without saying that I am responsible for all remaining shortcomings.

1 Related to the corpus results about "joy" and "happiness" reported above, another study found that subjects drinking something during the experiment were more likely to rate a radiantly smiling person as feeling 'joy,' while people actively searching for something in a library were more likely to rate the same person as feeling 'happiness' (cf. Bergen 2012: 202–203).

2 Recent research has hypothesized some of these to be innately given (Casasanto 2014b).

3 Within the Neural Theory of Metaphor, this is conceived of in terms of "neural binding," "a correlation in experience realized in the brain as the coactivation of distinct neural areas, which leads to the formation of circuits linking those areas" (Lakoff 2008a: 27; see also Lakoff 2014).

Part I

Metaphor in Cognition

2 Sources and Targets in Primary Metaphor Theory: Looking Back and Thinking Ahead

*Joseph E. Grady & Giorgio A. Ascoli**

Chapter Preview

Primary metaphors are deeply entrenched associations of "source" and "target" concepts, e.g. HEAVINESS and DIFFICULTY, that underlie numerous, extremely common metaphoric uses of language both within a given language such as English and across languages. Apart from reviewing relevant existing work on the conceptual and linguistic relationships referred to as "primary metaphors," especially claims about their unidirectionality and universality, this chapter also suggests a new avenue for future research on aspects of their neural organization/function, asking whether there may be neural correlates of "sourceness" and "targetness" that imply distinct processing profiles for the two sets of concepts, and suggesting plausible directions where such distinctions might be identified. More particularly, the chapter explores the hypothesis that source concepts might be correlated with localized cortical structures organized as neural maps as well as the complementary hypothesis that target concepts are not correlated with such localized structures and instead involve more widely distributed structures or processes, such as the action of diffuse modulatory neurotransmitters. In addition to considering the linguistic, conceptual, and neural distinctions to be drawn between "sourceness" and "targetness," we consider what the cognitive advantages might be of relatively unidirectional associations between such categories of concepts.

1 Introduction

Primary metaphors (Grady 1997a; Lakoff & Johnson 1999: 49–59) have proven an interesting focus for linguists and scholars in other cognitive disciplines (*this volume*: Casasanto; Cuccio; Winter & Matlock), since they form the basis for widely shared if not universal patterns of language and conceptualization, linking one idea (and element of experience) to another. In this section, we discuss the nature of primary metaphors, with a focus on previous characterizations, which will prepare the ground for the new proposals presented in the rest of the chapter. We begin with several examples of primary-metaphor patterns, which will serve as reference points for further discussion.

Examples (1) to (3) illustrate three common metaphorical patterns, associating 'difficulty' with 'heaviness' (DIFFICULT IS HEAVY), 'social dominance' with 'higher spatial position' (POWER/STATUS IS UP), and 'happiness' with 'brightness' (HAPPY IS BRIGHT), respectively.

(1) The New Orleans Saints' rookie offensive tackle was completely spent after *taking on a heavy workload* with both the first-string and third-string offenses during Friday's scrimmage. ("More highs, lows for Saints' Andrus Peat under heavy workload," ESPN.go.com, 8/7/2015)

(2) Plucked from the dirt in rural France by unexpected benefactors, Jean-Marie begins to *rise through the hierarchy* of an aristocracy which treats France as though she is their very own banqueting table. ("The Last Banquet, By Jonathan Grimwood," review at Independent.uk.com, 7/7/2013)

(3) Her *bright* demeanor is a marked contrast to Sichel, who frequently confesses her fears and anxieties directly to the camera. ("A Woman Like Me," film review at Hollywoodreporter.com, 7/7/15)

Like all other primary metaphors, these three patterns follow the basic template of "conceptual metaphors" as discussed in Conceptual Metaphor Theory (CMT) beginning with Lakoff and Johnson (1980): They constitute systematic conceptual associations that underlie both conventional and novel metaphoric usages of terms (originally) related to sensory domains. In (1) to (3), for instance, the words *heavy*, *rise*, and *bright* are used in their (highly conventional) non-sensory meanings of 'difficult,' 'gain in status/power,' and 'happy.'

CMT has assumed that the link between the concepts paired in a primary metaphor is rooted in highly regular correlations in experience, such as those between the weight of an object and our ease or difficulty in handling it in the case of DIFFICULT IS HEAVY. Similarly, the metaphor POWER/STATUS IS UP plausibly originates in the advantages offered by higher spatial position when it comes to dominating another (given the effects of gravity). In the case of HAPPY IS BRIGHT, there is a clear experiential correlation between personal mood and ambient brightness.

CMT has stressed from the beginning that examples like (1)–(3) are not isolated instances, neither within languages, nor across them. It is easy to identify many other English expressions illustrating the same three mappings, for instance: A difficult task can be *burdensome* or *weigh* a person *down*. Privileged social ranks are routinely referred to as *higher* or *upper* ones and the people in them as *higher-ups* or *superiors*. The face of a happy person *lights up* or *shines*. In other languages, words expressing sensorimotor experiences related to 'weight,' 'high spatial position,' or 'brightness' frequently refer to the same non-sensory domains, as do their English counterparts: Arabic *thaqiil* can mean both 'heavy' and 'oppressive.' Finnish *yli* ('high') also refers to high status, or position within a hierarchy. And the Hausa root *hask*, which basically refers to brightness, can also refer to happiness.

2 Looking Back: Primary Metaphors in Conceptual Metaphor Theory

2.1 On the Nature of Primary Metaphors

Both the source and the target concept of a primary metaphor are equally *basic* concepts, which differ from each other only with regard to whether they are ultimately grounded in a particular *sensorimotor* domain. Primary Metaphor Theory (PMT) claims that the connection between the two concepts is strongly *unidirectional*, such that the source is used to conceptualize and talk about the target, but not vice versa. In the following, we take up each of these aspects in more detail, also responding to recent findings and suggestions.

Basicness Primary metaphors are conceived as associations between fundamental concepts, e.g. defined as concepts that are grounded in universal (rather than culturally determined) aspects of human experience. Considering the three patterns offered above as illustrations, while the six relevant concepts are of course subject to cultural variation (e.g. different cultures might certainly be characterized by different understandings of 'happiness'), the spirit of the primary-metaphor proposal is that there is also a shared element of experience across cultures that forms the basis for these concepts.

That is, primary source and target concepts (such as HEAVINESS and DIFFICULTY, VERTICAL HEIGHT and SOCIAL DOMINANCE, or BRIGHTNESS and HAPPINESS), however they are elaborated in a given culture and language, should ultimately be grounded in what can plausibly be conceived as basic parameters of human physical, social, emotional, or intellectual experience. Other, more particular or culturally contingent concepts – 'house,' 'chair,' 'wife,' 'election,' 'priest,' etc. – do not participate in primary-metaphor patterns. On the other hand, primary metaphors may certainly play a role in figurative conceptualizations of such entities (see section 2.2).

Related to the discussion of possible neural substrates for aspects of primary metaphor in section 2 below, a more concrete definition of 'basicness' might entail that primary source and target concepts are grounded in experiences that are, in some meaningful sense, part of humans' innate cognitive repertoire. That is, a definition of primary source and target concepts might ultimately include the requirement that we are "pre-wired" to have the associated experiences.[1] While certainly not proven with respect to all such concepts, this proposal seems very plausible where concepts like 'difficulty,' 'heaviness,' 'social dominance,' 'vertical height,' 'happiness,' or 'brightness' are concerned – and there is even concrete knowledge of how the brain processes some of these aspects of experience, such as in the visual domain (see section 2).

It is worth considering an interesting challenge to the idea that primary metaphors should be stated at the level of basicness discussed in this section. Through a very clever series of experiments investigating SIMILARITY IS CLOSENESS, Casasanto (2008a) shows that spatial proximity on a screen causes abstract concepts to be judged more similar, but visual stimuli to be judged less similar. Based on these results, he argues that there is no conceptual metaphor linking proximity and similarity – the actual metaphor, on this account, only links proximity and *conceptual* similarity – and concludes that, "[i]f the present results are interpreted as validating conceptual metaphor theory overall, then the theory is rendered too vague to make falsifiable behavioral predictions" (ibid.: 1053). In other words, while people *talk* about perceptual similarity as closeness (as Casasanto observes, "two paint chips can be *close in color*"), they do not *think* in this way, and the experiments "directly contradict predictions that follow from conceptual metaphor theory" (ibid.).

We suggest an alternative interpretation of the experimental data that preserves the original metaphor analysis but requires a more layered consideration of cognitive processes – and one that is in fact closer to the "hierarchical" account offered by Casasanto (2014a, *this volume*): It is possible that there *is* a conceptual link between proximity and similarity (including perceptual similarity) but that this link is "trumped" in the context of a particular judgment task, and quite possibly in other contexts. While CMT is concerned with patterns of association, it does not assert that these associations are predominant in all cognitive situations. In fact, much is made of the finding that the very same target concept can be conceptualized in different ways. Grady (1997a), for instance, observes that moral goodness can be understood as either cleanliness or healthiness. Conceptual metaphors, including primary metaphors, do not *absolutely determine* how we experience or perceive a given topic, rather they create the possibility or probability that we may conceptualize it in this way.[2]

In short, we believe it is both intuitively helpful and consistent with linguistic and experimental data to preserve the idea of a primary metaphor that links the two very basic experiential dimensions of proximity and similarity.

Sensory vs. Non-sensory Concepts The three examples listed above all illustrate another central property of the patterns of association between one conceptual domain and another that constitute primary metaphors: They all include one concept, the source, that is associated with a particular aspect of sensory experience, and another concept, the target, that is not. While the target concepts – HAPPINESS, SOCIAL DOMINANCE, DIFFICULTY – can certainly be associated with experiences that include a sensory dimension (e.g. we might feel happy when we eat chocolate cake), they are not consistently grounded in one particular type of sensory experience and might be experienced independent of any relevant sensory aspect at all (e.g. in the context of the election of a favorite candidate). The relevant source concepts, however – BRIGHTNESS, HEIGHT, HEAVINESS – are each *defined* with relation to a particular aspect of physical, sensory experience. Given the basicness of these dimensions of experience, as just discussed, Grady (2005a) proposed that primary source concepts might in fact be usefully considered a subset of image schemas.

Overall, the distinction between "sensory" and "non-sensory" is obviously resonant with numerous previous claims (e.g. by Lakoff & Johnson 1980) that metaphors map the "concrete" onto the "abstract," for instance (but certainly *not* with various observations that metaphors map the "familiar" onto the "unfamiliar"). On the other hand, the dimensions of experience in which concepts like 'happiness,' 'difficulty,' and 'social dominance' are grounded seem intuitively just as basic as the source experiences they are associated with, though different in kind. For this reason, depending on how we understand the term, it may be misleading to describe primary target concepts as "abstract."

But is "non-sensory" an adequate label, with its implication that primary target concepts as a group are defined only by a quality they lack? Exploring the idea that primary target concepts may constitute a natural category of their own (not defined by exclusion from another category), and referencing his own earlier proposals among others, Grady (2005a: 47) offered the following brief characterization of the nature of primary target concepts and used the term "response content" to distinguish their referents from the sensory referents of associated source concepts: "[Primary target concepts] relate to our interpretations of and responses to the world, our assessments of the physical situations we encounter, their nature and their meaning."

Whether or not "response content" is a fitting label, the spirit of the primary-metaphor proposal has been that source and target are distinguished by a fundamental difference in kind between the two sets of concepts – a distinction that may even be amenable to characterization in neural terms, as we consider in the second part of this chapter.

Directionality The source–target relationship is unidirectional by definition, and in fact, there is a consistent directionality to the semantic extensions motivated by primary metaphors. In accordance with AFFECTION IS WARMTH, for instance, an affectionate person is *warm*, but there are no conventional usages that go in the opposite direction – i.e. with social-emotional terms mapped onto temperature; English speakers would presumably have difficulty guessing the intended meaning of "*affectionate* day," which reverses the direction of the source–target relation. Likewise, relative difficulty is talked about as relative heaviness, but not vice versa (ex 4a), physical height is not figuratively expressed as social dominance (ex 4b) and so forth. Importantly, this directionality is not only a characteristic of conventional linguistic usages, but also predicts whether novel usages are likely to be interpretable.

(4) a. ?? She kept the blanket from blowing away by placing a *difficult* stone on it.
b. ?? Picture A is hanging *in charge of* Picture B on the wall.
c. I have a *fifty-ton* task to complete this weekend.

By contrast, virtually any reference to weight is easily understandable as a reference to relative difficulty (ex 4c). Note that while the discussion here assumes English speakers will agree with judgments of interpretability, there is also experimental evidence regarding the (lack of) aptness of many "reversed" metaphors. For instance, though we know of no experimental evidence specifically focusing on primary metaphors, Chiappe et al. (2003) find that a variety of metaphors are judged uninterpretable when reversed.

A number of recent psychological studies (for reviews, see Lakoff 2014; Shen & Porat, *this volume*) have raised very interesting questions about the unidirectionality of primary metaphors. The key finding reported is that there is non-linguistic behavioral evidence for *two-way* associations between primary sources and targets so that a feeling of suspicion, for instance, can support the detection of a "fishy" smell (cf. SUSPICIOUS IS SMELLY). Lakoff (2014: 8, emphasis in the original) offers the following summary of findings from Lee and Schwarz (2012): "They showed not just that fishy smells induce suspicion, but that *by inducing suspicion in subjects, that subjects were better able to distinguish the smell of fish oil from other smelly oils*." Likewise, thoughts about morality can trigger a sense of feeling clean or unclean (cf. MORAL IS CLEAN); judgments of another individual's social-emotional stance can influence sensations of temperature (cf. AFFECTION IS WARMTH); judgments of relative importance can affect assessments of physical weight (cf. SIZE IS IMPORTANCE), or judgments about similarities influence assessments of spatial distance (cf. SIMILARITY IS CLOSENESS).

What do such bidirectional psychological relationships mean for the theory of primary metaphors? The answer depends in part on how we define "metaphor." One possibility is that we reserve the term for patterns that include lexical instantiation, i.e. usages of words or signs (in signed languages).

Casasanto (e.g. 2013) suggests helpfully that it is worth distinguishing between what he calls “linguistic” and “mental” metaphors, which may overlap and be related but can also be considered separately. In a review of experimental research on various cognitive correlates of handedness, Casasanto (2014a) points out that left-handed individuals, unlike right-handers, tend to associate positive valence with the left side rather than the right – e.g. when asked to rate the appeal of images presented on one side or the other – and that this particular “space-valence association” can even be acquired (unconsciously) by right-handers, through a few minutes of training that constrains action with the dominant hand, allowing the left hand to move more fluently (ibid.: 112). Such a cross-domain association, which is *not* evidenced in language, would be a “mental” metaphor in Casasanto’s terminology.

On the contrary, we propose that such patterns as the association between ‘left’ and ‘good’ – in certain individuals, or at certain times – *not* be considered metaphors per se. Rather, these often-unconscious, cross-domain patterns of mental association constitute, as Casasanto (2013) suggests, the basis for *potential* metaphors that may or may not arise, based on various environmental factors, such as the linguistic usages of other speakers. According to Casasanto (2014a), these patterns do obviously form the basis for the common, cross-linguistic metaphor pattern that associates the right side with good things, presumably because right-handedness is far more common than left-handedness. In fact, it might be helpful to refer to such patterns of cross-domain mental association as “pre-metaphors,” not least because of existing evidence of certain such cross-domain mental associations even in infants (e.g. Lourenco & Longo 2011).[3]

Returning to the question of bidirectional effects, if we reserve the term “metaphor” for the patterns that inform explicit conceptualization (“thinking”) *and* communication (a usage that we feel is consistent with widely shared and intuitive understandings of the nature of metaphors), as opposed to merely unconscious associations affecting behavior, then the directionality of primary metaphors is preserved. While we certainly expect correlated dimensions of experience to lead to cognitive and neural association (Hebb 1949), and while this means we should expect bidirectional effects of some kind related to these correlations (cf. also Lakoff 2014), this is not the same as calling these effects metaphors, which are most usefully and intuitively understood as patterns in language, (explicit) conceptualization, or both.

In sum, we propose that the recent psychological literature on bidirectional associations offers a rich and helpful context, but not counterevidence, for the idea of unidirectional primary metaphors. Certain kinds of correlation in experience (discussed next) lead to (bidirectional) patterns of mental association and to “pre-metaphors” (such as ‘side of the dominant hand is good’) that *may* in the end become (unidirectional) primary metaphors if they are regularly instantiated in conceptual and (consequently also reflected in) linguistic structure. The neurological basis for the directionality of these metaphors is the subject of section 2 of this chapter.

Correlation and Covariation The origins and motivations for primary metaphors are presumed to be related to recurring correlations in experience, as the three examples offered at the beginning of this section illustrate. Brightness in our environment is correlated with positive affect, the weight of an object is correlated with the degree of effort required to lift or move it, and so forth. Lakoff and Johnson (1980) pointed out such correlations as the basis for some metaphors, and Primary Metaphor Theory (Grady 1997a) takes the step of identifying primary metaphors as ones that are plausibly motivated in this way – as opposed to more complex, culture-specific metaphor patterns such as the conceptualization of THEORIES *as* BUILDINGS (Grady 1997b).

As Grady (2005b) points out, however, mere correlation between two aspects or dimensions of experience (one sensory, the other not) is not enough to predict a metaphorical relationship. These aspects must also be construable as sharing the same "superschematic structure":

> For instance, they must both be construable as states (viability – erect posture), as scalar properties (bright – happy), as atemporal relations (inside X – member of category X), or as actions (achieving a purpose – arriving at a destination), as events (failure – collapse; seeing – coming to know), as entities which can serve as landmarks, or as trajectors (state of affairs which is allowed to continue – physically supported object; fact – object which is seen), and so forth. (ibid.: 1606)

Even if eating is correlated with positive affect, for instance, we do not find conceptual patterns such as HAPPINESS (state) IS EATING (action/process). Additionally, to form the basis for a primary metaphor, the two correlated dimensions of experience must "covary":

> [A] difference in one domain, such as a difference in degree or quantity, for example, must be associated with a corresponding difference in the other. This is easiest to see in the case of scalar properties, and especially cases where either source causes target or vice versa. For instance, increased anger means increased heat, and increased heaviness means increased difficulty. (ibid.: 1607)

Finally, while these relationships predict the likely existence of a primary metaphor in most or all languages and cultures (see below), logical prediction is not the same as causal explanation. How exactly do primary metaphors arise? Are they natural products of experience and development, i.e. associations learned through repeated experiential correlations from infancy on? Might they be innate? Or are they culturally transmitted?

From the perspective of Primary Metaphor Theory, the most plausible general answer seems to be that experiences lead to natural cognitive associations ("pre-metaphors"), which then may or may not be established as conventional patterns of conceptual and linguistic associations, depending on the presence or absence of reinforcement from the surrounding linguistic and cultural environment. On the other hand, Casasanto (*this volume*) cites experimental evidence with infants, suggesting that at least some primary metaphors may in fact be based on innate patterns of cross-domain association, e.g. between magnitude in time and space, respectively. "Pre-metaphors" could thus be either learned or innate (for a detailed discussion of this, see Casasanto 2014a, *this volume*).

Wide Distribution across Languages Table 2.1 offers a number of additional examples of words from sixteen languages that follow five different primary-metaphor patterns, including two of the metaphors introduced above.

Evidence for primary-metaphor patterns is found in languages so widely distributed in space and time that borrowing is not a plausible explanation. Instead, as implied by the kinds of considerations discussed above, it seems that primary metaphors reflect universal aspects of human experience, cognition or neural structure, or a combination of these.

Note, however, that the universality of a set of motivations for primary metaphors does not imply that lexical patterns themselves must be universal. There are a number of intervening factors between experience, for instance, and linguistic conventionalization, including cultural mediation, so that even a conceptual association that is well motivated may not end up leading to a productive pattern of semantic extension. Bernárdez (2013: 417–420) reviews a number of studies and offers a compelling discussion of the fact that quite a few languages (in Australia, South America, and elsewhere) have a strong metaphorical pattern linking 'knowing' with 'hearing' but only a weak pattern, or none at all, linking 'knowing' and 'seeing' – the pattern familiar in usages of myriad English words such as *introspection*.

If particular patterns of conceptual association are well motivated yet not lexically conventional in a given language, it is an interesting question – not yet experimentally tested, to our knowledge – whether speakers of such a language might nonetheless easily grasp and learn these patterns. For instance, might speakers of an Australian language apparently lacking the KNOWING IS SEEING pattern nonetheless easily guess the intended meanings, related to knowledge, of novel usages of seeing verbs in their language? The discussion in this chapter, along with other discussions of motivations/origins for primary (or correlation-based) metaphors (e.g. Casasanto 2014a), predict such patterns would be easily learned.[4]

Bases for More Complex Conceptualization Grady (1997b) reexamined the pattern that Lakoff and Johnson (1980) had called THEORIES ARE BUILDINGS and concluded that, for several reasons, it is best understood as a

Table 2.1 *Cross-linguistic survey of linguistic polysemy motivated by primary metaphor*

	HEAVY → DIFFICULT, ARDUOUS	HIGH → SOCIALLY DOMINANT	LARGE → IMPORTANT	HOLD/GRASP → CONTROL	HOT → EMOTIONALLY AGITATED
Arabic	*thaqil* ('heavy')	*'ala* ('above')	*kabir* ('large')	*qabda* ('grip')	*harara* ('heat')
Basque	*pezütarzün* ('weight')	*goi* ('high')	*handi* ('large')	*esku* ('hand')	*bero* ('hot')
Finnish	*raskas* ('heavy')	*yli-* ('above')	*suuri* ('large')	*käsi* ('hand')	*kuuma* ('hot')
Hausa	*naunaya* ('make heavy')	*kai* ('top')	*'bagume* ('become large')	*dank'a* ('hand to')	*zafi* ('heat')
Hawaiian	*kaumaha* ('heavy')	*luna* ('above')	*nui* ('large')	*kaohi* ('hold')	*wela* ('heat')
Hungarian	*nehéz* ('heavy')	*magas* ('high')	*nagy* ('large')	*szorít* ('grasp')	*forró* ('hot')
Japanese	*omoi* ('heavy')	*ue* ('above')	*ookii* ('large')	*te* ('hand')	*netsu* ('heat)'
Malay	*berat* ('heavy')	*tinggi* ('high')	*besar* ('large')	*pegang* ('hold')	*panas* ('hot')
Mandarin	*zhóng* ('heavy')	*sháng* ('above')	*dà* ('large')	*ba* ('hold')	*rè* ('be hot')
Old Irish	*tromm* ('heavy')	*ós* ('above')	*mór* ('large')	*lám* ('hand')	*té* ('hot')
Russian	*t'azolıj* ('heavy')	*v'erx* ('top')	*krupnıj* ('large')	*d'erzat'* ('hold')	*gor'acij* ('hot')
Sanskrit	*guru* ('heavy')	*upári* ('above')	*mahâ-* ('large')	*grah-* ('grasp')	*usna-* ('hot')
Swahili	*-zito* ('heavy')	*juu* ('above')	*-kubwa* ('large')	*mkono* ('hand')	*moto* ('heat')
Tagalog	*mabigat* ('heavy')	*ipataas* ('raise')	*malaki* ('large')	*hawak* ('grip')	*mainit* ('hot')
Turkish	*agır* ('heavy')	*üst* ('top')	*büyük* ('large')	*tutmak* ('hold')	*kizgin* ('hot')
Zulu	*-nzima* ('heavy')	*enyuka* ('rise')	*-khulu* ('size')	*phatha* ('hold')	*-shis-* ('heat')

combination and special case of two more basic mappings: one relating CAUSAL/LOGICAL STRUCTURE (ORGANIZATION) TO PHYSICAL STRUCTURE (5a), the other relating VIABILITY/FUNCTIONALITY to ERECTNESS (Ex 5a, b, cf. Grady 1997b). Each of these patterns is easily motivated by the kinds of correlations associated with primary metaphors, and each leads to a wide range of linguistic usages that have nothing to do with buildings (instead making reference to textiles, works of art, etc.) and can apply to a wide range of concepts from target domains (besides theories), such as social relations or ecosystems.

(5) a. the *fabric* of society, an *array* of procedures, a *masterpiece* of logical construction
b. the *foundation* of marriage, the *collapse* of the Bay's ecosystem

Following up in a similar vein, Grady (2005b) discussed primary metaphors as a special type of input to conceptual integration (Fauconnier & Turner 2002). For example, a novel linguistic metaphor that frames aloofness as a "glacier, slow to melt away" (Grady 2005b: 1608) is an elaboration of the more basic (primary) association between 'temperature' and 'affect' (AFFECTION IS WARMTH). Likewise, many other complex and culture-specific metaphors are also based on and informed by primary patterns: Grady et al. (1999) discuss how the "Ship of State" metaphor pattern, while culturally determined to a significant degree, is also grounded in such primary (and widely distributed) patterns as ACTION IS SELF-PROPELLED MOTION, GOALS ARE DESTINATIONS, and SOCIAL RELATIONS ARE CONTAINERS.

In sum, primary metaphors are often the starting points for richer, more vivid, specific, and idiosyncratic conceptualizations (for a discourse-based illustration of this point, see Deignan, *this volume*).

2.2 *On the Function(ality) of Primary Metaphors*

Given that primary-metaphor patterns are so ubiquitous, both within English and across languages, it is natural to ask why. At least three broad categories of hypothetical answers to this question suggest themselves:

(i) *There is no "function"*: The patterns are epiphenomenal, not "useful," an accidental by-product of some other aspect(s) of experience or brain function that happen to lead to particular linguistic and conceptual associations. (The possibility that primary metaphors are epiphenomenal in this sense can be considered the null hypothesis with respect to function.)

(ii) *Primary metaphors offer communicative advantages*: Source concepts are sensory in nature, and by definition associated with particular "images" – in a broad sense that includes kinetic and auditory images as well as visual ones.

Thus, as basic elements of a communicative setting (as opposed to the internal, emotional world of the interlocutors, for instance), they might serve as "anchors" for communication, as speakers are able to point to and agree on their referents. If relatively more subjective or "abstract" target concepts such as 'happiness' or 'difficulty' can be linked with these concepts, there may be communicative advantages to these associations.

(iii) *Primary metaphors offer cognitive advantages*: If cognition related to source concepts is in any way different in character from cognition related to target concepts, then even if we were not communicating with others, primary metaphors might hypothetically play a useful role in conceptualization – namely by allowing us to harness cognitive capacities associated with source concepts when processing (in whatever sense) target concepts.

Any of these hypotheses may be true, and the last two are not mutually exclusive. But the third is arguably the strongest and most interesting. It suggests a reason to explore possible neural substrates for "sourceness" and "targetness," in case these point to processing differences that would lead to cognitive advantages of some kind when source and target are associated.

3 Thinking Ahead: A Proposal on the Neural Character of Primary Source and Target

While scholars in several fields have explored linguistic, psychological, and other aspects of primary metaphors (*this volume*: Casasanto; Cuccio; Mittelberg & Joue; Winter & Matlock), it is currently unknown whether primary metaphors reflect aspects of neural organization or function. But given the basic and (seemingly) universal nature of these patterns, it is potentially fruitful to speculate whether there may be neural correlates to some aspects of primary metaphor – possibly related to the cognitive characteristics referred to in the discussion of potential cognitive advantages above. More specifically, can neural signatures of sourceness vs. targetness be identified? We suggest in the remainder of the discussion that the answer may be yes and explore several related hypotheses, which may ultimately describe the neural signatures in question.

Lakoff (2014: 5) proposes that the asymmetry between source and target, and, in particular, the directionality between them, can be explained based on ordering: "The asymmetry of the mappings appears to arise via STDP – spike-timing dependent plasticity – from which metaphor sources and targets can be predicted."

To the best of our understanding, Lakoff is arguing that if (the experiences underlying) two concepts tend to be associated, according to STDP, the more frequent of the two would tend to become pre-synaptic and the less frequent would tend to become post-synaptic. It is useful here to recall the basic rule of STDP: If neuron A fires "just before" neuron B, the synapses from (the axons of) A to (the dendrites of) B are strengthened, while the synapses from (the axons of) B to (the dendrites of) A are weakened. Thus, Lakoff's STDP hypothesis makes assumptions about which neurons fire more frequently and also assumes that the neurons firing more frequently would tend to fire "just before" those firing less frequently.[5] We take no position on these assumptions except to suggest that they would need to be substantiated. In any case, we believe there are additional hypotheses worth exploring when it comes to the distinctions between source and target, and the possible cognitive advantages of linking one to the other.

For purposes of subsequent discussion, it will be helpful to distinguish four aspects of the complex set of experiential, cognitive, and social processes that ultimately yields semantic meaning:

stimulus ➔ (phenomenological) experience ➔ concept ➔ language

While the relationships among these are certainly not as simple as a linear, ordered chain, the ordering above is also not random and reflects an intuitive scenario in which the existence of a stimulus is a logical starting point and a fact about language is the end result. A given stimulus (e.g. an apple) is perceived in ways that lead to an experience of that stimulus (e.g. of the flavor, visual image, or weight of an apple); concepts, in turn (e.g. the concept 'apple'), are in some way connected with and refer to such experiences; and language, in turn (e.g. the English word "apple"), is built on and refers to such concepts.

There are endless possible ways of reinterpreting these relationships, but such discussions are not germane to the present chapter, and the schema above is presented only to clarify that the discussion is primarily concerned with neural structures and processing related to *experiences* – e.g. the neural processes that allow us to experience the look, feel, or taste of an apple, or any emotional responses associated with apple – as opposed to the neural substrates of concepts or language per se.[6] More specifically, our discussion will largely focus on the substrates for "primary source concept experiences" (source experiences, or SEs, for short) and "primary target concept experiences" (TEs).

3.1 Localized vs. Distributed Neural Substrates

Having established that we will be focusing on distinctions at the level of neural substrates of perception and phenomenological experience, there are several related hypotheses worth exploring regarding the ways in which the substrates for SEs may differ systematically from those of TEs. The main hypothesis we explore here is that the brain activity patterns representing source experiences are organized based on cortical positions (as sets of localized "hotspots"), which we will refer to as "neural maps." In other words, we propose that the experiences associated with source concepts such as HEAVINESS, HEIGHT, and BRIGHTNESS are more likely to have neural substrates characterized by neural maps, than are the experiences associated with target concepts such as DIFFICULTY, DOMINANCE, or HAPPINESS.

This position is generally consistent with the known functional organization of the mammalian neocortex pertaining to perception of the body and of the external world (Bednar & Wilson 2015). For example, the sensory cortex represents somatic sensation (such as touch, pain, and cold or hot detection) from skin receptors approximately preserving the local organization of the periphery. A similar "body map" in the motor cortex (known as the *homunculus*) codes for the planning and execution of intended movements (Graziano & Aflalo 2007).

One type of cortical localization is the case of so-called "topographic mapping," in which nearby cortical locations encode for similar stimuli (Chklovskii & Koulakov 2004). In other words, parts of the cortex are organized such that adjacent neurons respond to the same type of stimulus (e.g. edges of visual shapes or frequencies of sound tones), and the spatial positions of the neurons themselves encode variations that can be detected, such as relative inclination angles of an edge or the pitch of a voice. All primary sensory and motor maps in the mammalian neocortex are topographic, but higher associative areas such as the frontal neocortex are also known to follow a topographic architecture (Silver & Kastner 2009).

At the same time, due to the complex and far-reaching, tree-shaped structure of their input and output extensions (dendrites and axons, respectively), cortical nerve cells can also form non-topographic maps. That is, they can form complexes (so-called "cell assemblies") that act together to perceive, process, and represent particular types of stimuli in the way that topographic maps do, though they are not physically adjacent in the same sense. Among the most evolutionarily conserved examples of these non-topographic maps (i.e. showing significant similarities among species related to humans and to each other) are the neural systems responsible for spatial representation, which have also been shown to play a role in higher cognition and language (Landau & Lakusta 2009). Some of the most striking examples of these spatial maps are given by the so-called systems of "place cells" in the hippocampal formation. Place cells are neurons that are selectively active when the subject is in a particular location within an environment. For example, in the context of a residential setting, a specific hippocampal neuron might be systematically active when the subject stands by the stove in the kitchen, another neuron when the subject is in the shower, and yet another when the subject crosses the entrance doorway. The map is non-topographic because nearby locations are not reflected by nearby neurons and vice versa: the 'stove' neuron and the 'shower' neuron might be adjacent in the hippocampus (even if the kitchen and bathroom are in opposite locations in the house), whereas a neuron representing the medicine cabinet in the bathroom just next to the shower might be physically located in a relatively faraway position of the hippocampus.

Although the activity of all hippocampal neurons is spatially modulated (McNaughton et al. 1996), pyramidal cells (the main neuron types in the hippocampus) display the strongest and most reliable place fields. More generally, activity in the neural circuits of the hippocampus appears to be involved in spatial navigation (Hartley et al. 2014) and, of relevance to our proposal, in the spatial aspects of imagination (Bird et al. 2012).

In both topographic and non-topographic maps, the cortical representations of experience remain fairly localized and encoded in the actual positions of the activation foci. This survey represents only a greatly simplified account of the experimental neuroscientific evidence, as the extent of the topography (and even map-like character) of cortical representation may vary substantially depending on the considered level of analysis, from microscopic neuronal assemblies to macroscopic regional activation (Kanold et al. 2014).

The hypothesis we suggest here is that the neural representation of an SE (such as the pattern of activity necessary for representation of an experience of heaviness or brightness) corresponds to a significantly smaller set of such loci than the representation of a typical TE (such as difficulty or happiness). In this sense, the cortical representation of SEs would be substantially more *localized* than the representation of TEs. For instance, the physical brightness of a light stimulus is encoded as visual intensity in the primary cortex in the occipital lobe organized as a retinotopic map (that is, cortical positions actually reflect the locations in which light entered the retina at the back of the eye). Similarly, heat is encoded in temperature-sensitive patches of somatosensory cortex in the parietal lobe organized as a body map (the homunculus). Likewise, heaviness is encoded as force intensity during movement planning in the premotor cortex in the frontal lobe organized as a directional map.

If SEs are, as just discussed, associated with more localized representations, TEs appear to be associated with more distributed representations and *diffuse brain states*. As an extreme case of diffuse, distributed representation, many target concepts – specifically those associated with *affect* – appear to be considerably related to a system of neurotransmitters that modulate cortical activity across the entire cerebral cortex rather than locally (Zaborszky 2002). These modulatory neurotransmitters include, among others, acetylcholine (associated with states of purposeful arousal, as during a search activity), dopamine (positive and negative valence), serotonin (satisfaction or aversion to risk-taking), and noradrenaline (sudden and unexpected novelty). It seems that many TEs – such as those associated with happiness and difficulty – may consist of or include affective states represented by a combination of such diffuse representations throughout cortical areas. Although the literature on emotional representation in the brain is immense (and there has also been considerable study of the culturally determined dimensions of emotion), our specific emphasis on target concepts in primary metaphors leads us to focus on the neural correlates of *declarative* experience (Mitchell & Greening 2012), as well as the most basic psychological and physiological dimensions that experiences of happiness, for instance, might share across cultures.

It is tempting to speculate that other primary target concepts, including DOMINANCE or others related to social status, may also be less correlated than source concepts with localized areas of activity, and more correlated with diffuse cortical states (see Table 2.2). If true, such a pattern would add substance to previous suggestions (e.g. Grady 2005a) that primary target concepts encode aspects of our response to the environment, while source

Table 2.2 *Primary source and target, and potential neural substrates*

Source experience	Target experience	English examples	Neural map [sensorimotor "pre-wiring"]	Relevant neurotransitter(s)
HEAVINESS	DIFFICULTY	*work load, light duty*	primary motor	acetylcholine (Ach)
HEIGHT	SOCIAL DOMINANCE	*middle class, high officer*	visual topograpy	aoradrenaline (NA)
BRIGHTNESS	HAPPINESS	*sunny disposition, dark hours*	visual intensity	dopamine (DA)
HEAT	EMOTIONAL AROUSAL	*cool off, heated discussion*	somatic homunculus	serotonin (HT)
SIZE	IMPORTANCE	*a big day a small change*	secondary visual	NA/Ach
FORWARD MOTION	PROGRESS TOWARD GOAL	*getting there, one step forward, two steps back*	secondary motor	DA/HT
PROXIMITY	SIMILARITY	*close (e.g. in skills), far apart (e.g. in ideas)*	visual topograpy	Ach[1]

[1]Acetylcholine could be correlated with TEs for 'similarity' if these are in any way related to search tasks – that is, if detecting similarity between two objects of attention is related to identifying objects of search tasks.

concepts encode our physical perceptions of it. In effect, SEs would make up something like a "physical map" of a given scenario, i.e. reflect the physical aspects of the scenario, while TEs would make up a "goal-related map," i.e. reflect various aspects of our goal-orientation, correlated in turn with characteristic balances of neurotransmitters, and possibly other non- or less localized aspects of cortical activity.

3.2 Attentional Mechanisms

An interesting consequence of the proposed neural distinctions between SEs and TEs along the lines of cortical localization vs. neuro-modulatory diffuseness is that SEs may be more closely associated than TEs with *attentional mechanisms*, making it easier in some sense to focus on source concepts. According to this perspective, attention might be bootstrapped to target concepts via source concepts, potentially yielding a cognitive advantage of primary metaphors.

A brain region relevant to this consideration is the thalamus, which plays a crucial role in selective gating (Shipp 2004): the process of suppressing or allowing activity in a given set of neurons. The thalamus is robustly and bidirectionally connected with all areas of the neocortex and is believed to modulate relative levels of activity in various neocortical locations, giving rise to the ability to selectively experience/attend to some stimuli vs. others.[7] Given the previous discussion of cortical localization, i.e. the positional encoding of the neural correlates of SEs, it may be the case that the attentional mechanisms associated with the thalamus can act more directly on these localized representations than on the more diffuse states associated with TEs.

An additional notion worth considering related to the aforementioned attentional mechanisms concerns a micro 'aha' or 'eureka' effect, which may again involve bootstrapping of target concepts by source concepts. An intriguing possibility is that when we "successfully" attend to or focus on a concept – i.e. when the brain successfully stabilizes into a state representing a particular experience, which might happen on the order of many times per second – the resulting neural and cognitive events correspond in some sense to effective thought, as opposed to random noisy activity (Kounios & Beeman 2014). If it is easier to achieve this type of stabilization, and the resulting cognitive "reward," with source than with target concepts – e.g. due to attentional mechanisms discussed earlier – then linking the two may enable this effect with target concepts as well. In short, SEs may be associated with *more stable or identifiable representations* than target concepts, perhaps mediated in part by the neural map organization discussed above, and this stability could in turn lead to a cognitive distinction and advantage.

4 Conclusion

The speculation in the second part of this chapter is partly motivated by a desire to capture the intuition that metaphors are "helpful" in some sense, while also recognizing that primary target concepts, or at least TEs, are so basic to our experience that it is difficult to see how we would need help thinking or talking about them. The hope going forward is that further research may help clarify, possibly by following up on suggestions offered here, the types of cognitive advantage that could result from linking a concept correlated with localized neural map(s) on the one hand, with concepts correlated with more diffuse representation on the other.

The discussion is further motivated by questions regarding "sourceness" and "targetness" as real categories of concepts, and tries to build on the widely shared intuition that these concepts are of meaningfully different kinds. If so, can we expect the conceptual differences to be reflected in distinct types of neural signature? In at least some cases, there seem to be promising directions to look in for such distinctions.

An additional, related question not substantively addressed in the body of the chapter concerns "primary-ness" itself, and whether this too might be a meaningful category from a conceptual and/or neural point of view. For instance, it might be useful to define primary (source and target) concepts (like HEAVY, DIFFICULT, HIGH, DOMINANT, BRIGHT, HAPPY, etc. as opposed to more specific concepts like 'house,' 'marry') as those whose associated experiences the brain is pre-wired to process or represent. Neuroscience research is making promising progress in elucidating the molecular, physiological, and behavioral dynamics underlying the formation and alignment of topographic brain maps within and across representation modalities (Cang & Feldheim 2013).

Finally, all of the above hypotheses arise from looking at a small sample of primary metaphors. We hope that future research might follow up on some of the questions and hypotheses suggested here by looking more systematically at a broader set of patterns.

Notes and Acknowledgments

* The authors would like to thank an anonymous external reviewer and especially the volume editor for extremely helpful comments that improved the quality of the paper.

1 In fact, it may not even be unreasonable to suggest that the experience types at the root of primary source and target concepts are so basic that non-human primates such as chimps should also be pre-wired for them – e.g. to judge brightness, heaviness, relative height, and to have experiences corresponding to what humans know as happiness, effortfulness, social dominance – though not, of course, to have concepts or language related to these experiences.

2 We wonder whether an experiment could test the interpretation offered here, e.g. one that does not involve judging the similarity of two stimuli visible at the same time (a context that seems sure to override any influence of an association between similarity and proximity) but instead assesses whether visually similar objects are *placed* closer to one another, whether visually similar stimuli, seen at different times, are subsequently assigned to nearby locations in a placing task, etc.

3 Building on a comment in an earlier footnote, it might be possible, and would certainly be interesting, to experimentally test whether non-human primates show behavioral evidence of associations between, e.g., warmth and affect, weight and significance, etc. – i.e. whether they have pre-metaphors in the sense discussed above.

4 Casasanto (2014a: 13–14) offers indirect support for the idea that experientially motivated "pre-metaphors" might exist in the mind, in ways that could make learning of actual metaphorical (linguistic) patterns more likely. He reports experimental results according to which Farsi and Dutch speakers, after a brief period of training with pitch metaphors present in the respective other language but not in their own (the sources being relative 'height' vs. 'thickness' of a tone), showed similar non-linguistic behavioral (interference) effects (caused by the metaphor) as speakers of the respective other language. Such effects did not occur when learning another novel metaphor not supported by experiential correlation.

5 "Those neurons that fire more tend to develop greater firing capacities. And those involved in physical bodily functioning tend to fire more. For this reason, the metaphorical maps learned are asymmetric and tend to have physical source domains" (Lakoff 2008a: 28).

6 Criticizing PMT's tradition of taking the "modality of the constitution of perceptual experience" (which provides the source concepts of primary metaphors) for granted, Cuccio (*this volume*) makes suggestions based on Gallagher's distinction between "body schema" and "body image."

7 Note that diffuse neuro-regulatory mechanisms, e.g. involving acetylcholine, are believed to play an important role in *overall attentiveness* and ability to focus. In contrast, the thalamic gateway offers a mechanism for localized attention (as opposed to a state of attentiveness) that can be distinctly dissociated from emotional components of experience (Arend et al. 2015).

3 The Hierarchical Structure of Mental Metaphors

*Daniel Casasanto**

Chapter Preview

People think about abstract domains like TIME and GOODNESS metaphorically. This tendency may be universal. Yet the particular mental metaphors that people use can differ dramatically between individuals and groups, and may change from one moment to the next. Where do our mental metaphors come from, and how can they change so quickly in response to new patterns of experience? If mental metaphors are grounded in universal patterns of body–world interaction, how can different people have contrasting (and sometimes contradictory) mental metaphors? Hierarchical Mental Metaphors Theory (HMMT) provides an account of: (a) how mental metaphors are formed and changed, (b) how they can be fundamental to our understanding of abstract domains, yet at the same time remarkably flexible, and (c) how distinctive language-specific, culture-specific, and body-specific mental metaphors can arise from universal patterns of interaction with the physical and social world.

1 Introduction

According to theories of metaphorical mental representation, metaphors in language are more than just ways of talking, they are clues to a pervasive way of thinking (Lakoff & Johnson 1980). On this view, when people use expressions like a "*long* vacation," a "*high* price," or a "*close* resemblance," they are using mental representations of space (i.e. 'length,' 'height,' 'proximity') to scaffold mental representations in non-spatial conceptual domains (i.e. 'time,' 'value,' 'similarity'). Although initial evidence for metaphor theory was based on descriptive analyses of how people talk, there is now abundant experimental evidence that people also *think* metaphorically – even when they are not using any metaphorical language (or using language, at all) (for a review, see Casasanto & Bottini 2014a). That is, people often think in "mental metaphors" (Casasanto

2008a, b): point-to-point mappings between nonlinguistic representations in a "source domain" (e.g. SPACE) and a "target domain" (e.g. TIME) that is typically more abstract (i.e. hard to perceive) or abstruse (i.e. hard to understand; Lakoff & Johnson 1980), which support inferences in the target domain.

The term "mental metaphor" is used contrastively with "linguistic metaphor" here, the former designating a mapping between non-linguistic mental representations, and the latter between linguistic representations.[1] Distinguishing mental metaphors from linguistic metaphors becomes particularly important in contexts like the present chapter where I raise questions like: "Do people who use different linguistic metaphors think in correspondingly different mental metaphors?" and "Do people sometimes think in mental metaphors that are absent from language?"

Where do our mental metaphors come from? Does everyone use the same mental metaphors, at least when they are thinking about universal experiences like the passage of time? Once established, do our basic mental metaphors ever change? Some of the answers to these questions offered by metaphor theory's founders (Lakoff 1993; Lakoff & Johnson 1999) are at odds with a growing body of experimental results. In this chapter I first illustrate the tension between some core tenets of Conceptual Metaphor Theory (Lakoff & Johnson 1999) and experimental tests of metaphorical thinking. I then describe a proposed resolution, Hierarchical Mental Metaphors Theory (Casasanto 2008b; Casasanto & Bottini 2014a, b), and review three sets of studies that serve as testbeds for this proposal.

2 Origin and Universality of Mental Metaphors: Puzzles and Paradoxes

According to Lakoff and Johnson (1999), our most basic mental metaphors are universal because we learn them from universal correlations between source and target domains in the natural environment:

> We acquire a large system of primary metaphors automatically and unconsciously simply by functioning in the most ordinary of ways in the everyday world from our earliest years. We have no choice in this [. . .]
>
> When the embodied experiences in the world are universal, then the corresponding primary metaphors are universally acquired [. . .] Universal conceptual metaphors are learned; they are universals that are not innate. (ibid.: 47, 56–57)

Once acquired, these basic mental metaphors are said to constitute "fixed conceptual mappings" (ibid.: 149), implemented in "permanent neural connections ... across the neural networks that define conceptual domains" (ibid.: 46).

To summarize these points, our basic mental metaphors are proposed to be: (a) *learned* early in life on the basis of source–target correlations in the world; (b) *universal*, so long as the source–target correlations in the world are universal, and (c) *fixed*, by virtue of their implementation in permanent neural connections.

Yet the claims that basic mental metaphors are *learned*, *universal*, and *fixed* are all challenged by experimental data that have accumulated over the past decade. The claim that primary metaphors are learned early in life on the basis of observed source–target correlations was called into question by the most direct test to date. De Hevia and colleagues (2014) showed that neonates between 0 and 3 days old are already sensitive to relationships between spatial, temporal, and numerical magnitudes that are encoded in linguistic expressions like "a *long* time" and "a *large* number." At 0 to 3 days, these infants presumably had no understanding of linguistic and cultural conventions linking these domains, and had very little experience with correlations between them in the natural world. The data presented by de Hevia and colleagues thus suggest that cross-domain mappings between space, time, and number may be innate, not learned.

The claim that mental metaphors are universal is challenged by numerous experiments demonstrating crosslinguistic, cross-cultural, and cross-individual variation in spatial mappings for basic domains of experience. For example, some languages talk about musical pitch in terms of one-dimensional spatial height, whereas other languages metaphorize pitch in terms of multidimensional spatial thickness; speakers' mental metaphors for pitch differ accordingly (Dolscheid et al. 2013). Some cultures depict temporal sequences as unfolding rightward across calendars, graphs, and written timelines, whereas other cultures depict them as unfolding leftward; people's mental timelines follow the directions of these culture-specific SPACE–TIME mappings (Casasanto & Bottini 2014b; Fuhrman & Boroditsky 2010; Ouellet et al. 2010; Tversky et al. 1991). Right-handers implicitly associate positive ideas and emotions with the right side of space and negative ideas with the left, but left-handers show the opposite associations between space and emotional valence (Casasanto 2009a). These studies showing that mental metaphors can be language-specific, culture-specific, or body-specific also challenge the claim that cross-domain mappings in our minds are *fixed*; on the contrary, mental metaphors that are deeply entrenched and highly automatic can be changed – even reversed – after as little as 5 minutes of exposure to different cross-domain relationships. How can mental metaphors be grounded in universals of experience if they vary across people? How can they be fundamental to our conceptualizations of target domains if they can change in a matter of minutes?

3 A Proposed Solution: Hierarchical Mental Metaphors Theory

A solution to these apparent paradoxes emerges if we consider that even our most basic mental metaphors are constructed over multiple timescales, on the basis of multiple kinds of experience. According to Hierarchical Mental Metaphors Theory (HMMT; Casasanto & Bottini 2014a,b; see also Casasanto 2008b, 2014b; Dolscheid et al. 2013), the cross-domain mappings that people use at any moment are members of a *superordinate family of mappings*. The superordinate family is typically constructed on the basis of source–target relationships in the natural world. These relationships could be learned from early experiences with source and target domains, as Lakoff and Johnson (1999) suggest, or they could be part of infants' innate "core knowledge" (Srinivasan & Carey 2010). Cross-domain relationships like MORE TIME IS MORE DISTANCE are survival-relevant and could plausibly become encoded in the human genome. Whether learned or innate, each superordinate family of mental metaphors constitutes a set of mappings that can be used for scaffolding target-domain thinking and can be encoded in linguistic and cultural conventions. For a given target domain (e.g. PITCH), children acquire (or manifest) a superordinate family of source-domain mappings early in life. To the extent that source–target relationships in the natural world are found universally, superordinate families of mental metaphors should be universal.

Once learners are exposed to relevant conventions in language and culture, or to regularities in the way they use their particular bodies, a second process begins which can continue throughout the lifetime and gives rise to the diversity of mental metaphors found across individuals and groups. One of the mappings from a superordinate family (or a subset of the mappings) becomes strengthened through a process of competitive associative learning. For example, each time someone uses a linguistic metaphor, the corresponding non-linguistic source–target mapping is activated. Activating a mapping *strengthens* this source–target association and, importantly, also *weakens* the competing source–target mappings in the same family, as a consequence. The process of strengthening the frequently activated mappings within a family, and of weakening their "sibling" mappings, follows naturally from the dynamics of long-term memory networks for families of associations (e.g. Anderson et al. 2000).

The process of strengthening and weakening specific mappings within superordinate families can account for several otherwise mysterious properties of mental metaphors. First, this hierarchical model can explain how mental metaphors can be grounded in universal source–target relationships in the natural world and yet be variable across people. Even if superordinate families are universal, the specific mappings that get used most frequently or automatically can vary across individuals and groups. On this view, there is no single answer to the question, "Are our mental metaphors universal?"

Second, HMMT can explain how mappings can change rapidly in response to new patterns of experience. In the examples that will be reviewed below, participants are implicitly using "new" mappings that differ from – and in some cases directly contradict – the mappings they ordinarily use, after only brief experimental interventions. This rapid change is possible because the "new" mappings introduced during the experiment are not really new; rather, they are members of the same superordinate family as the mappings participants normally use and can become strengthened through repeated use to the point that they are (at least temporarily) stronger than the mappings that participants ordinarily use.[2]

Here I will focus on the three sets of mental metaphors mentioned above, whose use is conditioned by different streams of physical and social experience. Spatial representations of a particular dimensionality or directionality serve as the metaphorical source domain that structures people's mental representations in the target domains of MUSICAL PITCH, TIME, and EMOTIONAL VALENCE. These target domains are more "abstract" than the domain of space insomuch as they are impossible to see or touch; in the cases of time and valence, they are impossible to experience through any of the five senses. That is, we can see the spatial length of a rope or the height of a ladder, but we can never *see* the length of a vacation (i.e. its duration) or the height of a musical note (i.e. its auditory frequency).[3]

Spatializing these non-spatial domains in our minds may make our experiences of pitch, time, and valence easier to imagine, compare, or remember. It may be a human universal to conceptualize these domains in terms of space (cf. Eitan & Timmers 2010; Whorf 1956), but the particulars of these spatial representations vary across groups of people, according to the particulars of their linguistic, cultural, or bodily experiences. The mechanism underlying all of these effects of experience, I will suggest, is the same: Habitual experiences cause a certain mental metaphor to be activated frequently, strengthening this source–target association in memory, at the expense of competing associations within the same family of mappings.

4 Spatial Representations of Musical Pitch: Universals and Language-Specificity

In many languages, pitch is metaphorized in terms of vertical space: High-frequency pitches are "high" and low-frequency pitches "low." But this is not the only possible spatial metaphor for pitch. In other languages like Farsi, Turkish, and Zapotec, high-frequency pitches are "thin" and low-frequency pitches are "thick" (Shayan et al. 2011). Beyond talking about pitch using spatial words, do people think about pitch using spatial representations? Several studies suggest that speakers of "height languages" like English activate vertical SPACE–PITCH mappings when judging pitches (e.g. Pratt 1930; Roffler & Butler 1968). In one set of experiments, Dolscheid et al. (2013) investigated (a) whether people still activate SPACE–PITCH associations even when they are not using language, and (b) whether speakers of "height languages" and "thickness languages" tend to use the same non-linguistic SPACE–PITCH associations, or whether their mental metaphors for pitch are shaped by their experience of using linguistic metaphors.

Like English, Dutch describes pitches as *hoog* ('high') or *laag* ('low'), but in Farsi, high pitches are 'thin' (*nāzok*) and low pitches are 'thick' (*koloft*), as already noted. Dolscheid et al. (2013) tested Dutch and Farsi speakers on a pair of non-linguistic pitch reproduction tasks in which participants were asked to reproduce the pitches of tones that they heard in the presence of irrelevant spatial information: either lines that varied in their height (height interference task) or their thickness (thickness interference task). Dutch speakers' pitch estimates were strongly affected by irrelevant spatial height information. On average, a given tone was sung back higher when it had been accompanied by a line that was high on the computer screen, and lower when it had been accompanied by a line that appeared low on the screen. By contrast, lines of various thicknesses had no measurable effect on Dutch participants' pitch estimates. Farsi speakers showed the opposite pattern of results. Lines of varying heights had no measurable effect on Farsi speakers' pitch estimates, but tones accompanied by thin lines were sung back higher, and tones accompanied by thick lines were sung back lower.

4.1 Differences in Nonlinguistic Pitch Representations Not Due to Verbal Labeling during the Task

The pattern of spatial interference on people's pitch reproduction performance reflected the SPACE–PITCH metaphors in their native languages: Dutch speakers could not help incorporating irrelevant height information into their mental representations of pitch (but could ignore thickness), whereas Farsi speakers could not help incorporating irrelevant thickness information into their mental representations of pitch (but could ignore height). This pattern cannot be explained by differences in overall accuracy of pitch reproduction, or in differences in musical training between groups.

Importantly, this pattern also cannot be explained by participants using language covertly during the task: labeling the pitches they needed to reproduce as "high/low" or "thick/thin." This explanation was ruled out by the experimental design, in which nine different pitches were paired with each of nine different spatial heights or thicknesses. This "crossing" of all of the levels of pitch and of space meant that variation in each domain was orthogonal to variation in the other: There was no correlation between space and pitch in the stimuli. As such, covertly labeling high pitches as "high" (or "thin") and labeling low pitches as "low" (or "thick") could not produce the observed effects of space on pitch reproduction; on the contrary, labeling pitches using the spatial metaphors in one's native language during the task could only work *against* the effects we predicted and found.

Rather than an effect of using language "online" during the task, these experiments show an effect of people's *previous* experience using either one linguistic metaphor or the other, and thereby strengthening either one mental metaphor or the other (i.e. strengthening a non-linguistic HEIGHT–PITCH or THICKNESS–PITCH mapping in memory). To confirm that the observed effects did not depend on participants covertly labeling pitches during the task, Dolscheid et al. (2013) repeated the height interference task in Dutch speakers with the addition of a concurrent verbal suppression task. On each trial of the task, participants had to rehearse a novel string of digits while perceiving and reproducing the pitches. Secondary tasks like this have been used across many experiments to prevent participants from labeling the stimuli (e.g. Winawer et al. 2007). As predicted, verbal suppression had no effect on the results of the pitch reproduction task. Dutch speakers still showed strong height–pitch interference, consistent with an "offline" effect of participants' previous experience using language on their subsequent non-linguistic pitch representations (see also Casasanto 2008b).

4.2 *Does Using Different Linguistic Metaphors* Cause *People to Use Different Mental Metaphors?*

The results reviewed so far show a correlation between people's linguistic metaphors and their non-linguistic mental metaphors, but they do not provide any evidence that language *causes* Dutch and Farsi speakers to mentally represent pitch differently. Dolscheid et al. (2013) reasoned that if using THICKNESS–PITCH metaphors in language is what causes Farsi speakers to activate THICKNESS–PITCH mappings implicitly when reproducing pitches, then exposing Dutch speakers to similar THICKNESS–PITCH metaphors in language should cause them to reproduce pitches like Farsi speakers. A new sample of Dutch speakers were recruited and assigned to one of two training conditions: Participants in the "thickness training" group learned to describe pitches using Farsi-like metaphors (e.g. "a tuba sounds *thicker* than a flute"), whereas the other half in the "height training" group (i.e. the control group) described pitches using standard Dutch metaphors (e.g. "a tuba sounds *lower* than a flute"). After about 20 minutes of this linguistic training, participants in both groups performed the non-linguistic thickness interference task described above. Whereas "height-trained" participants showed no effect of irrelevant thickness information on their pitch estimates, "thickness-trained" participants showed a thickness interference effect that was statistically indistinguishable from the effect found in native Farsi speakers. Even a brief (but concentrated) "dose" of thickness metaphors in language was sufficient to influence Dutch speakers' mental metaphors, demonstrating that linguistic experience can cause the differences in non-linguistic pitch representations found across natural language groups.

Notably, Dolscheid et al. (2013) also included a training condition in which Dutch-speaking participants were taught to use "thick" and "thin" to describe pitches in a way that contradicts both the linguistic mappings in languages like Farsi and the relationships between thickness and pitch in the natural world (e.g. they learned to use expressions like "a tuba sounds *thinner* than a flute"). This training intervention was identical to the "Farsi-training" condition described above in every way except for the pairing of high/low with thick/thin. Although participants learned to use the "reverse-Farsi" mapping with high accuracy (95%), this linguistic training had no effect on their non-linguistic mental representations of pitch.

The contrast between the Farsi-like and reverse-Farsi training supports a prediction of HMMT: People should be able to adopt mappings that are included in a superordinate family of mappings (e.g. the SPACE–PITCH mappings that are evident in the natural world) more easily than they can adopt mappings that are not included in the superordinate family (i.e. mappings that run contrary to, or orthogonal to, the source–target mappings found in the natural world).

4.3 *When Does Language Shape* SPACE–PITCH *Mappings?*

The results reviewed up to this point leave open the question: Do SPACE–PITCH metaphors in language cause people to *develop* the corresponding non-linguistic SPACE–PITCH mappings, or does using linguistic metaphors change how likely people are to use a preexisting mental metaphor? To evaluate these possibilities, Dolscheid et al. (2014) tested 4-month-old infants on a pair of space–pitch congruity tasks. Infants heard pitches alternately rising and falling while they saw a ball rising and falling on a screen (height congruity task) or a cylinder growing thicker and thinner (thickness congruity task). For half of the trials, changes in pitch and space were congruent with the HEIGHT–PITCH and THICKNESS–PITCH mappings encoded in Dutch and Farsi, respectively, and for the other half of the trials they were incongruent with these SPACE–PITCH mappings. The data showed that infants looked longer at congruent SPACE–PITCH displays than at incongruent displays. This was true both in the height congruity condition (consistent with an earlier experiment by Walker et al. 2010) and in the thickness congruity condition. There was no difference in the magnitude of the congruity effect between conditions, suggesting that there was no difference in the strength of the HEIGHT–PITCH and THICKNESS–PITCH mappings in the infants' minds.

Four-month-olds are completely unable to produce SPACE–PITCH metaphors in language and are also, presumably, unable to understand them. Yet, they are sensitive to two of the SPACE–PITCH metaphors that are found in languages like Dutch and Farsi, and in their speakers' non-linguistic pitch representations. These results suggest that people who use different linguistic metaphors for pitch come to think about pitch differently, not because language instills in them one spatial mapping instead of the other, but rather because language strengthens one of their preexisting SPACE–PITCH mappings, at the expense of the other.

4.4 Hierarchical Construction of Spatial Metaphors for Pitch

How could infants who are sensitive to both HEIGHT–PITCH and THICKNESS–PITCH mappings turn into adults who appear to activate only one of these mappings when they represent pitch? This process can be understood in terms of HMMT. First a superordinate "family" of mappings is established, which in the case of space and pitch includes both the HEIGHT–PITCH and THICKNESS–PITCH mappings. These mappings may be constructed, over either ontogenetic or phylogenetic time, on the basis of observable correlations between space and pitch in the natural world. The HEIGHT–PITCH mapping reflects the fact that people involuntarily raise their larynxes, chins, and sometimes other body parts (e.g. their eyebrows) when they produce higher pitches, and lower them when they produce lower pitches. It also reflects a statistical tendency for higher pitches to originate from higher locations, and lower pitches from lower locations (Parise et al. 2014). The THICKNESS–PITCH mapping reflects a pervasive correlation between pitches and the size of the objects or creatures that produce them: Consider the different pitches produced by, for example, strumming thin vs. thick strings on a guitar; banging on a large steel oil drum vs. a small steel can; barking by a small dog vs. a big dog. Although Dolscheid et al.'s (2014) data confirm that both the HEIGHT–PITCH and THICKNESS–PITCH mappings are present in infants' minds, they leave open the question of exactly how and when these mappings become established initially.

Whatever the ultimate origin of SPACE–PITCH mappings in pre-linguistic children may be, when children learn metaphors in language, a second process begins. The findings in adults reported by Dolscheid and colleagues (2013) suggest that each time people use a linguistic metaphor like "a *high* pitch" they activate the corresponding mental metaphor, strengthening this mapping at the expense of competing mappings in the same family of SPACE–PITCH associations. As a consequence, speakers of height languages like Dutch and English come to rely on vertical spatial schemas to scaffold their pitch representations more strongly than on multidimensional spatial schemas, whereas speakers of thickness languages like Farsi come to rely on multidimensional spatial schemas, more strongly than vertical spatial schemas.

According to HMMT, the process of strengthening certain mental metaphors via the use of the corresponding linguistic metaphors results in the *weakening* of other members of the family of mappings – but this does not cause these dispreferred mappings to be extinguished. This aspect of the theory may explain the representational flexibility demonstrated in the training experiment by Dolscheid and colleagues (2013). Dutch speakers could be induced to use a non-linguistic THICKNESS–PITCH mapping (like Farsi speakers) after only a brief training intervention because no spatial mappings had to be created or destroyed; rather, the new pattern of language experience boosted the strength of the THICKNESS–PITCH mapping that had presumably been present in the Dutch speakers' minds since infancy, causing them to think about pitch in a way that was not new, just rarely used.

5 Spatial Representations of Temporal Sequences: Universals and Culture-Specificity

Spatial metaphors for time are common across languages (Alverson 1994). In English, time appears to flow along a sagittal (front–back) axis: the future is "ahead" and the past is "behind." No known spoken language uses the lateral (left–right) axis to talk about time conventionally: Monday comes before Tuesday, not to the left of Tuesday (Cienki 1998). Yet, despite the total absence of left–right metaphors in spoken language, there is strong evidence that people implicitly associate time with left–right space and that the direction in which events flow along people's imaginary lateral timelines varies systematically across cultures. In a seminal study (Tversky et al. 1991), children and adults were asked to place stickers on a page to indicate where breakfast and dinner should appear relative to the lunch sticker, in the middle of the page. Whereas English speakers placed breakfast on the left and dinner on the right of lunch, Arabic speakers preferred the opposite arrangement. This cross-cultural reversal in the lateral SPACE–TIME mapping has been corroborated by reaction time tasks (e.g. in English vs. Hebrew speakers; Fuhrman & Boroditsky 2010; Ouellet et al. 2010).

The sagittal mapping of time, enshrined in linguistic metaphors, has been proposed to arise from the canonical experience of moving forward through space (not backward or sideways) due to the construction of our feet, hands, and sensory organs all of which are directed toward the front of our bodies (Clark 1973). As we use these bodies to move forward through the world, objects that we will encounter in the future lie literally ahead of us, and objects we have already passed lie behind us. Thus, a correlation between anteriority and the future and between posteriority and the past is reinforced nearly every time we walk (or run, bike, drive, fly, etc.). But where does the lateral mapping of time come from?

The left–right mapping of temporal sequences has been hypothesized to arise from our experience with the written word. As we read or write, we move our eyes and attention through both space and time, from left to right for some orthographies (e.g. Roman script) and from right to left for others (e.g. Arabic script). In English, for each line of text we read we begin on the left side of a page (at an earlier time) and arrive at the right side (at a later time). Thus, reading English entails a correlation between "progress" through space and time, from left to right. To find out whether experience using one orthography or another is sufficient to determine the direction of the mental timeline, Roberto Bottini and I asked Dutch participants to perform a space–time congruity task on stimuli written in standard (left-to-right) Dutch orthography, mirror-reversed orthography, or orthography that was rotated either 90 degrees upward or downward (Casasanto & Bottini 2014b). When participants judged temporal phrases written in standard orthography, their reaction times were consistent with a rightward-directed mental timeline: Past-related phrases (e.g. "a day earlier") were judged faster with the left hand, and future-related phrases (e.g. "a year later") with the right hand. After a few minutes of exposure to mirror-reversed orthography, however, participants showed the opposite pattern of reaction times; their implicit mental timelines were reversed. When standard orthography was rotated 90 degrees upward or downward, participants' mental timelines were rotated, accordingly.

5.1 *Separating Effects of Language and Culture on* SPACE–TIME *Mappings*

These data show that the experience of reading is sufficient to determine the direction of people's implicit mental timelines (though they do not rule out the possibility that other culture-specific practices, such as gesturing about time or using calendars, could influence people's lateral representations of time, as well). But why is this an effect of *cultural experience* as opposed to *linguistic experience*? Language can be considered an aspect of culture, and in many cases it is difficult to disentangle linguistic and non-linguistic practices. At first glance, reading might appear to be an ambiguous case, since it is a cultural overlay on natural language. Yet it is notable that reading is extremely recent and rare in human history; although reading may seem integral to language use in our culture, only a tiny fraction of all of the humans who have ever used language have been able to read. More to the point, in Casasanto and Bottini's experiments, *language was held constant across the orthography conditions.* The words and phrases in natural language were invariant; all that changed was the direction and orientation of the orthography in which they appeared. Thus, changes in orthography determined the flow of time in people's minds independently of any changes in the structure or content of language.

5.2 *Hierarchical Construction of Spatial Metaphors for Temporal Sequence*

How could a few minutes of exposure to a new orthography completely reverse people's usual mental timeline, established over a lifetime of reading experience? As in the case of language, space, and pitch, HMMT may explain the flexibility of this culture-dependent mental metaphor. To elaborate, Casasanto and Bottini (2014b) proposed that people's implicit associations between source and target domains can be characterized, not just as families of mappings but alternatively as a set of nested *intuitive hypotheses* (Goodman 1983). At the top of the hierarchy is the *overhypothesis*, which comprises a family of *specific hypotheses*. In this case, the overhypothesis could be: "Progress through time corresponds to change in position along a linear spatial path." This correspondence could be learned as children observe the relationship between space and time in moving objects, or it could be innate (Casasanto 2010; de Hevia et al. 2014; Srinivasan & Carey 2010). Either way, the overhypothesized association between space and time is presumably universal across cultures, and it should be omnidirectional, since more time passes as moving objects travel farther in any direction.

Once children are exposed to cultural practices with consistent directionality, they accumulate a preponderance of evidence for one specific hypothesis. For Dutch children, reading and writing experience provides evidence for the specific hypothesis "Progress through time corresponds to rightward change in position along a linear spatial path," strengthening this hypothesis at the expense of its competitors and causing Dutch speakers to use a rightward-directed mental timeline by default. Exposure to a different orthography in the experimental setting increased the weight of evidence for one of the participants' overhypothesized (but culturally dispreferred) SPACE–TIME mappings, strengthening it to the point that it influenced behavior, transiently weakening their culturally preferred mapping as a consequence.

5.3 *Spatial Representations of Emotional Valence: Universals and Body-Specificity*

Several years ago I proposed a theory of *bodily relativity* (Casasanto 2009a), by analogy to the theories of linguistic and cultural relativity. By hypothesis, the contents of our minds are constructed, in part, through our physical interactions with the environment. People with different kinds of bodies interact with their environment in systematically different ways. Therefore, myriad aspects of their thinking should vary *relative* to the particulars of their bodies. The spatial mapping of emotional valence has provided one fruitful testbed for this proposal (for reviews, see Casasanto 2011, 2014a).

Across languages and cultures, good things are often associated with the right side of space and bad things with the left. This association is evident in positive and negative idioms like "my right-hand man" and "two left feet." Beyond language, people also conceptualize good and bad in terms of left–right space, but not always in the way linguistic and cultural conventions suggest. Rather, people's implicit associations between space and valence are "body specific." When asked to decide which of two products to buy, which of two job applicants to hire, or which of two alien creatures looks more trustworthy, right- and left-handers respond differently. Right-handers tend to prefer the product, person, or creature presented on their right side but left-handers tend to prefer the one on their left (Casasanto 2009a). This pattern persists even when people make judgments orally, without using their hands to respond. Children as young as 5 years old already make evaluations according to handedness and spatial location, judging animals shown on their dominant side to be nicer and smarter than animals on their non-dominant side (Casasanto & Henetz 2012).

Beyond the laboratory, the association of 'good' with the dominant side can be seen in left- and right-handers' spontaneous speech and gestures (Casasanto & Jasmin 2010): In the final debates of the 2004 and 2008 US presidential elections, positive speech was more strongly associated with right-hand gestures and negative speech with left-hand gestures in the two right-handed candidates (George W. Bush, John Kerry), but the opposite association was found in the two left-handed candidates (John McCain, Barack Obama).

In summary, a body-specific mental metaphor links lateral space and emotional valence, and influences the way people think and communicate about positive and negative ideas. The observed SPACE–VALENCE mappings cannot be explained by influences of language or culture since, in the case of the GOOD-IS-LEFT mapping in left-handers, the implicit mental metaphor goes *against* the explicit GOOD-IS-RIGHT mapping enshrined in linguistic idioms and other cultural conventions (e.g. raising the right hand to swear to tell the truth).

5.4 *Experiential Basis of Lateral* SPACE–VALENCE *Mappings*

Where do body-specific SPACE–VALENCE mappings come from? All of the results reviewed so far demonstrate correlations, but Casasanto (2009a) proposed a *causal* relationship between the way people use their hands and the way they implicitly spatialize 'good' and 'bad.' In general, greater motor fluency leads to more positive feelings and evaluations: People like things better when they are easier to perceive and interact with (e.g. Ping et al. 2009). Bodies are lopsided. Most of us have a dominant side and a non-dominant side and therefore interact with the physical environment more fluently on one side of space than on the other. As a consequence right-handers, who interact with their environment more fluently on the right and more clumsily on the left, come to implicitly associate 'good' with 'right' and 'bad' with 'left,' whereas left-handers form the opposite association (Casasanto 2009a).

To test this proposal, Evangelia Chrysikou and I studied how people think about 'good' and 'bad' after their dominant hand has been handicapped, either due to brain injury or to something much less extreme: wearing a bulky ski glove. In one experiment, right-handed university students performed a motor fluency task, arranging dominoes on a table while wearing a cumbersome glove on either their left hand (which preserved their natural right-handedness) or on their right hand (which turned them temporarily into left-handers, in the relevant regard). After about 12 minutes of lopsided motor experience, participants removed the glove and performed a test of SPACE–VALENCE associations, which they believed to be unrelated. Participants who had worn the left glove still thought RIGHT was GOOD, but participants who had worn the right glove showed the opposite LEFT-IS-GOOD bias, like natural lefties (Casasanto & Chrysikou 2011).

5.5 *Hierarchical Construction of Spatial Metaphors for Valence*

Even a few minutes of altered motor experience can change people's implicit associations between space and emotional valence, causing a reversal of their usual judgments. HMMT provides a potential explanation of this representational flexibility. In the case of mental metaphors linking lateral space and valence, the overhypothesis may be: "The fluent region of space is good." For right-handers, who act more fluently on the side of their dominant hand, typical motor experience provides a preponderance of evidence for the specific hypothesis that "the right side of space is good," whereas typical motor experience for left-handers increases the strength of the evidence for the hypothesis that "the left side of space is good." In terms of memory networks, this means that either the association between 'right' and 'good' or the association between 'left' and 'good' is strengthened at the expense of the competing associations – which are weakened but not lost and can therefore be strengthened again by new patterns of motor experience.

6 Hierarchical Construction of Language-, Culture-, and Body-Specific Mental Metaphors

The case studies described in this chapter illustrate ways in which mental metaphors can be constructed via similar mnemonic processes being driven by different kinds of linguistic, cultural, or bodily experiences. Early in ontogenetic time (or perhaps over phylogenetic time), *families of source–target mappings* are constructed, which reflect sets of observable relationships between source and target domains in the natural world. Specific members of these families are then strengthened according to an individual's language-specific, culture-specific, or body-specific experiences. As a result, other mappings in these families are weakened. This process of competition among mappings in long-term memory explains why *all* of the mappings within a given family are not active at once: for example, why adult Dutch speakers do not typically conceptualize pitch using representations of both height *and* thickness, even though both mappings appear to be equally active in infants' minds (Dolscheid et al. 2013; Dolscheid et al. 2014).

The hierarchical structuring of mental metaphors in terms of source–target families and their constituent members may also explain how spatial source–target mappings can be fundamental to our conceptions of non-spatial domains, yet also remarkably flexible. It is notable, for example, that about 5 minutes of exposure to mirror-reversed writing did not simply *modulate* the direction of participants' mental timeline, it *completely reversed* its direction, as indicated by a reversal of reaction–time congruity effects (Casasanto & Bottini 2014b). Had space–time congruity effects been extinguished by exposure to the new orthography, this would have been consistent with the possibility that people cease to represent time spatially when their preferred mental metaphor is challenged. Instead, the reversal of these effects indicates that participants did not abandon a spatial mapping of time; rather they rapidly adopted a *different* mental timeline, consistent with their new orthographic experience.

How are the various members of an overhypothesized family of mappings preserved in long-term memory, even though some of the mappings may never be reinforced explicitly (e.g. by the use of corresponding linguistic metaphors or by cultural conventions)? Presumably they are maintained by the recurrence of the same sorts of physical experiences that are ultimately responsible for the family's construction. Even in a language group that exclusively uses height metaphors for pitch in language, physical thickness–pitch relationships can still be observed (e.g. in the sound of thick vs. thin guitar strings). Even in a left-to-right reading culture, it should still be possible to observe moving objects progressing through space and time from right to left (and in all other directions). Even right-handers occasionally experience greater fluency with their left hand, or on their left side of space. The preservation of dispreferred mappings explains why they can be adopted so quickly when people are given new patterns of experience.

By seeking to understand common mechanisms by which our mental metaphors are shaped by language-specific, culture-specific, or body-specific patterns of experience, we can better understand the origins of our thoughts, the extent of cognitive diversity, and the dynamism of our mental lives.

Notes and Acknowledgments

* This research was supported in part by a James S. McDonnell Foundation Scholar Award (#220020236) and a National Science Foundation grant (BCS #125710). Thanks to Laura Staum Casasanto for helpful discussion.

1 This distinction is blurred by the use of the terms "conceptual metaphor" (Lakoff & Johnson 1980), "primary metaphor" (Lakoff & Johnson 1999), or just "metaphor" (Lakoff 1993) to refer to mental metaphors, since these terms are often used to refer to linguistic metaphors, as well.

2 HMMT concerns universals and variability within basic mental metaphors; this theory should not be confused with the "inheritance hierarchies" that Lakoff (1993) proposed to explain how complex metaphors (like LOVE IS A JOURNEY, A CAREER IS A JOURNEY, A LIFE IS A JOURNEY, etc.) are constructed and related.

3 A common objection to this claim is that we can see the length of a vacation as it stretches across the grid of our wall calendar, and the height of a musical pitch as it is notated on a musical staff. But in these cases, we are not seeing time or pitch, at all; rather, we are seeing a spatial representation of time or of pitch – consistent with the theory that we habitually use space to represent time and pitch metaphorically, both in the mind and on the page.

4 Metaphorical Directionality: The Role of Language

*Yeshayahu Shen & Roy Porat**

Chapter Preview

Verbal metaphors are fundamentally directional. For example, people commonly refer to social relations in term of temperature (e.g. "She is a *warm* person"), but the inverse metaphors in which we talk about temperature in terms of social relations are not usually found. Conceptual Metaphor Theory (Lakoff & Johnson 1980, 1999) attributes this directionality to an underlying unidirectional "conceptual mapping" between the respective domains, rooted in our bodily experience. However, recent psycho-physical experiments have shown these conceptual associations to be *bi*directional: Not only can manipulations of an individual's experience of physical warmth affect that individual's judgment of another person or situation as friendly or unfriendly, the reverse is also true, as thinking about a friendly or unfriendly social situation can alter an individual's judgment of room temperature. To account for this discrepancy, we propose that (i) verbal (unidirectional) metaphors rely on a pre-linguistic, non-directional, association between the two domains and that (ii) language plays an essential role in rendering this association into a directional target–source relation.

1 Metaphorical Directionality: Introduction

Verbal metaphors are fundamentally directional in that terms referring to more accessible ("source") domains are commonly used to talk about less accessible ("target") domains, but not the other way around (e.g. Lakoff & Johnson 1980, 1999). For example, a conventional metaphor people use in talking about SOCIAL RELATIONS (a less accessible domain) employs expressions referring to TEMPERATURE (a more accessible domain), as in "She is a *warm* person." However, inverse mapping in which we talk about temperature in terms of social relations, as in "This is a *kind/friendly* temperature," are not conventional and hard to interpret.

Conceptual Metaphor Theory (CMT) claims that the directionality of verbal metaphors (especially those labelled as "primary") reflects an underlying conceptual directionality in which more accessible (typically, more concrete) source domains provide the conceptual structure for conceptualizing less accessible (typically, more abstract) target domains. Thus, SOCIAL RELATIONS are *thought of* in terms of TEMPERATURE, and not merely talked about in that way (cf. Grady 1997a; Lakoff & Johnson 1980, 1999). It is further maintained that this "conceptual directionality" is rooted in our bodily interaction with the environment, in which cross-domain associations originate in the frequent correlation (and resulting experiential conflation) of subjective (abstract) and sensorimotor (concrete) experiences, such as the co-occurrence of infants' experience of affection and the physical warmth of their caretaker's body (Grady 1997a; Grady & Ascoli, *this volume*; Grady & Johnson 2002; Lakoff & Johnson 1999).

Regarding the origins of verbal metaphors as ultimately rooted in our bodily experience has become a central tenet of embodied-cognition approaches to metaphor (e.g. Boroditsky 2000; Casasanto & Boroditsky 2008; Lakoff & Johnson 1980, 1999; Williams et al. 2009), which propose that "our conceptual system recycles concrete concepts to help understanding the abstract. Representations of location, motion, size, color, brightness, weight, smell, temperature, and other perceptually based dimensions of experience are used to understand more abstract concepts as if, at least in part, the latter were examples of such concrete experiences" (Santiago et al. 2012: 1051).

2 Verbal vs. Conceptual Metaphors

2.1 Experimental Evidence for Conceptual Metaphors: The Directionality Problem

Until recently CMT relied primarily on *linguistic* evidence for the consistency of metaphorical expressions in language. Given that the occurrence of such clusters of expressions as "warm person," "chilly reception," and "cold shoulder" are unlikely to be a mere coincidence, it was suggested that such metaphors do not constitute an arbitrary group of isolated expressions but are rather the linguistic manifestations of a single, implicit mapping between concepts from different domains (e.g. TEMPERATURE and INTERPERSONAL RESPONSIVENESS), that is, a "conceptual" (or, more specifically, a "primary") metaphor (Grady 1997a; Lakoff & Johnson 1980). In other words, the existence of a pre-/non-linguistic metaphorical *mapping* was deduced from the regularity of mappings in some groups of verbal metaphors, an argument that was criticized for its circularity (cf. e.g. Murphy 1996).

In recent years, however, various psycho-physical studies in the area of embodied cognition have provided a growing body of *psycholinguistic/experimental* evidence in support of the theory, as manipulating one domain was found to implicitly affect the perception of another, metaphorically related one. For example, participants who held a warm (rather than a cold) beverage tended to judge target individuals as having a "warmer" (i.e. 'more friendly') personality, in accordance with the hypothesized conceptual (/primary) metaphor AFFECTION IS WARMTH (Williams & Bargh 2008a; see also Citron & Goldberg 2014). In another study, participants were found to be more likely to judge a currency to be more valuable when holding a heavy (rather than a light) clipboard, in accordance with the conceptual metaphor IMPORTANT IS HEAVY (Jostmann et al. 2009). These and similar studies were interpreted by CMT advocates as evidence for the extension of metaphorical relations beyond the realm of language and, consequently, as support for the CMT model (e.g. Gibbs 2014b: 175–177; Lakoff 2014).

However, these recent psycho-physical studies have also uncovered a puzzling discrepancy between the conventional verbal instantiations of such (primary) metaphors as AFFECTION IS WARMTH or IMPORTANT IS HEAVY and their conceptual/mental counterparts: In contrast to the clear unidirectionality of verbal metaphors, behavioral research on the kinds of cross-domain associations underlying primary metaphors in CMT consistently reveals *bidirectional* effects (IJzerman & Koole 2011; IJzerman & Semin 2009; Lee & Schwarz 2012). While evidence accumulated that manipulating a concrete domain affects individual's judgments in the correlated abstract domain – in accordance with the predictions of CMT – the reverse pattern was also found. For example, thinking about pleasant or unpleasant social situations likewise tends to alter judgments of room temperature as being warmer or colder, respectively (Zhong & Leonardelli 2008). Following the logic of the original study, this finding corresponds to the non-hypothesized conceptual metaphor *WARMTH IS AFFECTION, which defies the regular concrete-to-abstract pattern and has no conventionalized verbal equivalent.

The WARMTH-AFFECTION case is not an isolated example, as this bidirectional effect extends to many other associations between abstract (non-perceptual) and sensorimotor (perceptual) experiences (of the kind hypothesized to underlie primary metaphors), including moral judgment and physical cleanliness, verticality and positive or negative mood, importance and weight, and many others (Schneider et al. 2011; Zhong & Liljenquist 2006; for an overview, see Landau et al. 2010). In contrast, the corresponding verbal metaphors exhibit a robust unidirectionality, e.g. moral judgment is verbally described in terms of physical cleanliness but not vice versa, mood is described in terms of verticality but not the other way around, importance in terms of weight, and so forth (see also Grady & Ascoli, *this volume*).

We hold that the discrepancy between the unidirectionality of verbal metaphors and the apparent bidirectionality found in psycho-physical studies poses a serious problem for CMT, especially concerning primary metaphors. As CMT maintains that abstract concepts/domains are "embodied," i.e. conceptualized via bodily experiences, it predicts that manipulating the experienced source concept should impact the representation of the target concept, *but not vice versa*. To return to our example, if affection is represented in terms of temperature, then changing experiences of physical warmth should affect judgments about affection/empathy. Since physical warmth, in turn, is not conceived in terms of affection, however, perceiving it should not be affected by our social feelings.

In sum, despite CMT's long-standing claims that verbal metaphors are mere reflections of underlying conceptual mappings, the reported psycho-physical findings (taken as reliable indications of the properties of their mental/conceptual counterparts) suggest that there is a clear difference between the two, with the former being unidirectional and the latter bidirectional.

2.2 *Previous Attempts to Cope with the Directionality Problem*

Although largely overlooked, a small number of researchers have noticed this discrepancy and the challenge it poses to CMT. While Landau, Meier, and Keefer (2010: 364) "hold out the hope that future research can resolve this issue while preserving the benefits of a metaphor-enriched perspective," IJzerman and Koole (2011) as well as Schneider and colleagues (2011) take these findings as refuting the CMT notion of conceptual metaphors with a clear target–source distinction altogether; they do not attempt, however, to account for the directionality of verbal metaphors.

In contrast, Lee and Schwarz (2012) claim that the discrepancy can be fully accommodated within Lakoff's paradigm, relying on (a) the distinctions between the linguistic and the psychological consequences of conceptual metaphors; (b) the distinction between representational structure and online processing; and (c) the distinction between the two mechanisms involved in the formation of metaphors according to Lakoff and Johnson (1999: 55–57), "co-activation" and "projection."

The first two of these distinctions explore the discrepancy rather than fully explain it. No attempt is made, for example, to address questions such as why there should be a difference between the linguistic and psychological consequences of conceptual metaphors, and, in particular, why these two should differ in directionality. The third distinction presents a more convincing argument. According to Lakoff and Johnson (1999: 48–49), early life experience involves repeated conflation between different domains – for example, between the feeling of affection while being held or hugged as an infant and the physical warmth of the caretaker's body. These experiential correlations may lead to neural co-activation of the two domains, a bidirectional process by which experience in one domain activates the other and vice versa. In turn, these correlation-based associations form the basis for metaphors such as AFFECTION IS WARMTH, in which properties are projected from one (concrete) domain onto another (abstract) one. According to Lee and Schwarz's proposal, it is possible that both mechanisms remain active so that aside from the unidirectionality of verbal metaphors that derives from the underlying process of projection, there may also be a bidirectional metaphorical effect that results from an underlying (bidirectional) process of co-activation.

However, Lee and Schwarz's proposal does not constitute a full account of the issue at stake, since the very distinction between the two processes (which we fully agree with) does not provide an answer to such questions as: What is the relation between the two processes? How does one shift from one process to the other? And, most importantly, why do verbal metaphors reflect the (unidirectional) process of projection rather than the (bidirectional) process of co-activation? Lakoff (2014) himself, apart from pointing to a possible solution to Lee and Schwarz's findings in neural terms, concludes that their experiment points to the need to better understand the difference between metaphorical mapping and experimental effect.

To conclude, past references to the conflict between the CMT predictions and the empirical findings on directionality have led to unresolved attempts to reconcile the two, dismissal of the reliability of psycho-physical findings as "psychological consequences" of the original conceptual metaphors, or even to the rejection of CMT altogether. In contrast, we propose an alternative account that not only provides a simpler solution for the discrepancy but also allows us (i) to accept the experimental findings reported above as reliable representations of metaphorical relationships at the conceptual level, and (ii) to largely preserve CMT's central claim that verbal metaphors are reflections of a deeper pre-linguistic/conceptual relationship. The solution we propose relies on the commonly overlooked role of a central factor that distinguishes the conceptual level from the verbal one, namely, language itself.

3 Verbal Metaphors and Conceptual Associations

3.1 Two Phases of Metaphor Processing

We agree with the CMT model that verbal metaphors originate from a conceptual pre-linguistic level so that the relation between 'affection' and 'warmth,' for example, as represented by expressions such as "She is a warm person," does indeed reflect an underlying implicit association between the two domains. We disagree with CMT's claim that this implicit pre-linguistic association represents the same type of metaphorical relation as their corresponding metaphorical expressions. Instead, we claim that it represents a simpler, more symmetric type of linkage in which the two domains are simply "associated," and which involves no attribution of "target" or "source." We suggest that for this symmetrical "bare association" between the two domains to become a full-blown metaphor in which aspects of the source are unidirectionally "projected" onto the target, another process is required, in which language plays an essential role. In other words, we claim that the unidirectionality of metaphorical expressions in language is not a direct reflection of a corresponding unidirectionality of pre-linguistic metaphorical associations. Instead, we suggest that language is (at least partially) the generator of this unidirectionality, by turning a *latent* (conceptual) asymmetry between the two concepts/domains into an *active* one. As said, our suggestion relies on the separation of metaphor processing into two different phases to be elaborated on next: "bare concept/domain association" and "directional projection."

Bare concept/domain association is the initial phase of metaphorical association, which is derived from experiential correlation between two domains and corresponds to Lakoff and Johnson's suggested mechanism of co-activation. We use the word "bare" to emphasize that at this phase the two domains (e.g. 'affection' and 'warmth') are not assigned target and source functions but are merely associated with each other. Crucially, this bare association between the two domains is, in principle, bidirectional, in that each domain is associated with the other and can therefore prompt or interfere with it, as the aforementioned experiments show. We agree with CMT that this basic association between the two domains then motivates a more developed type of relationship which is expressed in full-blown metaphors such as AFFECTION IS WARMTH. However, we do *not* claim that the shift from this initial phase to the more developed one is triggered automatically, probably in early childhood (see Lakoff & Johnson 1999: 45–59). Rather, we claim that this bare association remains the prominent type of connection between metaphorically related domains – unless directionality is externally triggered, which occurs when the relationship between the two domains is expressed *in language*. Put simply, we propose that instead of assuming full-blown metaphors at the conceptual level, it would be more accurate to describe the pre-linguistic level as consisting of "conceptual (bidirectional) associations."

Directional projection refers to the process of mapping one domain onto the other. This type of relation is built on the simpler, bare association between the two domains and includes the additional components of (i) *assigning* the TARGET and SOURCE functions to the two domains and (ii) *projecting* some properties from the source to the target domain, which results in the conceptualization of the target *in terms of* the source. This relation is a *unidirectional* one, in that properties of the source are used to conceptualize the target, rather than the other way around.

Bearing in mind this separation between the two "types" of metaphor processing, we propose the following:

1. The bidirectional bare association between concepts from two domains is the initial phase of metaphor formation and comprehension, preceding unidirectional projection.
2. Language plays an essential role in changing this bare association into a directional relation of target and source.

Taken together, these two claims provide a fairly straightforward solution to the discrepancy discussed above: The bidirectionality found in the perceptual and sensorimotor experiments reflects the initial bidirectional relation between two domains. In contrast, the robust unidirectionality of verbal metaphors reflects the output of another, "higher" process, namely, the assignment of a target–source relation to the associated domains, whereby language plays an essential role.

This proposal has direct bearing on the debate about (the depth of) the level at which conceptual metaphors exist. The present proposal suggests a compromise between those who maintain the position that there are primary metaphors at a preverbal (conceptual or even embodied) deep level (Lakoff & Johnson 1980, 1999; *this volume*: Grady & Ascoli; Winter & Matlock; see also Casasanto's "mental" metaphors) and those who challenge this position by arguing that there is no evidence for this (e.g. Keysar et al. 2000; for conceptual metaphors generally, see also Murphy 1996).

3.2 *Evidence for the Distinction between the Two Phases of Metaphor Processing*

Since the empirical investigation of the conceptual level poses major methodological difficulties, the existence of the hypothesized bidirectional bare association between the two domains can only be deduced from converging pieces of evidence, e.g. through analytic reasoning (as done by CMT) *and* from the findings of relevant psycho-physical studies. However, there is another piece of evidence for the existence of two distinct mechanisms in the process of metaphorical comprehension, which seem much like the types we are proposing, that is, an initial symmetrical relation followed by a more developed, directional one.

For example, Wolff and Gentner (2011: 1456–1457) managed to reconcile two of the most dominant (and competing) views regarding the nature of metaphor in the last years, to which they referred as the "emerging commonalities" and the "directional projection" views: While the former claims that metaphor relies on the detection of commonalities in different domains, the latter states that metaphor is a process of projection, in which properties from one domain (the source) are conveyed to the other (the target).[1] Crucially, these two approaches differ in their view of directionality, since the process of projection is unidirectional by definition, but detecting commonalities is at least theoretically a bidirectional process.

Wolff and Gentner (2011) used a mix-deadline procedure (exposing subjects to the stimuli for either a short or a long time) to show that these two processes should not be taken as separate mechanisms, but rather as two stages of metaphor processing. Participants were asked to judge the comprehensibility of verbal (hence directional) A-IS-B metaphors, such as "some arguments are wars," and their reversed versions "some wars are arguments," in either short or long exposing time. In accordance with their model, forward and reversed orders did not differ in comprehensibility at the early stage of processing (600 ms), while at later stages forward metaphors were clearly more comprehensible than reversed metaphors (as demonstrated in numerous studies). These results indicate that, despite the common view of metaphor as inherently unidirectional, directionality is in fact attributed at a later stage of processing. As the researchers themselves point out (ibid.: 1480), their findings pose a problem to Lakoff's view, which predicts directional processing from early stages (both explicit *and* implicit). However, these findings are consistent with our modified version of CMT, which also claims that there is a shift from symmetrical to unidirectional processing. According to our model, therefore, the first 600 ms in Wolff and Gentner's study may be regarded as a "window" into a deeper conceptual level.

A few developmental studies provide further support for a "shift" from a symmetrical to an asymmetrical processing. For example, several studies indicated that children are insensitive to asymmetry in metaphors.[2] Most noticeably, one study showed that although 4-year-olds respond better to grammatically asymmetrical similes – e.g. are more likely to identify the metaphorical "ground" (i.e. the relevant metaphorical property) of "a boat is like a leaf" than of "a boat and a leaf are alike" – they are insensitive to the order of the two concepts: e.g. "a leaf is like a boat" and "a boat is like a leaf" were equally easy to extract a ground from.[3] These findings, too, support the notion that metaphorical directionality is a later development. Since young children do notice the asymmetry of grammatical structure, at least one possible explanation for these findings is that children at a young age simply do not use metaphorical projection but, rather, rely on the simpler association between the two concepts.

An even more long-term "developmental" shift was demonstrated in a study that compared cross-domain interference using human and non-human subjects (Merritt et al. 2010), which found that while humans demonstrate asymmetrical space–time interference (with spatial information influencing temporal judgments much more than temporal information influenced spatial judgments), rhesus monkeys demonstrate symmetrical interference (with spatial information strongly influencing temporal judgments, and vice versa). As the researchers point out, one obvious (but not necessary) explanation for the difference between the two species may be the availability of language, which could have long-term effects on the creation of asymmetrical mappings (ibid.: 199).

Combined with the discrepancy between the characteristics of verbal metaphors and the findings of psycho-physical studies, these examples provide some empirical support for the first claim of our model, i.e. that under the directional type of metaphor processing there is a more basic and simpler, non-directional linkage between metaphorically related domains. We now introduce some evidence supporting our second and major claim, namely, that language plays an essential role in enhancing, or even establishing, metaphorical unidirectionality.

4 The Impact of Language on Metaphorical Directionality

The distinction between the two types of cross-domain relations immediately raises the question of *how* the system changes the initial bare association into a unidirectional projection from source to target. According to CMT, the shift from non-directional to unidirectional processing occurs automatically due to differences in the relative accessibility of the associated concepts, their conceptual prominence, or some other conceptual asymmetry between the two: It is more natural to map properties from a more accessible concept to a less accessible one than the other way around, from a more familiar to a less familiar one, from a concrete to an abstract one, and so forth (e.g. Lakoff 2014; Lakoff & Johnson 1980, 1999; for a proposal in neural terms, see Grady & Ascoli, *this volume*).

According to that view, once the target-source relation has been established on the ground of this pre-linguistic asymmetry, expressions referring to source and target concepts respectively are placed in the respective slots of the grammatical templates that express this relation (for an in-depth study of this, see Sullivan 2007). In the (primary) metaphor "*warm* smile," for instance, the head noun ("smile") and the modifier ("warm") represent the target and source functions, respectively (as opposed to "*smiling* warmth"). Similarly, in "Our relation *has been in the doldrums* for a while," instantiating LOVE IS A JOURNEY, the clause is a statement about the subject NP, thus assigning the target role to it, while the predicate "be in the doldrums" constitutes the source. The same goes for fully explicit A-is-B metaphors like "libraries are goldmines," where the subject noun ("libraries") again provides the target and the predicate noun ("goldmines") the source. Changing the allocation of the nouns to the two slots ("Goldmines are libraries") also "reverses" source–target functions.

Crucially, under this account the bulk of the work is relegated to the conceptual, pre-linguistic level, while language itself plays the marginal role of merely providing the means of expressing this conceptual asymmetry between the domains in question. In other words, CMT assumes that the division of labor is determined *prior* to the representation of the metaphor in language, i.e. that the assignment of grammatical functions merely reflects a conceptual asymmetry that already exists and does not in itself contribute to the directionality of the metaphor. However, we suggest that this is only partially correct.

4.1 The Importance of Linguistic Form

First, linguistic form is by no means "transparent." Consider, for example, the way people interpret "reversed" metaphors, in which the more natural candidate for the source concept appears in the target position, as in the reversed (unconventional) A-IS(-LIKE)-B metaphor "An anchor is (like) a friend." The interpretation of such reversed metaphors may cause processing difficulties (e.g. Glucksberg & Keysar 1990; Ortony et al. 1985) or even produce new meanings (Shen 2008), as people rely on the grammatical form in determining the metaphorical target (and source) terms, even when this form is incongruent with the conceptual bias to map from more to less accessible concepts (e.g. interpreting the reversed metaphor "an anchor is like a *friend*" as 'an anchor is a *sailor's best friend*'). Arguably, these difficulties are caused by a clash between grammatical and conceptual asymmetries, that is, between the tendency to assign the target and source on the basis of the grammatical and the conceptual bias to map from more to less accessible concepts.

Second, in some cases linguistic form can even *determine* the target–source assignment, as in the case of conceptually symmetrical (metaphorically related) pairs, in which none of the concepts can be regarded as the natural candidate to the roles of target and source. A case in point is "This butcher is a surgeon," which yields a totally different interpretation (highlighting exaggerated precision and care) than its reversed version, "This surgeon is a butcher." In this case it is the grammatical form that determines the direction of mapping, given that both directions yield equally plausible interpretations (cf. Glucksberg & Keysar 1990).

Third and most importantly, grammatical asymmetry may not only trigger or enhance the corresponding conceptual asymmetry but rather necessitate it: Even if, as our model predicts, the fundamental (pre-linguistic) association between metaphorically related concepts is non-directional, then still the very placement of the two concepts in a grammatically asymmetrical form would impose *some* division of labor between them. Consider, for example, the butcher–surgeon case: The concepts of 'surgeon' and 'butcher' may be related in several respects (e.g. both cut flesh), and hence, in the absence of grammar (or some other directional cue, see also Forceville, *this volume*), both directions of mapping are possible, from 'butcher' to 'surgeon' or vice versa. Once grammatical asymmetry is employed, however – for example, when one is asked to verbalize the relation between two domains in a typical (i.e. grammatically asymmetric) metaphorical form, certain choices regarding the assignment of the target and source functions to the concepts have to be made, determining the direction of the mapping.

In that respect, we assume that expressing metaphors in a grammatically asymmetrical structure may illustrate a special type of "thinking for speaking" (Slobin 1996), where the very use of certain linguistic forms requires the speaker to apply a certain mode of thinking, in this case, assign target–source functions to an otherwise bidirectional association; the hearer, of course, is also forced to understand the metaphorically related concepts in the way determined by this linguistic form.

It is important to note that though all of these effects are easily demonstrated by using nominal metaphor or simile (A-IS-B/A-IS-LIKE-B) – as done throughout this section – we intend our arguments to equally apply to other types of grammatically asymmetrical constructions usually discussed in CMT, such as noun–adjective constructions of the type "a smooth person," "a big event," "a warm welcome," or "a heated debate" (which reflect the basic, correlation-based associations underlying primary metaphors), or the above-mentioned instantiation of a complex metaphor like LOVE IS A JOURNEY. The important point is that linguistic forms which are used to express metaphorical association are almost always grammatically asymmetrical and therefore impose *some* division of labor (between target and source functions) on the associated concepts.

4.2 *Language as a Prerequisite for Metaphorical Unidirectionality*

We have so far stressed that language may trigger, determine, and necessitate unidirectional mappings. But is it also a *prerequisite* for such mappings? Unlike the 'butcher'–'surgeon' example, the vast majority of metaphors do maintain some type of conceptual asymmetry between the two concepts/domains which determines a *preference* for a particular target–source assignment. As discussed above, such a division of labor between target and source is a sufficient condition, according to the CMT view, for the creation of a "full-blown" directional metaphor, especially one of the primary type.

But what if the arrangement of the two concepts within a grammatically asymmetrical structure did not merely reflect a pre-linguistic division of labor but rather led to this division of labor in the first place? In other words, could it be that the mere existence of conceptual asymmetry between 'fear' and 'cold,' for example, is not sufficient to trigger a directional process of mapping – and that, therefore, an *external intervention* in the form of grammatical asymmetry (or some other directional cue) is needed?

To test this prediction, we investigated the effect of grammar on directional judgments of novel metaphorical associations (of the A-IS-LIKE-B type) with a clear abstract–concrete asymmetry, such as "childhood memories" (coding for an abstract concept) and "migrating birds" (coding for a concrete concept).[4]

The experiment was conducted in two phases. In the first phase 10 independent judges (mean age 40) were presented with two directional comparisons for each pair of the aforementioned terms (e.g. a pro-hierarchical order in which the source term is more concrete than the target one, as in "childhood memories are like *migrating birds*" and the corresponding anti-hierarchical order, as in "migrating birds are like *childhood memories*"). They were asked to judge which of these comparisons seems more natural, and to rate (on a scale of 1–7) the degree of confidence in their choice. Unsurprisingly, the judges demonstrated a very strong preference toward pro-hierarchical ordering (91% of all choices, with average confidence level of 5.3), as would be predicted by CMT. This finding suggests that even without understanding the relation between two given concepts (the judges were not required to interpret those novel similes), the mere conceptual asymmetry between abstract and concrete by itself is sufficient to dictate a division of labor *if* (and, as soon to be explained, this is a big "if") grammatical asymmetry is involved.

In the second phase, 43 participants (mean age 33) were presented with the same set of metaphorical pairs. Half of pairs (the "asymmetrical condition") were embedded in a pro-hierarchical asymmetrical comparison ("A is like B," as in "childhood memories are like migrating birds"); the other half (the "symmetrical condition") were embedded in the corresponding symmetrical form ("A and B are alike," as in "childhood memories and migrating birds are alike").

Each experimental item was followed by two alternative contexts in which the comparison could have been uttered: the "pro-hierarchical context" (e.g. "a nostalgic writer speaking about his youth," which determines the abstract concept 'childhood memories' as the topic of the comparison), and the "anti-hierarchical context" (e.g. "an enthusiastic ornithologist describing the flight of birds," which determines the concrete concept 'migrating birds' as the topic of the comparison). Participants were asked to decide which was the more likely context for the comparison to be uttered, and to rate (on a 1–7 scale) their level of confidence in their choice. If indeed the preferred ordering of the two concepts reflects a directional mapping existing *prior to* its representation in language, then the pro-hierarchical context should be preferred *regardless of the grammatical form* (symmetrical or asymmetrical) representing it in language.

In contrast to this prediction, however, a notable difference between the two structures was found. Comparisons in the asymmetrical condition demonstrated a strong preference for the pro-hierarchical topic-assignment (95.1% of all cases, average confidence level of 5.3); in contrast, the comparisons in the symmetrical condition demonstrated a much weaker tendency for the pro-hierarchical assignment (69%, confidence level of 4.9). The difference between the two conditions was significant for both choice (Z = -4.739 $p <$ 0.001) and confidence level (t = -4.417, $p < 0.001$).

The results of this experiment suggest that the conceptual asymmetry alone was not sufficient to establish a clear division of labor between the two concepts. Rather, embedding the terms of these comparisons in a grammatically asymmetrical structure is required in order for this conceptual asymmetry (that is, the assignment of the target and source functions to the abstract and concrete terms, respectively) to be fully realized.

One might argue, however, that the novelty of associations in the previous experiment and/or the metaphor type chosen might have tilted the results, as they did not represent the metaphorical relationships discussed as "conceptual" or "primary" in CMT. In order to test this, we replicated the experiment (10 judges, mean age 40; 31 participants, mean age 35) using expressions reflecting conventional metaphorical associations that CMT would regard as instantiations of conceptual metaphors, both complex and primary ones. Example item pairs are given by "a political argument" and "a boxing match" (reflecting ARGUMENT IS WAR, Lakoff & Johnson 1980: 5), or by "fear" and "cold" (reflecting FEAR IS COLD, Kövecses 2005: 289).

This replication yielded a similar pattern of results as the previous experiment. As predicted, a strong preference for pro-hierarchical ordering (92% of all cases, average level of confidence 5.7) and pro-hierarchical topic-assignment was found in the asymmetrical condition (94%, level of confidence 5.5). In contrast, a much weaker tendency toward pro-hierarchical topic assignment was found in the symmetrical condition (72%, level of confidence 4.9). Again, the difference between the different (i.e. symmetrical vs. asymmetrical) verbalizations was significant for both choice (Z = −3.785, $p <$ 0.001) and confidence level (t = −3.604, $p < 0.001$).

From these findings it follows that even preexisting conceptual hierarchies such as abstract–concrete require a directional task for their actualization and are not in themselves sufficient to prompt a strongly unidirectional mapping. If the very existence of an abstract–concrete asymmetry was sufficient to trigger a directional process, as implied by CMT, we would expect to find the same topic assignment (preferring the abstract concept as the topic of the metaphor) regardless of grammatical structure, i.e. in both the symmetric and the asymmetric condition. The fact that the tendency toward a pro-hierarchical context was *much weaker* in the symmetrical condition may suggest that the actual division of labor between a given pair of concepts does not derive automatically from their conceptual asymmetry but, rather, are only actualized fully by their insertion into the grammatically asymmetrical form.

To conclude, presenting metaphorically associated words in a grammatically asymmetrical form strongly enhances (and in some cases even triggers) metaphorical directionality in two complementary ways. First, it may actualize a potential asymmetry between the two domains that otherwise might have been remained latent: by inserting relevant verbal expressions into the grammatical slots defining targets and sources, a clear division of labor is imposed. Second, the very placement of the two concepts in these slots may in turn serve as a cue for their metaphorical assignment regardless of their semantic content.

5 From Mental Associations to Words

This discussion raises a broader, related question, which concerns the impact of language on conceptual hierarchies. Many recent studies have investigated the various ways in which language may shape our experience, as even the perception of the most purely perceptual stimuli may be altered when they are verbalized (see Lupyan 2012; Wolff & Holmes 2011). It seems, however, that while the way in which language modulates the processing of single concepts has gained much attention (see, e.g., Lupyan et al. 2007; Winawer et al. 2007), very few studies have dealt with the impact of language on the relations between concepts.

In a serious of studies, Shen and colleagues (Shen & Gil 2017) examined the effects of language on the categorization of visual hybrids, i.e. images that are constructed from two or more entities from different domains (see Figure 4.1).[5] They asked, particularly, whether this categorization would be affected by the (conceptual) "animacy hierarchy" (with humans on top, followed by animals, plants, and inanimate objects). The animacy hierarchy plays a central role in general and linguistic cognition (Keil 1979; see also Deane 1992; Lakoff &

Figure 4.1 A visual hybrid (half man, half tree)

Turner 1989 about the "great chain of being"), as well as in the domain of metaphor comprehension (Connor & Kogan 1980).

The interesting finding was that this hierarchy affects the categorization of hybrids *only in verbal tasks*: When people had to describe the visual hybrid verbally, they tended to use the pro-hierarchal description (e.g. "a man with a lower part of a tree") rather than an anti-hierarchical one (as in "a tree with a man's upper part"). In contrast, non-verbal tasks, such as the categorization of the visual hybrid into one of two visually presented categories (e.g. 'humans' or 'trees'), yielded *no* hierarchy effect: Participants in those tasks did not show a preference for the higher (or lower) category. Moreover, this discrepancy between linguistic and non-linguistic tasks seems to be correlated with grammatical asymmetry, as grammatically symmetrical tasks (e.g. using descriptions such as "half-human, half-tree") reveal a lesser effect or none at all (Mashal et al. 2014).

This finding demonstrates a point parallel to the one discussed in the previous section: Although both parts of the hybrid clearly maintained a conceptual asymmetry (humans are "higher" on the hierarchy than plants), this asymmetry in itself was not sufficient to yield a preference to categorize the hybrid as belonging to the "higher" rank in the animacy hierarchy. That is, in the absence of any directional task, the two concepts were simply associated, and the conceptual asymmetry between them remained implicit. The fact that this effect of language was correlated with the degree of grammatical asymmetry (that is, grammatically asymmetrical descriptions yielded a stronger effect than their grammatically symmetrical counterparts) further supports the claim that in this case, too, grammatical asymmetry served as the relevant directional trigger.

These examples bring us back to the question of automaticity. As said earlier, in contrast to the common view that metaphorical directionality is a direct and automatic outcome of the linkage between conceptually unequal domains or concepts (Lakoff & Johnson 1999: 45–59), we suggested that a distinction should be drawn between the pre-linguistic, experienced "bare" association and its expression as a full-blown metaphor in language. To further illustrate this point, consider the following thought experiment: Suppose you look at a pictorial representation of only two entities, a tired runner and a wilted plant, which are associated in our perceptual experience based on their conceptual (and, possibly, perceptual) similarity (Figure 4.2).

While one of the two entities may still be perceived as more prominent than the other, richer in its inferential capacity, or demonstrating any other conceptual difference which makes it a better candidate for becoming the source concept of a metaphor, there is nothing in the actual experience of these entities that leads the perceiver to project properties from one to the other. However, if a person is asked to judge the "proper" way to assign these two entities into target and source (for example, in the grammatically asymmetrical form of the simile "An X is like a Y"), then a potential directional mapping is prompted, actualizing the implicit conceptual hierarchy between the two entities (e.g. the person chooses "The runner is like the wilted plant" rather than "The plant is like the exhausted runner").

Reconsidering the (primary) metaphor AFFECTION IS WARMTH ("a *warm* smile"), the same logic can be applied. The very association of the two domains does not necessarily yield a division of labor between source and target, that is, it does not impose a unidirectional mapping, at least not in the strict sense. Indeed, that is exactly what the psycho-physical experiments discussed above show: Just as warmth co-activates affection, affection co-

a. A tired runner b. A wilted plant

Figure 4.2 Example of associated entities[6]

activates warmth. According to the view proposed here, the metaphorical directionality does not therefore characterize a metaphorical relation from its early formation but rather originates at a later phase, in which this prelinguistic relation is "converted" into a unidirectional verbalized form, following the grammatical templates of source–target assignment.

Further support for this account comes from the following small-scale study, which used non-verbal stimuli.[7] Twenty-four participants were presented with 16 pairs of pictures representing metaphorically related concepts with a clear asymmetry between them (either human/non-human or abstract/concrete), such as the aforementioned 'tired person' and 'wilted flower' or more conceptually related concepts such as 'raging man' and 'volcano.' On each trial, one picture appeared on the left side of a computer screen and the other on the right side, as illustrated in Figure 4.3.

The participants were divided into two groups, the verbal and the non-verbal. In the verbal group, they were asked to decide which of the two pictures in each pair is more similar to the other, by expressing their choice in a full sentence (e.g. "The raging man is similar to the volcano" or vice versa) and rate their confidence in their choice (on a 1–6 scale). Participants in the non-verbal group were asked to express their decision by using only their pointing finger, without speaking (no preference was marked by "0" confidence on the scale).

a. A raging man

b. An active volcano

Figure 4.3 Example of associated entities[8]

As predicted, participants in the verbal condition showed a clear preference (83%) for pro-hierarchical ordering (by choosing, e.g., "the raging man is similar to the volcano" rather than the other way around); however, almost no such preference was exhibited in the non-verbal condition (54%). Furthermore, participants expressed greater confidence in their choice in the verbal than the non-verbal tasks (average of 3.1 and 1.9, respectively). The difference between the conditions was significant for both choice ($Z = -2.857$, $p < 0.005$) and confidence level ($Z = -2.049$, $p < 0.05$).[9]

These findings suggest that language is indeed a crucial factor largely determining metaphorical directionality: When encountering only the pictorial representations of 'raging man' and 'active volcano,' the participants did understand the conceptual relation between the two but had no preference for a mapping direction; when they were asked to express this relation in the form of a fully articulated metaphor, however, a clear pro-hierarchical preference emerged.

These findings strongly support the proposed model. First, it seems that in the absence of language, the relation between metaphorically related concepts tend to be processed non-directionally, even when a clear conceptual hierarchy is involved. Second, verbalizing such purely conceptual (or perceptual) metaphorical relations is sufficient to activate a directional process, thus turning the original relation between the two concepts into a full-blown (asymmetrical) metaphor.

6 Conclusion

Conceptual Metaphor Theory profoundly changed the way we think about metaphor. In contrast to the common traditional depiction of metaphor as a primarily linguistic phenomenon, Lakoff and Johnson (1980) suggested that verbal metaphors are merely the explicit manifestations of unconscious processes through which we relate different domains, thus depicting metaphors as a window into a more fundamental level of cognition. Naturally, the rising popularity of this view shifted the focus of attention from the linguistic to the conceptual components of metaphors, as the significance of language to its formation was largely pushed aside (for a noteworthy exception to the neglect of the relevance of language for CMT, see Casasanto 2013).

In this chapter we tried to reevaluate some of Lakoff and Johnson's fundamental claims by pointing out and addressing a challenge to CMT: While verbal metaphors tend to be clearly unidirectional in their mapping from metaphorical source to target, their pre-linguistic counterparts, as manifested in psycho-physical manipulations, are not. Under the account proposed here, this commonly overlooked discrepancy is accounted for by a revision of a central tenet of the CMT model: In the revised model, unidirectional mappings are no longer regarded as an inherent component of metaphorical relationships at the conceptual level. Instead, we propose that the bidirectionality demonstrated in the psycho-physical studies derives largely from the structure of pre-linguistic metaphorical relations, which (contrary to central tenets of CMT) are based on a *bare* association between concepts/domains, with no clear assignment of source and target. The unidirectionality of verbal metaphors, we argue, is largely determined by being instantiated in a linguistic form. Language, by *requiring* a unidirectional projection, should thus be regarded as an important contributor to the formation of full-blown metaphor.

Notes and Acknowledgments

* This chapter is partly based on a chapter of the second author's Ph.D. thesis, which is being written in Shirley and Leslie Porter School of Cultural Studies at Tel Aviv University under the supervision of Yeshayahu Shen and David Gil. We thank David Gil of the Department of Linguistics at the Max Planck Institute for Evolutionary Anthropology in Leipzig for many hours of intensive discussions during which he has made many insightful suggestions and invaluable theoretical and methodological observations that have substantially contributed to the formation of the chapter. We would also like to thank an anonymous reviewer of the present chapter, and, in particular, Beate Hampe for many invaluable suggestions. Many thanks also go to the Porter Institute for Poetics and Semiotics and Shirley and Leslie Porter School of Cultural Studies at Tel Aviv University, and especially to Orly Lubin for a generous financial support to the second author. This research was supported by *The Israel Science Foundation* administered by *The Israel Academy of Sciences and Humanities*, no. 1196/12 for Yeshayahu Shen.

1 According to one of the dominant projection models, "the attributive category view" (Glucksberg et al. 1997), the expression "My lawyer is a shark" can be taken as a non-literal form of class-inclusion statement in which "my lawyer" serves as a member of the metaphorical category that is exemplified by "shark" ('vicious and cunning entities'). According to the commonality-based approach, the metaphorical

meaning of this expression derives from the idea that sharks and lawyers have similar features (being 'vicious,' 'cunning,' etc.).

2 Kathleen Connor and A. J. Martin, "Children's recognition of asymmetry in metaphor." Paper given at the Meeting of the South-Eastern Conference on Human Development, Baltimore, 1982.

3 William Cerbin, "Young children's comprehension of metaphoric language." Paper presented at the *Biennial Meeting of the Society for Research in Child Development*, Toronto, 1985.

4 The experimental work reported here has partially been done for Roy Porat's doctoral thesis "The role of language in the process of metaphorical understanding" (Tel Aviv University, Israel) and partially by the authors in cooperation. A more extensive report of the latter is currently being prepared for publication (R. Porat and Y. Shen, "Language enhances conceptual asymmetry").

5 Y. Shen and D. Gil, "The perception of visual hybrids: The role of language." Paper presented at Cognitive Poetics and Rhetoric 1.0, University of Lodz, Poland, 2010; Y. Shen, D. Gil, and H. Roman, "What can hybrids tell us about the relationship of language and thought?" Paper presented at the IGEL conference. Munich, Germany, 2006. See also Mashal et al. (2014).

6 Figure 4.2a ("tired runner"), from: www.oksportsandfitness.com/. Figure 4.2b ("Wilt") by Scott Nelson, from: www.flickr.com/photos/scotnelson/19898115344/.

7 This study is part of the Ph.D. dissertation by Roy Porat, currently in preparation for publication.

8 Figure 4.3a ("raging man") by Sadeh Halbrecht. Figure 4.3b is a part of the photo "Sakurajima at Sunset" by Kimon Berlin, from: www.flickr.com/photos/kimon/4128149164 (last accessed June 9, 2016).

9 To rule out the alternative interpretation that the symmetrical judgments were the result of random choice due to misperceiving the items in the purely pictorial condition, the participants were asked after each trial whether or not they understood the conceptual linkage between the two pictures. No difference in comprehensibility between the two conditions was found, with cases marked as meaningless excluded from the overall analysis. Furthermore, for distracting items that relied on visually similar pictures that differed in prominence (e.g. an ordinary-colored and a particularly colorful fish), a preferred order was noted in both conditions, indicating that the task was understood as directional in both of them.

5 Body Schema and Body Image in Metaphorical Cognition

*Valentina Cuccio**

Chapter Preview

Neurologists, philosophers, psychologists, and also linguists frequently employ the notion of the 'body schema.' Many divergent definitions of this notion were provided till Shaun Gallagher (1986) clarified the terminological and conceptual confusion by proposing a clear distinction between the two concepts of 'body schema' and 'body image.' I propose that two different roles played by the body in cognition can be identified on the basis of this distinction, corresponding to two different levels of embodiment. In this account, a first level of embodiment is constituted by *invisible metonymies* that have aspects of the body schema as their source domain. *Visible metaphors* occur at a second level of embodiment and take their source domains from aspects of the body image. In the first case, the mapping is directly from sensorimotor abilities to perception; in the second case, the mapping is from concepts that are related to our bodily experiences to abstract concepts.

1 Introduction: The Role of the Body in Cognition

What is the role, if any, that our body plays in metaphorical cognition? No doubt, this question is of vital importance to research on conceptual metaphors and embodiment more generally. However, the answer is far from simple. A consistent answer to this question requires a clarification of what we mean by "body." Although defining the notion of body may seem trivial, the literature on this topic is quite controversial.

In the embodiment literature, the notion of body has been defined in many different ways; consequently, many different roles have been ascribed to the body in human cognition. According to some authors, for example, the body directly affects cognition. According to others it contributes to cognition by being the object of a representation. In this latter view, representations of the body, and not the body in itself, have a role in the structuring of our conceptual system (for a survey, see Alsmith & de Vignemont 2012).

Related issues concern the level at which the body plays a role in cognition. A relevant distinction is that between the "personal" and "subpersonal" level in the explanation of our experience (Dennet 1969): The personal level pertains to "the explanatory level of people and their sensations and activities"; the subpersonal level in contrast concerns "the level of brains and events in the nervous system" (ibid.: 93). Personal-level phenomena are thus those mental processes that characterize our lives as subjects, while subpersonal phenomena are physical processes. The issue is thus whether the role of the body is explicit and even conscious or implicit, subpersonal, and unconscious.

Particularly controversial in this debate has been the notion of the 'body schema.' It was first introduced by the French neurologist Pierre Bonnier to refer to an internal representation of the body (Bonnier 1905). Since then not only neurologists but also psychologists and philosophers have made frequent use of the notion (Merlau-Ponty 1945). However, there has been considerable conceptual as well as terminological confusion as to what precisely body schemas are. Not only have there been many contrasting definitions of the notion, it has also frequently been used interchangeably with the notion of 'body image.'[1]

In order to clarify, Shaun Gallagher (Gallagher 1986, 2005; Gallagher & Zahavi 2008) proposed a clear distinction between the two notions of body schema and body image. According to Gallagher and Zahavi (2008: 164), the body image "is composed of a system of experiences, attitudes, and beliefs where the object of such intentional states is one's own body." The body schema, in contrast, "includes two aspects: (1) the close-to-automatic system of processes that constantly regulates posture and movement to serve intentional action; and (2) our pre-reflective and non-objectifying body awareness. So, the body schema is a system of sensorimotor capacities and activations that function without the necessity of perceptual monitoring" (Gallager & Zahavi 2008: 165; see also Dijkerman & de Haan 2007; Gibbs 2006a: 27–39). Two neurological pathologies, "deafferentation" and "personal neglect," which selectively affect the body schema or the body image, have been cited in support of the theoretical distinction between these two notions.[2]

What can this distinction tell us about the role of the body in cognition and, more specifically, about the hypothesis of the metaphorical nature of human cognition? I propose that a first level of cognition relies directly on body schemas. I will define the relationship between body schema and cognition as having a metonymic nature. I further propose that a second level of cognition relies on body images. The relationship between body image and cognition has a metaphoric nature. Depending on the source domain, i.e. body schema or body image, the body thus plays different roles in cognition that correspond to two levels of embodiment.

The first is the level of metonymies that have the body schema as their source domain. The power of these metonymies can be explained by their function of structuring perception and, consequently, also our conceptual system. In this case, the body is not the object of our attention and explicit knowledge. It is, instead, the condition of the possibility of action and knowledge. At this level, our cognition is intrinsically metonymic, implying a foundational relation between sensorimotor abilities and perceptual experiences. This first level of embodied metonymic cognition is prior to any other level of metaphorical cognition in thought, language, and communication; its role is that of making possible perception and, hence, knowledge of the world.[3] I will describe the shift from sensorimotor abilities to perceptual experiences as "invisible" and "transparent," because our body becomes invisible to us during perception. Except in particular circumstances, we do not focus our perceptual attention onto our own body, otherwise we would lose what perceptual experiences are about. From now on, I will refer to this first level of embodiment as the *level of invisible metonymies*.

The second level of embodiment is the level of embodied metaphorical cognition. It is claimed here that embodied metaphors occur at this level. In this case our body as object of knowledge and attention (i.e. our bodily experiences, and attitudes and beliefs about the body) is the source domain of a metaphorical mapping. Thus, the contribution of the body to thought and language is not direct. The body contributes to our metaphorical cognition as an object of knowledge. Accordingly, its contribution is mediated by our cultural, environmentally situated, and linguistically structured representations of the body. Body images can be conscious representations, but they do not necessarily have to be. From now on, I will refer to this second level of embodiment as the *level of visible metaphors*. It will be argued that the definition of visible metaphors provided includes not just Grady's (1997a, *this volume*) "complex" metaphors, but also those described as "primary."

In contrast to the neural, phenomenological, and cognitive-unconscious levels of embodiment often postulated (e.g. Gibbs 2006a: 39–40; Lakoff & Johnson 1999), my proposal identifies two logically different processes: (1) the foundation of perceptual experiences (at the phenomenological level) on our sensorimotor abilities (including their neural basis), and (2) the foundation of the conceptual system (including what is called the "Cognitive Unconscious") on our representations of the body.

In the following, I will first discuss the notions of body schema and body image (section 2) and then take up in more depth the different mappings they give rise to (section 3). In doing so, I will also discuss in which way my notion of invisible metonymy differs from that of primary metaphor.

2 Body Schema and Body Image

As indicated above, the notion of body schema has been used inconsistently, both by several authors and even in the work of single authors (for reviews, see Gallagher 2005; Gibbs 2006a: 27–36; Tiemersma 1989). The most confusing and ambiguous aspect of the definitions of body schema and/or body image is related to consciousness (Gallagher 2005: 21). To what extent is consciousness a necessary feature of a schema or image of the body? The answers to this question have been quite divergent. Consequently, the notions of a schema or image of the body have been described (i) as a subpersonal phenomenon occurring at the neural level, (ii) as a conscious mental representation, (iii) as an unconscious representation, or (iv) as the way we organize our bodily experiences (ibid.: 23; see also Gibbs 2006a: 28–29).

This conceptual confusion points to a deeper theoretical problem: At least two different levels of embodiment have often been collapsed. A conceptual and terminological clarification, which also considers interactions/dependencies between the body schema and body image is thus a necessary and preliminary step to any discussion of the role of the body in cognition.

In what follows, I will discuss the distinction between body schema and body image with the aim of fostering a deeper understanding of the role of the body in human cognition that also takes into account possible interactions between different levels of embodiment.

2.1 The Body Schema

> The body-schema is a system of sensory-motor processes that constantly regulate posture and movements – processes that function without reflective awareness or the necessity of perceptual monitoring.
>
> (Gallagher 2005: 37)

In Gallagher's terms, the concept of body schema refers to the sum of the sensorimotor capabilities that allow us to move and constrain our movements, to navigate and perceive the world. In this sense, the body schema is not the result of our perception of our own body and does not refer to a perceptual or mental image of the body. With this definition, Gallagher refers to the motor abilities that are foundational to action and perception.

As such, the body schema does not usually involve awareness or constant perceptual monitoring. Unless something does not work in the right way or unless we are facing the task of learning a new motor pattern, for example a dance step, we do not generally focus our attentional awareness on the body and on the processes underlying action and perception. Let us think of what we normally do when we walk. We know that we need to move one foot after the other in a certain direction. However, while walking, we do not need to attend to our body and its fine movements, that is, we do not need to focus our attention on our legs and on our feet to calculate the exact distance of space we need to move or to estimate how to balance the weight of our body on one foot when the other is moving forward, and so on. So, even though we are not aware of what we do in order to walk, we are usually able to walk and to effortlessly adjust our movements to the ground. We do not continuously lose our balance if the surface where we are walking is not completely regular, and we do not fall down all the time. To make our movements faster and safer, there is a set of subpersonal mechanisms, proprioception *in primis*, that allow us to register the inputs we get from the outside and on this basis to regulate what we need to do in order to move in the environment. Of course, we can suddenly have a physical problem, such as a severe pain in a leg that will not allow us to move any more. In such a case we may lose our balance or even fall down, and then need to give conscious attention to our body and its movements to be able to walk again. But this is not the norm. Pain, together with other peculiar circumstances related, for example, to fatigue, sex, sickness, or even to philosophical introspection or medical investigation, are limiting cases in which the body itself becomes the focus of our attention. When the body enters our perceptual field, becoming the object of our conscious perception, we are already dealing with the body image. In sum, the body schema is not an image of the body but the condition of the possibility of action and, thus, also of perception (Noë 2004).

According to Gallagher (2005: 45), three functional subsystems constitute the body schema. The first is the system responsible for the processing of information about posture and movement. Information about posture and movement comes from different sources. Somatic proprioception is certainly the primary kind of information we use. We get proprioceptive information from kinetic, muscular, articular, and cutaneous sources. Vestibular and equilibrial functions and the visual sense are also sources of proprioceptive information. In the latter case, we automatically register visual information about the movement of our own body in the environment. The visual sense, however, can also be a source of *explicit* information in cases when we directly focus our perceptual attention on the position of our limbs. In these cases we are again already dealing with a form of body image. Note that proprioceptive information is defined here as a set of physiological, subpersonal, and unconscious processes that lead to proprioceptive awareness. In some pre-reflexive sense, we are always aware of the position of our body, but this awareness is not the result of an explicit act of reflection.

The second functional system of a body schema is responsible for the production of motor programs and movement patterns (output). We have a number of motor habits. Developmental studies suggest that some of these are innate, such as swallowing, while others are learned, such as writing (Meltzoff & Moore 1977, 1989; see also Gallagher 2005). At the neural level, a motor program can be described as the activation of some neural circuits in the motor cortex that enables the execution – at the behavioral level – of the single motor acts that together constitute the chain of a motor action. The processing of proprioceptive information is essential for the production of motor patterns. We constantly need feedback about our current body posture to efficiently move in the environment.

The third functional system of a body schema regards cross-modal communication. We have an innate ability to transform visual inputs into motor competence. This means that when we observe other people' actions, this visual stimulus is immediately and automatically translated into motor terms. This is achieved by means of mirror neurons, multimodal neurons in the pre-motor cortex which respond both to action observation and to action execution (di Pellegrino et al. 1992). The motor neurons that enable the movement of the hand when we grasp a cup, for example, will be activated not only when we effectively grasp a cup but also when we observe someone else grasping a cup. The somatotopic activation of motor neurons in the pre-motor cortex in the absence of a corresponding action has been considered as a "motor simulation" of the observed action. It has been suggested that motor simulation is a constitutive process of action understanding; we understand other people's actions by means of the activation of our own motor competence (Gallese & Sinigaglia 2011). Furthermore, it has also been hypothesized that motor simulation is involved in the process of learning by imitation (Rizzolatti et al. 2008). In this connection, the mirror mechanism determines automatic activation of the motor programs that are necessary to carry out the observed action.

It has lately been discovered that the mechanism of simulation is not limited to motor neurons in the pre-motor cortex. This mechanism is widespread in the brain, and it also characterizes perception- and emotion-related areas. When we see other people's facial expressions indicating their emotions, for instance, emotion-related areas of our brain will be activated. Furthermore it has also been observed that the mechanism of simulation is activated not only by direct observation of others but also by cognitive tasks such as mental imagery and language comprehension (Gallese & Sinigaglia 2011; for a discussion of the latter, see Ritchie, *this volume*). Given that the process of simulation is neither activated by action observation only nor confined to the motor areas of the brain, it is usually referred to by the more general term of "embodied simulation."

2.2 *The Body Image*

> The body-image consists of a complete set of intentional states and dispositions – perceptions, beliefs and attitudes – in which the intentional object is one's own body.
>
> (Gallagher 2005: 25)

As suggested by this definition, different types of intentional relations can be involved in the constitution of a body image. First, the body can be the object of a perceptual state ("body percept"). When we move around perceiving the world, for example when we look at a beautiful landscape from the peak of a mountain, we are usually not aware of our body. It becomes invisible to us while we are absorbed in the breath-taking beauty of the landscape. But if we suddenly have a terrible itch on our left foot, this will become the object of our perceptual attention and of our efforts to relieve the complaint. This intentional relation, clearly, also implies conscious awareness. We are perfectly aware of what our foot feels like when it itches. This kind of epistemic access to our body is from the first-person perspective (Pauen 2012).

Second, the body can be the object of our conceptual knowledge ("body concept"). This happens when it is accessed from the third-person perspective (ibid.). When we open a handbook of anatomy and we start to study the structure and composition of the human body, it becomes the object of our conceptual understanding. In this case, we cannot know how it feels to have neurons firing, but we have a scientific description of this neuro-physiologic process. This is clearly an intentional relation, also involving conscious awareness. Note that our scientific knowledge about the body does not always imply a conscious level of awareness: We do not always have the functions and processes of the nervous system or of other parts of the body consciously present in our mind. According to Gallagher (2005: 25), this knowledge is part of a set of beliefs and attitudes that – even unconsciously – entertains an intentional relation with the body considered as an epistemic object. Scientific knowledge is not the only source of conceptual knowledge about the body; commonsense beliefs are an equally important part of our conceptual understanding of the body. Common sense and scientific knowledge constantly interact with one another. Our beliefs are inevitably historically, linguistically, and culturally situated and the progresses and results of scientific knowledge are an integral part of our historical, linguistic, and cultural environment. What scientific research reveals about the body does, in a slow but constant process, influence our commonsense understanding of the body.

Third, the body can also be the object of an emotional attitude ("body affect"). This is the case when our feelings, positive or negative, have the body as their object. We look in the mirror every day, and this routine action is usually associated with a positive or negative feeling, according to our mood on that day and to many other variables. We do or do not like what we see. This feeling toward the body is an intentional relation that can be conscious but is very often unconscious. It is of great importance that our feelings and attitudes toward the body are inevitably mediated by our body concept, that is, by our beliefs about the body. If we live in a society where the standard of beauty is a thin and athletic body and we do not match that standard, this can lead us to have negative feelings toward our body. It is also possible and fairly common that our feelings toward the body influence and affect our perception of our own body and our beliefs and conceptualization of it.

Body affect, body concept, and body percept are three different but deeply interconnected aspects of our image of the body. The body image, then, is a set of interconnected intentional states, whereby each type of intentional relation with the body affects and influences the others and all of them are deeply situated in a historical, linguistic, and cultural environment. The image we have of our own body is inevitably the result of our being situated in a specific context including a particular physical, linguistic, and sociocultural environment.

Finally, it is important to note that the body image is almost always a partial representation of the body: Our perception, emotional attitude, or conceptualization of the body are usually directed toward a part or a single aspect of the body at a time, as in the example of the itch on the left foot discussed at the beginning of this section. We single out one aspect of our bodily experience and this aspect or part becomes the object of a representational state.

2.3 Relations between Body Schema and Body Image

I indicated in the previous sections that, although conceptualized as distinct, the boundary between body schema and body image is not rigid in human cognition, so that the body image can affect the body schema. This is the case when our beliefs and concepts about our own body affect perception and movement in space. Even a basic activity, acquired very early on in life, such as walking, can be affected by our beliefs and thus, in the range of the biomechanical possibilities, determined by the structure of our body, it can be to some extent culturally shaped.

Vice versa, it is also possible that in particular circumstances, for example, when we are facing a situation of particular physical effort (e.g. during some sports training), we focus our attention on specific motor patterns that are usually below the threshold of awareness. In such a case, body schema functions become the object of attention and perception.

Finally and most relevant to the present concerns, the body schema and the body image interact in embodied simulation. It has been proposed that embodied simulation is involved in the sensorimotor foundations of the conceptual system because metaphorical thought seems to directly recruit the sensorimotor system (Gallese 2009; Gallese & Cuccio 2016; Gallese & Lakoff 2005). The exploitation of the sensorimotor system, which is part of the body schema, in the structuring of the conceptual system by means of the mechanism of simulation highlights the tight interaction between body schema and body image (see section 4).

3 Two Levels of Embodiment

I have so far argued that an understanding of how the body contributes to cognition requires a clear distinction between body schema and body image. In this section I will distinguish between two levels of embodiment that are based on the body schema and the body image, respectively. I will argue that they provide the source domains of two different kinds of mappings, one metonymic and one metaphorical.

3.1 Invisible Metonymies: The Body Schema as a Source Domain

As previously defined, the notion of the body schema refers to the set of (partially innate) sensorimotor functions that enable our active interaction with the environment. In this section I will discuss in depth the hypothesis that the body schema is the basic and ontogenetically primary source of a metonymic mapping from sensorimotor abilities to perception (and, hence, ultimately to cognition, too).

Our perceptual experiences are always functions of our movements. This is the case even for vision, which is often taken to be the most passive of our perceptual modalities and has also served as the paradigm case for thinking about perception in general (cf. Noë 2004: 2). There is empirical evidence showing that a paralysis of the eyes causes blindness. Vision requires saccades and microsaccades (eye movements), many times per second, to make us able to see (ibid.: 13). These constant movements of the eyes are constitutive of vision. Furthermore, it has also been shown that perception does not only require bodily movements relative to the surrounding environment. It also requires self-actuated movements, i.e. movements that individuals actively perform, not passive movements (ibid.; Held & Hein 1963). From this point of view, perception is grounded in and constrained by our motor abilities (see also Gibbs 2006a: 42–78). In other words, perception is something that we literally act out (and thus cannot adequately describe as a passive reception of stimuli).

Calling this level of embodied metonymic cognition "transparent" emphasizes that, when we enact perception, our actions and the body that enables them are usually outside the focus of our attention and not visible to us. To have perceptual experiences, we need to map sensorimotor contingencies, here defined as the "interdependence between stimulation and movement" (Gibbs 2006a: 65), onto the stimuli we receive. Crucially, the stimuli we get from the environment are always partial and incomplete, but our perceptual experiences are not. For example, we usually see objects only from one side but we perceive them as three-dimensional. To do so, we project sensorimotor contingencies onto the partial stimuli we receive. A partial and incomplete stimulus is, thus, always seen in terms of the actions and movements that would allow us to have a more complete perceptual access to it.

The first and primary level of embodiment is at play in our perception of the world, being its condition of possibility, and it is, thus, foundational to any other level of cognition. This is particularly evident when we look at cognitive development. Our body schema is the primary source of knowledge because movement in space is our primary source of knowledge. On the basis of partial stimuli, we map from movement to complete perceptual experiences. This level of embodiment does not reveal itself in the linguistic dimension.

Although taking up vital aspects of Conceptual Metaphor Theory (henceforth CMT) and Primary Metaphor Theory (henceforth PMT), namely, their claim that metaphors are cross-domain mappings from sensory source domains onto more abstract domains (including social and affective ones), the present proposal also goes beyond CMT and PMT insofar as these do not account for the modality of constitution of sensory experiences. Sensory experiences (see Grady 1997a; Grady & Johnson 2002) seem to be a starting point that can be taken for granted. Whether the sensory experiences assumed to provide the source domains of primary metaphors belong to the body schema or to the body image is thus left open.

It is claimed here that we also need to account for the *constitution* of sensory experiences. A closer scrutiny of the constitution of sensory experiences will allow us to realize that this basic and primary level of cognition implies a metonymic description: The mapping goes from the body schema to perception. The body schema provides the structure to every perceptual experience: Although we are not aware of this, we map patterns of sensorimotor contingencies onto partial perceptual stimuli, and this allows us to have full perceptual experiences. This mapping is neither conscious nor directly visible to us, but it allows perceptual experiences to take place. The level of invisible metonymies is thus of a constitutive nature.

Clearly, the definition of this first level of embodied cognition is profoundly different from the level of primary metaphors introduced by Grady (1997a, 2005a). In Grady's account, primary metaphors are constituted by the association of sensory experiences, referred to as their "image content," with non-sensory "response" concepts, which include social and emotional assessments of the sensory experience. Both the source and the target of a primary metaphor are equally basic aspects of the holistic experience given by a so-called "primary scene":

> The correlation between emotion and skin temperature is real and experienced. We feel warm when our emotions are aroused, and we feel warm when we are close to other people, as we are when we interact intimately. There is a *conceptual association between coldness and lack of feeling*, not because interacting with a cold object and interacting with an unfeeling person are perceived as similar experiences, but because

> through recurring experience *we associate the conceptual domain of temperature with that of emotion.* (Grady 2005b: 1600, emphases inserted)

Though PMT does not distinguish between body schema and body image, Grady's remarks can be taken to place the association between the source and target of a primary metaphor already at the conceptual level. Hence, it can be concluded that, in PMT, the body contributes to cognition being already an object of knowledge, i.e. as body percept.

At the first level of embodiment, in contrast, the body is not an object of knowledge. It is, instead, the condition of possibility of knowledge because our motor abilities, together with the sensory apparatuses we are equipped with, are the condition of possibility of every perceptual experience. The relationship between the physical body and motor abilities, on the one hand, and perceptual experiences, on the other, is constitutive and considered to be metonymic. To have perceptual experiences, we map sensorimotor contingencies onto the partial stimuli we get from the environment. Only this allows us to build complete perceptual experiences.

However, the boundary between this level of embodied metonymic cognition and the level of visible metaphors is not so rigid. The lived body and its motor abilities can enter our perceptual field in different situations and can be exploited, by means of the mechanism of embodied simulation, to carry out cognitive tasks that also involve the use of representations of the body. I will discuss this in more detail in section 4.

3.2 Visible Metaphors: Body Image as a Source Domain

The power of metaphors having a body image as a source domain can be considered audible and visible, in comparison with the silent and transparent power of embodied metonymies based on the body schema. To be more precise, in metaphors from the body image the source of the metaphor is our body as an object of representation and knowledge (i.e. a body percept, body concept, or body affect), and the metaphorical mapping takes place independently of the presence of these metaphors at the level of language, although language may reflect them. As such, the metaphorical mapping is now from one representation to another representation, and the contribution of the body is mediated by our cultural, environmentally situated, and linguistically structured representations of the body itself.

According to my proposal, Grady's (1997a) primary and complex metaphors both take their source domains from the body image. As noted before, a primary metaphor is based on a correlation between a concept in the conceptual domain (matrix) of sensory experiences and another one in an abstract conceptual domain. The metaphorical mapping takes place at the conceptual level, and hence, in this account, the body contributes to metaphorical cognition as an object of knowledge. Metaphors such as INTIMACY IS CLOSENESS or AFFECTION IS WARMTH are classic examples of experientially motivated primary metaphors in which we associate two different conceptual domains.

Complex metaphors are not considered to be directly experientially motivated. They are a combination of primary metaphors recruiting wider frame knowledge (including believes, norms, etc.) (e.g. Grady 2005b; Lakoff 2008a). Standard examples of complex metaphors are long-discussed conceptual metaphors such as LOVE IS A JOURNEY or THEORIES ARE BUILDINGS. In these cases, the metaphorical mapping doubtlessly takes place at the conceptual level. It is thus suggested here that both primary and complex metaphors imply a mapping that takes place at the conceptual level and have (aspects of) the body image as a source domain.

A key element to discuss with respect to the difference between primary and complex metaphors is the notion of context. I propose that both primary and complex metaphors are contextually determined, although in very different ways. In order to highlight the contextually mediated nature of metaphors from the body image, we need to address a classic and hotly debated topic in CMT, which concerns the universal or nearly universal nature of conceptual metaphors, especially primary ones (e.g. Lakoff 2008a). However, universality claims seem to be undermined both by theoretical considerations about the role of context in metaphorical conceptualization and by the huge amount of data on cross-cultural variation.

Kövecses (2005, 2010a) stressed that there is a great amount of data on universal conceptual metaphors, and their universality seems to rely precisely on the universality of our bodily experiences. As Lakoff (2008a: 26) suggested, we all have the same bodies and almost the same relevant environments, and during our childhood the same connections between domains are likely to be built. We all have lived the physical experience of being up when we are happy. We all have lived the physical experience of warmth when feeling affection. Hence, this first level of metaphorical conceptualization is universal and deeply grounded in our bodies – although, in Lakoff's account, it does not follow that those conceptual metaphors are expressed exactly in the same way in all languages. Nor does it follow that cross-cultural variation does not play any role at higher levels of conceptualization. In Lakoff's view (2008a, 2014), primary metaphors are atomic units that can be the basis for wider systems of contextually determined complex metaphors.

However, empirical evidence abounds on the side of cross-cultural or within-culture variations that can even be applied to primary metaphor (Kövecses 2010a).[4] According to Kövecses (ibid.: 204), this tension between universality and cultural variations in conceptual metaphors is the result of two different and concomitant pressures underlining our metaphorical conceptualization: One is the *pressure of embodiment* that forces metaphorical conceptualization toward its universal characterization; the other is the *pressure of context*, which is determined by local culture and forces metaphors in the direction of cross-culture and within-culture variations. To reconcile these different pressures, Kövecses (ibid.) proposes the notion of 'differential experiential focus.' Based on the idea that our bodily experiences consist of many different components, it assumes that we can single out and emphasize different aspects of that experience when using the same bodily experience as the source domain of a metaphor – depending on the context in which the metaphorical conceptualization takes place. Context is defined broadly by Kövecses (ibid.: 204) as the set of physical, social, cultural, and discourse aspects, the last of these also in relation to factors such as topic, audience and medium, that can affect the conceptualization of metaphors. Differences in experiential focus result from the role of context in the creation of primary metaphors. Although we all share a large number of physical and subjective experiences, which of these experiences that we focus on when establishing a primary metaphorical connection depends on the context in which these experiences are embedded. Hence, at this level, the role of context is that of selecting some aspects of our universally shared experiences. The context works as a lens that allows us to isolate some features of primitive universally shared human experiences that often and very early on occur together in our life (for a related view, see Casasanto, *this volume*).

Things are different with complex metaphors. Here, the role of context is much more pervasive. The blending of elements (primary metaphors, frame knowledge, beliefs, other complex metaphors, metonymies etc.; see Grady 2005b; Lakoff 2008a; Ruiz de Mendoza, *this volume*) that is involved in building complex metaphors is largely determined by contextual factors. Complex metaphors completely rely on cultural practices.

Issues related to the universality vs. culture-specificity of metaphorical conceptualization clearly need to be addressed in great detail because the metaphorical mappings take place at the conceptual level, from concept to concept – and even in the case of primary metaphors – from a conceptual representation of the body to another conceptual representation.

When considering the mapping from motor abilities to perception, the issue of the different pressures applied by embodiment and culture has a very different import. On the one hand, it is true that there are motor activities that are deeply culturally embedded and that these activities, for example, the practice of a specific dance or sport, have specific motor programs underlying them. As such, these motor programs are culturally determined.

In this context, it should furthermore be noted that the mechanism of embodied simulation is sensitive to these cultural differences. If I have never seen someone dancing the capoheria, I will likely not have any motor simulation of the observed action or a very low activation of the corresponding motor areas when I finally watch someone dancing it. The motor programs that in our motor system implement and underlie any culture-specific practices are the product of our learning activities in specific contexts.

On the other hand, when considering the contribution that our body schema makes to cognition, we primarily think of the set of processes and mechanisms that are the condition of possibility of any learning activity. These mechanisms and processes are innate and universal. Hence, the contribution the body schema makes to perception is the matrix of species-specific and universal aspects in human cognition.

4 Embodied Simulation

By means of the mechanism of embodied simulation, the metonymic mapping from motor abilities to perceptual experiences can be exploited to support cognitive activities at the level of the body image even when we are not carrying out any overt movement (Gallese & Cuccio 2016; Gallese & Lakoff 2005). Indeed, both thought and language recruit the mechanism of simulation. It is important to highlight that the mechanism of simulation allows us, in particular circumstances, to go from the activation of motor areas of the brain to the level of bodily sensations (Cuccio 2014, 2015), and this further highlights the foundational relation that connects actions/movements and perception.

This hypothesis is confirmed by empirical data. For example, Costantini and colleagues (2005) carried out an fMRI study to investigate the potential simulation elicited by the observation of both possible and biomechanically impossible movements of fingers. The authors of this study observed the activation of a motor simulation in both conditions. Additionally, data from this study also showed the activation of the Posterior Parietal Cortex (PPC), an area of the brain that is involved in the processing of bodily sensations, in both experimental conditions, but the PPC was significantly more activated in the biomechanically impossible movement condition. Moreover, particular circumstances – e.g. related to attention, emotion, pain or pleasure – can amplify the simulation effect. The experimental stimulus in the condition with the biomechanically impossible movements clearly suggested to the participants a potentially very painful situation. The simulation, in this and analogous cases, is not confined to the motor areas but also involves areas related to the experience of bodily sensations. This involvement of brain areas related to bodily sensations led participants of the study to report that they felt "sensations" that were determined by the observation of the experimental stimuli.

It has also been found that the mirror-neurons system is involved in action prediction: To predict other people's actions, we recruit our motor system (cf. Abreu et al. 2012). An fMRI experiment by Abreu and colleagues (ibid.) studied the ability of basketball players, both expert athletes and novices, to predict the outcome of free throws performed by others. Abreu and colleagues investigated whether other neural regions are also involved in predicting others' actions. They found that in both expert basketball players and novices, the observation of the experimental stimuli (free throws performed by others) not only led to the recruitment of the mirror system and, hence, to motor simulation but also determined the activation of the sensory cortex. "Motor simulation," the authors say, "may imply a mapping of specific sensory features" (ibid.: 1652). The specific experimental task of this study required participants to pay attention to the action features carried out by basketball players observed in short movies. The task performed led both to the activation of a motor simulation and to the involvement of the sensory cortex. Very likely, bodily sensations were directly recruited in solving the cognitive task the participants were asked to perform (to predict the outcome of free throws performed by others). The involvement of the sensory cortex is, thus, considered to be task-dependent.

In other words, embodied simulation does not always determine the activation of bodily sensations. There are cases, for instance, in which it has the function of preparing us for an action we can potentially carry out. A good example is tool-use behavior. Our interactions with tools are usually underpinned by the activation of the mechanism of simulation (Caruana & Cuccio 2015). In these cases, embodied simulation does not have the role of helping us understand others, and it likely does not lead to the experience of any bodily sensations. In this case, the cognitive role of simulation is to "suggest" to us the right action and prepare our motor system to perform it. Bodily sensations are not required for this.

The mechanism of simulation seems to be able to determine bodily sensations, even though this does not always happen (and when it happens, these bodily sensations are not always nor very often conscious).

In the hypothesis proposed here, embodied simulation allows us to exploit the metonymic mapping that goes from the body schema to perceptual experiences. Interestingly, Raymond Gibbs (2005b) reconsidered the notion of 'image schema,' defined in CMT as recurrent patterns of/in our sensorimotor experiences (Johnson 1987), in terms of their role in the mechanism of Embodied Simulation. For him, they are psychologically real experiential "gestalts," construed "on the fly," and not abstract mental representations unconsciously recalled during linguistic processing.

The hypothesis that image schemas play a crucial role in embodied simulations does not contradict the two levels of embodiment proposed here. In Gibbs' account, embodied simulation is defined not as a merely neural phenomenon but as the experience of bodily feelings activated by an imaginative process. Embodied simulation, so conceived, can be considered as the mechanism that allows us to *exploit* the first foundational level of embodied metonymic cognition. In other words, the direct and unmediated contribution of the body to cognition that characterizes the first level of embodiment can be recruited to carry out cognitive tasks that involve the use of representations of the body (as part of the imaginative process, that is).

5 Conclusions

To summarize, I have proposed that – on the basis of the distinction between body schema and body image – it is possible to identify two levels of embodiment. The first level is the level of invisible metonymies that are foundational to every possibility of perception and cognition. They have (aspects of) the body schema as a source domain. The power of these metonymies is silent and transparent because in this case our bodily capabilities are the glasses through which we look at the world. The body is not the object of our attention and explicit knowledge. It is, instead, the condition of possibility of perception and knowledge. In this first case, the contribution of the body to thought and language is direct.

The second level of embodiment is the level of visible metaphors. They take source domains from the body image. In comparison with the silent and transparent power of metonymies based on the body schema, the power of these metaphors can be considered audible and visible. In this case our body, i.e. our bodily experiences, attitudes, and beliefs about the body, becomes the object of explicit knowledge and attention. The body is thus explicitly considered as an object of knowledge, and the contribution of the body to thought and language is mediated by our cultural, environmentally situated, and linguistically structured representations of the body itself.

Notes and Acknowledgments

* I wish to thank an anonymous reviewer for most valuable comments and suggestions on an earlier version of this chapter. I wish to express my deepest gratitude to Gerard Steen for helpful comments on an earlier draft of this chapter and, most of all, for his invaluable help and support during these years. I wish to thank Beate Hampe for her constant and invaluable help during the writing of this chapter. Her inspiring and thought-provoking comments have, sometimes, been hard to address but were certainly fundamental to reaching the final version of this work.

1 For surveys of the use of the terms in psychology, see Gibbs (2006a: 27–28) and de Vignemont (2010).
2 For details on deafferentation, see Cole (1995), Cole and Paillard (1995), and Gallagher and Cole (1995). For details on personal neglect, see Denny-Brown et al. (1952).
3 This chapter views perception as having a fundamental role in the structuring of conceptual knowledge but does not address the likewise fundamental role of language in conceptual knowledge.
4 Diverging from earlier work, Kövecses (2015) views primary metaphors as near-universal.

6 Primary Metaphors Are Both Cultural and Embodied

*Bodo Winter & Teenie Matlock**

Chapter Preview

Cognitive linguists have argued that metaphors are anchored in our embodied experiences. Cultural, linguistic, and gestural representations are often seen as reflections of underlying conceptual mappings. On the basis of three different metaphors, MORE IS UP, SIMILARITY IS PROXIMITY, and SOCIAL DISTANCE IS SPATIAL DISTANCE (aka INTIMACY IS CLOSENESS), we argue for a more active role of external representations in individual cognition. Rather than being mere "reflections" of the respective conceptual associations, external representations actively enhance and support these. Since two of the metaphors we discuss associate the same source domain (SPATIAL DISTANCE) with different target domains (SIMILARITY and SOCIAL CLOSENESS), we also discuss to what extent primary metaphors are (by necessity) interrelated, and whether these metaphors can be treated as distinct conceptual entities at all.

1 Introduction

Metaphor is far more than a rhetorical tool used in poetry and literature. Metaphors of all shapes and sizes permeate our everyday communication, written and spoken. They also appear in visual media, including sculpture, paintings, and architecture, as well as in music. Metaphors, as argued by cognitive linguists, are anchored in our embodied experiences and recruited to help us make sense of abstract and complex entities and situations in the world (Gibbs 1994; Johnson 1987; Kövecses 2002; Lakoff & Johnson 1980).

Metaphors can be analyzed in different ways, depending on the goals of the researcher. One common distinction made among cognitive linguists is between "primary" versus "non-primary" metaphors (Grady 1997b, 1999, 2005b; Grady et al. 1999; Grady & Ascoli, *this volume*). Primary metaphors are thought to arise from our most basic physical and perceptual experiences in the world. On this view, the metaphor MORE IS UP, for instance, emerges from repeatedly observing the natural correlation between verticality and quantity (e.g. stacking cookies, piling up rocks, filling up glasses) (Lakoff 1987: 276–277). Repeatedly creating or observing a "higher" stack of cookies comes to be associated with a greater amount of cookies. The same goes for a "higher" pile of rocks or for "rising" water levels.

Cognitive linguists often contrast primary metaphors like these with "non-primary" metaphors, an example of which is THEORIES ARE BUILDINGS, which underlies statements such as, "He destroyed my theory" or "My theory rests on solid ground" (Grady 1997b; cf. also Kövecses 2002: 108–110). Conceptual metaphor theory in particular maintains that, in understanding such statements, people map the source domain of BUILDINGS onto the target domain of THEORIES (for an extensive discussion of this point, see Steen, *this volume*). In contrast with MORE IS UP, there is no obvious embodied correlation associated with THEORIES ARE BUILDINGS; the presence of buildings does not necessarily correlate with the presence of theories. Rather, there is a perceived resemblance between THEORIES and BUILDINGS. Moreover, primary metaphors such as MORE IS UP are assumed to be universal because the correlation between verticality and quantity is a fact of the natural world. By contrast, THEORIES ARE BUILDINGS presupposes a specific cultural context, a context where people theorize and talk about creating and maintaining theories (see also Cuccio, *this volume*).

This is not to say that primary metaphors are *acultural.* Primary metaphors have abundant cultural reflections. With MORE IS UP, for example, measuring cups, thermometers, and graphs reflect the mapping of verticality onto quantity that we often see in Western cultures. In this chapter, we argue that such cultural reflections of primary metaphors do not merely signal metaphorical content but also play a more active role, actively shaping the conceptual systems of people who witness those reflections (for closely related views, see Gibbs 1999; Kövecses 2015; Marghetis 2015). Once primary metaphors, perhaps originating from experienced embodied correlations, take hold and become part of multiple conceptual systems (i.e. of multiple speakers), the linguistic and cultural structures that emerge from this help maintain and strengthen the underlying metaphorical relationship. Linguistic and cultural reflections of primary metaphors may thus "feed back" into the underlying conceptual structure. This view resonates with approaches in cognitive science that emphasize the role of cultural artifacts in scaffolding conceptual knowledge (e.g. Hutchins 1995, 2005) and with the view that primary metaphors are not always purely "embodied" but may have different origins (e.g. also linguistic, cultural ones) (Casasanto 2014b, *this volume*). Cognitive linguists could benefit from a broader perspective of metaphor, one that embraces the complex web of interactions between language, culture, and embodied experience.

Here we focus on three primary metaphors: MORE IS UP (section 2.1), SOCIAL DISTANCE IS PHYSICAL DISTANCE (section 2.2), and SIMILARITY IS PROXIMITY (section 2.3). For each, we discuss linguistic reflections (for a larger crosslinguistic survey, see Grady & Ascoli, *this volume*), gestural reflections, and non-linguistic cultural reflections, as well as the relevant evidence from behavioral experiments. In section 3, we argue that linguistic, gestural, and cultural representations of metaphor should not be viewed merely as passive indicators of underlying conceptual mappings but, rather, as building blocks for creating and re-creating metaphor (cf. Gibbs 1999; Kövecses 2015; Marghetis 2015; Winter 2014). In section 4, we discuss how primary metaphors overlap and interact.

2 A Complex Web of Language, Culture, and Cognition

2.1 MORE IS UP

We first discuss linguistic, gestural, cultural, and cognitive reflections of primary metaphors with MORE IS UP. This metaphor is expressed when English speakers make statements like "high tax rates," or when German speakers make statements like "Die Preise sind gestiegen" ('The prices have risen'). Besides these linguistic reflections, MORE IS UP is expressed via gesture. Metaphor is often expressed in manual gestures (Chui 2011; Cienki 1998; Cienki & Müller 2008b; Sweetser 1998). Figure 6.1, a still image from the TV News Archive, shows a gesture by Michael Hayden, former CIA director (2006–2009).[1] Hayden is talking about employment in the CIA and, specifically, about a division of the CIA that he classifies as "core support." According to Hayden, there is a "disturbingly high number of contractors" in this core support division. In Figure 6.1, the palm of his left hand is facing toward the audience and toward the camera. As he says "high number," he moves the hand upward. This movement is consistent with MORE IS UP. That the movement is time-locked with the verbal phrase suggests that gesture and the metaphorical semantics are tightly coupled in this example (for a close discussion of further examples, see Winter et al. 2013).

Cultural reflections of MORE IS UP are pervasive. Floors in tall buildings are numbered with smaller numbers at the bottom. Doctors measure humans using scales with smaller numbers at the bottom and increasingly larger numbers going upward. Beakers and measuring cups have small numbers at the bottom and large numbers at the top, and so do thermometers. Cultural reflections of MORE IS UP are prevalent in graphs (Tversky 2011), where it is

a. (...) disturbingly *high number* ... b. ... of contractors in core support

Figure 6.1 MORE IS UP expressed in co-speech gesture on the phrase "high number." The hand starts low and moves up to a higher position (a), with the end point shown in (b).[2]

a convention to put larger numbers higher on the y-axis than lower numbers. This characterizes particularly bar plots and line graphs, which are often used in science and newspapers. Empirical work on the understanding of graphs has furthermore shown that vertical bar plots that embody MORE IS UP are easy to interpret, more so than horizontal bar plots (Fischer et al. 2005).

Some researchers have pointed out exceptions in the cultural patterns of MORE IS UP (e.g. Holmes & Lourenco 2011; see also Tversky 2011). Consider numbers on cell phones, where smaller numbers are at the top rather than the bottom, or the rank orders of tournaments, where the first rank is listed at the top and lower ranks at the bottom. However, crucially, these number uses contrast with measurement cups and thermometers in that they do not imply a true sense of quantity, which is commonly called a "cardinal" use of number. Instead, cellphones present a primarily "nominal" use of numbers (e.g. the phone number +1-998-532-9193 is not "more" than the number +1-138-777-6124), while tournament ranks represent an "ordinal" use of number (see Nieder 2005 for excellent discussion). Hence, cultural reflections that do map true quantity onto verticality tend to obey the MORE IS UP principle (see Winter et al. 2015).

Experiments have provided abundant behavioral evidence to support the claim that people have a *mental* association between verticality and quantity (for a review, see Winter et al. 2015). For example, when people are asked to generate a sequence of numbers as randomly as possible, they tend to generate larger numbers after having moved their eyes upward (Loetscher et al. 2010), or after having moved their head upward (Winter & Matlock 2013). Similar associations between verticality and quantity have been found in more classic button-press paradigms. For example, when participants are asked to indicate whether a number is "even" or "odd" through using two buttons, they tend to respond faster to a larger number when the button is located at a relatively higher position (Hartmann et al. 2015; Ito & Hatta 2004; Müller & Schwarz 2007).

2.2 *SOCIAL DISTANCE IS PHYSICAL DISTANCE*

People often talk about social distance in terms of physical distance. For example, in discussing friendships or romantic relationships, English speakers make statements such as "The couple is slowly *drifting apart*," or "Bill and Marco have *gotten closer* lately." Such cases imply a change in social distance, not physical distance. German speakers also do this, as seen in "Wir waren uns einmal sehr nah" ('We were very close once'). In these and other linguistic reflections of the primary metaphor SOCIAL DISTANCE IS PHYSICAL DISTANCE (aka INTIMACY IS CLOSENESS), people talk about aspects of social relationships in terms of physical space. More precisely, the amount of space separating people reflects the nature of their relationship, such that larger distances indicate larger degrees of estrangement/alienation, etc.

An example of gesture related to SOCIAL DISTANCE IS PHYSICAL DISTANCE is shown in Figure 6.2, also from the TV News Archive. In this example, Sir Paul McCartney is being interviewed by David Letterman. In describing his relationship with pop star Michael Jackson he says, "So, we

a. (...) so we kinda *drifted*... b. ... *apart*

Figure 6.2 Co-speech gesture expressing SOCIAL DISTANCE IS PHYSICAL DISTANCE. First the hands are close together (a), then farther apart (b).[3]

kinda drifted apart." He describes how the relationship deteriorated, and in doing so, he gestures. He raises both hands to his chest, where they are momentarily held close together, and quickly moves them away from each other. Critically, the distance between McCartney's two hands is smaller at the beginning of the gesture than it is at the end, reflecting increased distance, showing how people spontaneously use the spatial modality of gesture to express state changes in social relationships.

Above and beyond gesture, we see other cultural reflections of SOCIAL DISTANCE IS PHYSICAL DISTANCE. Social scientists have discussed "segregation effects" and "peer effects" in the context of human relationships.[4] Segregation effects refer to cases in which people physically move closer to others they perceive as similar to themselves (Miller & Page 2007: 143–146; see also Bishop 2008). Peer effects refer to cases when people get physically close to each other and then begin to pick up certain behaviors from each other (Christakis & Fowler 2009). So people tend to move toward others they perceive as similar, and to become more like them once they are physically close. These two tendencies can lead to large-scale correlations of social distance and physical distance. This principle is not only characterizing modern societies but has also been shown for old hunter-gather settlement sites (Wiseman 2014). Thus, culture at large reflects the principle of SOCIAL DISTANCE IS PHYSICAL DISTANCE.

The association between 'social distance' ('intimacy') and 'physical distance' is also reflected in film, another form of cultural representations. Here we discuss a scene from *Before Midnight*, the third movie in a trilogy about two characters in stormy relationship.[5] The main characters, Jesse and Celine, husband and wife, are on vacation on a Greek island and, instead of having a romantic evening, have a heated discussion about Jesse's teenage son, Henry. The argument drags on for 20 minutes, spanning a wide range of heated topics, such as irrational thinking in men versus women, personal sacrifices in marriage, and infidelity. This part of the argument fluctuates in emotional intensity, becoming very loud and caustic at times, but calm and subdued, at others. In the end, Celine leaves the room when she becomes enraged with Jesse.

Over the course of the argument, the physical distance between Jesse and Celine changes in ways that are consistent with SOCIAL DISTANCE IS PHYSICAL DISTANCE. When the argument becomes aggressive and heated, there appears to be greater physical distance between the characters. Figure 6.3 shows two successive moments at the beginning of the argument. Jesse sits on the bed in (a), and Celine, on a couch in the adjacent room, in (b). Jesse pointedly asks, "So this is how you want to be spending this evening? I mean, this is what you wanna do tonight?" to which Celine curtly responds, "Well, you started it!" At this time, Jesse and Celine appear to be as far from each other as possible in the hotel room. Importantly, the distance between the

a. So this is how you want to be spending this evening? (...) b. Well, you started it!

Figure 6.3 Spatial positions of characters expressing SOCIAL DISTANCE IS PHYSICAL DISTANCE in *Before Midnight.* (a) Jesse criticizes Celine for arguing when they should be making love instead; (b) Celine retaliates by blaming Jesse for having started it.

viewer and the characters in the film is also accentuated via the camera. In (a), Jesse appears to be very far away, both from Celine and from the viewer. The physical distance is highlighted by the fact that the door frame is included in the shot, showing physical separation between the two. Moreover, both shots in (a) and (b) show the full body (total shots). In the previous scenes where the couple was intimate, there were more close-ups, focusing on the face and suggesting physical proximity. Thus, both the relative positioning of the characters and the position of (and perspective taken by) the camera adhere to SOCIAL DISTANCE IS PHYSICAL DISTANCE.

Figure 6.4 shows two shots from before the argument, where physical (and hence also social) distance appears to be smaller, even when Jesse and Celine do not share the same frame. One way that physical proximity is suggested is by the size of the characters in each shot: Rather than the full total shots in Figure 6.3 (showing each body almost entirely), the characters are shown up close, with most of the image space taken up by their bodies. Further, Figure 6.4b shows the same door frame as Figure 6.3a, but separation seems less because Celine is standing at the door.

So far, we have talked about linguistic, gestural, and cultural reflections of SOCIAL DISTANCE IS PHYSICAL DISTANCE. Several experimental studies suggest that the domain of physical distance is automatically accessed when thinking about likeability and intimacy. For example, in Matthews and Matlock (2011), people drew a path through a park depicted by a map. On the map, stick figures represented characters described as "friends" (low social distance) or "strangers" (high social distance). On average, lines intended to represent paths were closer to the "friends" than to the "strangers" on the map. In another experiment, Williams and Bargh (2008b), people drew two points on a sheet of paper, either very close to each other or very far away from each other. People in the "far" condition reported that they felt less of an emotional

a. Stefanus and Ariadne got us a bottle of wine and a couple's massage.

b. They are so nice. We have to give them a present.

Figure 6.4 Spatial positions of characters expressing SOCIAL DISTANCE IS PHYSICAL DISTANCE in *Before Midnight*. Jesse (a) and Celine (b) in a friendly interaction about a gift from their friends.

attachment to family members than did people in the "close" condition (although Pashler et al. 2012 report a failure to replicate this result). These and other studies indicate that when performing spatial tasks or when making social judgments, people automatically consider social distance and physical distance together. Such work supports the idea that SOCIAL DISTANCE IS PHYSICAL DISTANCE is not merely expressed in linguistic, gestural, and cultural content but is part of our conceptual system.

2.3 *SIMILARITY IS PROXIMITY*

English speakers often talk about SIMILARITY in terms of how PROXIMAL or DISTAL things are relative to each other. For example, your friend describes her political views as being "very far from" or "very close to" your political views (cf. examples in Casasanto 2008a: 1047), or a chef tastes her sauce and says, "It's getting close now," referring to how similar the sauce is to the sauce she made a week ago. A comparable German example is seen in statements such as "Diese Ansichten sind weit voneinander entfernt" ('These views are far away from each other').

Just as with SOCIAL DISTANCE IS PHYSICAL DISTANCE, the primary metaphor SIMILARITY IS PROXIMITY can be expressed through gesture. The speaker in Figure 6.5, Michael Powell, CEO and president of the National Cable & Telecommunications Association, is asked by an interviewer whether wired and wireless markets should be regulated in the same way. He responds that regulations should be "harmonized" and that wired and wireless markets are "increasingly trending toward being more similar, not more different." When he is talking about wired and wireless technologies becoming "more

a. They are increasingly trending toward being more similar ...

b. ... not more different.

Figure 6.5 Co-speech gesture expressing SOCIAL DISTANCE IS PHYSICAL DISTANCE. Both hands move toward a location in the center of the body for expressing SIMILARITY (a). For expressing DIFFERENCE, the hands move apart (b).[6]

similar," he moves his hands, palms facing toward each other, toward the middle of his body. While saying "not more different," he moves his hands apart. This sequence is integrated, with his hands continuously approaching each other and retracting again, beginning with "increasingly" in the utterance. The gesture makes it clear that two spatial positions are prominent, one being close (coinciding with the "similar" part of the sequence) and one being far (coinciding with the "far" part of the sequence). In this example, distance is primarily marked through dynamic movement toward or away from the midpoint of the body. The amount of distance between the hands is associated with the degree of similarity or difference.

SIMILARITY IS PROXIMITY also appears in the spatial location and configuration of cultural artifacts. We see this in how rooms in houses are arranged. Things that are similar by virtue of function are grouped together. For instance, substances for cleaning the body are co-located in bathrooms. Edible things are found in kitchens. Clothing items are found together in bedrooms. This pattern is also seen in design, including web design, where things that perform similar functions, such as menu buttons, are positioned close to each other. This pattern is also seen in the design of virtual worlds (e.g. Waterworth et al. 2003). Humans intentionally use space to sort things in their environment according to similarity (cf. Kirsh 1995). Grouping like things together in space helps people perceive them as similar (Wertheimer 1938).

Again, these are relatively small-scale reflections of a larger cultural principle that is evident in society-wide scales. For example, people within a city tend to self-organize into districts that are relatively homogenous with respect to factors such as ethnicity or socioeconomic status (Schelling 1971;

Bishop 2008). Often, similar people are located near each other because of necessity. Students are located near other students because they attend the same university and live near campus. Nurses are located in or close to hospitals or other medical facilities because they provide care for patients. Commuters are near other commuters because they share the same road or mode of transportation.

What is the experimental evidence for the conceptual nature of the metaphor SIMILARITY IS PROXIMITY? Casasanto (2008a) asked participants to rate unrelated words while they were being presented on a computer screen at varying distances. When participants were presented with two words that were close to each other, they rated them as more similar than when they were presented with words that were relatively far from each other. Boot and Pecher (2010) found that participants were quicker to judge colors (e.g. two shades of blue) as being similar when the colors were presented close together, and quicker to judge them as different when they were presented relatively far apart (see also Breaux & Feist 2008). Winter and Matlock (2013) showed that cities or people that were described as similar were subsequently placed closer to each other in a drawing task. Finally, Guerra and Knoerferle (2012) showed how visual depictions of various distances can affect the comprehension of sentences involving similarity. In their task, participants were shown concepts, i.e. words such as "stupidity" and "wisdom," on two cards that were near or far from each other, and then read the sentence, "Stupidity and wisdom are certainly different." Sentences about differences were read more quickly when the words "stupidity" and "wisdom" had been far from each other. Conversely, sentences about similarity were read more quickly when the concepts had been presented close to each other. Similar to our discussion of MORE IS UP and SOCIAL DISTANCE IS PHYSICAL DISTANCE, such research on SIMILARITY IS PROXIMITY suggest that this primary metaphor is deeply entrenched in our cognitive system, and there is much convergent evidence to support the hypothesis that SOCIAL DISTANCE IS PHYSICAL DISTANCE is a mapping not just in language and culture but also in our conceptual systems.

3 A Cultural Feedback Loop

In the preceding section, we reviewed MORE IS UP, SOCIAL DISTANCE IS PHYSICAL DISTANCE, and SIMILARITY IS PROXIMITY. Of key interest was how these exemplary primary metaphors are not purely conceptual. They are also expressed through language, gesture, and culture. In this section, we discuss some implications from this co-expression through multiple channels (for related arguments, see Gibbs 1999; Kövecses 2015; Marghetis 2015; Winter 2014). We begin by discussing the traditional view of primary metaphors.

Primary metaphors are thought to come from repeatedly experiencing a set of embodied correlations. This is a plausible proposal given that we know that children are exceptionally good at detecting statistical regularities in their environment (Kirkham et al. 2002; Saffran et al. 1996; Saffran et al. 1999). Moreover, there is a plausible neuronal mechanism that can readily explain the cognitively entrenched nature of conceptual metaphors. This mechanism is "Hebbian learning" (Hebb 1949), often summed up in the slogan "neurons that fire together wire together" (cf. Lakoff 2012). For example, repeatedly experiencing the correlation between verticality and quantity will repeatedly activate neurons associated with the perception of space and neurons associated with numerical estimation. Over time this pattern strengthens the connections between the neurons thus frequently co-activated. Tapping into and entrenching such correlational structures is generally thought to be the source of primary metaphors (for more discussion, see *this volume*: Casasanto; Grady & Ascoli).

Yet, from the perspective of a learning child, there is no principled difference between environmental correlations commonly subsumed under the "embodied origins" of primary metaphors and the cultural correlations discussed above. That metaphors come to be expressed in language, gesture, and culture means that language, gesture, and culture yield a new set of correlations that provide input to a child's metaphor system. Children grow up in a cultural world where they are surrounded by metaphors becoming expressed in cultural artifacts, gestures, and metaphorical verbal language.

These correlations may continue to play a role once a particular metaphorical mapping has been learned in childhood. While growing up in a metaphor-infused culture, people are constantly "reminded" of the metaphorical mappings they learned at a young age. Such an argument is presented in Winter (2014) in an analysis of a specific cultural reflection: horror movies.[7] The argument is that horror movies often reflect the primary metaphors BAD IS DOWN and BAD IS DARK (or EVIL IS DARK). This is even evident in DVD stores: DVD covers get obviously darker as one goes from the comedy section to the horror section. Within a given horror movie, shifts in darkness and verticality are frequently expressed over the course of the narrative. For example, the 2012 movie *The Cabin in the Woods* follows a downward trajectory as things become progressively worse for the protagonists. Often, these primary metaphors are expressed more locally in a single shot, such as the camera panning down to a dark hole from which a monster emanates. So, nearly every time people watch such a movie, they (re-)experience (old, already entrenched) correlations between the source domains of VERTICALITY and DARKNESS and the target domain of GOOD/BAD. On this view, the horror movie serves as a reminder of the metaphorical mapping already engrained in the general cultural context, but it also extends and elaborates those mappings by giving them concrete, entertaining, and emotionally engaging cultural representations (see also Forceville 2008).

This general principle is not limited to horror movies of course. All kinds of cultural reflections of metaphors (e.g. posters, advertisements, books) function as such reminders, further strengthening the mapping and maintaining it in our culture. When we discussed MORE IS UP, SOCIAL DISTANCE IS PHYSICAL DISTANCE, and SIMILARITY IS PROXIMITY in section 2, we talked about linguistic, gestural, and cultural "reflections" because the representations are often analyzed as merely reflecting underlying conceptual content. In particular, in the domain of media, "multimodal metaphors" are often seen as passive reflections of our internal conceptual world, a view that is driven by the largely cognitive orientation of Lakoff and Johnson (1980), which sees underlying conceptual structures as the ultimate cause of metaphorical language. However, metaphor theory has to acknowledge that verbal, gestural, and cultural reflections are witnessed by others, and when they are, external representations of metaphor affect the cognitive systems of those observers.

Marghetis (2015) discusses a similar concept in what he calls "gestural contagion," the idea that co-speech gestures help to propagate metaphorical concepts. His research experimentally demonstrates that seeing a particular metaphor expressed in gesture changes the subsequent understanding of the target domain in a non-gestural task. For example, seeing a gesture in line with ARITHMETIC IS MOTION ALONG A PATH (Lakoff & Núñez 2000) activates spatial representations where small numbers are to the left of larger numbers more so than seeing a gesture in line with ARITHMETIC IS OBJECT COLLECTION.

A useful way of looking at the influence of culture and external representations of metaphor is presented in Kövecses (2002), who distinguishes three levels at which metaphor should be investigated: the "sub-individual" level (i.e. embodied experience), the "individual" level (i.e. cognitive mappings inside single minds), and the "supra-individual" level (cultural representations). Some metaphor theorists maintain that direction of causality goes from the sub-individual to the individual to the supra-individual level, in a feedforward manner (but see *this volume*: Casasanto; Gibbs). Winter (2014), in line with Gibbs (1999), Marghetis (2015), and others, argues that it is important to remember that cultural representations of metaphors (understood broadly as including artifacts, gesture, and linguistic expressions) *feed back* into the cognitive systems at the individual level. That is, if we view metaphor as a multi-scale phenomenon distributed across different levels, we should not assume that metaphors in the "underlying" conceptual systems (the individual level) lead to cultural representations (supra-individual), but that the connection between individuals and representations is a two-way street.

The precise ways through which cultural representations interact with cognitive metaphorical systems are still underexplored. Winter (2014) proposes at least three different ways in which culture and cognition come together with respect to metaphor. First, cultural representations elaborate on metaphors and enrich them with specific examples, e.g. a monster in a horror movie that instantiates the more general BAD IS DARK in a highly specific and concrete way (cf. the many examples in Forceville 2006a, 2008, *this volume*; Forceville & Urios-Aparisi 2009). Second, cultural representations (including artifacts) may strengthen metaphorical representations, i.e. act as *reminders* in different ways and at different time points. Third, cultural representations may create new metaphorical representations, or re-create metaphorical representations that already exist in a new generation of speakers in a culture. In contrast to gesture and language, non-verbal cultural representations (e.g. artifacts, movies) play a special role because they are less ephemeral (e.g. a movie can be watched again and again) and distributed more widely (e.g. movies are watched by millions of people). Thus, these cultural representations have a way of stabilizing metaphorical representations throughout a culture, and hence also in the minds of its members.

Similar ideas have been offered by Daniel Casasanto, who argues against the idea that all metaphors are embodied and proposes that metaphors have diverse origins. In discussing CONSERVATIVE IS RIGHT/LIBERAL IS LEFT, Casasanto (2014b) argues that – given the lack of any obvious embodied correlations in the natural world for this association – this metaphor must be acquired on the basis of language use, specifically, exposure to phrases such as "the right-wing party" or "his political views are left-leaning" (and would thus not count as "primary"; see Grady & Ascoli, *this volume*). Casasanto (2014b) also proposes that the left–right orientation of time (in Western cultures), which is not reflected by linguistic metaphors (and would thus not count as "primary" either), is influenced by the frequent use of calendars and other cultural representations of time. Finally, he argues that GOOD IS RIGHT/BAD IS LEFT emerges from individual embodied experience (ibid.), namely people's handedness (see also Casasanto 2009a; Casasanto & Henetz 2012), essentially through correlations of feeling positive emotions when performing actions fluently with their dominant hand, i.e. the right one in the vast majority of cases. This metaphor – in contrast to THE FUTURE IS RIGHT/THE PAST IS LEFT – has some linguistic reflections (e.g. "this is the *right* thing to do," "He is not in his *right* state of mind"), but language does not reflect that left-handed people mentally associate GOOD with LEFT.

So, although embodiment is a powerful explanatory tool in metaphor analyses, we should avoid immediately defaulting to it, especially at times when evidence for it seems to be lacking (cf. Casasanto & Gijssels 2015).

Some claims about the embodied origin of primary metaphors would be difficult to test experimentally (see also Casasanto 2014b: 249). For instance, what experiment would be capable of testing whether MORE IS UP is derived from perceiving the natural correlation of quantity and verticality and nothing else? This would require factoring out all cultural reflections associated with this mapping, which is likely to be impossible. As previously discussed, because our environment is so infused with metaphor, it is challenging to tease apart the relative contributions of various correlations.

4 Interactions and Gradations between Primary Metaphors

If, as we argue, children and adults are sensitive to metaphorical correlations in the natural world, in language, including gesture, and culture, then we have to acknowledge that some correlations do not correspond as clearly to particular metaphors as we might expect. There is a tendency in metaphor research to characterize metaphors as discrete entities (see also Gibbs 2011c). Yet, it is precisely the "embodied correlations view" that, when turned to its full logical conclusion, can lead us to question the discreteness of metaphors (see also *this volume*: Gibbs; Jensen).

Imagine a bar graph next to an upward-pointing arrow of green color, a form of visual representation that features prominently in TV and online reports of sales, revenues, and the stock market. In these financial contexts, the upward-pointing arrow and the bar graph are conventionally interpreted in terms of numerical quantity, e.g. increased revenues. However, an affective or evaluative component may also come into play, with the upward arrow indicating that things are going in a POSITIVE direction, i.e. UPWARD. This emotional message is highlighted by the fact that frequently in news reports, such arrows are in green color if they point upward and in red color if they point downward. In other words, the color scheme emphasizes the evaluative component on top of the association between quantity and verticality. A metaphor analysis of such a visual display thus needs to recognize that there is the potential for MORE IS UP and GOOD IS UP being co-present.

Similar cases of co-present metaphors are SIMILARITY IS PROXIMITY and SOCIAL DISTANCE IS PHYSICAL DISTANCE (INTIMACY IS CLOSENESS), discussed in section 2. The target domains SIMILARITY and SOCIAL DISTANCE are both correlated in the social world and covary with the source domain of PHYSICAL DISTANCE. People who are more similar to each other tend to like each other more. People who like each other tend to become more similar. And people who like each other and are similar to each other tend to be in close physical space. Hence, in the social world, the metaphors SIMILARITY IS PROXIMITY and SOCIAL DISTANCE IS

PHYSICAL DISTANCE are often conflated, and this carries over to the linguistic instantiations of the respective metaphors.

Take, for example, the sentence "We're headed in opposite directions" (Gibbs 2011c: 531), commonly discussed as an instance of the metaphor LOVE IS A JOURNEY. Depending on the intentions of the speaker and nature of the situation, this example reflects LOVE as a MOVEMENT ALONG A PATH, with "headed" and "directions" implying motion. Increased distance is also inferred, suggested by the physical movement of the two people in two different directions. The sentence also conveys the negative status of the relationship, with loss of intimacy and increased social distance. Thus, this specific instantiation of the complex metaphor LOVE IS A JOURNEY reflects SOCIAL DISTANCE IS PHYSICAL DISTANCE, in addition to such primary metaphors as ACTION/PROGRESS IS MOTION, STATES ARE LOCATIONS, and PURPOSES ARE GOALS (see Lakoff 2008a). In addition, SIMILARITY IS PROXIMITY may play a role, as the experiential contexts overlap with those motivating some of these primary metaphors, such as RELATIONS ARE CONTAINERS and INTIMACY IS CLOSENESS. A couple that goes in different directions often does so because of insurmountable differences in attitudes, tastes, lifestyles, opinions, or beliefs. Moreover, once "apart," the members of the separated couple are likely to become more dissimilar from each other over time because of the lack of frequent interaction. The statement "We're headed in opposite directions," said with the intended LOVE IS A JOURNEY reading, is likely to lead to inferences about intimacy and similarity consistent with both SOCIAL DISTANCE IS PHYSICAL DISTANCE and SIMILARITY IS PROXIMITY. The same argument applies to other instances of LOVE IS A JOURNEY, as in "our relationship is at a crossroads" (cf. Gibbs 2011c).

Let us consider non-linguistic cultural representations that conflate coherent conceptual metaphors. Timelines, such as calendars, can represent both THE FUTURE IS TO THE RIGHT as well as MORE IS TO THE RIGHT. As one goes from left to right on a timeline, temporal distance increases concomitantly with numerical quantity (for discussion, see Winter et al. 2015; Marghetis 2015; Marghetis & Youngstrom 2014). In a similar fashion, MORE IS BIG often correlates with IMPORTANCE IS SIZE because bigger quantities of any object are generally more important.

So, culture, language, and gesture provide speakers with many correlations, along with environmental/natural correlations. But just what is being correlated may not always be clear, and this transfers over to metaphors, where there is ambiguity about which metaphor is highlighted in a given situation. This is also in line with Gibbs' dynamic systems approach to metaphors in discourse:

> A given conceptual metaphor is not just activated, and employed as a single entity, to help interpret a metaphorical utterance. Instead, multiple conceptual metaphors, which may have arisen to prominence at a specific moment in time, given the particular dynamics of the system at that moment, may collectively shape the trajectory of linguistic processing so that no one conceptual metaphor has complete control over how an utterance is interpreted. (Gibbs 2011c: 553)

Observational evidence for the simultaneous co-activation of metaphor comes from Walker and Cooperrider (2015), who show for time metaphors that English-speaking gesturers simultaneously move their hands forward and to the right when talking about the future, and backward and to the left when talking about the past. Thus, in interactions about time, gestures indicate that speakers simultaneously conceptualize the target domain in terms of two distinct metaphors, one in which time is thought to extend along a front-to-back axis and one in which time is thought to extend along a left-to-right axis (as on a calendar). This discussion is not intended to criticize labels such as "MORE IS UP" or "SIMILARITY IS PROXIMITY." Delineating metaphors gives us a convenient way to talk about the recurrent patterns that they entail. Still, we need to remind ourselves that metaphors such as MORE IS UP, SOCIAL DISTANCE IS PHYSICAL DISTANCE, and SIMILARITY IS PROXIMITY are not discrete entities.

5 Conclusions

In this chapter, we reviewed evidence for three primary metaphors: MORE IS UP, SOCIAL DISTANCE IS PHYSICAL DISTANCE, and SIMILARITY IS PROXIMITY. Apart from being entrenched conceptually, these are jointly expressed through language, gesture, and culture. We have taken this multitude of multimodal metaphorical "reflections" to argue that primary metaphors have multi-causal origins and that embodied experience of natural correlations cannot be the only story.

We have argued that the conflation of (different, but coherent) metaphors in the natural and the sociocultural world is mirrored by a conflation in linguistic expressions of metaphor, as well as the manifestations of metaphor through other modalities. Finally, these considerations suggest that it is fruitful to focus on the interactions between different modalities of metaphorical expression, as well as interactions between different metaphors, rather than to focus exclusively on particular modalities or particular metaphors in isolation.

NOTES AND ACKNOWLEDGMENTS

* We thank Daniel Casasanto and Beate Hampe for extensive review and feedback on an earlier version of this chapter.

1 The TV News Archive is a vast online repository of American TV News broadcasts that can be freely accessed online (https://archive.org/details/tv). The database is searchable so that one can look for specific metaphorical expressions such as "we drifted apart." Over 400,000 news shows are already online, representing over five years of US television (2009–2015). On specific uses of the archive for gesture research, see Winter et al. (2013).

2 The video is archived at: https://archive.org/details/CSPAN_20090821_100000_Today_in_Washington?q=disturbingly+high+number+of+contractors+in+core+support#start/2178/end/2238 (still images taken on June 2, 2016).

3 The video is archived at: https://archive.org/details/HLN_20090716_160000_HLN_News#start/660/end/720 (still image taken on June 2, 2016).

4 This characterization is adapted from Scott Page's *Model Thinking* (cf. discussion in Miller & Page 2007: 143–146).

5 Movie (US, GR) directed by Richard Linklater, starring Julie Delpy and Ethan Hawke, released June 2013.

6 The video is archived at: https://archive.org/details/CSPAN_20111210_233000_The_Communicators?q=increasingly+becoming+more+similar+but+different#start/978/end/1038 (image taken June 2, 2016).

7 For other insightful discussions of metaphors in horror movies, see Eggertsson and Forceville (2009) and Ortiz (2011). For discussions of darkness-related primary metaphors in films, see Coëgnarts and Kravanja (2012), Forceville and Renckens (2013), Forceville, *this volume*.

Part II

More than Metaphor

7 Source Actions Ground Metaphor via Metonymy: Toward a Frame-Based Account of Gestural Action in Multimodal Discourse

*Irene Mittelberg & Gina Joue**

Chapter Preview

This chapter starts from the observation that metaphoric understandings expressed monomodally through gesture tend to rely on "primary metaphors" (Grady 1997a). Asserting that gestures draw on basic, experientially motivated, embodied construal operations, we detail how primary scenes and subscenes (Grady & Johnson 2002), image and force schemas, metonymy, and frames (Fillmore 1982) interact in situated meaning-making. We propose that by shifting the focus from object-oriented schemas, source domains, and mappings to what we call "source actions" and "embodied action frames," we can account for the pragmatically minded nature and specific mediality of communicative gestural acts integrated in natural multimodal discourse. We argue that coverbal gestures recruit frame structures metonymically, singling out elements of "scenes" (Fillmore 1977), especially those underpinning correlated metaphoric meanings. We back up our theoretical claims with evidence from neuroscientific studies and outline a frame-based approach that helps trace avenues for further research into embodied cognition and multimodal discourse processes.

1 Introduction

Our understanding of the world and the discourses we participate in integrates pieces of information presented in different sensory modalities into dynamic meaningful wholes. As embodied semiotic beings, we observe our conversational partners while listening to what they are saying, we sense emotional qualities in their articulation, and we might reach out verbally and gesturally to them or hold ourselves back. Oral communication clearly involves more than language use; it combines various sign systems such as words, gestures, eye gaze, head movements, and body posture. Naturalistic discourse thus typically consists of concerted *multimodal acts of contextualized meaning-making*, i.e. of dynamic "semiotic contextures" (Jakobson 1956) or "contextures of action" (Goodwin 2011b). As physical actions of the human body influenced by cognitive and affective states, gestures have been shown to provide valuable insights into the physical grounding and sociocultural situatedness of embodied cognition and language use. Since speakers tend to be mostly unaware of their gestural behavior, gestures may also reveal less monitored aspects of cognitive and emotional processes during communication, including mental simulation and metaphorical construal (e.g. Cienki & Müller 2008a; Gibbs 2006a; Mittelberg 2006; Müller 1998, *this volume*; Sweetser 1998, 2007).

This chapter puts the human body and its communicative behavior at the very center of studying embodiment, discourse, metaphor, and ad-hoc meaning construction. We bring together several theoretical constructs to help us understand why the communicating body during spoken discourse production has a strong tendency to simulate deeply entrenched physical routines including motor programs and object manipulation, regardless of whether the discourse topic is abstract or concrete. This approach allows us to account for our observation that metaphors expressed monomodally through gesture alone tend to be "primary metaphors" drawing on "primary scenes" (Grady & Johnson 2002) as well as on basic "scenes" and "frames" (Fillmore 1977, 1982).[1]

Following the frame-based account of metaphor and metonymy advanced by Dancygier and Sweetser (2014), we will apply the notion of frames to gesture and draw connections to interrelated embodied construal operations. Shifting the focus from object-oriented source domains to the actions of the human body, we introduce the notion of "source action" in metaphorically construed semiotic acts, which may or may not involve (imagined) persons, objects, or surfaces. Our approach is based on the assumption that metaphor in gesture is tightly linked to metonymic modes. In fact, metonymy grants access to meaning, including metaphorical meaning (Mittelberg & Waugh 2009, 2014).

In more general cognitive terms, we propose that metonymy can be seen as a mechanism through which top-down (cognitive) control filters out irrelevant bottom-up (sensory) features perceived during the comprehension of multimodal discourse. In reducing the features requiring attention for further processing, cognitive control via metonymy provides a means of integrating features with each other and establishing associations with existing semantic frames. Without such a mechanism, the numerous sets of semantic frames that are involved in metaphor understanding, especially in multimodal communication, could be computationally intractable.

We illustrate these premises mainly with data from academic discourse and film retellings in American English and German, and also bring in additional evidence from neuroscience studies. Our findings attest to the tight junction of action and perception and of physical and mental processes. They also shed light on people's speech-independent understanding of metaphorically motivated actions performed by others who are speaking (Gallese & Lakoff 2005). Zeroing in on "the meaning of the body" (Johnson 2007), that is, speakers' semiotic actions and semanticized gesture spaces as the immediate, natural media and loci of recurring interactions with the material and social world, our intent is to provide gestural support for the idea that people engaged in discourse *do* metaphor (*this volume*: Gibbs; Müller; Jensen).

2 Pragmatic Foundations of Metaphoric Processes in Multimodal Discourse

2.1 Embodiment: Bodily Semiotic Acts Mediate between Experiential Grounding and Conceptual Schematicity

Embodiment, gesture, metaphor, and metonymy are intimately linked. Embodiment theorists generally agree that our higher cognitive and linguistic abilities are shaped by the architecture of our bodies and by the ways in which we interact with our physical and social environment (e.g. Gibbs 2006a; Hampe 2005a; Johnson 1987, 2007; Lakoff & Johnson 1999). Obviously constrained by the morphology of the human body, gestures are also shaped by the forms and affordances of our material habitat and by social interactions in both personal and institutional settings (e.g. Kendon 2004). In particular, many of the basic habitual actions of object manipulation, tactile exploration, and sensorimotor routines that humans use to comprehend the world and to function in it manifest themselves in gestural hand movements performing communicative actions (e.g. Calbris 2011; Müller 1998; Streeck 2009; Streeck et al. 2011).

Questions of how multimodal communicative acts may be driven by embodied conceptual structures and construal operations have inspired a growing branch of gesture research within cognitive linguistics (for overviews, see Cienki 2013a; Sweetser 2007). Building on the premises of embodiment, Mittelberg's (2008, 2013b) notion of the "exbodied mind," or the mind externalized through the body, captures this perspective; it accounts for how embodied cognitive-semiotic principles (e.g. iconicity, metaphoricity, indexicality, conventionality, image and force schemas, metonymy, and viewpoint) may not only motivate and structure observable patterns of gestural sign constitution but also guide how gestures are interpreted due to the embodied nature of their motivation. Given the above observations, we expect gestures to exhibit a natural tendency to evoke the kinds of metaphors, metonymies, frames, and other construal operations that rely on a high degree of embodiment and reflect their inherent indexicality (e.g. Mittelberg & Waugh 2014).

2.2 *Multifunctionality of (Primarily Metaphoric) Gestures*

Most gesture scholars agree that gestures do not lend themselves to being assigned to a single category (e.g. McNeill 1992, 2005; Müller 1998); hence, the term "metaphoric gesture" does not do justice to this medium's versatility. While space limitations do not allow for a detailed discussion of gesture functions, the polysemous and multifunctional nature of gestural signs is briefly addressed here, as it feeds directly into the multidimensional fabric of multimodally expressed metaphoricity.

Consider, for example, the following metaphorically construed gestural portrayal of a grammatical category. During a German language course for beginners, the instructor asks her students about the properties of the grammatical category "infinitive" (Figure 7.1a–c): "You are looking at an … infinitive … can you say … ah, this is … present, perfect, past perfect [tense]?"[2] In Figure 7.1a, the instructor is enacting what she wants her students to do, namely, to contemplate the grammatical category "infinitive" that she is speaking about ("you are looking at an infinitive") and seemingly holding in her hands. She subsequently directs her gaze toward her audience (Figure 7.1b) and continues to hold the bimanual gesture while asking the students whether infinitives may be marked for tense ("can you say … ah, this is … present tense, perfect tense, simple past?"). While she is waiting for a response, her right hand forms into a Palm-Up Open Hand (PUOH, Müller 2004; Kendon 2004), and her left hand also opens up slightly (Figure 7.1c). She remains silent in this position for about four seconds. This PUOH qualifies as an interactive *seeking gesture* (Bavelas et al. 1995) signaling the speaker's wish to receive an answer. The open hand may also indicate that the reified infinitive – now construed as a smaller, imagined object sitting on the open palm – is still available for inspection.

This multimodal teaching performance illustrates both the strikingly dynamic, multidimensional character of embodiment (Gibbs 2006a) and the multifunctional nature of gestures mediating metaphoric understandings. Following Jakobson (1960), we assume a hierarchical ordering of semiotic modes and discourse functions in gestural sign processes (Mittelberg 2013b: 755). The metaphoric dimension of the gesture in Figure 7.1a pertains to the *referential* or *cognitive* function by evoking or referring to an idea. Additional subordinated functions are *emotive* (expressing the speaker's attitude and intentions), *conative* (making the students think and respond), *phatic* (maintaining the connection with the students, keeping their attention focused on the question),

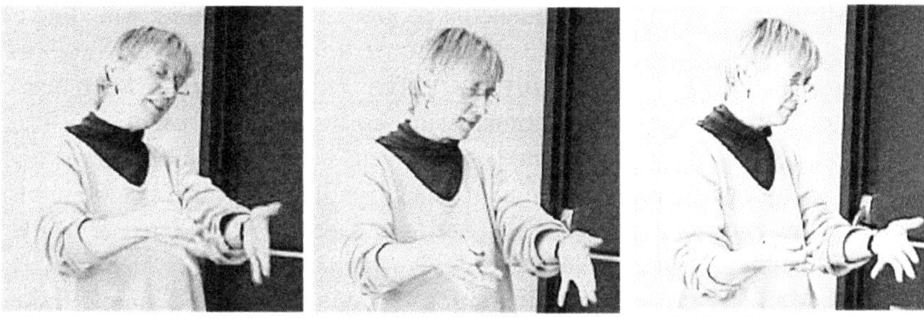

a. Holding an *infinitive* b. Asking about *infinitive* c. Waiting for an obvious answer

Figure 7.1 Multimodal instruction about the grammatical category infinitive

and *meta-linguistic* (defining the technical term "infinitive"). The speaker's facial expressions and head movements further enhance and contextualize these functions. Importantly, all these facets of action and interaction may also be observed when people actually handle and exchange physical objects. We will revisit this example to highlight how metonymic and metaphoric modes tend to interact in such experientially motivated, action-based processes of multimodal meaning-making.

3 Strongly Embodied Construal Operations Motivating Metaphoric Processes

In multimodal discourse, metaphorical conceptualizations themselves are often multimodally expressed (e.g. Forceville & Urios-Aparisi 2009). The same metaphoric understanding can be concurrently reflected in both speech and gesture. Different metaphors can also manifest themselves in the two modalities. Additionally, metaphorical understandings may be expressed only in the verbal or only in the gestural modality, thus giving rise to *monomodal* metaphoric expressions (e.g. Müller & Cienki 2009). When basic physical actions and/or the implied objects are set in a metaphorical frame through the concurrent speech and other contextual factors, as in the example of the monomodal metaphor discussed above (Figure 7.1a–c), the tight correlation between basic recurrent physical experiences and metaphorical processes becomes literally tangible. In this section we discuss experientially basic construal operations that give rise to bodily expressed metaphoric processes integrated in multimodal discourse.

3.1 Experiential Basics: Primary Metaphors and Scenes

Grady (1997a, see also Grady & Ascoli, *this volume*) coined the term primary metaphor for metaphorical mappings that arise through recurrent perceptual and sensorimotor experiences influencing people's subjective understanding of the physical and social world (e.g. AFFECTION IS WARMTH; IDEAS ARE FOOD; CAUSES ARE FORCES; DIFFICULTIES ARE BURDENS). Such basic metaphors have first-order relations with corresponding, often physical, experiences. They have been found to motivate both linguistic and gestural expressions in spontaneous discourse about, for instance, abstract domains, moral values, emotions, and mental states (e.g. Cienki 1998; Cienki & Müller 2008b; Mittelberg 2008; Müller 2008b, *this volume*; Parrill & Sweetser 2004; Winter & Matlock, *this volume*). In particular, body posture and kinetic action may reflect essential facets of metaphorical understandings of ideas, categories, events, or relations even when the concurrent speech is non-figurative (e.g. Mittelberg 2006).

Other basic construal mechanisms such as primary scenes (or recurrent experiential scenarios) and subscenes (e.g. Grady & Johnson 2002) may also become manifest mono- or multimodally. They provide ways of deconstructing experiential types into their constitutive parts and dimensions. For example, for the primary scene "manipulation of complex object" (ibid.: 537), gestural practices may pick out a particular subscene. We can imagine someone pretending to carry a huge monitor or to hold a small brittle vase. As pointed out by Grady and Johnson, primary metaphors and scenes are akin to what Slobin (1985), in his work on the acquisition of grammatical categories, refers to as "prototypical events," which also include object manipulation and object transfer. Prototypical events "could include grasping, pushing, squeezing, pulling apart, etc., each of which would be a distinct subscene" (Grady & Johnson 2002: 548).

3.2 *Varying Levels of Abstraction: Mimetic Schemas, Image Schemas, and Force Gestalts*

As for language development, Zlatev's (2005) notion of "mimetic schema" (e.g. KICK, JUMP, GRASP, EAT, HIT, KISS) as well as Andrén's (2010) notion of "action gestalt" and "action-based gestures" capture intermediate levels of abstraction regarding the understanding and communicative use of actions and objects. Mimetic schemas are "dynamic, concrete and preverbal representations, involving the body image, accessible to consciousness and prereflectively shared in a community" (Zlatev 2005: 334). An interesting question is how these schemas and actions are used metaphorically (Cienki 2013b). In adults, higher levels of abstraction can be found in certain "gesture families" (e.g. Calbris 2011; Kendon 2004; Müller 2004) and in "recurrent gestures," which tend to be more conventionalized (e.g. the cyclic gesture, Ladewig 2011).

As embodied patterns of recurrent experiences with the physical and social world, "image schemas" (e.g. Hampe 2005a; Johnson 1987; Lakoff 1987) are more abstract and schematic than the bodily action routines from which they, at least partly, derive. They have been attested a prominent role not only in structuring our bodily experience but also in motivating metaphoric expressions in diverse modalities (Forceville & Urios-Aparisi 2009; Gibbs 2006). A growing body of research suggests that gestures and body postures may also reflect a range of image schemas, such as PATH, CONTAINMENT, CYCLE, OBJECT, and SUPPORT, as well as "force-dynamic" gestalts (Talmy 1988) such as FORCE, BLOCKAGE, and GRAVITY (e.g. Cienki 2005, 2013b; Ladewig 2011; Mittelberg 2006, 2010, 2013b; Sweetser 1998). In fact, there seems to be a certain structural similarity between image/force schemas and gestural forms and movements. While gestures are physical, they also are schematic gestalts of experiential essence: They typically consist of reduced hand configurations, motion onsets or traces that minimally suggest, for instance, a PATH, an OBJECT (Figure 7.1), CONTAINMENT, or an IN-OUT spatial relation (Figure 7.3). Likewise, subtle shifts in body posture may evoke the sensation of physical forces impacting the speaker's body, thus recruiting, for instance, the BALANCE schema in construals of mental states (e.g. Mittelberg 2013a).

Both mimetic schemas and image schemas motivate gestures and connect the meaning of conventionalized linguistic expressions to physical actions ("symbol grounding problem," Barsalou 1999). They are different, however, in that the image schema framework focuses more on the links between actions and embodied conceptual structures, whereas the focus in mimetic schemas is on the actions themselves, bringing in imitation, or mimesis, to explain how symbolic meanings arise. Both kinds of schemas are thus congruent with Piaget's proposed role of schemas in cognitive development, namely, as basic cognitive units developed through action and perceptuo-motor interaction (Piaget 1967).

3.3 Mental Representations, Modality, and Body Schema

Being inherently physical, coverbal gestures provide a link between mental representations of sensory patterns and symbols characteristic of communication, including embodied abstract concepts. With gesture understanding, where visual input arguably needs to be matched with action representations, there is a more direct computational motivation to maintain fidelity to the "body schema" (Blanke 2012; Gallagher 2005), which can be glossed as the dynamic sense of one's own body (for a discussion of "body schema" vs. "body image," see Cuccio, *this volume*). We saw this fidelity when we asked healthy adults to demonstrate transitive actions while pretending that a part of their body, e.g. their hand, was the tool, when a tool was required (e.g. to slice an apple). They failed to do so 77.5 percent of the time despite repeated prompts, with only 3.7 percent of the participants correcting themselves automatically (Grandhi et al. 2011). However, these results do not clarify the relationship among more abstract representations, even those involving gestures. In an unpublished fMRI study where our volunteers watched videos of an actor speaking and gesturing, we found greater activity in brain networks for processing metaphorical and grooming gestures that have been implicated in studies on the body schema. We also found support for a generic network for amodal metaphor processing: Multimodal and monomodal metaphoric gestures do not seem to require distinct cognitive processes, but both may recruit a common semantic processing network (see also Straube et al. 2011). Although this is not definitive support, it is consistent with our proposal (to be detailed in sections 4 and 5) that gestural information creates additional features for semantic frames, reinforcing frames through manual actions.

Making a stronger claim, Barsalou has suggested that symbols are grounded in units of perception and are stored in such schematic building blocks, or perceptual symbolic units, which can be pieced into holistic frames (Barsalou 1999; Barsalou et al. 2003). In his solution of the symbol grounding problem, "perceptual symbolic units" are reminiscent of prototypical events (section 3.1) and "holistic frames" are akin to semantic frames. A criticism of Barsalou's account is that even if symbols were grounded in modality-specific experiences, it does not automatically follow that the maintained representations have not evolved away from them. However, numerous studies have suggested that body schema and gesture influence mental representations (e.g. Cook et al. 2013).

4 Gestures Evoke Embodied Frames and Scenes: Metonymic Bases of Metaphoricity

We develop our notion of "embodied physical action frames" based on Fillmore's (1982) idea of frames as conceptual systems originating from patterns of experience and practice. Frames have been shown to underpin not only lexical semantics but also mental spaces, metaphor, metonymy, constructions, and the understanding of discourse, to mention only a few central areas of linguistic structure and meaning construction (e.g. Coulson 2001; Dancygier & Sweetser 2014; Sullivan 2013; Ziem 2014). They represent the interlocutor's dynamic holistic representations of the world and impose a filter in her interactions with the world and other interlocutors. We will back this view with support from neuroscience below (section 4.2). Frames do not only underpin our pragmatic action-based account of entrenched metonymic and metaphoric processes but also (i) illuminate the relation between meaningful gestural acts and the semantics of the concurrent speech and (ii) allow us to describe how basic physical actions may be used and understood metaphorically without necessarily assuming conceptual mappings.

4.1 Frames and Scenes Evoked in Multimodal Discourse

Words evoke frames. Besides determining the meaning of linguistic expressions, frames also guide their use:

> A "frame," as the notion plays a role in the description of linguistic meanings, is a system of categories structured in accordance with some motivating context . . . The motivating context is some body of understandings, some pattern of practices, or some history of social institutions, against which we find intelligible the creation of a particular category in the history of the language community. (Fillmore 1982: 119)

Similar to the frame functions outlined by Fillmore, gestures may provide a "description of linguistic meanings" and are "structured in accordance with some motivating context" such as "some pattern of practices." Gestures, too, are often shaped by "some history of social institutions" (ibid.). For instance, the TEA-DRINKING frame entails culturally defined constellations of persons, objects, and ingredients, as well as sequences of actions and interactions, which no doubt influence how one can gesturally ask someone to refill one's tea cup.

So while frames are abstract conceptual structures, gestural frame evocation may illustrate that at least a subsection of them is grounded in physical actions. Crucially, like frames, gestures are also shaped by contexts and habits, or "scenes." Fillmore (1977) applies this term to real-world experiences, situative factors, and non-linguistic conceptual dimensions feeding into semantic frames (see also Ziem 2014). Scenes are particularly relevant to how interlocutors construct and interpret processes of online meaning constitution: "In most natural conversations, the participants have, already 'activated,' a number of shared, presupposed, scenes that we can speak of as being in their consciousness as they speak" (Fillmore 1977: 126).

Semantic frames can become salient or dominant when reinforced through repeated activation. Similarly, features of a frame can become salient through repeated activation. Processes of lexicalization (Fillmore 1982) exemplify these dynamic dimensions of frames, for example, when a neologism enters the dictionary or a novel metaphor is conventionalized. Conventional metaphoric mappings can be so salient that they dominate, even when they are irrelevant in a particular context and interfere with the appropriate semantic understanding (Glucksberg et al. 1982). Likewise, this should apply to emblems or other conventionalized or habitual gestures. This dynamic and experience-rooted nature of representations occurs even on the neuronal level: When a familiar input (frame) is disused, its mental representation loses functionality and hence salience (Wang et al. 1995). That is, experience induces long-term structural reorganization of mental representations.

We propose that coverbal gestures that recruit frame structures have a natural, pragmatically entrenched tendency to single out elements and dimensions of "prototypical instances of scenes" (Fillmore 1977: 63), in addition to primary scenes and subscenes. Gestures may metonymically profile salient dimensions of an action or object; that is, they may enact aspects of the motivating contexts of frames (see also Mittelberg 2017).

4.2 *Frames and Metonymy*

We consider frames as networks of metonymic relations that may be partially or wholly activated during frame-based reasoning, language use, and discourse understanding (e.g. Dancygier & Sweetser 2014; Fillmore 1982). An example of semantic frame activation is evoking the EMAIL frame through a simple gestural action (i.e. typing) that allows the addressee's embodied mind to associate not only a keyboard with the movement but also possible contents of the email message and the receiver's reply. This email example is a multimodal instantiation of what Dancygier and Sweetser (2014: 134) call "frame metonymy" and define as "the use of some entity A to stand for another entity B with which A is *correlated*" (ibid., italics in the original). Drawing on Langacker's (1987) notion of *active zone* as the profiled part of a whole, Dancygier and Sweetser (2014: 108) emphasize that a certain degree of salience is needed to clearly associate a term with a frame: "the part centrally or directly involved in an activity stands for the whole. The hand, for example, is the part of the arm used for holding, touching, etc.; hence it is the active zone of the arm for many purposes" (e.g. "field hands": 'people who do mainly physical work'). This naturally applies to the gesturer's hands, the body parts involved in both physical actions and communicative gestures and hence in evoking frames. In such cases, the following metonymic processes may apply: SALIENT PART OF FORM FOR WHOLE FORM (Barcelona 2009: 395) or SALIENT ASPECT/PHASE OF ACTION FOR WHOLE ACTION. Through frame metonymy, contiguity relationships between gesturing hands and the adjacent semanticized spaces and imaginary entities implied in their actions may become meaningful (Figures 7.1, 7.3). That is, they draw on metonymic correlations such as ACTION FOR OBJECT INVOLVED IN ACTION, PRESENTATION FOR PRESENTED, or LOCATION FOR OBJECT (Mittelberg & Waugh 2009, 2014; Panther & Thornburg 2003).

Metonymy helps evoke relevant semantic frames (schemas) or parts of them when input is noisy or incomplete, as is common in face-to-face communication. To make sense of an environment, bottom-up sensory feature input is integrated and matched to features of semantic frames. Input might be grouped into categories, such as discourse events, or remain as perceptual units (Barsalou 1999). Features become relevant when they can be set in a semantic frame that has been determined as relevant for a given context.

This integration or frame setting is important even at a neuronal level, where bottom-up stimulation from the environment alone is insufficient to change cortical representations. Instead, cortical changes (mental representations) depend on the interplay between bottom-up experiences and attention-modulating top-down goals (Ahissar et al. 1992).

Activating a culturally (including linguistically) defined frame includes the "co-activation" of its features. Co-activation also has bases in neuroscience where synchrony of neuronal firing creates mental representations and learning (i.e. reorganization and creation of representations). Groups of cells that "fire together" have been argued to "wire together" in Hebbian's theory of learning, providing an explanation of how contiguity can lead to mental representations. For example, separate mental representations of previously separate sensory inputs will merge when the inputs subsequently occur only in temporal synchrony (Wang et al. 1995). Similarly, the subscenes constituting a primary scene are associated in this way (see section 4.3 for further discussion of primary metaphors).

4.3 Interaction of Metonymy and Metaphor

Metaphor and metonymy interact to varying degrees in language and other sign systems (e.g. Jakobson 1956; Köveczes 2013; Radden 2000; see also *this volume*: Littlemore; Ruiz de Mendoza). Investigating how indexical and iconic principles jointly guide the interpretation of predominantly metaphoric gestures, Mittelberg and Waugh (2009) suggest two distinct but intertwined mappings in which metonymy leads into metaphor. For instance, to reconstruct the meaning of the gesture evoking an infinitive (Figure 7.1a), we can first assume a process of metonymic inferencing. The metonymic source – i.e. the two hands involved in the source action of holding something – points to the immediately contiguous metonymic target: the virtual object involved in the action. Second, the same imaginary object serves as the source of the metaphoric mapping whose target is the abstract notion of "infinitive" referred to verbally (see also Taub 2001: 94ff.).

Though cognitive, experiential, or functional "domains" (e.g. Croft & Cruse 2004) can also be understood in frame-semantic terms, Dancygier and Sweetser (2014) convincingly argue that, compared to domains, the structural organization of frames allows for a more systematic and fine-grained account of correlations, not only *within* a frame – giving rise to frame metonymy – but also *between* two frames that are partially mapped onto each other – giving rise to metaphor. It is central to the present perspective on frame-based multimodal (primary) metaphor involving gesture that "[f]rame metonymy is closely tied to the kind of correlations which are involved in experientially based metaphors, in particular Primary Metaphors . . . It is precisely the development of a complex frame out of a correlated simpler frame which makes a primary scene so powerful" (Dancygier & Sweetser 2014: 137).

Also reinforcing our embodied account of frames and gestural frame evocation are brain imaging findings that have implicated the temporo-parietal junction (TPJ) not only in controlling semantic frames (Rennig et al. 2013) but also in supporting the body schema. In our own unpublished neuroimaging studies, we have also found the TPJ to be involved in more complex metonymic resolution in coverbal gestures. Moreover, we have found the TPJ to exert top-down modulation of semantic network areas previously implicated in the metaphoric processing of multimodal discourse involving speech and gestures, regardless of the modality in which the metaphor is expressed. Other studies have implicated the TPJ in roles that are consistent with the function of metonymy in multimodal communication, namely, in attentional control or updating top-down control (Geng & Vossel 2013). This is not surprising, as the TPJ has been argued to be a hub that integrates inputs from different sensory modalities. Thus, body schema, sensory integration, top-down attention modulation, and more complex metonymy resolution are all linked to one neuronal structure. However, as such reverse inference can only attest to the *plausibility* of our proposals, future studies focusing on the role of metonymy and frames in multimodal communication are needed. Studies could capitalize on gestures being an "exbodiment" (Mittelberg 2013b) and physical realization of meaning construction.

5 Gestural Frame Evocation: *Source Actions* as Sources of Meaning and Understanding

Throughout the chapter, we have highlighted how aspects of physical action feed into basic embodied construal operations and dynamic semantic structure. In line with the stance that interlocutors "do metaphor" while speaking, we advocate shifting the focus from object-oriented schemas, source domains, and mappings to *action-based source domains*, or what we call "source actions." Tapping into both literal and metaphoric meanings via the action-based nature of communicative gestures, we distinguish between two types of frame structures with varying degrees of abstraction and complexity: "basic physical action and object frames" and "more complex abstract frame structures." For the present exposition, basic action and object frames are particularly relevant.[3]

Basic physical action and object frames are strongly grounded in bodily experience, involving physical action and interaction with the social world and material culture. These basic embodied frames encompass Slobin's (1985) notion of prototypical events, Andrén's (2010) action gestalts, Zlatev's (2005) mimetic schemas, and what Lakoff (1987: 270–271) calls "basic-level actions" (e.g. running, walking, eating). In multimodal discourse, gesturing hands often pretend to hold, place, move, group, or else create reified abstract entities (e.g. Mittelberg 2013b; Müller 1998; Streeck 2009). Speakers evoke basic frames through such gestures and postures, through imitating walking up a steep slope with the torso leaning forward and supporting arm movements, or toasting to someone (pretending to hold an imaginary glass). Many of these actions may also function as source actions in more specific metaphoric linguistic expressions, as in "I'll walk you through the text" (THOUGHT IS MOVEMENT) or "she grasps new concepts without problems" (UNDERSTANDING IS GRASPING; Lakoff & Johnson 1980). In each instance, two different frames that are correlated partially map onto each other (Dancygier & Sweetser 2014).

In a similar vein, Hostetter and Alibali's (2008: 502) *gestures-as-simulated-action* framework "asserts that gestures emerge from the perceptual and motor simulations that underlie embodied language and mental imagery." That is, schematic or abstract scenes are assumed to function as blueprints for gestures that simulate actions involving the whole body or parts of the body (see also Mittelberg 2017). When gestures simulate actions or scenes in schematic ways, the question is under what circumstances what kinds of actions gain metaphoric meaning.

5.1 Source Actions *with Different Communicative and Cognitive-Pragmatic Functions*

We call deeply embodied patterns of experience with the physical and social world that activate a basic physical action frame "source actions." They range from intrinsic sensorimotor routines to actions involving people, objects, surfaces, and/or tools. As such, they may illustrate or partake in intransitive, transitive, or ditransitive clause constructions (Goldberg 1995; Hopper & Thompson 1980). In ongoing discourses, speakers may employ source actions to perform different kinds of communicative, cognitive-pragmatic tasks:

(i) iconically enact aspects of *basic action frames* also evoked through speech (see section 5.2);
(ii) perform a *gestural framing action* by manipulating entities evoked through speech (see section 5.3);
(iii) carry out a *discourse-structuring activity* at a meta-level, such as sorting speech contents by placing them in different regions of gesture space.

Source actions provide cues to interlocutors' intentions and to which aspects or moments are made salient in a dynamically evolving and intersubjectively shared multimodal discourse contexture (e.g. Goodwin 2011b; Jakobson 1956;

Mittelberg & Waugh 2014; Müller & Tag 2010; Streeck 2009). Importantly, source actions may be used and understood literally or metaphorically, depending on the interlocutors' mental frame, the subject matter, the speech content, and the overall context. Different kinds of metaphoric source actions will be illustrated next.

5.2 Basic Physical Action Frames *Evoked through Speech and Iconic Gestures*

The most essential kind of source actions encompasses basic intransitive and (di-)transitive *physical action frames* evoked through the concurrent speech and iconically simulated via gesture. Let us first consider an intransitive action (Figure 7.2).

The speaker in Figure 7.2 describes how she experienced watching a short film in which sound effects take center stage: "No, well ... as a matter of fact I felt pulled directly into the film."[4] She expresses the feeling of being pulled into an emotional space, created by watching the film, with the intransitive clause, "I felt pulled directly into the film" while gesturing inward with both hands, palms facing her body, and pointing slightly upward and toward her torso. Interestingly, she conceptualizes the space close to her own body as the area into which she felt that she was being pulled, adopting an allocentric view. Her subtle inward movement is metaphorically contextualized through the

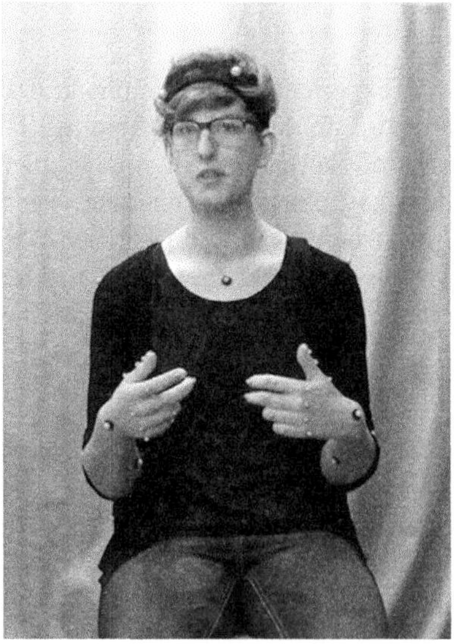

Figure 7.2 Feeling pulled into a film

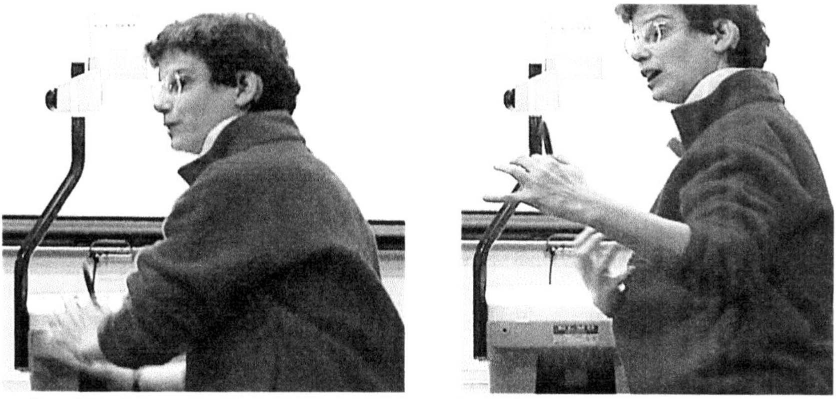

a. *Reaching into* a constituent b. *Pulling out* a sub-constituent

Figure 7.3 Explaining constituent structure

discourse context: She is talking about her subjective viewing experience and emotional reaction. It may count as a metonymic "emotive" (Jakobson 1960) gestural enactment of a prototypical event or mimetic schema PULL, subtly instantiating the FORCE schema ('being pulled') as well as the image schemas IN-OUT and NEAR-FAR (Lakoff & Johnson 1999). The primary conceptual metaphor MENTAL/EMOTIONAL STATES ARE CONTAINERS may be pragmatically inferred. These interacting embodied construal mechanisms are triggered by evoking the basic action frame PULL (IN), which functions here as a source action that metonymically and metaphorically correlates physical movement and space with mental/emotional experiences and states.

The next example contains both an intransitive and a transitive construction (Figure 7.3). A linguist is explaining the hierarchical relationship between two kinds of constituents: "So, 'invite John's sister' is a constituent, but we can reach into it and pull out a sub-constituent." While the main constituent is metaphorically construed as a CONTAINER with a profiled interior and the sub-constituent is construed as a smaller OBJECT (to be pragmatically inferred), it is the gestural actions interacting with these imaginary constructs that are perceptually salient.

These dynamic enactments function here as source actions anchoring two object-based primary metaphors via metonymic correlations between gesturing hands and contiguous spaces or objects. The speaker verbally and gesturally evokes (i) an intransitive basic action frame (REACH INTO) and the correlated (implied) spatial goal or target space (a CONTAINER), as well as (ii) a transitive basic action frame (PULL OUT) and the correlated (implied) contiguous, hand-held imaginary OBJECT (the patient). Note that the physical (iconic) source actions of reaching and pulling get a metaphorical reading through cross-modal interaction of gestural action and linguistic information about the implied imaginary, abstract categories. The ways in which semantic roles (Fillmore & Baker 2009) factor into these bimodal instances of frame evocation still requires further investigation.

5.3 Gestural Framing Actions *Not Mentioned in Speech*

Unlike source action frames, *gestural framing actions* typically are not specified in speech, that is, they do not enact a linguistically evoked frame. However, such iconic bodily actions can be constitutive and perceptually salient components of multimodal performances.

Returning to our first example (Figure 7.1), we see an instance of a monomodal (i.e. only bodily expressed) metaphor. Although the accompanying speech is not figurative, the gestures portray an 'infinitive' as a generic physical object that can be touched and manipulated through drawing on the object-oriented primary metaphors IDEAS ARE OBJECTS and CATEGORIES ARE CONTAINERS (Lakoff & Johnson 1999). Crucially, this portrayal of an abstract category is semiotically contextualized and *framed* by an enactment of holding a tangible item. In our view, such strongly grounded, prototypical transitive source actions may function as gestural framing actions that evoke the metonymically correlated, contiguously handheld – or otherwise manipulated – imaginary items mentioned in the affiliate speech (Mittelberg 2006; Mittelberg & Waugh 2009).

One needs to remember that, even with the aid of body schema or body image, no single gesture has an unequivocal interpretation. Without the affiliate speech, interpreting gestures is rendered even more difficult: An ambiguous bodily sign does not effectively evoke the appropriate semantic frames that lead to understanding the intended meaning. Moreover, ineffective or weak, and hence non-salient, metaphors tend to be ignored (Glucksberg et al. 1982). Thus, in order for monomodal metaphoric gestures to be communicatively effective, they would need to recruit strongly embodied primary metaphors (and the related image and force schemas), for instance, via metonymically correlated gestural framing actions.

5.4 Some Implications

The fact that non-emblematic, spontaneous coverbal gestures seldom have unique interpretations reminds us of the importance of how the overall sum (i.e. the intended meaning communicated) in multimodal communication is greater than the sum of its parts (i.e. the meanings derived from each modality, taken separately). This phenomenon is known as "superadditivity" in physiological and neuroscience research of multisensory integration. Superadditivity also hints at the workings of metonymy or frames: "Parts" or features can map onto more complete "parts" (themselves semantic frames, combining a number of features), which, in turn, are parts of yet more complex, holistic semantic frames. Hence, it might appear that the sum of the parts leads to greater activation than the parts in isolation. In multimodal discourse, understanding is a distributed (inter-)subjective, cognitive process requiring grounding in experientially motivated frames and scenes that are strongly perception- and action-based. Monomodal metaphoric gestures seem to rely on this process even more heavily.

Along with the semantic frames involved in processing spoken utterances, some additional frames seem to be needed to process actions in multimodal discourse. These frames, like gestures, could be related hierarchically. As features are weighted according to how essential or salient they are for an entrenched pattern of experience, this hierarchy seems to be determined by the capacity of a given feature or scene to cue for a particular frame (see also Dancygier & Sweetser 2014). This lets us assume that the more (salient) features are profiled, the more complete and hence more strongly the frame is activated.

The intended meaning of coverbal gestures is strongly determined by the context, which is often greatly shaped by the accompanying speech (see Müller, *this volume*). However, when the speech does not aid in resolving the intended meaning of a gesture, its decodability relies on its ability to convey features that are salient or embodied enough to be able to activate frames on their own. Without attentional control and a mechanism as a conduit to handle noisy input, these features remain as noise. Metonymy provides a means to "fuzzy match" in order to activate relevant frames with less effort on the part of the speaker. Without cues in the affiliate speech, people seem to follow a set of strategies, based on body schema and action routines that are part of these schemas, to interpret gestures representing, for instance, literal transitive actions (e.g. Grandhi et al. 2012).

We have argued that metaphoric understandings expressed through gestures, especially gestural framing actions involving metaphorically construed items, tend to – via metonymy – involve primary metaphors (in particular for monomodal metaphoric gestures) or other very salient, strongly embodied conceptual metaphors that recruit primary scenes (Grady & Johnson 2002), prototypical events (Slobin 1985), basic-level actions (Lakoff 1987), basic image and force schemas, certain mimetic schemas (Zlatev 2005), and in particular, basic embodied frames and scenes (Fillmore 1977).

6 Concluding Remarks

We have laid out the foundations of a frame-based account of gestural action. The *basic action frames* and *source actions* we have presented may function as bodily sources of meaning, experience, and understanding (Johnson 2007) in multimodal discourse where speech, gestures, and other modalities contextualize one another. As emphasized, metonymic modes allow us to infer full action routines, emotive qualities, and interactive dimensions from schematic gestural articulations, as well as correlated imaginary objects or traces from visible gestural actions (Mittelberg & Waugh 2009, 2014).

When such gestural actions occur in discourses about abstract knowledge domains, mental processes, affective states, or other kinds of subjective experiences, they may receive a *contextually driven* metaphorical interpretation (see also Müller & Cienki 2009). This resonates with research on language processing showing that certain linguistic contexts cause a metaphorical reading of verbal expressions that, in principle, could have either a literal or a figurative meaning (e.g. Giora 2008). Once interlocutors are in an abstract or emotional mind-set, gestural actions, including framing actions, can mediate between physical and cognitive processes and thereby provide experiential grounding, for instance, through “imaginary material anchors” (Hutchings 2005), such as imagined objects, even if the concurrent speech is non-figurative.

Our frame-based account of how gestural source actions may profile “prototypical instances of scenes” (Fillmore 1977: 63) – or enact relevant aspects of “scenes basic to human experience” (Goldberg 1995: 5) – allows us to better understand why metaphoricity that is monomodally expressed through the communicating body relies on metonymy and tends to involve primary metaphors (Kövecses 2013). Working out how scenes and frames may also motivate multimodal constructions is one ensuing step of inquiry (e.g. Barcelona 2009; Mittelberg 2017; Sullivan 2013).

The gestural and neurocognitive patterns discussed in this chapter further attest to the psychological and semiotic reality of internalized conceptual operations, entrenched metaphorical understandings, and social practices (Gibbs 2006a; *this volume*: Gibbs; Winter & Matlock; Müller). Complex conceptual networks do not necessarily translate into neural network fingerprints. Although grounded strongly in bodily experience, the interplay of this bodily experience with other contextual factors makes linguistic and multimodal cognition a multidimensional process requiring further studies before an integrative understanding can be gained. Here we have outlined a theoretical account, anchored in empirical findings across different disciplines, in order to help shape goals of future cognitive-linguistic and neuroscience research into linguistic cognition, discourse processes, and the role of the body.

Perhaps the most intriguing question re-arising from these body-centered and action-based insights is whether, or rather in which cases, we actually need to assume conceptual metaphorical mappings when deeply embodied, basic frame-based correlation metaphors are recruited for communicative purposes via their metonymic bases. From a discourse pragmatics perspective, it indeed seems likely that such intuitive communicative acts directly simulate sensorimotor routines, environment-oriented actions, and sociocultural experience (e.g. Arnheim 1969; Hostetter & Alibali 2008; Gibbs, *this volume*) and may be understood literally or metaphorically – depending on various contextual factors.

Notes and Acknowledgments

* We thank the editor and an anonymous reviewer for a very helpful discussion of a number of critical points. The research presented in this chapter was supported by the Excellence Initiative of the German Federal and State Governments.

1 This approach builds on Fillmore's notion of "frame," as developed before the FrameNet project (Fillmore & Baker 2009).

2 German original: "Sie schauen einen (. . .) Infinitiv an, können sie sagen *ah*, das ist, (. . .) Präsens, Perfekt, Plusquamperfekt?"

3 For a discussion on gestures evoking complex, abstract frame structures, such as discourses and theories, see Mittelberg (2017).

4 German original: "Nö, das also . . . also ich fühlte mich schon direkt reingezogen in den Film."

8 Metaphor and Other Cognitive Operations in Interaction: From Basicity to Complexity

*Francisco J. Ruiz de Mendoza Ibáñez**

Chapter Preview

By combining three complementary perspectives, the present chapter goes beyond previous treatments of figurative language in general and of conceptual metaphor in particular. Besides viewing metaphor in terms of the basic cognitive processes underlying it, it also investigates how metaphor combines with other metaphors and with metonymy and in what way it is related to other cases of figurative meaning construction. The present chapter paves the way toward an encompassing theory of meaning construction that employs a highly restricted set of principles to account for a broader range of phenomena than previous accounts have done.

1 Introduction

By combining three complementary perspectives, the present chapter goes beyond previous treatments of conceptual metaphor: It looks at metaphor in terms of more basic cognitive processes; it relates metaphor to other cases of figurative meaning construction; and it investigates how basic cognitive operations interact, focusing especially on combinations of metaphor with other metaphors and with metonymy. The ultimate goal is an encompassing theory of meaning construction that is based on a more restricted set of principles than previous theories and that accounts for a broader range of phenomena while making explicit their interrelations.

Starting out in section 2 from an overview of knowledge organization in terms of cognitive modeling, I present linguistic evidence supporting the claim that metaphor and metonymy are cover terms for more basic cognitive operations and introduce these in section 3. Section 4 demonstrates the explanatory power of an account of meaning constructions in terms of cognitive modeling by showing how metonymies and metaphors combine into more complex constructs. It also addresses other cases of interaction between cognitive operations involving metaphor, simile, hyperbole, and irony. The major conclusions are summarized in section 5.

2 Conceptual Structure

As internally consistent conceptual networks representing world knowledge, Fillmore's (1985) "frames," Johnson's (1987) "image schemas," as well as Lakoff and Johnson's (1980) "conceptual metaphor and metonymy" have all been subsumed under Lakoff's (1987) notion of "idealized cognitive model" (ICM). The focus here is on how the last two differ from the first in their operational rather than merely descriptive nature.

Frames are conceptual characterizations of entities, states, situations, and events. For example, the skiing frame in the domain of sports represents encyclopedic knowledge about sports people (agent role) who employ skis as special equipment (instrument role) in order to move speedily and effortlessly (purpose/manner roles) on snowy ground (circumstances/location role). Image schemas are different in that they are schematizations of sensorimotor experience capturing spatial orientations (UP/DOWN and FRONT/BACK), regions and positions (IN/OUT, ON/OFF, AT/AWAY FROM), the part–whole structure of complex entities, etc. A hollow three-dimensional physical object like a parcel, for example, instantiates the CONTAINER image schema ("Put the book in the parcel") or may invoke the SURFACE schema ("Wrap up the parcel").

Metaphor is a mapping of conceptual structure from a source to a target domain in which the structure and logic of the target partially determine the choice of the source. The source in turn is used to reason and talk about the target. To illustrate, we can talk about gradable abstract concepts like 'importance,' or 'complexity'/'difficulty' in terms of such gradable physical properties as size ("a big discovery") and depth ("a deep issue"), respectively. Conceptual metaphors like these arise from ubiquitous experiential correlations (cf. Grady 1997a; Grady & Ascoli, *this volume*) and are to be distinguished from metaphors based on perceived similarities between objects or scenarios, which are very close to similes: "Her hair is (as soft as) cotton" (cf. Grady 1999). Metonymy, finally, is a conceptual relation between two elements where one stands for the other. More specifically, the source domain supplies a conceptual point of access to the target (cf. Kövecses & Radden 1998). As a consequence, the target is seen from the perspective of the source. In the case of "hand" for 'help' (INSTRUMENT FOR ACTION), we primarily think of the help provided as involving manual work ("We need a hand on the farm"), though intellectual ability ("Could you give me a hand or two with my homework?") can also become relevant through a further metonymic shift from manual work to any form of work.

By viewing metaphor and metonymy as cases of idealized cognitive models, Lakoff (1987) stressed that they provide coherent representations of our experience. In the metaphor "be at a crossroads in life," for instance, the source domain activates frame knowledge about real crossroads. When faced with a crossroads without a clear indication of "where to go," people may feel confused, fearful, or frustrated. They may decide to "retrace their steps" or "take the risk" of following one path at random. This logic models our understanding of the actions people take when similarly faced with decisions about how to best reach their goals in life. Though perhaps less obviously, metonymy also models thought. In "Sadam Hussein invaded Kuwait," where the ruler stands for the army under his command, the metonymy does more than refer to the army by mentioning the ruler: It draws attention to the Iraqi dictator as fully responsible for the invasion. Metaphor and metonymy are thus different sources of inferences, both with communicative consequences.

It is argued here that metaphor and metonymy differ from frames and image schemas in that they act on frames and image schemas, i.e. they have an operational nature. Thus, metaphor and metonymy create frames (i.e. new ICMs) from other frames. For example, through metonymy, "hand" has acquired various meanings: 'manual laborer' ("a farm hand"), 'member of a crew' ("a ship's hands"), 'person that specializes in a given pursuit' ("an old hand at negotiations"), etc. Through metaphor, "hand" has come to mean 'pointer on a dial or the face of a watch.'

The "invariance hypothesis" (Lakoff 1990) states that metaphorical mappings respect the image-schematic properties of their source domains. By contrast, metonymy can change an image-schematic construct into a related one. This is what happens in so-called image-schema transformations (Lakoff 1987). In the transformation called PATH-FOCUS TO END-POINT FOCUS, for example, we imagine the path of a moving object and then focus on the point where it will come to rest, as in "She lives over the bridge." The relationship between "over" as an overt marker of a motion trajectory and its intended meaning ('at the end of the path that one can trace by walking over the brige') is evidently metonymic (cf. Peña & Ruiz de Mendoza 2009).

3 Cognitive Operations

In cognitive psychology, a cognitive operation is any mental activity with an identifiable effect resulting from the brain's response to human interaction with the world. The literature (Anderson 2010) cites cognitive operations of various kinds which can be grouped into at least three broad categories. First, *sensorimotor operations* underlie the bodily aspects of interaction with the world and they may influence concept building (e.g. motor programs and their execution; for a discussion of this latter point, see Cuccio, *this volume*). Second, *concept-*

building operations result in the creation and internal manipulation of bodily-based knowledge stores (e.g. memory encoding and retrieval; tactile, visual, and auditory encoding; mental imagery manipulation). Third, *representational operations* produce constrained meaning representations by putting into different perspectives elements of preexisting knowledge stores relative to other elements or by giving prominence to some elements of a conceptual construct over others (e.g. figure–ground alignment and windowing of attention). Representational operations can also produce new meaning through inferences (e.g. different kinds of metaphor). The first two of these constitute *construal operations*. The third comprises a variety of *inferential operations* (see Figure 8.1).

Concept-building operations and sensorimotor operations affect meaning production differently from representational operations. In fact, representational operations include cognitive operations whose activity ranges over the output of concept-building operations and of those sensorimotor operations that relate to the creation of knowledge structures. These last two categories give rise to organized knowledge stores consisting of interconnected frames and image-schematic categories.

These knowledge stores can, in turn, constrain the activity of representational operations because they are rooted in bodily experience. This is demonstrated by well-known psycholinguistic work on embodied simulation and its effects on metaphorical thought. There is increasing evidence that motor programs are related to how people understand concepts. The understanding of concrete non-metaphorical language – and even of (at least some)

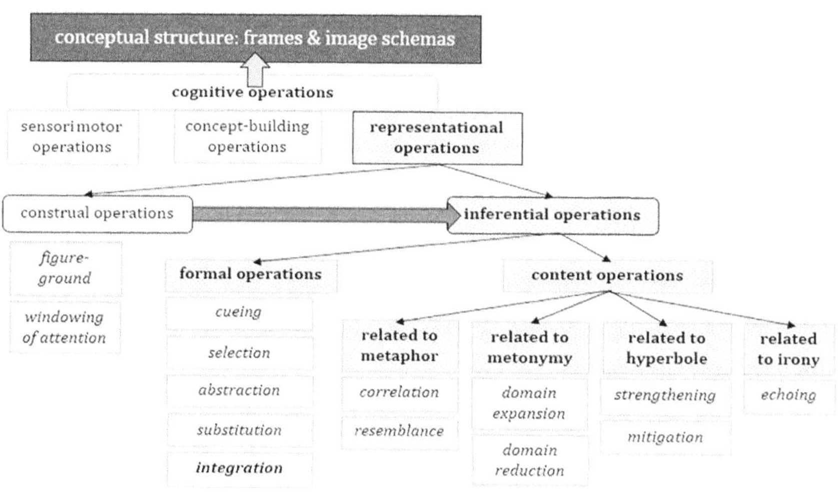

Figure 8.1 Survey of cognitive operations working on frames and image schemas

metaphorical language – draws on the embodied simulation of actions, which recruits the same brain areas, e.g. the motor cortex (cf. Bergen 2012; Lakoff 2014; Ritchie, *this volume*).

3.1 Construal Operations

Construal affects linguistic expression. A case in point is *figure–ground alignment* (cf. Talmy 2000), which determines the position of one object, called the figure, in relation to another, the ground, with the former usually being smaller and more likely to move than the latter. From this, well-known interpretive constraints arise: "The box is on the desk," for example, exhibits a natural figure, the box, while "The desk is under the box," where the desk is the figure, is decidedly odd. Another case of construal relates to *shifts of attention* (cf. ibid.), which can constrain the use of verbal predicates. Consider the behavior of movement verbs in the alternation between the highly productive agent-subject construction (ex 1) and the tightly constrained locative-subject construction (ex 2, 3). As with other alternations, not all movement verbs participate in it. "Dance," for instance, is excluded (2b). However, this restriction does not hold for its figurative uses (2c).

(1) a. Children *swarmed* in the playground.
b. Lovely couples *danced* on the stage.
c. They *danced* around in excitement.
(2) a. The playground *swarmed* with children.
b. *The stage *danced* with lovely couples.
c. His head *danced* with great memories.
(3) a. The stage *filled* with lovely couples.
b. The playground *filled* with children.
c. *Two or three children *swarmed* in the playground.

A perceptual constraint rules out (2b) (cf. Rosca 2012): The locative-subject construction captures unorganized motion covering a whole region in space, thus requiring a multitude of wildly moving entities (3a, b). Since dancing usually involves rhythmic, ordered motion, literal uses of "dance" are disallowed. However, through an attention shift, it is possible to use "dance" with a special focus on leaps and jumps (1c). This slightly shifted meaning of "dance" supplies the right construal for its metaphorical use with a construction requiring unorganized motion.

In short, metaphoric mappings give rise to inferences on the basis of the previous construal of conceptual characterizations. It is therefore possible to use metaphor as a test for construal options. The adjectives "wealthy" and "rich," for instance, denote the same attribute ('having an abundance of material possessions') and can often (4a–c) – but not always (5a–d) – be used interchangeably. All uses of "rich" in (5) are metaphorical extensions from 'abundance of property' to 'abundance in crop yield, food, natural resources, and ingredients.' Evidently, of the respective foci of rich on 'above-average quantity' and of wealthy on 'above-average value,' only the first licenses the metaphorical extensions in (5).

(4) a. She is so *wealthy/rich* she doesn't need to work.
b. He wants to marry a *wealthy/rich* woman.
c. Sometimes *wealthy/rich* people are unhappy.

(5) a. a *rich/*wealthy* harvest ('abundant')
b. a *rich/*wealthy* banquet ('lavish')
c. a *rich/*wealthy* region ('productive')
d. a *rich/*wealthy* chocolate shake ('full of valuable ingredients like cocoa')

We have shown that construal operations are preliminary to inferential activity and will discuss inferential cognitive operations next.

3.2 *Inferential Cognitive Operations*

There are two broad types of cognitive operations that play a direct role in making inferences by working on (perspectivized) conceptual material: *formal* and *content* operations (cf. Ruiz de Mendoza 2011). Formal operations manipulate concepts structurally; they can either prepare conceptual structure for the activity of content operations or interact with them:

Cueing prompts the activation of conceptual material on the basis of conceptual consistency. Such selected activation can take the form of what Langacker (2008) has termed an "active zone," a relevant meaning facet of a profiled (or designated) concept. Compare "There are *cigarettes* on the pavement" ('stubs') and "Put out your *cigarette*" ('burning end of cigarette').

Selection opens cued conceptual structure to a content operation. In metonymy, relevant structure is selected on the basis of the efficient search for conceptual consistency. In metaphor the target domain sets requirements to – and thus limits – source-structure activation: "My wife really *mothers* me" has a pampered husband in the target. This requires the nurturance model of 'motherhood' to the detriment of other models, while "Necessity is the *mother* of invention" exhibits a target domain (a creative source or origin), requiring the 'bringing-into-existence' dimension of the birth model (for ICMs of 'motherhood,' see Lakoff 1987).

Abstraction consists in deriving generic-level structure from lower-level structure. It underlies the creation of generic-level concepts like 'action,' 'agent,' 'instrument,' etc. Among other functions, this operation is necessary to preserve image-schematic structure in metaphors based on similarity: "The posts are strung out across the desert" maps the image of stretched strings onto the overall shape of posts (as seen from a distance) by topological abstraction of source and target elements.

Substitution occurs when (a part of) a cognitive model is replaced by (a part of) another cognitive model. It is a prerequisite for a number of phenomena, among them metonymy ("They broke the *window*": 'the pane'), euphemism ("She's *ample*": 'fat'), and referential metaphors ("Here comes the *rat* that betrayed me": 'despicable traitor') (cf. Ruiz de Mendoza & Galera 2014).

Integration consists in the principled merging of conceptual structure from any number of cued items. In "She went into a depression," the PATH schema combines with the CONTAINER schema, which fills in the 'end-of-path' slot, in both the source and the target of the metaphorical use of "go into." This operation relates to Fauconnier and Turner's (2002) notion of "conceptual integration" (or "blending") but has a narrower scope of application. While blending is a pervasive process that holds for all aspects of cognition, cued integration refers to the simple unification of compatible elements and – like all formal operations – is a prerequisite for the full-range activity of content operations.

Content operations are lower-level operations used to make inferences on the basis of the cues provided by a linguistic expression or the context in which it is produced.

Content Operations Related to Metaphor The first operation is "correlation" (cf. Grady 1999). When two events co-occur frequently in our experience, they are strongly associated and we may even experience them as being the same. Correlation underlies conflation, which is a stage in concept acquisition where the infant is not able to distinguish between the perceptual aspect and the subjective-response aspect of one and the same situation, a so-called "primary scene." Correlation gives rise to metaphor (cf. Grady 1997a; Lakoff & Johnson 1999: 46–59). A case in point is GOALS ARE DESTINATIONS. We commonly talk about achieving goals using the verb "reach," whose core meaning ('to touch or grasp by stretching out') involves physical distance ("He couldn't reach the shelf"). Other meanings obtained by extension retain this element of 'physical distance' (6a–c). The intentional component of the primary scene in which people go to places they want to reach provides a highly plausible reason why people talk about "reaching goals," namely, that reaching a destination literally involves achieving the goal of so doing.

(6) a. They finally *reached* ('arrived at') their destination.
b. The shadow *reached* ('extended up to') the wall.
c. The sound of falling rocks *reached* ('traveled as far as') our ears.

The second operation is "resemblance" (Grady 1999). It consists in detecting similarities between discrete conceptual domains. In contrast to correlation metaphors, resemblance metaphors are very close to similes. A well-known example of a resemblance metaphor is PEOPLE ARE SHARKS ("My lawyer is a shark"). It results from thinking about ruthless social behavior in terms of a shark's predatory behavior, which, when compared to human standards, is perceived as ruthless.

Content Operations Related to Metonymy I distinguish two converse operations which relate to PART–WHOLE and WHOLE–PART metonymic relations, namely, "domain expansion" and "domain reduction." Domain expansion broadens the scope of a conceptual characterization (in the sense of evoking larger frames that include the frame against which the source concept is defined). In combination with the formal operation of substitution, it results in metonymy if general conditions of "relevance" (Sperber & Wilson 1995) hold. Within the domain of musical performance, for example, a musical instrument can afford access to the person playing the instrument. If textual and contextual conditions make this broadening interpretively relevant, the musical instrument can substitute for the instrument player ("The violin came late to today's rehearsal"). In other contexts, it could refer to other concepts through expansion. In a workshop where different workers are specialized in making different instruments, for instance, the person making violins could be called "the violin" by his co-workers.

Domain reduction reduces the scope of a conceptual characterization, endowing a textually and contextually relevant portion of the initial conceptualization with focal prominence. This is called "domain highlighting" (Croft 1993), which consists in giving primary status to a secondary characterization. For example, interpreting the sentence "Tie your shoes" requires highlighting the shoelaces, which are not a central element of the notion of 'shoes' (not every shoe has shoelaces). The present account of cognitive operations puts domain highlighting into a broader perspective: First, it is seen as complementary to domain expansion – not just because it brings a part of the designated conceptualization to bear upon interpretation but also because it gives focal prominence to that part (while the conceptualization to be broadened in domain expansion has focal status by default and never loses it). Second, it is seen as naturally combining with formal substitution operations that are typical but not exclusive of metonymy.

Content Operations Related to Over- and Understatement The conversely related operations of "strengthening" and "mitigation" operate on scalar concepts like 'distance,' 'weight,' or 'height.' Their function is to place such concepts at the highest or lowest ends of their respective scales – or as close to either end as is contextually relevant. In other words, strengthening upscales and mitigation downscales concepts.

Hyperbolic meanings are based on upscaled concepts. If saying that an object we want to carry, e.g. a suitcase, weighs "a ton," we actually mean that this object is unexpectedly, and perhaps frustratingly, weighty. Hearers take the opposite perspective. For them, recognizing the difference between the hyperbolic and the real-world situation involves downscaling the previously upscaled representation to make it match a plausible real-world representation. Understatement, in contrast, requires mitigation: "The shop is just round the corner," uttered in a context where the shop is actually farther than what "round the corner" would normally suggest, could be used by speakers to mitigate the impact or seriousness of a situation and appease the hearer.

Content Operations Related to Irony The notion of "echoing," treated here as yet another content operation, is taken from Relevance Theory (Sperber & Wilson 1995). An echo is the repetition of someone's thoughts, or of an utterance containing such thoughts. Echoing is typical of irony, where it serves the function of repeating thoughts that contradict the actual situation. Imagine someone thinks that the speaker's neighbor is very generous, but then the neighbor's actions prove the opposite. In this situation, a remark like "Yes, very generous indeed" is an ironic echo of such misled thought. Echoes are not restricted to irony. They are also found elsewhere, as in reported speech, where the echoed thought is not posed as contradicting reality.

Summary The content operations discussed account for a number of central aspects of what is traditionally called "figurative" language use. I have shown that formal operations have the function of either preparing conceptual structure for meaning-bearing cognitive activity resulting from content operations, or cooperating with content operations to give final shape to such activity.

4 Complexity

Conceptual integration creates more complex structures with emerging novel properties, as blending theorists have shown in relation to a number of phenomena, including metaphor and other cases of figurative language use (cf. Dancygier & Sweetser 2014; Fauconnier & Turner 2002). When discussing the processes involved in integrating concepts, this section will contrast the descriptive nature of frames and image schemas with the operational nature of metonymy and metaphor. In particular, the section focuses on the ways in which one formal operation, *integration*, interacts with other lower-level operations, thereby giving rise to conceptual complexes of various kinds. In order to make apparent the explanatory value of the cognitive operations introduced above, hyperbole and irony will be discussed in addition to metaphor and metonymy.

4.1 *Frame Complexes and Image-Schema Complexes*

Frames can be elaborated on in conventional and unconventional ways. Conventional elaboration occurs when schematic frame elements (agent, action, instrument, purpose, condition, etc.) are specified in accordance with preestablished feature values. Concerning the skiing frame mentioned above, for instance, people share the knowledge that the shape of the skis, the use of additional equipment and the sort and speed of movement vary in accordance with the terrain (steep hills, soft slopes, or flat plains) and type of snow.

Blending Theory (Fauconnier & Turner 2002) has dealt with how frames can be blended, yielding new conceptualizations that retain elements of the input frames but also show emergent structure of their own. The history of sports provides examples of such unconventional "frame complexes": Snowboarding is an instance of an unconventional development of the skiing frame. Apparently, it was invented several times in the 1960s, inspired by aspects of the surfing frame, the skateboarding frame, and the waterboarding frame, respectively.

"Image-schematic complexes" result from the integration of two or more image schemas. In "The wind blew the bullet off its course," one MOTION schema combines with another co-dependent one causing a change of PATH in the other. The configuration is captured by the DIVERSION schema, which results from (and is thus subsidiary to) this specific combination of MOTION and PATH (Peña 2008). Obviously, the conceptual package activated by this sentence makes only partial use of the full range of possibilities provided by the image-schematic complex associated with the notion of 'motion.' A more complete expression of the same motion scenario (employing a larger window of attention) could depict the entire path: "The wind blew the bullet off its course into the policeman's back." Here the CONTAINER schema is incorporated into the 'end-of-path' slot of the PATH image schema. Note that the CONTAINER schema is not necessary to foreground the 'end-of-path' ("The bullet *reached* the kidney").

Image schemas differ from frames in that the conventional/unconventional distinction cannot be applied to them. Unlike frames, image schemas cannot be elaborated on in any way, but remain schematic. As "skeletal" sensorimotor structures, they support reasoning processes that involve much richer frame knowledge. Thus, although 'motion' requires a moving entity that can be conceived of in a less schematic way (e.g. a bullet, a car, a missile, a leaf, etc.), the image schema captures only the basic outline and logic of a motion event, which will always involve a source, a course, a speed of movement, and an end of path. Elaboration, both conventional and unconventional, can only take place at the level of knowledge frames.

4.2 Combining Content Operations

Two or more cognitive operations of the same or of different kind can combine either simultaneously or in succession. Owing to the multiplicity of inferential cognitive operations, a full account of all interaction patterns cannot be given here. We will address only the following types: (i) metaphtonymy, (ii) metonymic chains, (iii) metaphoric chains, (iv) metaphoric amalgams, (v) hyperbole through metaphor or simile, and (vi) strengthened irony through hyperbole.

Metaphtonymy Goossens (1990) distinguished four cases of interaction between metaphor and metonymy and subsumed all of them under the label of "metaphtonymy": (i) metaphors from metonymy (e.g. "beat one's breast" for 'openly displaying sorrow'), (ii) metaphor within metonymy to enhance the latter's expressiveness (e.g. "stand on one's hind legs to defend one's views" for 'defend one's views emphatically'), (iii) metonymy within metaphor (e.g. "bite one's tongue" for 'refrain from speaking'), and (iv) metonymy lost within a metaphoric frame (e.g. "pay lip service" meaning 'express support without acting accordingly' and not 'pay service by using the ability to talk').

When looked at from a situational perspective, these cases of metaphtonymy correspond to only two broad interaction patterns (cf. Ruiz de Mendoza 2014). The first pattern includes cases (i) to (iii). The only difference between (i) and (ii) is that the intended source is cued by the metaphor PEOPLE ARE ANIMALS in (ii), i.e. that this metaphor is inserted into the source domain of a metonymy which maps 'standing' onto 'defending.' An alternative analysis of (iii) would simply state that a forced inability to talk is metonymically represented by the tongue-biting it entails, which in turn maps onto refraining from speaking more generally.

The second pattern is exemplified by the expression "pay lip service." Contrary to Goossens's analysis, the concept 'lip,' which generally stands for 'speaking' (INSTRUMENT FOR ACTION), does not lose its metonymic character. The interaction of the metonymy with the metaphor "pay service" is what defines the nature of the 'service' in the target (as one that will not be given). The source domain of the metaphor contains a payer making his payment to a payee. These source elements map onto corresponding elements in the target, i.e. a person doing something for another person. In this context, the metonymy from 'lip' to 'using the lips to make a promise' acts on the metaphoric target by reducing the 'service' element to the promise itself, which thus turns from a real act into a false promise. Of the two major patterns thus established, one involves the *metonymic expansion of a metaphoric source domain*, while the other requires the *metonymic reduction of a metaphoric target*.

However, there are two further interaction patterns which make use of the converse metonymic operations on either the source or the target domains of the metaphors involved, namely, the *metonymic reduction of a metaphoric source* and the *metonymic expansion of a metaphoric target*. An example of the former is supplied by paragons. A paragon is a model of excellence, a perfect example. From a cognitive perspective, it can be analyzed as a combination of metonymy and metaphor. Consider "Steven Pinker is the Einstein of psycholinguistics." Perhaps *the* leading physicist of the twentieth century and doubtlessly an extremely intelligent person, Einstein has thus come to stand for intellectual excellence. This metonymy is based on domain reduction, in effect giving focal prominence to Einstein's intellectual attributes over others (his sense of humor, musical talent, anti-war sentiments, etc.). In the paragon, this metonymy is built into the source of a metaphor which views Pinker's intellectual achievements in the domain of psycholinguistics in terms of Einstein's in theoretical physics. The present work complements previous analyses within the blending account (Fauconnier & Turner 2002) by identifying the specific cognitive operations involved in establishing the counterpart relations and locates this particular configuration within a greater survey of possible patterns of interaction between metaphor and metonymy.[1]

The remaining pattern, i.e. the metonymic expansion of the target of a metaphor, can be exemplified by the transparent idiomatic expression *knit one's eyebrows*.[2] In the source domain of making clothes, knitting requires intertwining thread in a series of loops that hold together to form a piece of fabric. In the target a person frowns, i.e. brings her/his eyebrows down and together so that they appear intertwined. However, the meaning expressed relates to deep thinking or displeasure, which cannot be obtained from the domain of knitting (the metaphoric source) but comes from that of frowning (the metaphoric target) by means of a metonymic inference: People frown (metonymic source) when angry or in thought (metonymic target).

Metonymic Chains It is well known that metonymy is used to shift referential meanings. Among other possible things, the polysemous word "paper," for instance, may refer to the material made of cellulose pulp ("a sheet of *paper*"), to an essay written on this material ("Turn in your *papers* on Monday"), to a scholarly article ("He is the author of numerous *papers* on Frege"), to a collection of letters, diaries, and writings by one person ("the Jefferson *papers*"), to a newspaper ("He bought his daily *paper*"), and to a wrapper made of paper together with its contents ("a *paper* of pins"). These referential shifts involve either metonymic expansion, indicated by < in (7a–d), or metonymic reduction, indicated by >:

(7) a. 'sheet of paper': material > sheet (individual object) made of this material
b. 'essay/article': material > sheet (individual object) made of this material < homogeneous collection of such sheets > contents preserved on them
c. 'a person's personal writings': material > sheet (individual object) made of this material < homogeneous collection of such sheets > contents preserved on them
d. 'wrapper': material > sheet (individual object) made of this material > sheet made of this material used for wrapping loose contents together with these contents

An account of the actual semantic impact of metonymy-based linguistic expressions requires an understanding of the operational value of metonymic chains. Compare "Where is Abbey Road?" with "What's Abbey Road doing about this problem?" As Abbey Road is the famous place where EMI Studios were located, the question "Where is Abbey Road?" could be a question about its location or, metonymically, about where the studios are located. This metonymy is based on domain reduction. The question "What's Abbey Road doing about this problem?" involves a metonymic chain containing a second domain reduction from the studios to their staff. As is well known, the name of a salient location like a legendary street is a convenient way of affording access to the conceptual domains associated with that location.

Communicatively, the metonymic chain is effective to the extent that it is capable of compacting a large amount of conceptual material into a simple expression. The chain helps speakers to avoid excessively elaborated expressions like: "What is the staff working for Emi Studios in their buildings on Abbey Road doing about this problem?" At the same time, Abbey Road, as the starting point of the metonymic chain, highlights the emblematic aspect of the place, with all its sociocultural associations. This focus is absent from the paraphrases that spell out the various target meanings in the chain.

Non-conventionalized chains can also exhibit metonymic sequences combining domain expansion and reduction. Compare "I am reading Shakespeare" with "You can find Shakespeare in the upper shelves." By means of a domain reduction from everything we know about Shakespeare to his works, his name comes to stand for his literary production in the former example. In the latter, there is an additional domain expansion from Shakespeare's literary works to the books containing them:

(8) 'printed edition of Shakespeare's works': author of literary works > author's literary works < medium of presentation of author's literary works

Sometimes a metonymic chain needs metaphoric support to be completed. This contrasts with metaphtonymy, which requires the metonymic development of either the source or the target domain of a metaphor. By contrast, the metaphoric support of a metonymic chain simply adds one more step to the chain. For illustration, consider the use of the zero-derived verb "head" in "She heads this administrative unit." Kövecses and Radden (1998: 55) have argued that zero derivation is a grammatical manifestation of metonymic shifts (9):

(9) "to *porch* the paper" (DESTINATION FOR MOTION), "to *summer* in Paris" (TIME PERIOD FOR ACTION), "to *blanket* the bed" (OBJECT FOR ACTION), "to *shampoo* one's hair" (INSTRUMENT FOR ACTION)

It is not possible to account for the meaning implications of zero derivation without investigating its conceptual motivations. The verb "to head" derives from the noun "head" and has several meanings. Two common ones pertinent to this discussion are 'go toward' ("We are heading north") and 'be at the front' ("to head the field"). However, these do not stem directly from the central meaning of the noun "head" as a body part, but from its extended meanings, which are grounded in experience. When people run, the head points forward. It is also the body part to first reach a goal in quick forward motion. The head is thus associated in our minds both with forward motion and with front position ("at the head": 'at the front'), creating the chains given in (10a, b):

(10) a. 'to go toward': head as upper part of the body, oriented to the front < a person's manner of forward movement toward a destination, including a forward-oriented head < movement toward a destination
b. 'to be at the front': head as upper part of the body, oriented to the front < front position
c. 'to lead': head as upper part of the body, oriented to the front < front position < person that takes the front position < person that takes a front position in order to lead others <=> person that takes a leading role independent of relative location in space < action of taking the leading role

The chain in (10c) makes explicit that this front position can, in turn, stand for the person taking it. Since people at the front are usually leading people, this last metonymy can become the source domain of a correlation metaphor where a person takes a leading role whether actually at the physical front or not (indicated by the double arrow). From this extended meaning, the verb "head" in the sense of 'to lead' is obtained.

Metaphoric Chains Metaphors can combine in chains where the target of one metaphor becomes the source of another (Ruiz de Mendoza & Galera 2014). Polysemy is again a useful source of insight. Let us take the English phrasal (-prepositional) verb "break off (from)." Based on the meanings of "break" ('divide into pieces') and "off" (image-schematic 'separation'), it is used to convey total, often abrupt, separation of one part from the whole ("He broke off a large piece of clay," "The iceberg broke off from the glacier"). In addition, there are at least two different figurative uses (11a, b).

(11) a. She just broke off from an emotionally draining relationship.
b. A number of dissenting groups broke off from the main Church.

(11a) is grounded in a correlation metaphor conceiving of human relationships in terms of physical bonds between people (SOCIAL BONDS ARE PHYSICAL CONNECTIONS), which is coherent with the spatial-distance metaphor INTIMACY IS CLOSENESS: People who feel affection for each other tend to be literally in touch, and hence also physically close. Discontinuing a relationship can thus be treated metaphorically as separation resulting from physical fragmentation. (11b) requires a particular construal of source-domain material in which a group of individuals is conceived of as a whole (through the MASS-COUNT image-schema transformation), endowed with PART–WHOLE structure. In "A branch of his men broke off from the main group and traveled north," the physical separation of some members from the group is seen as a physical fragmentation and subsequent removal of one of the parts from the whole. The target domain of physical separation can then act as the source domain for an additional metaphoric mapping, because of another correlation in experience, namely, physical separation as a frequent effect of social dissent, motivating DISSENT IS PHYSICAL SEPARATION. The metaphoric chain resulting from this elaboration of the initial metaphor is presented in (12).

(12) separation of part of an object from the whole object (source) <=> physical separation of part of a group of people from the whole group (target/source) <=> institutional separation of a group of people from the whole group due to dissent

Metaphoric Amalgams Metaphoric amalgams are non-chained combinations of primary metaphors that are integrated into a single conceptual package (Ruiz de Mendoza & Galera 2014). As such they are at the bottom of what is called "complex metaphor" in Primary Metaphor Theory (e.g. Grady 2005b). Here, the focus is now how amalgams are grounded in the integration and correlation of cognitive operations.

Ruiz de Mendoza and Galera (2004) distinguish between "single-source" and "double-source" metaphoric amalgams. Single-source amalgams are characterized by the incorporation of a freestanding metaphor into the source–target layout of another freestanding metaphor. In this process source domains are built into source domains and target domains into target domains. This can explain how a metaphorical expression like "My boss is a pig" can be used to refer to a person's immoral and abusive behavior:[3]

Pigs are often seen as foul-smelling, filthy animals that can cause disgust. Unless the subject-referent is literally dirty, however, mapping this view of pigs onto corresponding features in the speaker's boss does not yield that

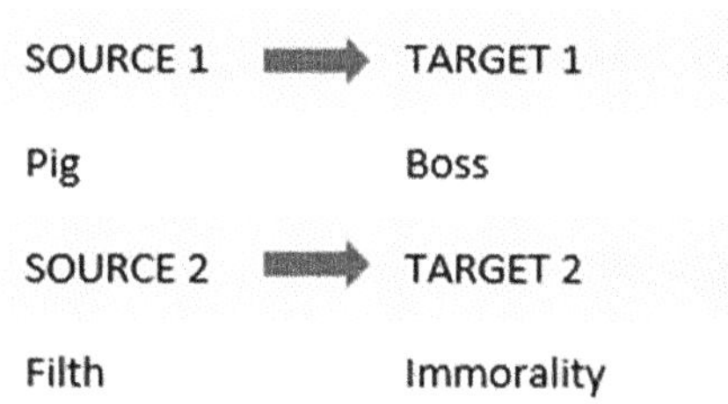

Figure 8.2 Single-source amalgam for "My boss is a pig"

interpretation. The conventionalized interpretation in the social domain refers to the improper use of authority or power. Since pigs are not immoral or abusive, the question is what cues for the activation of this interpretation or, in the terms of Blending Theory, for the novel properties emerging in the blended conceptualization. Primary Metaphor Theory (Grady 2005b) suggests that primary metaphors support complex ones by acting as domain connectors. In the example, these are the conversely related primary metaphors MORALITY IS CLEANLINESS/IMMORALITY IS FILTH ("He has a *clean/filthy* heart"), which arise from such experiential correlations as the following: Clean environments (including clean food and water) preserve our health and well-being, while dirty environments (and rotten food) relate to ill health and discomfort (cf. also Lakoff 2008b). The incorporation of IMMORALITY IS FILTH into the pig-boss metaphor is licensed by the existence of parallel cause–effect relationships between the metaphoric source and target: Abusive behavior can be emotionally (and even physically) revolting as much as pig's filth can be physically revolting. Furthermore, to the extent that experiential correlations are "compressed" into a unique property in a blended conceptualization (Grady 2005b), the effects of a pig's revolting physical appearance become practically indistinguishable from the effects of an abusive person's repulsive behavior (see Figure 8.2).

Double-source amalgams, in contrast, work by mapping two compatible source domains onto one single target domain in a complementary fashion. For example, the sentence "Mary slapped some common sense into her son" conveys the idea that, by slapping him, Mary managed to have him make an adequate judgment. "Common sense" in the target is simultaneously seen as the object of the caused motion and the resulting possession of Mary's son's. Figure 8.3 spells out how the complementary primary metaphors (CAUSED) CHANGE IS (CAUSED) MOTION and DEVELOPING A (NEW) PROPERTY IS ACQUIRING AN OBJECT are integrated:

SOURCE 1	TARGET	SOURCE 2
Motion caused by physical impact	Change motivated by psychological impact	Changing possession
Causer of motion	Causer of psychological change	Initial possessor of object
Causing motion	Causing psychological change	Transferring possession
Destination of motion (seen as a container)	Psychologically affected entity	New possessor of an object
Moving object	New psychological property	Possessed object
Reaching destination	Developing psychological change	Gaining possession of an object
Manner of causing motion	Manner of causing psychological change ('slapping')	Manner of transferring possession

Figure 8.3 Double-source amalgam for "Slap some common sense into someone"

Unlike single-source amalgams, this amalgamation pattern does not require any special licensing factor because the two source domains are intrinsically complementary with respect to the requirements of the target. In the example, the target demands a source-domain configuration that deals with two aspects of psychological change, namely, its causation and its lasting effect. Caused motion covers the first aspect while gaining possession covers the second.

Amalgams vs. *Blends* The two amalgamation processes postulated are not identical with "single-scope/double-scope" blends, as postulated in Blending Theory (Fauconnier & Turner 2002). In single-scope blends, two input spaces (partially activated knowledge constructs) are combined by adapting the structure of one to that of the other. A person's long nose could be called a "trunk," for example, because the (topology of) the relation between a nose and human head is preserved in that between a trunk and an elephant's head so that the length of the nose can be assessed in terms of that of a trunk.

In double-scope blends, the integration of structure borrows selected elements from the two input spaces (i.e. activated knowledge frames) with the blend producing its own structure. The invention of snowboarding discussed above as an instance of frame complexes requires double-scope blending. The same holds for the linguistic metaphor "My surgeon is a butcher," where the butchery and surgery frames contain incompatible means–ends relations. In the domain of butchery, the goal is to kill the animal and prepare the flesh as food. In the domain of surgery, the goal is to heal the patient. The butchery and surgery frames, however, also share conceptual structure (namely, that a person uses a sharp instrument to cut flesh). This shared structure is traced in a "generic" space and projected into the "blended" space. There, the means of butchery are combined with the ends and roles in the surgery frame yielding a blended conceptualization where a surgeon goes about operating on a living patient the way a butcher would go about cutting the meat of a dead animal. The incongruity between the butcher's means and the surgeon's ends leads to the central inference that the surgeon is incompetent. This inference becomes an "emergent" property that cannot be captured as precisely in a traditional source–target analysis (Grady et al. 1999).

Amalgams are not themselves blends, since they work directly on what Fauconnier and Turner call the "input spaces" (e.g. the metaphoric source and target), preparing them for the correlation- or resemblance-based metaphoric operation. If we accept the blending account of metaphor (for criticism and alternative analyses, see Ruiz de Mendoza & Díez 2002), amalgams are prior to the blending of input spaces. Moreover, metaphoric amalgams always involve primary metaphor, even in cases in which a resemblance operation is at work, as in the pig example analyzed above. Two resemblance-based metaphors cannot be integrated into one single construct the way correlation-based metaphors can, since resemblance operations do not lead to conceptual conflation but keep the domains to be compared distinctly separate. For example, saying that a person is the "black sheep" of his family marks that person as the odd one out, in the same way as a black sheep relates to the rest of a white herd. Similarly, the interpretation of "My boss is a pig" depicting the person as dirty involves only a resemblance metaphor based on two discrete domains (people and pigs). By contrast, the interpretation in which we regard the boss as behaving abusively requires an amalgam that builds a primary metaphor into a resemblance metaphor.

In sum, the present work extends existing work about the supporting role of correlation metaphors in resemblance metaphors by offering a systematic discussion of the different ways in which primary metaphors may do so and by locating the resulting configurations within a larger survey of patterns of "figurativity."

Hyperbole through Metaphor/Simile Researchers have long noted that metaphor and simile can be used to convey hyperbolic meaning. Claridge (2011: 41) distinguishes between "basic" and "metaphorical" hyperbole and characterizes the former as "domain-preserving," i.e. as making use of a single domain ("I'm freezing": 'very cold'). Metaphorical hyperbole involves switching domains. In "He was petrified" ('paralyzed with terror'), the relevant domains are those of terror and petrification (or fossilization of organic matter).

Against Claridge (2011), it is argued here that just switching domains does not suffice and that the manifold meaning effects of hyperbolic expressions cannot be accounted for without an explanation of hyperbole in terms of a cross-domain mapping. In other words, achieving hyperbolic meaning through metaphor requires reasoning about the target in terms of the source. In the example above, petrification maps onto fear-induced paralysis, which, as a conspicuous symptom of fear, is metonymic for it. The metaphor is thus used as a way to communicate the exacerbated nature of the fear by exaggerating its most noticeable symptom beyond proportion (when comparing it to a corresponding feature in the target).

By treating this latter aspect as the hallmark of so-called hyperbolic metaphor, this proposal clearly motivates the frequent use of metaphor to convey hyperbolic meaning. Along these lines, consider the hyperbolic effects in the sentence "You're the best dancer in the world." Among other attributes, an excellent dancer combines supple, well-coordinated movements with grace and elegance of expression. Literally, the skills of the "best" dancer are entirely unsurpassed, and thus sure to produce the deepest feelings of reverence, respect, and wonder in the audience. In the hyperbolic use, the cause–effect relationship between the addressee's real dancing skills and the feelings they produce in the speaker are mapped onto a corresponding imaginary situation in which the addressee is the best dancer in the world. In this way, an imaginary situation is used to reason about a real situation.

Many resemblance metaphors are inherently hyperbolic, namely, when the source is used to emphasize a gradable attribute in the target domain. The social-relations interpretation of the BOSS-AS-PIG metaphor discussed above can contain a hyperbolic ingredient in so far as the default assumption is that the aversion caused by an abusive boss is (at least physically) less intense than the repulsiveness caused by a pig's filth. Uses of the pig metaphor that highlight actual dirtiness bring out even more clearly a source–target discrepancy concerning the degree to which this attribute holds.

Strengthened Irony through Hyperbole Irony has been studied from many different perspectives. Within inferential pragmatics, Attardo (2000) has explained irony in terms of "relevant inappropriateness," i.e. as the flouting of one or more Gricean maxims, which requires reinterpretation in compliance with the Cooperative Principle. Pretense Theory (Clark & Garrig 1984) contends that irony results from the speaker pretending to perform a given speech act. Relevance theorists (Wilson & Sperber 2012) base their account on the notion of "echo," the repetition of someone's previous words or their attributed thoughts or beliefs.

All of these theories recognize a mismatch between what is said and the real situation. But explanations of how this mismatch is created and solved differ.

The most integrative approach is perhaps the relevance-theoretic account, which recognizes the existence of a clash and an echo, while highlighting the speaker's (usually skeptical) attitude to the echoed thought. In this view, pretense can arise from the speaker "echoing" a previous thought from which he dissociates him-/herself. A skeptical son, for instance, who does not believe that his father will attend his graduation ceremony may ironically repeat his father's false promise, "Son, I will be there."

As these inferential accounts focus on the communicative aspects of irony, a complementary approach should deal with its cognitive aspects. Under the assumption that hearers play expected interpretive roles which speakers can figure out beforehand, our discussion of the cognitive operations at work in figurative language has so far only taken into account the speaker's perspective.

To consider the hearer's, imagine again the pig metaphor (combining PEOPLE ARE PIGS and IMMORALITY IS FILTH) used in a context where a young lady is telling a friend about a male police officer who has harassed her ("He is a real pig!"). To her addressee, the word "pig" cues for the same metaphorical combination. Based on textual cues, the addressee constructs a meaning or mental representation akin to the speaker's. The case of irony is different, since the speaker's mental representation needs to take into account not only what the speaker him-/herself believes is the case with respect to a given situation but also what s/he thinks others believe to be the case. The speaker's utterance echoes such attributed beliefs, which are often the addressee's. In doing so, the addressee's perspective on the situation in question is taken into account in a very special way: The addressee's echoed assumptions and the speaker's own assumptions clash. The speaker, when making an ironic remark, hopes that the hearer may notice the clash and become more skeptical about his own assumptions. A cognitive account of irony, therefore, must proceed along the following lines: First, the speaker builds two incompatible scenarios. One echoes someone's thoughts, which are metonymically developed into a richer representation framing the echoed material. This representation contains an attitudinal element that is highlighted in a second metonymic shift. The other scenario is based on the speaker's observation. Its conceptual structure is incompatible with corresponding structure in the first scenario, including a highlighted attitudinal element that cancels out the one in the first scenario. This cognitive activity takes the form of a cross-domain metonymic chain whose second target is realized in the second scenario. Second, and following regular conceptual-integration principles, the two scenarios combine into one, which contains the speaker's knowledge of the situation and his dissociation from the hearer's attributed beliefs. This structure clashes with a corresponding structure built on the basis of what the speaker believes the hearer has in mind (which was previously echoed). If the clash becomes manifest to the hearer, s/he may accept the speaker's beliefs and attitude as her/his own.

Figure 8.4 below applies this proposal to the ironic use and interpretation of "Yeah, right, Mary is an angel!" The analysis shows how metaphorical hyperbole enhances irony. Metaphor serves to construct a hyperbole, which in turn is used to intensify the clash between the speaker's integrated scenario and what others believe or have said about it.

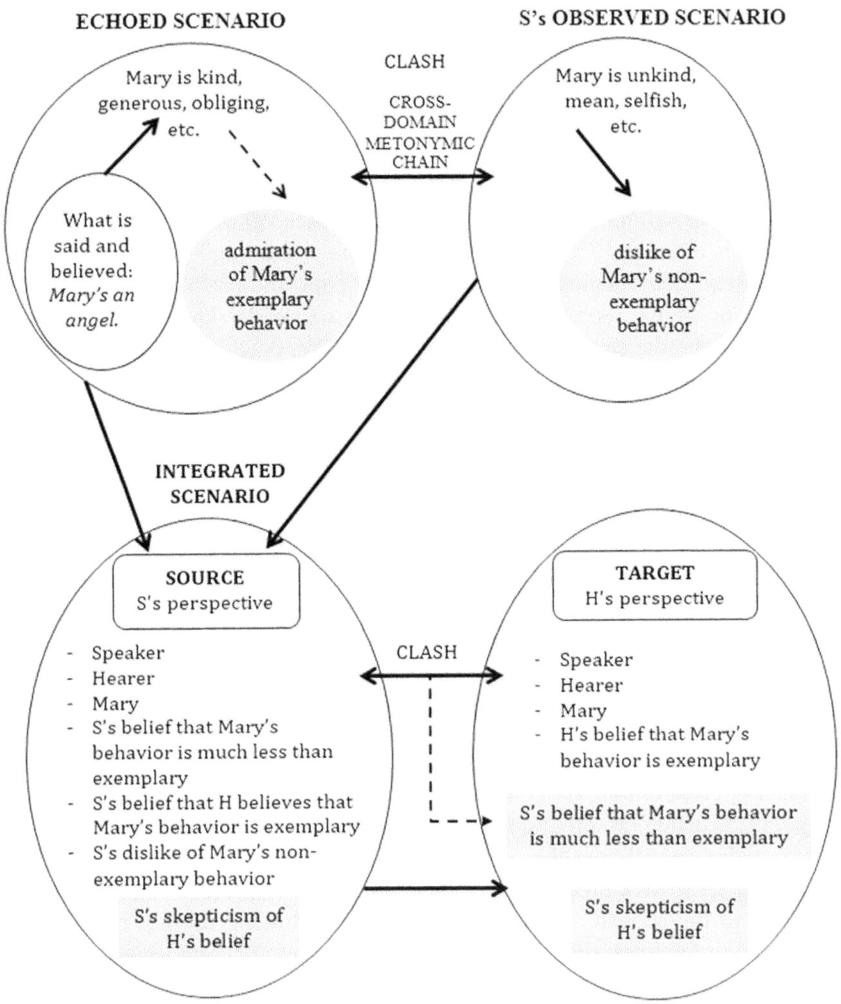

Figure 8.4 Creation of irony in "Mary is an angel"

5 Conclusion

The present chapter has integrated into a single account analytical proposals on several major figures of thought, such as metaphor, metonymy, simile, hyperbole, and irony. By examining the activity of basic cognitive operations on cognitive models, it has identified distinct interaction patterns for each of those figures and shown how they give rise to conceptual complexes of various kinds. The study of basic cognitive processes has made possible an improved understanding of complexity in its many manifestations.

Notes and Acknowledgments

* The research for this chapter has been financed by the Spanish Ministry of Economy and Competitiveness, grant no. FFI2013-43593-P. I would like to thank Professors Klaus-Uwe Panther and Beate Hampe for their valuable comments on the first version of this chapter. I would also like to express my appreciation to the editor for her meticulous editorial work. All remaining flaws are, of course, my own responsibility.

1 Blending Theory has dealt with literal and figurative uses of the "X is the Y of Z" configuration (Fauconnier & Turner 2002: 142). In the blending account, X ("Pinker") and Y ("Einstein") are counterpart elements. An implicit element ('theoretical physics') needs to be identified as the counterpart of Z ("psycholinguistics") to create a blend modeling X's role in Z in analogy to Y's role in physics.

2 The idiom is already found in, e.g., Chaucer (*Knight's Tale*: "This Palamon gan nit his brows tweye") and Shakespeare (e.g. *Henry the Sixth*, Part 2: Act 3, scene 1).

3 On a traditional cognitivist account (Lakoff & Turner 1989), animal metaphors are based on attributing human features to animals and then reattributing these features back to specific humans. This is only part of a more complex picture.

9 On the Role of Embodied Cognition in the Understanding and Use of Metonymy

*Jeannette Littlemore**

Chapter Preview

The majority of the chapters in this book focus on the symbiotic relationship between embodied cognition and metaphor. In contrast, this chapter focuses on the relationship between embodied cognition and *metonymy*. It argues that metonymy is also embodied, but in a different way, and that the social, environmental, dynamic, and developmental aspects of embodied cognition can be expected to play an important role in shaping metonymic meaning. It is suggested that the relative transparency of the role played by embodied cognition in metonymy creation is influenced by the presence of movement and emotion, with increases in the amount of movement and emotion leading to increases in the transparency of embodied cognition. Following Deignan et al. (2013), it is also suggested that the transparency of the role played by embodied cognition is affected by features of the genre (communicative purpose, staging, and discourse community membership) and the register (field, tenor, and mode).

1 Introduction

A key claim in the embodied cognition hypothesis is that "people's subjective, felt experience of their bodies in action provides part of the fundamental grounding for language and thought" (Gibbs 2003: 2). As other chapters in this book show, it follows from this that some metaphorical expressions will evoke actual bodily responses that correspond to the more "basic" or "literal" senses of those expressions. Considerable empirical support has been found for this proposition, with numerous neuroscientific experiments showing that metaphor comprehension does indeed often have a sensorimotor basis, particularly for those metaphors that have sensory source domains (Feldman & Naranayan 2004; Gibbs 2014b). For example, in

(1), taken from the British National Corpus (BNC), the word "grasp" is used metaphorically to mean 'understand':

(1) Swann displayed a much firmer *grasp* of the significance of socio-economic circumstances (BNC: FAY)

Studies have demonstrated that when people hear metaphorical uses of words such as this, sensory-motor responses are triggered that correspond to those that would be triggered when hearing them used in their more literal or basic senses. For example, it has been shown that people comprehend metaphorical phrases, like "grasp the concept," more quickly when they first make, or imagine making, a relevant bodily action, such as a grasping motion (Wilson & Gibbs 2007). As other chapters in this volume show, expressions such as this rely on correlational, primary metaphors which stem from an initial conflation of a perceptually defined concept and a subjective response to it, which later becomes dissociated (Grady 1997a; Grady & Ascoli, *this volume*).

However, there have, to date, been no such empirical investigations into the embodied nature of *metonymy*. Whereas metaphor is often defined as involving some sort of similarity or correlation between the source and target domain, metonymy involves a relationship of contiguity, or in cognitive linguistic terms, it provides mental access to another part of the same domain – or "idealized cognitive model" (ICM) (Lakoff 1987) – rather than evoking a different domain or ICM. It has been shown that primary metaphors have a metonymic basis, insofar as they begin life as metonymic extensions from bodily experiences, which are then projected onto abstract domains (Kövecses 2013). There is also work in gesture studies showing that gestural realizations of primary metaphors have a metonymic basis (Mittelberg & Waugh 2009). In these cases, one would expect metonymy to be embodied to some extent, by virtue of its association with embodied primary metaphor. However, no studies of the type described above have been conducted on metonymy when it stands alone, independent of metaphor. The principal reason for this is that metonymy does not relate concrete to abstract concepts in such a clear-cut way as metaphor and therefore does not lend itself well to this kind of experimentation. We can see this in the following examples of metonymy from the BNC:

(2)
a. *Dickens* is full of such characters (BNC: A06)
b. you could *boil your vegetables* in the saucepan and *boil the kettle* at the same time (BNC: D8Y)
c. when *Germany* defeated *France* and caused lasting resentment (BNC: CLX)

In (2a), "Dickens" metonymically represents 'stories written by Dickens,' the word "boil" in (2b) refers to the water containing the vegetables and the water in the kettle, respectively, and in (2c) "Germany" and "France" refer to the German and French armies. Evidence from eye-tracking studies has shown that when faced with metonyms such as these, participants develop an underspecified, schematic representation of the word's meaning and then home in on the appropriate sense (literal or metonymic) once sufficient contextual cues have been provided (Frisson & Pickering 1999). It is therefore not really relevant to ask whether any full-blown literal meaning of the word is activated, and then to compare this with its metonymic sense – the two senses, or uses, are too close together in the first place. With metonymy, there are different questions to be asked when it comes to the role of embodied cognition.

In order to explore the role played by embodied cognition in the processing of metonymy, it is necessary to draw on an extended definition of embodied cognition which incorporates an understanding of the fact that human cognition is not confined to the individual. Rather, it is shaped by one's physical and social environment as well as one's personal and social history. It is thus environmentally, socially, and temporally "distributed" (e.g. Clark & Chalmers 1998; Semin & Cacioppo 2008; Zhang & Patel 2006; Jensen, *this volume*). The notion of distributed embodied cognition emphasizes the fact that embodied cognition takes place in a world populated by other people and things, and that it changes over time. It has the following three dimensions:

(i) *Environmental embodied cognition* emphasizes the coordination between internal embodied cognition and the physical environment.
(ii) *Social embodied cognition* emphasizes the distribution of embodied cognitive processes across the members of a social group.
(iii) *Dynamic/developmental embodied cognition* emphasizes the ways in which current cognitive processes are affected by earlier processes, and change over time.

In sections 2, 3 and 4 of this chapter, I look at how each of these features of distributed embodied cognition is involved in the processing and production of metonymy. In section 5, I discuss ways in which contextual features, such as genre and register, may affect the salience of embodied cognition within metonymy.

2 Metonymy and Environmental Embodied Cognition

Environmental embodied cognition emphasizes the relationship between internal embodied cognition and the physical environment. It takes as its starting point the fact that we understand things in terms of what they mean to us and how we can best make use of them or interact with them (Glenberg 1999). In this section, I explore four aspects of environmental embodied cognition that have a direct bearing on the processing of metonymy. These are: affordances, perceptual salience, part–whole processing, and cognitive off-loading.

2.1 *Affordances*

A number of scholars have pointed out that when we encounter an object, one of our first (automatic) responses is to think about what that object means to us and what we can use it for. In other words, we think about what "affordances" the object might offer us in terms of its purpose and function (Gibson 1979; Glenberg & Robertson 2000). Thus, if we see a chair we perceive of it first and foremost as something that we can sit on; if we see a glass, we understand it first and foremost as something that we can put liquid in and drink from. This view of the physical world affects the way in which we use metonymy and the direction of the metonymy; the responses to the objects just described involve OBJECT FOR ACTION and CONTAINER FOR CONTAINED metonymic relationships (e.g. Radden & Kövecses 1999). These relationships license linguistic metonyms, such as "would you like a glass?" (meaning 'would you like a glass of wine?'). Affordances also license discourse-community specific metonyms, such as the utterance "you've got a foot there, out to the left," which might be said by one climber to another to mean that there is a hold nearby where they can put their foot. Incidentally, the word "hold" in this explanation is also metonymic, as it involves an ACTION FOR OBJECT relationship, which reflects a human affordance of the object in question.[1]

There is some evidence to suggest that affordances such as these have a neuro-physiological basis in that they generate corresponding synaptic connections in the brain (Bierwiaczonek 2013). In other words, certain clusters of neurons are specifically designed to relate the physical properties of objects to the most suitable cognitive motor programs that will allow us to interact with them manually in a purposeful way (see also Cuccio, *this volume*). Thus, when we see a teapot, or even a picture of a teapot, neuro-synaptic connections are activated so that we automatically prepare to take hold of the handle and pour the tea. Strong synaptic connections develop between the sight of the teapot and the action of making tea. It therefore follows that metonymic relationships which involve a link between PERCEPTION AND ANTICIPATED CORRESPONDING ACTION have a clear neurological substrate.

Related studies have shown that if one concept is used to refer to another on a regular enough basis, a synaptic link will form between those two concepts, and this synaptic link will become stronger as the association between the two concepts becomes more conventionalized. For example, fMRI studies have shown that words denoting activities, such as "smile," "hit," or "kick," activate the face, arm, and leg regions in the motor and pre-motor cortex (Hauk et al. 2004). Moreover, as infants, we develop powerful cause–effect relationships, which we then use to infer a cause from an effect and vice versa. For example, Michotte (1963) showed that if people see one object making contact with a second object and the second object then starts to move after a short delay, then they assume that the movement of the second object is the direct result of its contact with the first object, even if this is not the case. Similarly, when we hear a sound related to a particular action, the pre-motor cortex associated with that action begins to fire (Kohler et al. 2002). These synaptic relationships are likely to underlie many RESULT FOR ACTION or CAUSATION metonyms (such as "the car screeched to a halt"). There is even evidence to suggest that these synaptic connections exhibit some of the characteristics of embodied cognition that were described in the introduction; the activation of a social stereotype has been shown to cause the unintended mimicry of behavior that is strongly associated with the stereotyped group. For example, if people are asked to think about old people, they are more likely to start to walk more slowly (Bargh et al. 1996). This finding suggests that some of the metonymic shorthand that underlies social stereotyping (here SALIENT FEATURE FOR CATEGORY) is embodied, in that it is both perceptual and conceptual.

2.2 *Perceptual Salience*

A second aspect of environmental embodied cognition that is involved in metonymy creation is perceptual salience. When we survey our environment, some features will inevitably stand out more than others. This can be because of their distinct physical features (for example, if they are brightly colored, well delineated, or moveable) or because they have particular relevance to us (for example, for a human viewer, in most situations, other humans are more likely to stand out than animals or inanimate objects). The fact that we are more prone to notice things that are of immediate relevance to us, and that this drives the way we process information, is likely to play an important role in the relationship between embodied cognition and metonymy. The phenomenon of perceptual salience explains why, for example, the metonym "being at the wheel" is readily understood by speakers of English to mean 'driving a vehicle' (Littlemore 2015), though the exact nature of the vehicle that is evoked (be it a car, a lorry, a tractor, or even a boat) will depend on both the context and the hearer's previous experience with different sorts of vehicles (Giora 1997).

Perceptual salience also explains, for example, the choice of the words "summer" and "winter" rather than "spring" and "autumn" to stand metonymically for the idea of an event occurring year round in the following example:

(3) She always has a log fire in the hearth, *summer and winter* (BNC: A61)

Here, summer and winter are more perceptually salient in that they are respectively hotter and colder than spring and autumn, which is presumably why they are chosen as metonymic vehicles (Panther & Thornburg 2012: 465). This phenomenon, in which two or three words stand for a larger entity, is referred to as "merism" and is typical of ancient Hebrew poetry (Watson 1986: 321).[2] Shi-xiong Wu has found this to be widespread in Chinese, where, for example, the term "have young, have old, have tall, have short" means 'people of different ages and heights.' Similarly, "have long, have short" means 'all lengths' and "have fat have thin" means 'people of all sizes.' These expressions all focus on the people or objects that would be the most salient in a crowd or in a collection of items because they are the most extreme instantiations. These extreme instantiations stand for the entire scale. There are also more abstract examples of this phenomenon in Chinese: "good, bad" is used to refer to 'quality' and "cold, hot" refers to 'temperature.'[3] The semantic interpretation of such expressions can be attributed to metonymic inferences triggered by the co-occurring antonym pairs.

2.3 *Part–Whole Processing*

A third aspect of environmental embodied cognition, which has been shown to play a key role in metonymy creation, is part–whole processing. In life, we rarely see the whole of an object in a single viewing: We usually see it only from a particular angle and have to use our world knowledge to make assumptions about what the rest of the object will look like. As humans, we are very good at doing this. Gestalt psychologists have used a number of studies, both linguistic and non-linguistic, to show that when pieces of information are missing from a pattern, people will complete the pattern for themselves, sometimes not even noticing that there are pieces missing. People need to see only parts of a shape such as a square or circle to recognize the whole shape intended. In a study designed to demonstrate the power of part–whole processing, Cutting and colleagues (1978) found that when people are taken into a dark room and asked to observe the movements of someone dressed in black, but with lights attached to various points of their body, they can tell what the person is doing, their gender, and (if they know them) who the person is simply by watching the movements of the lights. This finding reflects the strength of the PART–WHOLE schema in humans. We are able to perceive a whole object, scene, or event, when we have only been shown parts, and we are able to use the whole object, scene, or event to infer the presence of parts that were not even there. This skill is necessary for us to understand and interact with our environment, as it is virtually impossible to view all aspects of an object, scene, or event at the same time. These connections underlie two of the most basic metonymic relationships: the PART FOR WHOLE relationship and the WHOLE FOR PART relationship. These two relationships have been found to account for a substantial number of the metonyms discussed in the literature (Radden & Kövecses 1999) and, according to some accounts, are thought to explain all cases of metonymy (Ruiz de Mendoza & Diez 2002). There is clearly a strong relationship between the ability to complete patterns ("gestalts") and the ability to relate the functional parts of a complex entity to the entity itself, as both of these involve the ability to perceive and process part–whole relationships.

I would like to end this section with an example of metonymy that displays the three aspects of environmental embodied cognition discussed thus far. In British Sign Language (BSL), the sign for 'computer' involves both hands being held next to each other in front of the body with palms facing down, with fingers wriggling up and down. This sign evokes the act of typing, which is perceptually the most salient act associated with a computer, and foregrounds what a human actually does with a computer, thus drawing attention to one of its main human affordances. There is also PART FOR WHOLE processing involved as typing is only one of the many things that one might associate with working on a computer. Others might include turning on the computer, clicking on the mouse button, or looking at the screen.

2.4. *Cognitive Off-Loading*

An important consequence of the environmental nature of embodied cognition is that it facilitates the off-loading of cognition onto physical or environmental artifacts. A good example of the role played by cognitive off-loading in metonymy can be found in a study by Deignan and colleagues (2013) of the language and gesture employed by a lecturer in international development. In this study, the lecturer was explaining management models to two interlocutors, one of whom was a colleague (and therefore a member of the same professional discourse community) while the other one was not. One of the models that she was explaining to the interlocutors was the Competing Values Framework. This model is used to describe different types of organizations in terms of how centralized or decentralized they are, and how inward or outward-focused they are. The lecturer illustrated this framework by means of a diagram which she drew on a flip chart before the arrival of the interlocutors. In this diagram, she drew the two variables sitting along two intersecting axes. Each of the four resulting quadrants represented a particular type of organization, namely: 'bureaucracy,' 'human relations,' 'open systems,' and 'goal-oriented.' Organizations that were 'open' and 'outward-looking' sat toward the top and the right of the diagram, whereas centralized and inward-looking organizations sat toward the bottom left.

In both the exchanges, the lecturer described the framework by referring specifically to previous bosses in her department, with each boss metonymically representing one of the four styles of management. In both exchanges, the lecturer metonymically "off-loaded" the management styles onto the diagram that she had drawn on the flip chart. She used the diagram metonymically to locate the bosses according to their management styles, pointing to various parts of the diagram, explaining to her interlocutor that the various heads of department were "definitely over here," "over to this side," "probably toward the left," or remarking that "we made loads of money when that boss was in charge."

3 Metonymy and the Social Nature of Embodied Cognition

Social embodied cognition, which involves the distribution of embodied cognitive processes across the members of a social group, is an important concept, as bodily experiences are interpreted very differently according to the sociocultural meaning resources that are available to us (El Refaie 2014). These meaning resources provide the framework within which embodied experience is interpreted.

There are a number of socially sanctioned ways of interpreting embodied metonymy, which affect what we do with our own bodies. One important factor is gender. In all languages, there are strong social conventions concerning what males and females are *supposed* to do with their bodies, and what these actions *mean*. In her study of the role played by body language in Dickens' novels, Mahlberg (2013: 112–113) shows how the expression "standing with his back to the fire" is often used to portray male characters in powerful positions. As Mahlberg points out, the fact that the fireplace is a prominent part of the room means that standing with one's back to it puts these men in a prominent and powerful position. They are also, rather selfishly, absorbing all the warmth from the fire. Women, in contrast, are almost never portrayed as standing with their backs to the fire, but they are occasionally portrayed as *sitting* with their backs to the fire. There is only one instance in Dickens of a woman standing with her back to the fire, and this is Mrs. Pipchin, in the novel *Dombey and Son*,[4] who runs a strict children's boarding house, which she rules with a rod of iron. She is a widow and a "marvellous, ill-favoured, ill-conditioned old lady" (ex 4):

(4) [. . .] and Mrs Pipchin, *with her back to the fire*, stood, reviewing the newcomers, like an old soldier.

Mahlberg points out that by presenting Mrs. Pipchin in a male pose, Dickens is emphasizing the fact that she is in charge, without a man in her life. These examples demonstrate the important role played by social embodied cognition in metonymy. "Having one's back to the fire" works as an embodied metonym for certain types of behavior and characteristics, but the precise meanings that are intended differ considerably according to gender, and according to whether the person is standing or sitting, and whether these meanings are socially sanctioned.

In another example, Mahlberg (2013: 102) compares occurrences of "putting a hand on one's shoulder" in the Dickens novel *Nicholas Nickleby*. When this action is carried out by male characters, it serves as metonymic shorthand for friendship, emphasis, or control. In the one case where this act is carried out by a female character, it is used in the literal sense and the character (Mrs. Snevellicci) is holding onto someone for physical support (ex 5).[5] Again, there is evidence of embodied cognition in both cases, but the precise metonymic meanings that apply to each gender are determined by social conventions.

(5) She actually *laid her hand upon the shoulder* of the manageress.

Another place where we can see the impact of socially constructed body roles on metonymic thinking is in the area of "enclothed cognition," the idea that one's body schema can be extended to the clothes that one wears.[6] For example, Adam and Galinsky (2012) conducted a study in which they had participants complete an experimental task wearing a white lab coat. Half of the participants were told that it was a doctor's coat and half were told that it was a painter's coat. There are metonymic connections here between the coats and the types of people who wear them. The participants who were told that they were wearing a doctor's coat performed the task with considerably more attentiveness than those who were told that they were wearing a painter's coat. In a previous study these researchers had found that participants who had been asked to wear a lab coat outperformed those who were not asked to wear a lab coat. Their findings suggest that the behavior of the participants was affected by the symbolic meaning of the coat, as well as by the physical experience of wearing it.

Social embodied cognition also operates in metonymic entailments of conceptual metaphors. We can see an example of this in Musolff's comparison of the way in which the BODY POLITIC metaphor is exploited in English and Chinese.[7] He found that English speakers conceptualize the political system as a body, following a hierarchical approach. In contrast to this, the Chinese also have the political system as a body, but the different cities are viewed as different parts of the body through a process of metonymic extension. For example, he found that Chinese participants in his study referred to Guangzhou as "the guts" and "the feet" ("where the peasants are perpetually bound to the soil"); Tianjin as "the hands" ("because there is manufacturing"); Shenzhen as "the eyes," and Tibet as "the stomach" ("because it makes Chinese people feel uncomfortable"). Thus, we have metonymic links in the source domain of the metaphor (for more on this point, see Ruiz de Mendoza 2014, *this volume*), with the focus of the cities and their respective contributions to the Chinese economy being grafted onto the BODY POLITIC metaphor.

4 Metonymy and the Dynamic/Developmental Nature of Embodied Cognition

Embodied cognition is by no means stable, straightforward, or permanently fixed in early childhood. It is more appropriately viewed as a highly complex, dynamic, and developmental process, whose nature varies according to the specific situations in which we find ourselves, and the extent to which we are consciously aware of our bodies at any given moment. The nature of our embodied cognition is also likely to develop as we grow older. The dynamic/developmental view of embodied cognition therefore encapsulates its characteristics as both a developmental and an adaptive process. In any study of the way embodied cognition impacts on the way we use metonymy, we need to consider how it changes over time and in accordance with changing circumstances.

We can see evidence of the developmental nature of embodied cognition in the comprehension of metonymy by young foreign language learners. Piquer Piriz (2005) explored how 5-, 7-, 9-, and 11-year-old Spanish learners of English understood and reasoned about the meanings of figurative extensions of the words "head," "hand," and "mouth." She found that the children's reasoning strategies varied significantly according to their ages. Her findings for the word "head" are particularly interesting. She discovered that, in comparison with younger children (aged 5 and 7), who reasoned metaphorically, using a vertical schema, with the head at the top, the older children (aged 9 and 11) displayed a strong tendency to reason metonymically using the BODY PART FOR FUNCTION (i.e. HEAD FOR GIVING ORDERS) metonymic relationship. Whilst this metonymic reasoning was helpful in interpreting expressions that were congruent with that schema, expressions that were incongruent with the schema (for example "head of the stairs") were more likely to be misunderstood by the older children than by the younger children. This particular expression was understood correctly by 82 percent of the 7-year-olds, but only 58 percent of the 11-year-olds. Piquer Piriz found that the deployment of preferred reasoning strategies gave rise to correct and incorrect responses at all ages. These findings show that children's domain knowledge develops as they experience more bodily and psychological interactions with the world, and these interactions make some metonymic relationships more accessible. However, although the children's domain knowledge becomes more elaborate as their knowledge of the world increases, the elaborate nature of this knowledge is not always advantageous. Piquer Piriz's finding complements findings from laboratory studies (e.g. Rundblad & Annaz 2010) in that it emphasizes the complex and developmental nature of metonymic reasoning.

I would like to close this section with an example that not only displays the dynamic nature of embodied cognition in relation to metonymy but also reflects the other two characteristics of embodied cognition just discussed. In other words, the metonymic meaning in this example appears to be shaped by the environmental, social, and dynamic features of embodied cognition. In British English, the words "upstairs" and "downstairs" can be used to refer respectively to 'bosses' and 'workers.' In the Bank of English (BofE) corpus, bosses are nearly always "upstairs" and workers are nearly always "downstairs" (ex 6, taken from Deignan et al. 2013: 179):

(6) a. . . . whizz kid managers '*upstairs*' don't take any notice of experienced people.
b. Tell them *downstairs* that I have specifically requested you.
c. If the *upstairs* don't get you the *downstairs* will.

We do not know whether, in practice, managers are more likely than workers to be located upstairs rather than on the ground floor, although a simple Google search for the expression "the boss upstairs" yields three times as many hits as "the boss downstairs"; and the expression "the manager upstairs" yields twice as many hits as "the manager downstairs." The fact that usage tends to reflect what is actually the case suggests that there is a complex interaction between real social experience (including the role of the vertical axis in buildings) and the embodied metonymies drawing directly on it. In addition, a range of primary metaphors coherently map the UP/DOWN image schema onto the social hierarchy (POWER IS UP, STATUS IS UP, CONTROL IS UP), presumably reinforcing the power of the metonyms (see also *this volume*: Matlock & Winter; Ruiz de Mendoza).

This interaction is likely to be motivated by the environmental, social, and dynamic features of embodied cognition. The environmental contribution to this apparently "embodied" metonymy accounts for the relationship between the location of the individuals and who they are. However, as we have just seen, the explanation does not get us very far, because it does not account for the fact that we are more likely to refer to the bosses as "upstairs" even when, in reality, they are just as likely to be located downstairs. In order to explain this pattern, we need to appeal to the social and dynamic features of embodied cognition.

The social contribution comes from the British class system and the idea of the manor house, where the rich owners lived upstairs (possibly for reasons of security) and their servants lived downstairs. This arrangement has arguably been reinforced in the national consciousness by the popularity of British television costume dramas, such as *Upstairs Downstairs* and, more recently, *Downton Abbey*, where, week after week, viewers are exposed to this spatial and class division.[8] Programs such as these may serve to "distribute" this particular metonymy among British speakers of English, thus reinforcing our existing cultural schemas. Interestingly, these metonymic usages appear to be virtually nonexistent in American English. A search of 200 corpus lines containing the term "upstairs" in the Contemporary Corpus of American English (COCA) reveals no such uses of the term. A search of 200 corpus lines containing the term "downstairs" reveals only one instance, and, somewhat ironically, this is a reference to the British costume dramas just mentioned:

(7) The wealthy and upper-class folks of Downton Abbey and Upstairs Downstairs long ago outsourced their kitchen and scullery work to *downstairs* staff (COCA: 2011 MAG)

The dynamic contribution comes from the time lag between a time in Britain, when people really did live like this, and nowadays, where, for the most part, they do not. Deignan (2003) has shown that there is often an indirect link between figurative expressions and the culture they represent.

In this section, we have seen how the environmental, social, and dynamic features of embodied cognition shape its role in metonymy. The extent to which these different features are highlighted in metonymy is likely to depend on a number of factors, such as the context in which the metonym is used, one's reasons for using it, and the relationship between the individuals who are using it. In different contexts, one would expect to find considerable variation concerning the intensity and transparency of the role played by embodied cognition in the creation of metonymy. In some instances, the role will be clear, in others it will be harder to identify. In the following section, I explore some of these contextual factors.

5 The Influence of Genre and Register on the Transparency of Embodied Metonymy

The range of ways in which language use varies according to context is encapsulated by the notions of 'genre' and 'register.' Genre and register have a significant effect on the ways in which both metaphor and metonymy are used (Deignan et al. 2013). Deignan and colleagues propose a framework for analysis which allows for an accurate and complete description of the ways in which figurative language use is shaped by the genre and register in which it appears. They illustrate the effectiveness of this framework by applying it to a range of datasets that vary in terms of genre and register. In this section, I draw on examples from different datasets to show how the transparency of the role played by embodied cognition in metonymy is shaped by both genre and register. Although I do not conduct a detailed analysis of a single dataset using Deignan et al.'s framework, I do make use of the essential elements of the framework. That is to say, I focus on the three defining characteristics of genre and of register.

The three defining characteristics of a genre are its discourse community, its communicative purpose, and the way in which ideas are "staged" (Swales 1990). The three identifying characteristics of a register are its "field" (what is being talked about), its "tenor" (the relationship between the interlocutors), and its "mode" (whether it is written, spoken, visual, or gestural, and whether the language is ancillary or constitutive) (Halliday 1985). Although to date no studies have directly investigated the ways in which genre and register affect the transparency of the role played by embodied cognition in metonymy, a number of findings do point toward some possible patterns. In this section, I examine these findings and propose some tentative hypotheses concerning the ways in which the salience of embodied cognition within metonymy might be affected by genre and register.

5.1 Genre

Communicative Purpose Beginning with genre, an example of the way in which the embodied nature of metonymy appears to vary according to communicative purpose can be found in a study by Hodder and Houghton,[9] in which they compared the language used on Twitter by the British University and College Union (UCU) during strike periods with the language used during non-strike periods. During non-strike periods, the main communicative purposes of UCU Tweets are to create and develop a feeling of community, to relay news of what is happening in different universities across the UK, and to maintain and increase membership of the union. During strike periods, the Tweets serve more as a "call to action," in which members are exhorted to join the strike. Using corpus linguistic techniques, Hodder and Houghton found that during strike periods, there was a significant increase in the number of words that related to the human body, including action words. The majority of the words in this category were used metonymically and appeared to involve explicit references to the body, in such a way as to imply that embodied cognition is involved (ex 8).

(8) a. Want to know *just how much money our universities are sitting on*?
b. Another *big shout out* to all our pickets this morning
c. To those Vice Chancellors who say they'd like to pay their employees more, *you know where the phone is.*

The use of metonymy in all of these tweets adheres to Radden and Kövecses' (1999) "human over non-human" principle of vehicle selection, which is inspired by Langacker's (1991: 306–307) "empathy hierarchy" and places humans above physical objects in terms of their potential to attract empathy, and by extension attention. The first tweet personifies the universities, allowing them to be construed as living organisms that can physically "sit on" money, and thus involves a "metaphtonymy" (see Ruiz de Mendoza 2014, *this volume*). The second contains a CAUSE FOR EFFECT metonym in which the word "shout" is used to indicate a desire for a large number of people to hear and respond to the message being conveyed, and the third refers a hypothetical phone via an OBJECT FOR ACTION metonym; it is highly unlikely that a vice chancellor would, in person, get on the phone to the UCU. These metonyms are all emotive to some extent. What we have here is a possible indication that embodied metonymy is likely to be more prevalent in instances where there is high emotional intensity. The "physicality" in the text reflects this intensity of feeling. There are also elements of personification in these texts, which also underscore the embodied nature of metonymy.

One possible explanation for the sudden increase in the salience of embodiment in these metonyms relates to the physical relationship between metonymy and motion itself. When our bodies are actually moving, or when we are witnessing or talking about movement, the language that we use reflects that movement (El Refaie 2014). Evidence for this contention can be found in the large amount of embodied metonymy that exists in football commentary (Levin 2008). Deignan and colleagues (2013: 191–229) also analyzed figurative language use in texts produced by a group of people associated with a children's football club, comparing the language used by supporters standing on the touchline at the matches with that used in the online post-match reports. They were thus comparing two related genres with slightly different communicative purposes. They found that twice as much metonymy was used by the supporters (although the figures were low in both corpora). Much of this metonymy appears to have involved embodied cognition in the broad sense discussed in section 1. For example, they found that in the supporters' discourse the players were frequently defined metonymically by their position on the pitch, as in the following example (ex 9, cf. ibid.: 211):

(9) Matthew, you're *centre midfield*

Here the centre of the pitch is used metonymically (via a PLACE FOR PERSON relationship) to stand for the player who is supposed to be based there.

They also found that the word "ball" was often used metonymically (via an OBJECT FOR ACTION relationship) to refer to an especially good piece of play, or to a missed opportunity for good play (ex 10, cf. ibid.: 214). There were also some hyperbolic uses of metonymy (ex 11, cf. ibid.):

(10) Boys that was a *great ball*, and we're not attacking it

(11) Patrick, Patrick, Patrick, *stand on it*

In example (11), the boys are being exhorted to get *near* the ball, rather than actually "on" it. Here an extreme action metonymically represents a related, less extreme action (for further discussion of hyperbolic uses of metonymy, see Ruiz de Mendoza, *this volume*). The exaggerated feel of the utterances reflects the urgency of the situation and makes the embodied feel of the utterances even more salient. The increased salience of the embodied cognition underlying these metonyms is likely to be related both to the overall communicative purpose of the genre (to exhort the children to play well) and to the fact that it involves a need for immediate action.

Stage Evidence for the effect of the stage of the genre on the transparency of embodied cognition within metonymy can be found in Deignan et al.'s (2013: 128–164) study of an academic exchange, discussed in section 2. They found that in both of the exchanges, dense clusters of metonymy were found toward the end of the exchange, and in both cases, these clusters served a summing-up function, drawing together themes that had been covered in the earlier part of the discussion. Similar findings have been made for metaphor by researchers looking at academic lectures (Corts & Pollio 1999; Low et al. 2008), reconciliation talk (Cameron 2007b), and religious sermons (Corts & Meyers 2002). These researchers identified dense clusters containing both metaphor and metonymy, which were found at the end of the lecture or sermon, and whose purpose was to combine the various threads that have been proposed during the lecture or homily into a kind of summing-up paragraph. These clusters were often accompanied by increased levels of gesture use (Corts & Meyers 2002; Corts & Pollio 1999).

These findings are also partially mirrored by findings in English literature. Toolan observes that, at the end of a short story or novel, we often find a powerful passage, in which the key ideas are summed up, with references back to earlier themes.[10] When commenting on the typical characteristics of these passages, he observes that, among other things, they include a high density of lexical and structural repetition and para-repetition, picking up on themes that have occurred previously in the novel, strong internal rhythms, a slight confusion caused by a loss of grammaticality, words and feelings of strong intensity, and single sentences that combine an externally reported event with a report of the protagonists' state of mind. Most importantly, Toolan reports such passages have a high emotional intensity. Example (12) provides a passage from "Passion" by Alice Munro,[11] which was used by Toolan to illustrate his point:

(12) She'd thought it was touch. *Mouths, tongues, skin, bodies*, banging *bone* on *bone*. Inflammation. Passion. But that wasn't what had been meant for them at all. That was child's play, compared to how she knew him, how far she'd seen into him, now.

The first sentence in this passage contains a number of metonyms whose embodied nature is highly transparent. This is also true of some of the other passages he discusses. The italicized body part metonyms work together to build a vivid scene; a scene that has been at the back of the protagonist's mind throughout the second half of the story. The scene is then negated in the following sentence. The salience of embodied cognition within these metonyms provides extra force to this already powerful summing-up passage.

Discourse-Community Membership In order to focus on discourse-community membership, we need to return to Deignan et al.'s (2013: 128–164) study of academic conversations. Among other things, they observed that whereas the colleague picked up on the metonyms and used them to extend the discussion of different management styles, the outsider failed to do so. The shared use of metonymy here appears to have both resulted from and, perhaps, helped to develop a sense of shared understanding between the lecturer and her colleague. Similarly, in their football study, they found that many of the embodied uses of metonymy had meanings that were specific to that particular discourse community, and that were different from mainstream meanings.

5.2 *Register*

Register can also affect the transparency of the role played by embodied cognition in metonymy. Deignan and colleagues (ibid.: 191–229) found higher levels of metonymy in the supporters' discourse than in the match reports, which they attributed to the fact that the language in the former was spoken and ancillary, and that there was a need for rapid communication. These factors may also have contributed to the embodied feel of the metonyms used in this context. The increased salience of embodiment may also have resulted from the fact that the *tenor* was more informal and the *mode* was more ancillary; there was also a high level of immediacy to this situation, the metonymy being in and of the moment. Moreover, the relationship between the parents (mostly fathers) on the touchline and the children was more familiar, less formal, and less hierarchical than the relationship between the manager and the players. The *field* of the discourse may also have increased the salience of embodied cognition within the metonyms used: The focus is very much on the action, and action is, by necessity, embodied. Finally, as with the UCU Tweets mentioned above, there is a high level of emotional intensity in these "calls to action"; many of the fathers are highly competitive; they want to see their sons win the match; levels of "personal involvement" are high.

Mode Of all the genre and register features likely to affect the degree to which embodied cognition is salient in metonymy, the strongest is probably mode. The embodied nature of metonymy is much more visible in modes of expression that involve the body, such as gesture (Mittelberg & Waugh 2009), sign language (Taub 2001), and dance (Gibbs 2014b) than it is in spoken or written language, simply because these forms of communication involve the body itself. A good example of the transparency of embodied cognition in metonymy in gesture can be found in the data used by Deignan and colleagues (2013) in their aforementioned study of academic communication. Although they do not report it in their chapter, there is an interesting episode in which the lecturer imitates the act of writing really small letters in order to illustrate the activity of "doing paper trails." Here, the most salient, physical action metonymically represents the complex process with which it is associated.

Müller (*this volume*) demonstrates how the use of gesture can foreground and thus intensify the "metaphoricity" of an expression or an entire passage by emphasizing the embodied nature of the metaphor. Here we see a similar phenomenon with respect to metonymy. Moreover, within these modes of expression, when a communicator becomes more passionate about the topic, the metonymic gestures, signs, and dance movements become bigger and more elaborate, thus making the role played by embodied cognition in the creation of metonymy even more transparent.

In this section, I have proposed a number of hypotheses concerning ways in which genre and register features may affect the transparency of the role played by embodied cognition in the creation of metonymy. In addition to genre and register features, the amount of *movement* (or *motion*) and by extension the amount of *emotion* that is involved are both likely to affect the transparency of the role played by embodied cognition in the creation of the metonyms that are being employed.

6 Conclusion

I have looked at a number of ways in which metonymy is likely to be motivated by embodied cognition. I have shown how a broader, extended notion of embodied cognition allows us to focus on its environmental, social, dynamic, and developmental features, and to explore the ways in which these features manifest themselves, in different ways, in metonymy. I have also suggested a number of ways in which the involvement of motion and the intensity of emotion may increase the transparency of the role played by embodied cognition in the creation of metonymy. Finally, I have shown how this relationship is mediated by genre and register. More research in this field should be conducted in order to shed further light on the fundamental question of how and why we think and communicate using metonymy.

Notes and Acknowledgments

* I would like to thank John Barnden and Fiona MacArthur for their extremely useful feedback on an earlier version of this chapter.

1 Joe and Oscar Malt, personal communication.

2 Thank you to Francisco Ruiz de Mendoza for this observation.

3 Shi-xiong Wu, "A metonymic interpretation of Chinese antonym co-occurrence constructions: The case of 'have X have Y.'" Paper presented at the International Conference of Cognitive Linguistics and Pragmatics, Nanjing University, China, 2014.

4 "Dombey and Son," in *The Works of Charles Dickens,* Vol. III, New York: D. Appleton and Company, 1868, p. 44.

5 Charles Dickens, *The Life and Adventures of Nicholas Nickleby*, Chapman and Hall, 1839, p. 288.

6 Cuccio (*this volume*) provides an extended discussion of the notions of 'body schema' and 'body image.'
7 Andreas Musolff, "Is Taiwan the HAIR of the Body Politic or the Queen its HEAD? Cultural differences in the interpretation of the NATION-AS-BODY metaphor." Paper presented at the University of Birmingham Translation Studies Research Forum, University of Birmingham, UK, 2013.
8 Fiona MacArthur, personal communication.
9 Andrew Hodder and David Houghton, "Linguistic markers of Tweets: Giving unions a voice." Seminar presented at the University of Birmingham English Language Research Seminar Series, October 2014.
10 Michael Toolan, "Making sense of narrative text." Seminar presented at the University of Birmingham English Language Research Seminar Series, March 2015.
11 "Passion," in Alice Munro, *Runaway*, London: Vintage Books 2006.

Part III

Metaphor in Discourse

10 The Cancer Card: Metaphor, Intimacy, and Humor in Online Interactions about the Experience of Cancer

*Elena Semino & Zsófia Demjén**

Chapter Preview

Employing a dynamic systems approach, this chapter investigates the use of one particular metaphor – the "cancer card"– on an online forum dedicated to cancer. Far from being a common Card Game metaphor with a stable source–target mapping, the metaphor is collaboratively developed (i.e. used, re-used, adapted) to express the idea that patients can use their illness to their advantage in a variety of situations, while also reflecting a broader tendency to employ humor as a strategy for coping with adversity. An analysis of all 106 instances of "(cancer) card(s)" on one of the threads of the forum shows that, though related to English expressions like "play the [. . .] card" and to conventional conceptual metaphors like LIFE IS A GAME, its use is specific to the interactions among the members of this online community. Our analysis of the "cancer card" as a group-specific "metaphoreme" (Cameron & Deignan 2006) emphasizes that multiple interacting factors must be considered to account for such rich and complex phenomena as the use of metaphors in online interactions.

1 Introduction

Consider the following extract, from a UK-based online forum for people with cancer:

(1) I am sorry, but I do have to report a Failed cancer card incident: (HoneyBee, date="2011-08-22 22:43:00")[1]

The writer goes on to relate a conversation with her brother in which she tried to use her cancer as an excuse to get him to make her a cup of coffee, but without success. Even without further contextualization, it is likely to be clear that the noun "card" is used metaphorically to refer to the writer's attempt to get her own way by mentioning that she has cancer. The use and interpretation of this metaphor can be explained in part with reference to conventional conceptual and linguistic metaphors, such as LIFE IS PLAYING A GAME (Ching 1993) and the metaphorical idiom "play the [X] card," where X tends to be a noun referring to a sensitive characteristic such as race or gender, i.e. something that people do not want to be seen to be insensitive about. However, these explanations do not fully account for the idiosyncratic way in which the metaphorical expression "card" is used in the extract, and for the humorous effects to which it contributes. Additional explanations are necessary, involving a number of other factors, such as the nature of the particular online forum thread in which the utterance occurred, the relationships among the contributors to that thread, the status of this particular writer within the group of contributors, and previous uses of "(cancer) card" by that writer and other contributors to the thread.

In this chapter we analyze this dynamic use and development of the "(cancer) card" metaphor on one particular online forum thread and reflect on why contributors might use this metaphor in the ways that they do. The thread is hosted within the open community forum of a UK-based cancer charity and is entitled "For those with a warped sense of humour WARNING – no punches pulled here" (henceforth "Warped"). The thread, in the 13 months of contributions we downloaded (2011–2012), includes over half a million words and 106 occurrences of "(cancer) card." We show how the creative and humorous ways in which this metaphor is collaboratively developed by contributors to the thread can only be adequately explained in terms of the interaction of multiple factors, from conventional conceptual metaphors that may be shared by all speakers of English to the local interpersonal goals of individual contributors interacting on the particular forum on a particular day about a particular topic. We propose that this interaction of factors in metaphor use is best accounted for within the dynamic systems approach proposed by Gibbs, Cameron, and Deignan (e.g. Cameron & Deignan 2006; Gibbs 2017b; Gibbs & Cameron 2008). From this theoretical perspective, the use of the "(cancer) card" metaphor in our data can broadly be captured by the notion of "metaphoreme," defined as "a bundle of stabilized but flexible word-meaning links that incorporate particular affective and pragmatic values with particular lexico-grammatical forms and cultural preferences, and seem to work as emergent attractors in the dynamics of speech community talk" (Gibbs & Cameron 2008: 73).

Metaphoremes may be observed at the level of a whole speech community (e.g. the metaphorical use of the noun "baggage" in English), or at the level of specific discourse communities (e.g. the use of "lollipop trees" to describe a particular way of drawing trees in a primary school class) (cf. Cameron & Deignan 2006; Deignan et al. 2013). In this chapter we suggest that the notion of metaphoreme is particularly useful when accounting for the latter phenomenon.

2 The Dynamics of Communication, Metaphor, and Humor

Human communication is a highly complex and coordinated enterprise. Acknowledgements of its complexity underlie the increasing number of studies that try to combine analysis of multiple modalities and those that minimally take into consideration, but increasingly also start from, various aspects of context broadly defined, including physical, cognitive, affective, interpersonal, institutional, sociocultural, and historical factors. All of these different aspects of context are seamlessly coordinated not just by an individual speaker, but also between different interlocutors (Dale 2015).

The dynamic systems approach aims to account for how this coordination happens (e.g. Gibbs & Van Orden 2012), emphasizing that the whole complexity of communication cannot be accounted for by considering a single factor on its own, or even the combination of a small subset of factors (ibid.). Although this approach is still in its infancy in terms of operationalization, especially at the discourse level (Dale 2015), dynamic systems are also being evoked to understand variation, patterns, and relationships in smaller units or subcomponents of discourse, such as the ways in which metaphor use develops and adapts in communication (e.g. Cameron et al. 2010; Gibbs & Cameron 2008).

Gibbs and Cameron (ibid.) propose a variety of factors (bodily, cognitive, linguistic, social, cultural) that may influence "metaphor performance" in interaction, i.e. affect how people employ certain words and phrases metaphorically. Among these are: (i) "enduring metaphorical concepts," including conventional conceptual metaphors; (ii) "previously understood metaphorical utterances," i.e. what has been said or written before; (iii) "body movements and gesture"; (iv) "gender and occupation" – which may be generalizable to 'who we are in the world'; (v) the negotiation of intimacy and social distance between interlocutors; (vi) "conventional talk in specific socio-cultural groups," or "discourse communities" (Deignan et al. 2013); (vii) "specific language and culture." Gibbs (2017b) also mentions a variety of discourse-level goals, including (i) taking into account previous non-metaphorical utterances, (ii) coordinating with others in the moment, (iii) mitigating incompatibility between expectations and what occurred, and (iv) potentially (re-) establishing some equilibrium with others in context. However, the point of this approach to metaphor (and indeed to communication more broadly), at least for now, is not to list all the possible factors that influence its use, but to recognize and begin to take account of the fact that metaphor use is always and continually shaped by a potentially infinite number of factors.

As a result, the dynamic systems approach is able to integrate into a coherent whole multiple theoretical views of metaphor, including cognitive approaches with discourse-based approaches (ibid.). Conceptual metaphor, for example, can be recognized as one influencer (or "basin of attraction") of metaphor use in a given interaction, alongside previous instances of a metaphor in the same interaction and other uses of the same expression within the relevant discourse community. Furthermore, it is acknowledged that in addition to the "downwards force" of conceptual metaphors and cultural norms, metaphor use is also influenced by "upwards forces" from the individuals involved and their goals in particular interactions, in a process of "reciprocal causality" (Gibbs & Cameron 2008). In the case of Warped, the main goal of the interactions is implied in the title of the thread and outlined in the first post: coping "by being irreverent and silly and able to laugh at all the bad stuff." Individual contributors explicitly orient to this purpose and the humorous frame (Coates 2007; Kotthoff 2006) in their posts (ex 2, 3). We will show that the goal of coping by means of humor is one of the key upwards forces affecting the use of the "(cancer) card" metaphor.

(2) so I hope i've passed the warped test and can join you haha. (Sue2, date="2011-09-16 11:20:00")

(3) don't say we didn't warn you about the warped humour. (HoneyBee, date="2011-08-01 09:06:00")

We take a broad view of humor as mental and verbal play "involving a lighthearted, non-serious attitude toward ideas and events" (Martin 2007: 1). However, our data more specifically displays examples of "conversational" humor, where humor is "relevantly interwoven into conversations" (Dynel 2011b: 4). The concept applies equally even when conversations are asynchronous and computer-mediated (Dynel 2011a), and a key element is that the humor is always co-constructed by participants reacting to each other (Coates 2007).

While research specifically on metaphor and humor is sparse (Dynel 2009), most scholars who do investigate both phenomena point out that humor and metaphor have several things in common. First, they both combine two disparate ideas or concepts to create meanings and effects, such as new understanding or laughter, at least in the case of humor based on incongruity (e.g. Attardo 1994; Ritchie 2013). Second, both are seen as multifunctional and are attributed overlapping social and discourse functions, particularly in relation to group cohesion and intimacy. Conversational humor, for example, as a collaborative enterprise, is seen as both signaling and contributing to group bonding (Dynel 2011a), solidarity, and intimacy through the "play frame" (Coates 2007; Hampes 1992; see also Jefferson et al. 1987). Metaphor use can also have these effects. Goatly (1997), for example, includes intimacy as one of the main functions of metaphor. A number of studies have indeed found that metaphor use in conversation is perceived as signaling closeness or intimacy between the interlocutors

(Bowes & Katz 2015; Horton 2007), especially when the metaphors are creative (Horton 2013). Additionally, metaphoremes also help to delineate and thereby bind discourse communities.

Specifically in the context of illness, humor has another important function. It is recognized as facilitating tension release, making it easier to conduct difficult or embarrassing conversations and to cope with adversity or serious illness (Chapple & Ziebland 2004; Demjén 2016; Heath & Blonder 2003). The uses of "(cancer) card" on Warped are manifestations of the humor that contributes to this coping function.

Besides the overlap between the phenomena of humor and metaphor described above, another similarity between them is the way in which they occur in discourse and interaction: Both can be seen as developing dynamically. In discussing conversational humor, Norrick (2003: 1338) talks about "the flexibility and protean character of conversational joking [...] joke punchlines turn into wisecracks, witty repartees grow into anecdotes, anecdotes develop into jokes, and so on" (see also Coates 2007). The dynamic systems view of communication makes much the same point about metaphor.

While in this chapter we cannot claim to account for all or even most of the bodily, cognitive, linguistic, social, and cultural forces influencing the use of "(cancer) card," we can acknowledge the vast array of possible factors and focus specifically on the interactions between conceptual, interpersonal, intertextual, topical, and discourse-goal factors. In this way, we attempt to map systematically how stability and variation in the use of "(cancer) card" emerge from and shape the topic of Warped, the roles and relationships of the particular individuals involved, the sequencing of posts, and contributors' desire to stay true to the humorous mission of the thread. In particular, we will structure our analysis around one key transition point in the thread, a so-called "perturbation" (Gibbs & Cameron 2008), and discuss how "(cancer) card" is used humorously before and after this point.

3 The Data

Warped was one of the longest threads on the host forum: Spanning thirteen months from the years 2011–2012, the thread exhibits 106 occurrences of "(cancer) card" in a total of 530,055 words. It consists of 2,544 posts by 68 different individuals, and 90 percent of the content is contributed by people who describe themselves as having cancer (vs. people who care for someone with cancer).

Research on online interactions among people with different medical conditions has shown how online fora such as the one of which Warped is part provide valuable spaces in which people share information, validate one another's illness experience, support one another, form strong bonds of intimacy and companionship, and empower themselves and others (e.g. Allen et al. 2016; Prestin & Chou 2014). However, in contrast with other threads on the forum and patient fora more generally, the primary function of Warped is not the exchange of information and experiences on the disease and treatment options (see Armstrong et al. 2012). Instead, it provides a designated space for verbal play as a way of coping with cancer, as outlined in its first post:

(4) we need a place to say what we need to say without worrying about offending people so you have been warned!!!! This is for those of us who cope by being irreverent and silly and able to laugh at all the bad stuff. (HoneyBee, date="2011-07-24 13:38:00")

The contributors to Warped posted with relative regularity, touching on everyday topics like their pets, Jehovah's Witnesses at the door, gardening, needing to buy new clothes, their jobs and annoying colleagues, getting drunk, etc. They also discuss aspects of their lives related to their illness: things that "used to" be different, how people react to their cancer, physical consequences of cancer and cancer treatment. All of this is done in line with the humorous tone of the thread.

The contributors to Warped can be described as a "discourse community" – a group of people "who have texts and practices in common" (Barton 2007: 75) – not least because of the clear mission of the thread which sets it apart from the rest of the forum. Deignan et al. (2013) show that the members of specific discourse communities may share, among other things, particular ways of using figurative language. From a dynamic systems perspective, the interactions on Warped can be seen as a self-organizing system which evolves over multiple timescales as a result of complex interactions between internal and external forces. What Gibbs and Cameron (2008) call "metaphor performance" emerges as part of these interactions.

"(Cancer) card" is one of several humorous metaphors and in-jokes shared by the contributors to this thread. In what follows we discuss the dynamic ways in which the "(cancer) card" metaphor is used by cancer patients on Warped. We look at its flexible use as both a metaphorical phrase and a concept, potentially drawing from other source domains/scenarios than CARD GAMES, and occurring within different types of lexico-grammatical structures. We show its development into a context-specific metaphoreme that is shared by the thread contributors and is specific to them, and also examine a number of interesting cases of semi-literalization and how these relate to the metaphorical uses. Throughout the discussion, we also reflect on why contributors might be doing what they are doing.

We suggest that a satisfactory account of these patterns requires a consideration of a variety of interacting factors and hence the combination of insights from cognitive and discourse approaches to metaphor.

4 Analysis: "(Cancer) Card" on the Warped Thread

Contributors on Warped often joke about the (sometimes hypothetical) benefits of having cancer, as in the following two references to possible alternative uses of colostomy bags (that are sometimes required as a result of treatment for colorectal cancer):

(5) If baggy had farted lots then HoneyBee would have shot across the pool ... jet propulsion! (Smelly, date="2011-11-09 20:49:00")

(6) I am having the windy bean and lentil stew for lunch tomorrow at school ... I am getting nervous that even invincible pants won't be able to hold that lot in when it finally blows! Could get messy. Maybe I can strategically aim [the colostomy bag] ha ha (HoneyBee, date="2011-10-09 20:34:00")

There is "incongruity" here between the discomfort and embarrassment associated with colostomy bags and the imaginary exploitation of gas accumulated in the bag for antisocial purposes and to amuse oneself. This, along with the breaking of social taboos through references to breaking wind, results in humor. These examples involve "an alternative interpretation of the stressor" (Heath & Blonder 2003: 99), a strategy that stroke survivors with lasting disabilities have also been found to adopt. The reappraisal of the negative potentially allows people with serious illnesses to empower themselves by means of the language and attitude they decide to adopt for negative aspects of their lives that they have little or no control over. The "(cancer) card" metaphor is a way of "looking on the bright side" of cancer and using it to one's advantage.

The Warped thread contains 106 instances in which "card" is used to indicate a strategic reference to having cancer as a way to obtain some kind of special treatment, from being excused from unwelcome tasks at work to jumping a queue while coming out of a stadium. From a chronological point of view, however, a particular post by a contributor we will call HoneyBee marks a transition point in the use of this expression that we need to take into account in our analysis. This post, which occurs early on in the history of the thread, was entirely devoted to the 'cancer card' itself, and, as we argue below, caused a change in the way in which "(cancer) card" is subsequently used by contributors to the thread. From a dynamic systems perspective, this post caused a perturbation in the system that resulted in new patterns of stability and variation, with respect to both the first part of Warped and metaphorical uses of "card" in English generally.

4.1 *Idiosyncratic Use of a General Metaphoreme: '(Cancer) Card' in the First Part of Warped*

The Warped thread starts on July 24, 2011. The "transition" post was uploaded in the evening of August 19, 2011. Overall, the posts that precede this point amount to a total of approximately 25,000 words, i.e. 5 percent of the whole half-a-million-word thread. This first part of the thread contains 13 metaphorical uses of "(cancer) card," 12 of which are by the same contributor, HoneyBee. HoneyBee has an instrumental role on Warped: She started the thread and was the most prolific contributor throughout its existence. Her leading role is acknowledged when someone refers to the group as "HoneyBee clan," and she is responsible for initiating a number of in-jokes (see Demjén 2016) along with the "(cancer) card." Examples (7) to (9) provide three examples by HoneyBee, in chronological order:

(7) what's funny is someone just rang and asked me to do some stuff from this meeting today and email it round and I said I was too tired to do it tonight (cancer card used up for today now) when actually what I wanted to do was write this... (HoneyBee, date="2011-07-24 14:46:00")

(8) he [her husband] 'doesn't do gardening' so its me or it doesn't get done.. cancer card doesn't work with him I'm afraid... (HoneyBee, date="2011-07-24 15:50:00")

(9) Trolley service [on a train] got off half way up and the next trolley didn't come on (no one turned up he said...) gasp, pant, dying of thirst, no sandwiches etc... nearly thought of playing the cancer card, but resisted... and they found someone by Newcastle, so card reserved for brother making me coffee later... (HoneyBee, date="2011-08-13 21:37:00")

These uses of "(cancer) card" can in principle be seen as a specific application to cancer of the general metaphorical idiom "play the [...] card," which could in turn be described as a language-wide metaphoreme involving a Card Game scenario. In this idiom, the idea of playing a particular card to win a card game is used to capture the use of a reference to a socially and culturally sensitive topic in order to gain some advantage in the social interaction. More broadly, this idiom can be seen as consistent with a conventional conceptual metaphor such as LIFE IS PLAYING A GAME (Ching 1993), within which winning in a game corresponds to different kinds of success in life.

The first use of "cancer card" in example (9) is indeed clearly marked as a Card Game metaphor through the use of the verb "play." The other uses, however, occur as parts of different expressions, which have more specific implications. "Used up for today" in (7) and "reserved for brother making me coffee later" in (9) suggest that HoneyBee only has one cancer card available each day, perhaps due to a sense of self-restraint on the part of the person, who feels it is acceptable to use her cancer as an excuse only once a day. From the point of view of the source Card Game scenario, this is potentially compatible with the cancer card as a single "joker" in a round of play, which needs to be reserved for the most appropriate point. In example (8), the claim that the cancer card "doesn't work" with HoneyBee's husband reflects the influence of the literal topic over the source scenario of Card Games. In card games, the rules are fixed and apply regardless of who is involved. In contrast, in the target domain of living with cancer, different people react differently to the person's references to her illness as a reason why she should not have to do something she does not want to do.

All three examples are also light-hearted and humorous. This is partly signaled by the language used around the metaphors, e.g. "funny" in (7) and the hyperbolic "gasp, pant, dying of thirst, no sandwiches, etc." in (9), and partly a result of the kinds of relatively trivial situations in which HoneyBee uses (or considers using) the cancer card to get special treatment that is not strictly necessary from people who are not ill: a job she would prefer not to do in (7), household chores such as gardening in (8), and having someone provide refreshments or a coffee for her in (9).

In the first part of Warped, the "(cancer) card" metaphor is also extended to include the possibility of "trumping." HoneyBee introduced this idea in response to someone who says that one more person in her family has cancer:

(10) You are going to have to have some trump system for your cancer cards... shouldn't terminal trump remission?? (HoneyBee, date="2011-07-25 10:43:00")

Here the contrast is not between people with cancer and healthy people, but between people who are more or less seriously ill with cancer. This is captured metaphorically by the idea of a "trump system" (still consistent with the generic Card Game metaphor) in which people who are more seriously ill have cards of higher value than people who are less seriously ill. The "trump" version of the metaphor is reused by HoneyBee on several occasions and is then adopted a few weeks later by a contributor we will call Smelly, in response to a post where HoneyBee says that she would like to have all Warped members join her family at a party in Sweden:

(11) ...but if we all came over there would be too many of us playing the cancer card...and then would the fact that I had 4 relapses, lost some hearing, went loopy, peed a rainbow, stem cell transplant, filled in poo charts for days, had radiotherapy and was hospitalised with suspected swine flu trump all of you??? (Smelly, date="2011-08-19 14:55:00")

In spite of the light-heartedness of expressions such as "peed a rainbow," here the humor is arguably closer to "gallows humor," as it involves degrees of seriousness of a life-threatening illness. This seems to subvert the conventional Card Game metaphor, where having cards of a higher value is always positive. Indeed, HoneyBee's reply to Smelly a few hours later reuses the trump-system metaphor in an uncharacteristically somber way:

(12) Actually, I'm not looking forward to seeing us lot trying to outdo each other on the cancer card trump system ... that's one game I would happily lose, (HoneyBee, date="2011-08-19 18:43:00")

The preference for "losing" the metaphorical "game" is due to what is required for "winning" in the specific target domain, i.e. being more seriously ill than anyone else.

Overall, in this first section of the Warped thread the "(cancer) card" metaphor is used flexibly and creatively, mostly by one particular individual, to refer humorously to a range of ways in which she tries to use her cancer to her advantage in everyday situations. These specific uses of the metaphor are broadly consistent with the conventional metaphorical idiom "play the [. . .] card" but also differ from conventional uses of this idiom: they are not just humorous, but also reflect in various ways the specific situation of being ill with cancer, such as feeling that cancer should not be mentioned too often, and accounting for situations in which more than one person has cancer. Smelly's adoption of HoneyBee's "trump card" version of the metaphor, and HoneyBee's own use in an immediate response, also suggest that the metaphor is beginning to become a shared resource for defusing with humor some very serious situations (e.g. several people with cancer in one family or coming together). This potential of the metaphor is clearly realized after HoneyBee devotes a whole post to the cancer card.

4.2 *A Perturbation in the System: The "Cancer Card Services" Post*

We now come to the point in the thread where the "(cancer) card" is focused on and developed in several novel ways, causing a perturbation in the Warped dynamic system. In the post from which example (12) is taken, HoneyBee jokingly comments on Smelly's earlier reference to media reports that the psychoactive drug ecstasy might help treat cancers such as her own:

(13) As for the ecstacy, have you thought of entering a trial for preventing it coming back? You could try that one in court... well, you see m'lord, I was on this website for loonies and they suggested that I took drugs and... OH...

I've got cancer ... here's my card ... run away ... (HoneyBee, still 19 August 2011 6:43pm)

Here HoneyBee outlines a hypothetical scenario in which Smelly is being tried in court for using illicit drugs. In this scenario, the "card" is a literal object which Smelly can exhibit to prove that she has cancer, and thus to justify her illegal behavior before "running away." This imaginary card is therefore not a playing card. Rather, the hypothetical context and the expression "Here's my card" suggest something like a business card, a membership card or a medical note. Later on the same day (August 19, 2011), HoneyBee posts a new contribution that is entirely devoted to the idea of cards that make explicit references to cancer, and that can be used by patients or their relatives in a variety of situations:

(14) I was going to do this with illustrations, but no photoshop etc here and too much gin, so sorry- you will just have to imagine them xxxx

Feeling Tired? Fed Up? Listless? Hairless?

Or just can't be bothered ...

You need the Cancer Card!

HoneyBee Cancer Card services for all your cancer card needs ...

In our IGC range (I've got cancer)

or

ICFSWC range (I'm caring for someone with cancer)

We have a wide range of cards to suit most occasions...

Please note: All Cancer Cards are prefixed by either of the above IGC or ICFSWC please state clearly which type you require on the order form.

So for example the BMST card would read ... I've got cancer, buy me shiny things or

I am caring for someone with cancer, buy me shiny things.

Our featured cards this week are the ones for those days when let's face it, when you just need a bit of a perk from this cancer lark ...

The GOODWILL card- Get Out OF Doing What I Loath Lots

The WISH card- What I Say Happens

The BMST- Buy Me Shiny Things

The HNC- Housework? No Chance

The IHTW- I Have To Win

The IGWIW- I Get What I Want

The INC- I'm Not Cooking

And the multi purpose- DDTM card- don't do that to me.

This next card comes in handy packs of 3 and is particularly useful if your car breaks down, or you just need something doing for you ...

The FISH card- Free Instant Sympathy Here

Or why not try one of our themed ranges?

The Toilet humour range proving popular this month with those that want a bit of understanding for those hiding under the duvet days or pre check up days ...

POO- person out of order

PUBES- Person Under Bl**dy Enormous Stress

SH*T- Sympathy Here Instantly Thank you

Our new Medical themed cards are also proving popular with a certain clientele

GP- Gin Please

GMC- Give Me Cake/Chips/cocktails (delete as appropriate)

NHS- No Housework Stupid!

> And2 for those exasperating moments ...
>
> The STAYGAS card- Say That Again- You'll Get A Slap
>
> And HoneyBee's personal favourite ... which is on special offer of buy one get one free this week ... the ever popular...
>
> The IMLWBPDKTMTWYHTCIDMHI card
>
> (I Might Look Well, But Please Don't Keep telling Me That With Your Head Tilted Cos It Does My Head In!)
>
> All available to buy at honeybeecancercards.com
>
> Please note: Credit Terms not available
>
> We are always on the look out for new ranges so any suggestions please forward for inclusion in our autumn brochure coming soon.
>
> HoneyBee x
>
> Click here to find out more (HoneyBee, date="2011-08-19 23:25:00")

Although we cannot go into detail here, this post parodies the genre of (online) advertisements (e.g. "to suit most occasions," "featured cards") and makes explicit references to humor ("Toilet humour range"). More importantly, it sets up an imaginary online shop which sells cards that people with cancer (or carers of people with cancer) can use to get special treatment in situations that include avoiding domestic chores ("I'm Not Cooking"), being given presents ("Buy Me Shiny Things"), and generally getting one's own way ("What I Say Happens"). As in some previous posts by HoneyBee, there is humorous potential in the contrast between these mundane and sometimes frivolous requests and the seriousness of cancer. The use of lengthy acronyms for the various demands is also humorous, especially when the acronyms form words referring to taboo entities in the "Toilet humour range" ("PUBES").

As mentioned earlier, what HoneyBee does in this post can be described within a dynamic systems approach as a perturbation in the system formed by the group of people that interact on the Warped thread. On the one hand, there is some degree of continuity with previous metaphorical uses of "cancer card" on the thread and with the conventional metaphorical idiom "play the [. . .] card," as the cards described in this post (at least up to "FISH") are all used to exploit a difficult, sensitive issue for the person's advantage. This continuity also includes the fact that HoneyBee had already started to exploit other literal meanings of "card" and had mostly used the notion of the "cancer card" humorously, as is consistent with the nature of the thread as a whole.

On the other hand, the invention of an online shop selling imaginary cards with humorous cancer-related acronyms clearly marks a dramatic change in what "(cancer) card" potentially means on the Warped thread. Apart from the fact that they are mostly intended to be used to get special treatment, these cards have little in common with the playing cards of the idiom "play the [. . .] card." First, the expression "Cancer Card services for all your cancer card needs" is reminiscent of advertisements for other types of cards, such as credit cards or business cards. Second, the variety of cancer-related messages that can be printed on the cards is reminiscent of greeting cards, or, again, business cards. Third, as the post progresses, there is increasing variety in what the cards can be used for. While most can still be used to get some kind of special treatment, others can be used to explain patients' own behavior ("POO: person out of order") or deter unwanted behaviors in others ("STAYGAS: Say That Again- You'll Get A Slap"). In other words, HoneyBee creates a new concept by combining different literal and metaphorical associations of "card" with the literal experience of dealing with cancer, against the background of previous uses of "(cancer) card" on the Warped thread and its general humorous slant.[2] By means of this post, HoneyBee also strengthens her own identity as one of the main contributors to the thread, and one of the leaders in creating and developing different lines of humor on the thread.

After this post, the meanings and uses of "cancer card" change on the Warped thread, not just for HoneyBee but for other contributors too, as we show in the next section. In other words, the perturbation that example (14) creates in the dynamic system shifts the way in which "(cancer) card" works and results in what is best described as a context-specific metaphoreme that is only shared by members of the Warped discourse community.

4.3 *A Group-Specific Metaphoreme: The "Cancer Card" in the Rest of Warped*

Apart from HoneyBee, seven contributors use the "(cancer) card" metaphor in the rest of Warped (for a total of 79 instances). These uses exhibit some degree of variation, and both reflect and develop the version of the "cancer card" introduced in the previous section. The way in which the notion of the cancer card is adopted and developed by other contributors confirms HoneyBee's leading role on the thread but also shows how other members of the Warped community perform their own identities, both as "followers" in HoneyBee's humorous footsteps and as creators of (metaphorical) humor in their own right.

Literalization The first "phase" in the rest of Warped corresponds to the ten days immediately following HoneyBee's "Cancer Card services" post, up to August 29, 2011. This phase includes 70 posts overall and involves an intense focus on the new "cards" as literal entities in imaginary scenarios.

Smelly responds to the "Cancer Card services" post on the following day: She explicitly points out the humorous aspect of the cards by describing them as "so funny" and declares that she cannot think of any better ones. Another contributor, however, joins in and invents a set of cards around the theme of sex. He justifies the theme with reference to his own maleness and expresses the wish not to be "banned":

(15) Viagra card? Vital internal action gone right arye
Impotent Impossible, might point or try, entry not tonight
Limp Card Lost Interest My Pet
Tidy Card Think its dead Yet
pissed Card Penis is so sore, erectile disfunction
Big balls card Body is good but all lust last seconds !! (Tom, date="2011-08-21 16:06:00")

Here the humor results from the use of inventive acronyms to make reference to the taboo topic of male sexual dysfunction. However, what Tom describes here is arguably one of the most uncomfortable and embarrassing side effects of the illness and treatment, and although humor results from the reference to taboo subjects, it simultaneously facilitates the mention of these embarrassing consequences of treatment in the first place (see Demjén 2016). An important feature of humor generally is precisely that it allows us "to explore things which are difficult or taboo" (Coates 2007: 32).

In the following days, HoneyBee encourages anyone on the thread to contribute their own ideas for cards but also responds to similar invitations from other contributors by inventing new cards herself, and imagining new situations in which they can be used. One of these situations is traveling abroad with the cards in place of a passport:

(16) take the I get my own way card to the airport and sod the passport- you need a holiday. They are not going to refuse you with the cards now are they? (HoneyBee, date="2011-08-21 08:43:00")

This idea is collaboratively developed by HoneyBee and Smelly, who tell a series of stories in which a member of the group shows up at an airport with one or more cancer cards, which they use to get away with taking forbidden items in their luggage. In this phase of the interaction, the cards continue to be primarily literal entities in fantasy scenarios, or in fantasy versions of real scenarios. Within this phase, the notion of the cancer card is literalized in other ways too. Smelly talks about cancer patients in England having a "cancer card for life" in reference to a new policy whereby these patients are entitled to free prescriptions for the rest of their lives. Here the "cancer card" could be seen as semi-literal if it refers to the document that proves that someone has indeed had a cancer diagnosis. HoneyBee, on the other hand, imagines a situation in which she and others actually turn her idea into a concrete object:

(17) Maybe we should do a book of the cancer cards and we could all contribute to it ... we could do tear out pages maybe so you could actually use them? (HoneyBee, date="2011-08-22 19:21:00")

Even during this phase, however, the "(cancer) card" can still be exploited as a metaphorical concept. Our opening example ("Failed cancer card incident") is by HoneyBee herself and dates from three days after the "Cancer Card services" post. Moreover, ten days after that post, HoneyBee reasserts the metaphoricity of the card (ex 19) in response to a contributor who seems to be constrained by a literal interpretation when talking about a self-indulgent shopping spree:

(18) I should have had one of your cards with me HoneyBee. (Sarah, date="2011-08-29 18:13:00")

(19) Anyway, hoorah Sarah for buying shiny things ... you are allowed you've got the card remember? (HoneyBee, date="2011-08-29 19:37:00")

In (18), the writer regrets not having one of HoneyBee's cards to justify her purchases. This suggests that she is treating the cards as literal, if imaginary, entities. The use of "the card" in HoneyBee's response is metaphorical, however: she reminds Christine that, as a cancer sufferer, she always has the "card," i.e. she can always use the illness to justify pampering herself.

The Development of '(Cancer) Card' as a Discourse Community-Specific Metaphoreme After the first ten days of frequent and mostly imaginary-cum-literal uses, the "(cancer) card" once again starts to be regularly used and developed as a metaphor by several contributors to the Warped thread. This arguably results in the emergence of a group-specific development of the general "play the [. . .] card" metaphoreme.

The invention of new acronyms for cancer cards peters out on the Warped thread within about two weeks of the "Cancer Card services" post. However, the idea of cards with acronyms is still available and gets used as a metaphor, as in this extract from November 2011:

(20) Although I played the cancer card AIFTISSFTAE* at the beginning of the meeting, no worthwhile opportunity came for a strop, so sorry Valerie, I've let you down.

*Although I've finished treatment I still suffering from the after effects! (Lakedweller, date="2011-11-03 14:21:00")

More generally, the contributors to the thread also continue to use the "(cancer) card" metaphor, without references to acronyms, but nonetheless in ways that are distinctive to the group and that reflect a new balance of stability and variation following the perturbation caused by the "Cancer Card services" post. While the expression "play the cancer card" is regularly used, there are other patterns that vary from this structure and that reflect a new shared concept among group members. One type of variation involves the noun phrase itself where "card" is the head noun. In some instances the indefinite article ("a") is used with the singular noun "card" (ex 21–23). In other cases, the noun is used in the plural ("cards") (ex 24, 25):

(21) I threw a strop and played a cancer card today and came home early ... impressed? (HoneyBee, date="2011-11-01 20:18:00")

(22) [NB: in response to (21)] You have such a busy schedule, i'm glad you played a card and opted out of the meeting. (Sue2, date="2012-01-12 20:42:00")

(23) Whilst walking out of the stadium I got my brain cells working and thought about playing a cancer card, and so as I walked down to the train station I started to make my way toward the disabled entrance. (Sam, date="2012-08-05 12:01:00")

(24) I will also play the cancer cards if needed to get out of stuff (HoneyBee, date="2012-01-01 20:12:00")

(25) will keep the [naughty] step warm . . . I am sure you will be paying it a visit as spending time with normals is a sure way of bringing out the worst so enjoy play the cards and try not to behave (Pretzel, date="2012-01-02 08:46:00")

Both the singular indefinite and the plural use of "card" rely on the idea that the contributors to the thread have multiple cards to play as a result of their cancer, rather than a single "cancer card." This is both a reflection and a development of the acronym cards first proposed by HoneyBee. The status of the cards as common ground among contributors is also evident in uses where "card" occurs in the singular or plural without a determiner, as in: "So played cancer card!" (Lakedweller, date="2012-01-29 15:12:00"), and "I have to go and play cancer cards" (HoneyBee, date="2012-01-03 21:44:00"). In contrast, the 100 million-word British National Corpus contains no instances of play the cards (with a plural noun) and only five instances of "play a [. . .] card." However, none of the five instances of the latter expression involves a reference to a sensitive topic (e.g. "Yet fate was to play a strange card").

In addition, the noun "(cancer) card" is also used by several contributors in structures that do not involve the verb "play," e.g. "Failed cancer card incident" in (1). These uses vary in the extent to which they suggest Card Games scenarios, with a few cases potentially evoking different scenarios:

(26) First, may i hold up my cancer card, the one for being too sesitive. I thought i had offended when infact i hadn't and now i feel silly, silly, silly. (Sue2, date="2011-10-12 20:58:00")

Here the writer uses "hold up my cancer card" to introduce an acknowledgment of having over-reacted to something, which now makes her "feel silly." The use of "hold up" is reminiscent of idiomatic expressions like "hold up the white flag" and "hold up my hand," where the flag and the hand stand metonymically or metaphorically for an admission of defeat or responsibility for a mistake. In this example, therefore, the metaphorical card seems to function both as an acknowledgment of guilt and as an excuse for making the mistake in the first place, due to having cancer. The former meaning is consistent with the scenarios suggested by the idioms. The latter meaning is consistent with some of the previous uses of "(cancer) card" on the Warped thread (cf. our earlier comments on cards such as "POO – Person out of order," providing an excuse for otherwise inappropriate/unacceptable behaviors). In addition, the gloss for the card in (26) ("the one for being too sesitive [*sic*]") alludes to the availability of many different (cancer) cards from which one can pick the one that is suitable to a particular occasion. This meaning originates from HoneyBee's "Cancer Card services" post. In (27), a thread contributor uses another structure involving the verb "hold" in a post addressed at HoneyBee:

(27) it's about time you threw a strop, you need to remind people you hold a cancer card because the way you go babbling on nineteen to the dozen ti's easy for them to forget (Lakedweller, date="2011-11-02 00:02:00").

The reminder that HoneyBee "hold[s] a cancer card" may suggest both a playing card and a different type of card, such as a membership card that entitles someone to benefits due to their age or other characteristic.[3]

All these examples also show the multiple functions that the cancer card performs on the Warped thread, including not just creating humor (e.g. in the queue-jumping scenario of (23)) but also expressing mutual support (e.g. "I'm glad you played a card" in the second part of (22)) and – through humor – strengthening intimacy and group cohesion, as in the reference to healthy people as "normal" in the scenario in which (cancer) cards are played in (25).

Overall, after a brief literalization phase immediately following HoneyBee's "Cancer Card services" post, the "(cancer) card" develops into a group-specific metaphoreme with distinctive lexico-grammatical forms and particular affective and pragmatic values. In formal terms, the most distinctive structures involve the indefinite singular uses, the plural uses, and the occurrence of "(cancer) card" without the verb "play" and within a range of structures that do not (or not only) suggest a Card Game scenario. In terms of affective and pragmatic values, "(cancer) card" is used humorously to recount and justify the many different ways in which having cancer can be exploited to the person's advantage, not just by getting special treatment but also by excusing potentially unacceptable behaviors. This arguably helps to demystify a negative and often overwhelming experience, and to empower the individual both in their daily life and in how they conceive of themselves and of their illness: If having cancer can be joked about and even presented as beneficial to the self, its status as a frightening life-threatening illness is reduced. In other words, "if something is ridiculous then it cannot be serious or threatening" (McCreaddie & Wiggins 2008: 589).

At a group level, the joint ownership and development of a humorous metaphoreme both reflects and enhances intimacy, complicity, and mutual relationships. Contributors to Warped do not just share an in-joke and in-group metaphor that they have co-created and that only they can fully understand and exploit; they also use the notion of the "(cancer) card" to encourage one another to be kind to themselves and assertive with others, and to congratulate one another when they report having acted in these ways. And finally, the fact that the "(cancer) card" is mostly used humorously is consistent with the play frame of the Warped thread and contributes to maintaining the distinctiveness of the thread and the community of contributors.

5 Conclusions

We hope that our analysis of the use of "(cancer) card" by people with cancer contributing to an online forum thread has clearly shown the need to take multiple interacting factors into account in order to do full justice to the rich and complex ways in which metaphors can be used in discourse, and particularly in online interactions among tightly knit discourse communities such as the contributors to our forum thread. We have suggested that a dynamic systems approach is ideally suited to account for how a range of different factors are involved in metaphor use, as it makes it possible to bring together insights from different theoretical and analytical perspectives.

The notion of the *metaphoreme* has proved to be particularly appropriate to describe both stability and variation in the bundle of connections between the different linguistic structures in which "(cancer) card" occurs and the affective, pragmatic, and interactional functions that these structures perform in the interactions among members on the Warped thread. More specifically, while there is value in describing general semi-fixed expressions such as "play the [. . .] card" as language-wide metaphoremes, we would argue that the notion of metaphoreme comes into its own when dealing with uses of metaphor that are specific to particular contexts and discourse communities, such as the contributors to Warped. This specificity generates additional associations between forms, meanings, and functions that cannot be properly accounted for in terms of realizations of static conceptual mappings or in terms of general usage patterns of metaphorical idioms.

The analytical breadth and depth that a dynamic systems approach allows also has the advantage of making it easier for metaphor scholars to address issues that are relevant to researchers and practitioners from other fields. In our case, this applies not just to scholars interested in the interaction between metaphor and humor but also to the different kinds of researchers and professionals who are interested in online communities, and particularly online communities involving people with serious and/or long-term illnesses.

There is increasing evidence that it is important to understand the functions that such online interactions and communities perform in the lives of people with a variety of illnesses (e.g. Allen et al. 2016). Our analysis has shown how people with a life-threatening illness such as cancer can exploit the easy accessibility and relative anonymity of an online forum thread to co-create and develop a humorous metaphor in ways that can both contribute to their individual well-being and strengthen their sense of community.

Notes and Acknowledgments

* The research presented in this chapter was supported by the UK's Economic and Social Research Council (ESRC grant number: ES/J007927/1).

1 Original spellings and punctuation are retained throughout when quoting from our data. The nicknames, electronic "handles," and other identifiers of forum contributors have been changed. In each case, we provide the precise date and time of posting, as these are relevant to our analysis.

2 In Fauconnier & Turner's (2002) terms, this new concept could be described as the emergent structure of a blend resulting from the merging of different card-related and cancer-related input spaces.

3 Both HoneyBee and Smelly also reuse the notion of a "trump card" in humorous reflections on how cancer relates to other types of illnesses as a reason to get special treatment.

11 Mappings and Narrative in Figurative Communication

Alice Deignan

Chapter Preview

Showing how metaphors are used to talk about entities, relations, and attributes in one domain by drawing on another, Conceptual Metaphor Theory has sometimes been used in language analysis to highlight and explore fixed correspondences between domains. Another perspective is given by Schön (1993), who suggested that metaphors can draw a relationship between the topic and a common sequence of events – i.e. that metaphors can impose a narrative sequence on their topic – and by Musolff (2006, 2007), who described "scenarios," metaphors based on fragments of experience, incorporating a culturally shared evaluation. In two case studies, these complex relationships are further explored: The first examines three artifacts apparently realizing LIFE IS A JOURNEY, initially in terms of correspondences between domains. The second provides a detailed analysis of two speeches about education, analyzing them both in terms of metaphorical mappings and correspondences, and as narratives. The exploration of narratives is informed by a reference corpus, which is used to provide data from the language at large about the behavior of words and phrases from the education speeches.

1 Introduction

Gibbs and Cameron (2008) view metaphor as an emergent and dynamic phenomenon. They stress that conceptual mappings such as LIFE IS A JOURNEY are one of the forces that shape metaphor in use, but not the only one. Gibbs and Cameron (ibid.: 65) describe the mappings postulated by Conceptual Metaphor Theory (CMT) as "enduring metaphorical concepts," and write that the other forces that shape metaphor-in-use include previous metaphorical utterances in the ongoing discourse, intimacy, and distance between participants as it is adjusted during the discourse, and sociocultural norms. The ongoing and shifting influences of these and other forces result in figurative language that is, they claim, "soft-assembled in the flow of talk" (ibid.: 70).

El Refaie (2014) also contends that CMT has tended to present a static picture. In her discussion of embodiment, she notes critically that bodily experience is often assumed to be universal, albeit filtered by culture. In fact, she argues that embodied experience is dynamic, varying between different individuals according to factors such as gender, age, culture, and context, and within the same individuals over time, for example through experiencing the effects of ageing, injury, or illness.

In a number of case studies, Deignan et al. (2013) have shown that figurative language use varies significantly across different genres and registers. The same authors (Semino et al. 2013) have also explored how the meanings and use of apparently the same metaphorical expressions evolve and change over time in the telling and retelling of stories and ideas.

Cameron and Deignan (2006) have discussed how the dynamic, emergent view of metaphor contributes to the analysis of figurative expressions in text. They claim that figurative language use tends to stabilize into highly restricted linguistic phrases, which they term "metaphoremes," such as "walk away from," meaning 'abandon an ongoing responsibility.' Metaphoremes are defined as "the bundle of stabilizing linguistic, semantic, pragmatic, and affective patterns in the use of the word as metaphor, together with its possibilities for variation" (ibid.: 679). As this definition suggests, metaphoremes are shaped by forces that include conceptual metaphors, previous uses in the ongoing discourse, genre, register, and other sociocultural factors. The authors also note that metaphoremes may be temporary and sometimes specific to a particular discourse or context. An in-depth illustration of this is provided by Semino and Demjén (*this volume*), who explore a highly genre- and situation-specific metaphoreme, "the (cancer) card."

The present chapter embraces this dynamic approach to metaphor in communication. Here, I begin by considering my data in terms of cross-domain conceptual mappings, an approach which has been variously critiqued by the writers cited above as static, suggesting a universality and permanency that does not exist, or concerned with the cognitive at the expense of the social and local. I use this approach in analyzing a number of texts and other artifacts, and I demonstrate that it offers some useful insights. I then compare it with a narrative approach, informed by Musolff's (2006, 2007) "scenarios" and Cameron and Deignan's (2006) construct of the metaphoreme.

I begin by discussing three artifacts: a collection of related spoken texts, a drawing with written labels, and a photograph, all apparently realizations of

LIFE IS A JOURNEY. In the following section, I overview important work linking metaphor and narrative. I finally illustrate the two analytical approaches in more depth, through a text and corpus analysis of two recent texts on educational policy.

2 LIFE IS A JOURNEY realized

2.1 Example 1: JOURNEY Metaphors in Talk

A study of 14 men who had suffered spinal chord injuries causing paralysis through playing the sport of rugby union provides the data for my first set of realizations of LIFE IS A JOURNEY (Sparkes & Smith 2005). The injured men were interviewed about their lives before and after the accidents that had changed these completely. The researchers found that the men used three different narratives in constructing their life histories. These were "Restitution," used by 11 men, "Chaos," used by one, and "Quest," which two of the men used. Restitution narratives focused on the possibility of a medical cure, while Chaos was despairing, and without structure. Quest narratives, according to the authors, seemed to indicate acceptance of what had happened and a willingness to make it meaningful in itself. The narratives by David and Doug, for example, include many JOURNEY metaphors. However, these are used in notably different ways (ex 1, ex 2).[1] The two men also describe the importance of other people, especially other disabled people, who they both call "guides," thereby extending the conventional JOURNEY metaphor (ex 3).

(1) I've *covered a lot of ground* . . . I've *made a lot of progress*, but there are a lot of *ups and downs* on the *journey* I'm on. It isn't easy. (David, ibid.: 85)

(2) Along the way there are a lot of problems that can force me *off the track* . . . I can't take life for granted. For one, I know that there will be a *rocky road ahead* of me at some point and *obstacles* to think about. For now, I have to contend with everyday *barriers* placed by society, and the occasional emotionally bad day, but who knows what the future will bring, (Doug, ibid.)

(3) People are like *guides*, helping and *guiding* people along their journey. (Doug, ibid.)

2.2 Example 2: JOURNEY Metaphors in Text and Picture

The above example of realizations of LIFE IS A JOURNEY consists of transcribed spoken language. My second example, provided in Figure 11.1, is multimodal, consisting of drawn pictures and written commentary. It is, in El Refaie's (2017) terms, a verbo-pictorial metaphor and was produced in a single sitting of a few minutes, without preparation, by an English school student aged 13 in a lesson for religious studies (a compulsory subject in the national

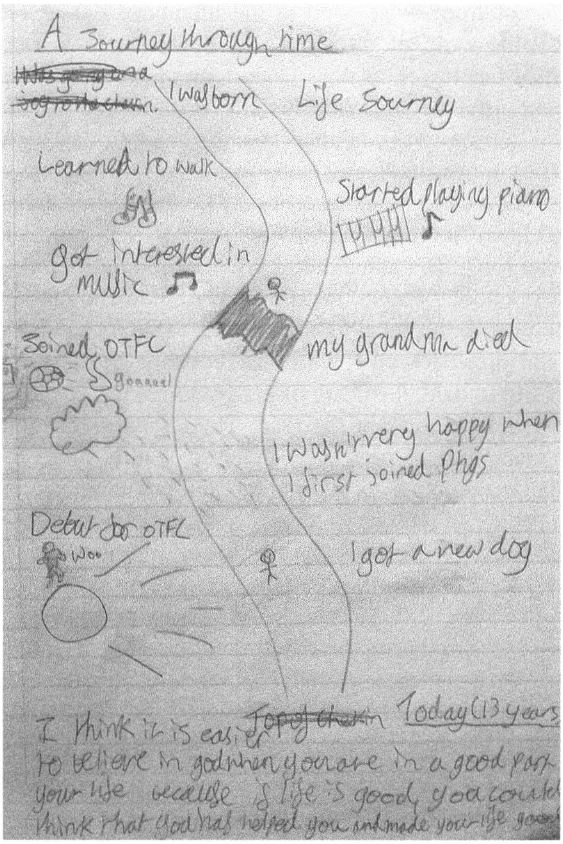

Figure 11.1 Life as a journey through time[2]

curriculum for England). To start a discussion about beliefs and values, the teacher told the students to write and draw their life so far "as a journey." I have looked at the drawings done by several students taught by the same teacher and discussed the task with them. They reported that they were told to draw a road, to think about their major life events to date, and to represent them alongside the road. All the drawings I saw had the road in common, and the text "I was born." Initially, this particular student misunderstood the teacher's instructions and started writing about a literal journey, as seen in the crossed-out text at the top and bottom of his drawing of a road (the *Chevin* is a local hill, which in his first version, he jogged up).

The drawings done by the students all demonstrated the ability to use the JOURNEY conceptual metaphor. Some of the correspondences that they produced are different from those cited in the literature. Lakoff (1993) and Gibbs (2013b, 2014b) write of difficulties as obstacles in a journey, and success as smooth or fast travel, as does Doug, one of the disabled men cited above. This student does not describe his life in terms of difficulties and success in quite the same way as examples taken from adult discourse. Rather, he lists sad and happy times, and many emotional events are shown in terms of the weather, which for a child or adolescent may be more immediately related to his prototypical literal journey (perhaps his walk to school) than physical characteristics of the route. His unhappiness when he moved from his primary school to secondary school ("PHGS") is shown as a cloud and rain; happiness, when he started playing for his local football team ("OTFC") and got a new pet dog, is shown as sunshine. However, what was probably the most intense time emotionally in his life to date, the death of his grandmother, is shown pictorially as an obstacle, a dark break in the road. These data give support to the CMT claim that metaphorical mappings are used readily and on occasion creatively by all language users, to think about and communicate experience and emotion.

2.3 *Example 3:* JOURNEY *Metaphors in an Image*

My third example is purely pictorial. It demonstrates a more specific version of the JOURNEY mapping, and one often mentioned by research students in Britain, A PHD IS A JOURNEY. My university's Virtual Learning Environment includes a folder of materials for Ph.D. students. A colleague offered the photograph reproduced in Figure 11.2, which she had taken

Figure 11.2 The Ph.D. journey[3]

herself, as a cover picture for the folder. Staff and students on the working group agreed that the photograph illustrated Ph.D. work well, so it has been used for several years.

I have discussed this image with colleagues and Ph.D. students, and asked whether they think that it is a suitable image for the content of the folder, and if so, why. There is wide agreement that the image, suggesting a journey on foot following this pathway, depicts the Ph.D. process reasonably well. Quotations from current and former Ph.D. students include those given in (4). In (4d–e), they talk about the limitations suggested by the image, phrasing their criticism in terms of the metaphor:

(4)
a. It shows *the ups and downs.*
b. I'm *in the dark wood at the bottom* at the moment.
c. It's good the way *you can't see the end,* just like you don't know where your research will take you.
d. There should be *paths that go off sideways.*
e. This makes it look like *the path is set out for you* but actually you have to *find your own way.*

2.4 *Correspondences in* LIFE IS A JOURNEY

The three examples discussed demonstrate the versatility and accessibility of the JOURNEY mapping. People are able to develop and expand metaphorical mappings, sometimes inventively, and to use them to express their own experiences. In Example (1), a paralyzed sportsman uses it to describe how he makes sense of his vastly changed future, in Example (2), an adolescent uses it to convey his feelings of sadness and happiness at events of significance in his life so far, while in Example (3), students can use it to describe the difficulties of the research process.

In none of the three cases do the users of the metaphor have any specialist knowledge or experience of metaphor study or the use of metaphors in text or image production; neither were they given time to reflect or prepare their thoughts. The comments made in Example (3) also document the user's ability to reflect consciously on using the metaphor.

What is more, all three of these examples show the users' ability to generate correspondences creatively. Gibbs (2014b: 169) describes some established correspondences for LIFE IS A JOURNEY: "entities in the domain of life (e.g. the people, their goals, the ways they try to obtain these goals) correspond systematically to entities in the domain of journeys (e.g. the traveller, the vehicle, destinations etc.)." Table 11.1 surveys some of the correspondences in the above examples that have been generated creatively.

The explanation of these examples in terms of correspondences allows for creativity and adaptation, and can thus be considered a dynamic one. However,

Table 11.1 *Creative correspondences of* LIFE IS A JOURNEY

Source domain entity or experience	Target domain experience	Example
Rocky road	Persistent difficulties in life associated with disability	Example 1
Dark gap in the road preventing further movement	Inability to act due to bereavement	Example 2
Periods of sunshine during the journey	Periods of happiness	Example 2
Being lost in woods	Struggling with conducting research	Example 3

this approach tends to lead to a focus on structural analogy, that is, the fixed points of relationship between source and target domains, and thus on paradigmatic relationships between entities in each domain. These are, of course, important, but they present only one of the possible perspectives on a domain mapping. In the next section, I discuss the analysis of metaphorical mappings from a different angle.

3 Narratives and Metaphoremes

Sparkes and Smith (2005), authors of the study reported in section 2.1, view metaphors as a component of a narrative: The narrative organizes the speaker's telling of their life history, and each narrative has characteristic metaphors. They refer to metaphors as being "within" a specific narrative (ibid.: 5). The JOURNEY metaphors that they describe, cited above, are situated within a Quest narrative in their model. In the discourse of other informants, they identified metaphors of sport and of war, which they situated within a narrative which they term "Restitution."

The study of narrative and the study of metaphor have separate histories, but Sparkes and Smith are not the only scholars bringing the two together to explore people's understandings of complex issues. Hanne (2015) has analyzed the use of medical metaphors and narratives in politics. While stressing that narrative and metaphor frame political thinking in different ways, he claims that "in political discourse, narrative and metaphor both have cognitive and emotive dimensions . . . we regularly slip backwards and forwards between the two" (ibid.: 4–5). Similarly, Elena Semino has shown how narrative and metaphor interact in the talk of patients suffering from chronic pain and from cancer and that they both have important interactional and emotive functions (see also Semino & Demjén, *this volume*).[4]

A related position is to see metaphor and narrative as being different sides of the same coin. Schön's (1993) analysis of housing policy discourse uses a precursor of the now-standard CMT technique of looking for semantic themes in the linguistic metaphor vehicles to propose a source domain. In one of the texts he analyzes, the literal meanings of "blight," "health," and "cycle of decay" set up a source domain, HEALTH AND DISEASE, or in his terms, a "frame," through which the target domain, INNER-CITY HOUSING, is conceptually structured and viewed: "things are selected for attention and named in such a way as to fit the frame constructed for the solution ... they describe what is wrong with the present situation in such a way as to set the direction for its future transformation" (ibid.: 146–147). In other words, the mapping of DISEASE onto INNER-CITY HOUSING not only gives the target domain a structure but can draw a relationship between the topic and a common sequence of events. In this way, metaphors can impose a narrative sequence on their topic.

Ritchie (2010b, *this volume*) has also argued that metaphors can imply or reference stories, and stories can be used metaphorically. He begins his chapter in this volume by quoting part of a speech made by Barack Obama in 2008 (ex 5):

(5) And if we *walk away* now, if we simply *retreat* into our respective corners, we will never be able to *come together*.

Emphasizing that looking for correspondences is not enough, Ritchie (*this volume*) claims that the passage can be fully understood only if taken as a "metaphorical story." He argues, here and elsewhere, that many figurative expressions can be understood more fully, and their extended, associative meanings can be better described and explored, if they are considered in terms of the shared stories that they index.

Several scholars have noted that specific metaphors reference narratives that are culturally shared. Gibbs (2011a: 122) discusses a group of idioms which include "skate on thin ice" and "get away with murder" and which he calls "isomorphic idioms," because (the components of) their literal and discoursal, figurative meanings are systematically and transparently related. Gibbs remarks that these idioms frequently evoke "mini-narratives," that is, they have a figurative meaning that is accessed through knowledge of the more extended story hinted at in the literal meaning.

With his work on "scenarios," Musolff (2006, 2007) captures a similar insight. A scenario is "a set of assumptions made by competent members of a discourse community about 'typical' aspects of a source-situation, for example, its participants and their roles, the 'dramatic' storylines and outcomes, and conventional evaluations of whether they count as successful or unsuccessful, normal or abnormal, permissible or illegitimate, etc." (Musolff 2006: 28). As his definition indicates, scenarios importantly include not just a bare sequence of events but associated beliefs and evaluations. Musolff (2007) reports a corpus investigation into the figurative use of "dinosaur" using the

Bank of English. He reports the "basic scenario" about dinosaurs, namely, that they became extinct, but shows how a more complex narrative has developed around the metaphorical use of the term, taking target-domain features in what appears to be an example of conceptual blending:[5]

> This extinction outcome is usually linked to a set of stereotypical attributes of the prehistoric animals, i.e. that they were very big, slow, not quick-witted and, crucially, failed to adapt to changing conditions in their environment. In melodramatic, moralistic presentations of the scenario . . . the failure to adapt is interpreted as a "culpable" lack of concern or even disdain for one's own species' survival. (Musolff 2007: 82)

Schön (1993) commented that the framing of housing in terms of disease, discussed above, suggests a particular solution. Similarly, Musolff (2007) claims that the choice of metaphorical scenario strongly leads the reader or hearer toward a particular conclusion.

I have discussed two broad approaches to the study of figurative expressions: In the first they are seen in terms of domain correspondences, in the second as mini-narratives (or as referencing known narratives). In the next section, I describe a detailed text and corpus study of political speeches about government policy on the training of school teachers. In accordance with the general approaches outlined in this chapter so far, I analyzed the figurative expressions in the speeches in two ways: first by looking at the structural mapping and (potential) correspondences, and then by looking at the narratives that they may tell or index.

4 Figurative Language in Political Speeches

4.1 Methods and Data

The following speeches were analyzed:[6]

(i) "Towards a school-led education system" (2,837 words): speech to teachers, head teachers, and other education professionals given on January 18, 2013 by Charlie Taylor, a former head teacher who was at the time Chief Executive of the National College for Teaching and Leadership (the body that leads teacher training in the UK);

(ii) Untitled speech about the teacher education scheme "Teach First" (2,037 words): speech given at the "Impact Conference," Leeds, UK, on July 29, 2015 by Nicky Morgan, at the time of the speech and still at the time of writing the Secretary of State for Education in the UK.

Employing the "Metaphor Identification Procedure" (MIP, Pragglejaz 2007), I analyzed the two speeches by hand in order to identify words and phrases used metaphorically. Using MIP, the analyst considers the contextual meaning of each lexical unit, decides whether the word has a more basic meaning, and if so, whether the relationship between these two meanings is one of comparison. MIP works at the level of the lexical unit which, in most cases in the Pragglejaz examples, is the individual word. Given the growing body of work stressing the importance of fixed expressions in language (e.g. Hunston 2013), I took a more phraseological perspective on the text than earlier MIP-led work. That is, in a number of places I consider strings of words to be a single lexical unit where other analysts might have split them into separate words. I then analyzed these figuratively used words and expressions from two different perspectives, as now described.

4.2 *Analysis of Structural Mappings and Correspondences*

Having identified individual figurative expressions, I explored how they might be connected through underlying systematic mappings. To do this, I followed the procedures developed by Cameron and Low (2010; see also Maslen 2017). Figurative expressions are identified and labeled as "vehicles," and vehicles are then grouped semantically into "vehicle groups." The analyst then examines the topics of the various vehicle groups in order to construct "systematic metaphors." While Cameron and Low use this term deliberately, namely, to avoid the commitment to mental mappings entailed in the term "conceptual metaphor," this difference in theoretical outlook is not one that is a direct concern of this chapter. I have employed the systematic-metaphor procedure because of its rigor and clarity, rather than from a commitment or otherwise to the status of either systematic or conceptual metaphors.

Table 11.2 presents an example of the data, sentences 7–13 from Charlie Taylor's speech. The words and phrases that I identified as figuratively used are in italics. Table 11.3 shows how these lines were analyzed using the framework developed by Cameron and Low (2010).

One such table was created for each of the two speeches. I then grouped and counted the vehicle groups. Relatively few vehicles in my analysis belonged to a second vehicle group, but where these were found, they were included in the count. Using this procedure, I identified 173 metaphor tokens and 7 metonym tokens in the Taylor speech, and 153 metaphor tokens and 1 metonym token in the Morgan speech (I used the definition of metonymy provided by Littlemore, *this volume*).

One vehicle group that was used fairly frequently is CONCRETIZE, to describe the use of a metaphor denoting a physical attribute or process to refer to something abstract, where a more specific vehicle group is difficult to establish; this corresponds to the CMT category of "ontological" metaphors (e.g. Lakoff & Johnson 1980; Ruiz de Mendoza & Pérez Hernández 2011). While this is not a very satisfactory label, it seems preferable to using a more

Table 11.2 *Sentences [7] to [13] from speech (i) by Charlie Taylor*

[7] . . . I'd like to discuss in this speech *our direction of travel* in each of them. [Teacher training, school improvement and leadership]

[8] **Teacher Training**

[9] Too often, even now, schools have got a *blind spot* when it *comes to* teacher training. [10] It is something that is done somewhere else, by someone else – *remotely*, without schools' *input*. [11] Ask many *head* teachers about teacher training and they won't have a lot to say about it. [12] They don't know what goes on or how it is done. [13] In the past teachers were often *parachuted* into schools *from on high*.

Table 11.3 *Applying the "systematic-metaphor" framework to data from speech (i)*

Sentence	Vehicle	Vehicle Group 1	Vehicle Group 2
7	*direction of travel*	JOURNEY	
8	*blind (spot)*	SEEING	JOURNEY/DRIVING
9	*comes to*	GOAL-ORIENTED MOVEMENT	
10	*remotely*	DISTANCE	
10	*input*	COMPUTER	
11	*head*	BODY	
13	*parachute*	WAR	JOURNEY
13	*from on high*	UP/DOWN	

specific label but perhaps over-interpreting the linguistic data. Table 11.4 presents the ten most frequent Vehicle Groups identified in this way.

The next stage in the procedure is to group topics with vehicle groups to identify systematic metaphors, which some analysts would consider to be cognitive mappings. In discussing this analytical procedure, Maslen (2017) notes that "systematicity emerges through repeated, coherent connections between topics and vehicles." If the topics are not examined in detail, a temptation for the analyst at this stage could be to construct connected meaning from the vehicle groups, but in some cases this may not be justified. For example, there are a number of instances of BODY AND BODILY ACTION vehicles used to talk about the topics of SCHOOLS and EDUCATION. Out of context, this could suggest a systematic mapping EDUCATION IS A PERSON, or A SCHOOL IS A PERSON. Most of the seventeen linguistic realizations in the Taylor speech are "head" or "head teacher," which would fit with the latter. However, other examples seen in context do not fit with this. They include:

Table 11.4 *Most frequent vehicle groups in the two speeches*

Speech (i) by Taylor			Speech (ii) by Morgan		
Vehicle group	Frequency	Example linguistic metaphors	Vehicle group	Frequency	Example linguistic metaphors
JOURNEY	29	*toward, lead, direction of travel, way, barrier, progress, fall behind, blaze a trail*	JOURNEY	28	*heading, came, return, way, toward, progress, go, every step of the way*
SEE	18	*see, clear, illusions, focus, views, blind (spot)*	SEE	13	*see, focus, clear, look at, regard*
CONCRETIZE	17	*merged, coalesce, scale, take on*	CONCRETIZE	10	*ownership, produce, make, ounce*
BODY AND BODILY ACTION	17	*head, face, sit, itch,*	LOCATION/ SPACE	10	*(comfort) zone, in line with, widespread*
BUSINESS	15	*turnover, customers, partnerships*	FORCE	7	*driving, impact, pushed, energy*
UP/DOWN	10	*from on high, low, down, under, on top of*	BUSINESS/ MONEY	5	*wealth, rewards, outcomes*
CONSTRUCTION	9	*build, structure, support*	MACHINE	5	*works, engage*
METONYMY	7	*pots of money, comes calling, fingers crossed*	UP/DOWN	5	*highest, highly, raised*
SIZE	4	*reduce, huge*	WAR/FIGHT	4	*tackling, battle, on the ground, frontline*
SPORT	3	*performance, goal*	BODY AND BODILY ACTION	4	*heads, body*

(6) a. . . . the changing *face* of teacher training (Taylor, sentence 54)
b. . . . the expectation of employment does not *sit with* an individual school (Taylor, sentence 38)
c. . . . get teachers through that *three year itch* that often leads to them leaving the profession (Taylor, sentence 63)

These figurative expressions share some elements of meaning, but it seems unlikely that there is underlying systematicity here, in the sense of one mapping that could be expressed as something like A SCHOOL IS A PERSON. The metaphors seem to be much more local than this, and to understand them we need to understand in much more detail what is referenced by them.

The same applies to the UP/DOWN vehicle group. Things that are UP in the two speeches include "standards," "the regard in which teachers are held," "pupils' expectations," and "the government" (which is metaphorically positioned as above schools), and things that are DOWN include "staff turnover." It is not even possible to construct a very general GOOD IS UP mapping, because, as I show below, sometimes expressions such as "on high" seem to have negative connotations in context, while "staff turnover" is an example of something where DOWN is good (cf. Hampe 2005d; see also Winter & Matlock, *this volume*).

Another vehicle group behaves differently, however: most FIGHT/WAR metaphors could actually be seen as realizations of a coherent mapping, expressed as TEACHING IS A BATTLE, and A SCHOOL IS A WAR ZONE. These occur in both speeches, for example:

(7) a. Teachers were often *parachuted in* (Taylor, sentence 13)
b. The real *battle* is about changing behavior (Morgan, sentence 33)
c. *Frontline* professionals (Morgan, sentence 40)

The majority of the vehicle groups of figurative language expressions do not, however, constitute sufficient evidence for the existence of a coherent mapping, at least within these two texts. Singling out figurative expressions and presenting them side-by-side in tabular form, as I have done, is an informative exercise but runs the danger of suggesting a connection within vehicle groups that may not actually exist. I then undertook a second kind of analysis, informed by the work on narrative and scenarios, informed by metaphoremes, discussed above.

In the following section, I describe how I analyzed figurative expressions from the text as individual expressions, attempting to understand any narratives that these may reference.

4.3 *Analysis of Narratives and Metaphoremes*

The second analysis aimed to consider any syntagmatic, sequential, or narrative relationships constructed by figurative language in the texts, as opposed to the analysis of potential networks of structural correspondences described above. An analysis like this is subjective when considering a single use or small numbers of uses of a term in a single text. I therefore used reference corpora to compare the uses in the speeches with uses of the expressions across a range of other texts. Here, I describe this analysis of the following figurative words and expressions: "were often parachuted in" (Taylor, sentence 13), "from on high" (Taylor, sentence 13), "every step of the way" (Morgan, sentence 23), "wall" (Taylor, sentences 58, 60).

BE + parachuted + in Verbal "parachute" is used by Taylor in the phrase "teachers were often parachuted into schools from on high." Intuition suggested that *BE parachuted in(to)* indexes a WAR narrative, but used figuratively it has negative connotations. This would contribute to the central message of Taylor's speech, which is an argument against the university-based training of teachers and in favor of a government scheme by which training largely takes place in schools under head teachers.

The software Sketch Engine was used to search the Oxford English Corpus, which consists of approximately 2 billion running words. *BE + parachuted + in(to)* (all inflected tokens) occurs 1,073 times, of which 500 were randomly sampled.[7] Of these, in 214 "parachuted" was the simple past form or the past participle used in a perfect tense, that is, active voice; only 5 of these were metaphorical uses. Disregarding these citations left 286 citations where "parachuted" was the past participle used in a passive voice structure, as in the use in the speech. Of these, a further 13 were discounted, where the subject (the entity that was parachuted) was something non-human, such as "aid supplies." Of the remaining 273 citations referring to people, 71 were literal and 202 metaphorical.

The literal citations overwhelmingly referred to a WAR narrative, with "parachuted" often collocating with expressions such as "enemy lines" and "enemy territory." The metaphorical citations all describe someone being put into an organization or situation from outside. In a small number of these, the evaluation seems neutral, especially when the context is business (ex 8).

(8) ... the industry veteran who was *parachuted in* as company chairman last July. (*The Sunday Times*, September 18, 2005)

More frequently, the implication appears to be that the person is arriving at a position that they either are not qualified for or do not know well because they are an outsider. In this scenario, a powerful agent, who is either indifferent or actively hostile to the interests of those within the situation or organization has placed them there, either to privilege that person or to actively change the way the organization or situation works. While this evaluative orientation cannot be identified objectively for single citations, the cumulative evidence from context across a large number of citations enables the analyst to identify a scenario, in Musolff's terms, with its typical evaluations (ex 9).

(9) a. But other local activists have warned against an outside candidate *being parachuted in* by the party's leadership in London. (*The Telegraph*, February 16, 2010)
b. All three are fine players but does their presence on the staff suggest that it is easier to get into Yorkshire's first team by *being parachuted in* from elsewhere rather going through the Academy? (The Press, York, January 2002)

Given that this use of "parachute" is closely associated with a specific lexico-grammatical structure, *BE + parachuted + in(to),* this is also an instance of a metaphoreme, which, as discussed above, "take a limited though variable form and have tightly restricted semantic and pragmatic meaning" (Cameron & Deignan 2006: 686–687).

The narrative (scenario/metaphoreme) approach also enables the analyst to see evaluative meaning that cannot be derived from a structural-mapping analysis. Examination of the semantic relationships within the source domain, presumed to be WAR, does not suggest a negative evaluation. Similarly, the corpus citations of literal *BE parachuted in(to)* do not have a negative evaluation; indeed, they often appear in narratives of courage. The narrative/metaphoreme approach does not, however, offer any explanation as to why the evaluative polarity is reversed between literal and figurative.

From on High In Taylor's speech, "parachuted in" is followed by "from on high." In the analysis of vehicle groups, this expression was described as an UP/DOWN metaphor, probably realizing the mapping IMPORTANT IS UP, given that it seems to refer to central government. There are 907 citations of the string "from on high" in the Oxford English Corpus, of which a sample 500 were analyzed. The collocates list generated by Sketch Engine for the string suggests that it often has a religious meaning (10a). Frequent collocates also include nouns referring to speech acts or written messages (10b):

(10) a. savior, decreed, tablets, revelation, blessing, judgment, divine, Spirit
b. decree, directive, orders, commands, instructions

A few citations literally describe a commandment or other action issued from a God to his followers. However, in the majority of the metaphorical citations, "from on high" is used with a highly negative meaning, probably derived ironically from the meaning 'given by God,' as in (11):

(11) a. Opinion is one thing; pronouncements *from on high* without taking into consideration any of another person's points or commentary is valueless. (*The Tyee*, Canada, 2004)

b. Isn't journalists taking intelligence handed down *from on high*, at face value and without question what got us into trouble the last time? (J. McKeating, Chicken Yoghurt, current affairs weblog, 2005)

This is another instance of an analysis in terms of narrative and metaphoremes showing an evaluative orientation that is not found through an analysis of vehicle terms. I now analyze an example of the JOURNEY group using the same approach.

Every Step of the Way Morgan's praise of a teacher training scheme called *Teach First* includes the following:

(12) I know that another one of the fantastic things about Teach First is that you'll have experienced mentors to help you *every step of the way*. (sentence 23)

"Every step of the way" occurs 1,736 times in the Oxford English Corpus, of which a random sample of 500 citations were analyzed. There are just 17 citations in which the expression is used literally, which is not surprising given that "way" itself is only rarely used with literal meaning (Stubbs 2003). The figurative citations tend to suggest that the metaphorical journey referred to by "way" is a difficult one. There are three discernible subgroups, those that mention fighting or protesting along a path to a negative outcome (e.g. "we've fought them every step of the way"), those that write about negative behavior happening at every stage of a process, and those that mention support in difficult times. The latter is the semantic pattern that Morgan's use follows (ex 13).

(13) a. His illness covered a time frame of about eleven weeks. Sheila was there with him almost *every step of the way* in Galway. (*The Western People*, local newspaper, Ireland, 2004)

b. . . . it won't be easy. It will take time and effort. There will be suffering and setbacks but I can promise you this: America will be with you *every step of the way*, as a partner, as a friend. (speech by Barack Obama, July 2009, from CNN transcript)

c. It's not an easy thing to do and there were many times when I didn't want to go on, but my husband encouraged me *every step of the way*. (*Manchester Evening News*, July 2004)

Unless Morgan's speech-writers are breaking the usual semantic pattern of this metaphor, it seems that teaching as a novice is being presented as a difficult and lengthy journey. As for the previous examples discussed, the narrative account gives an insight into the evaluative stance, confirmed by an examination of these citations from the reference corpus.

Wall The final example I discuss here, "wall," is isolated, in that it does not appear to be part of a larger vehicle group, and there are just two tokens. It could perhaps be seen as being nearly synonymous with "barrier," and thus part of a LIFE IS A JOURNEY mapping, but, noting Cameron and Low's (2010) caution not to over-generalize on slim evidence, it has been treated as a one-shot metaphor and therefore does not appear in Table 11.5, listing the most frequent vehicle groups. The context is as follows:

(14) There has in some cases been an artificial *wall* between universities and schools. The universities do the training, but after that the school takes over. This is changing, *the wall is coming down* and there is movement in both directions. (Taylor, sentences 58–60)

I was interested to explore the narrative potentially referenced by "the wall is coming down" and searched for other instances of this string. In the Oxford English Corpus, there are 3,595 citations where the lemma *COME* occurs in the same citation as *WALL*. I filtered the concordance to eliminate the plural form "walls," leaving 2,809 citations. Of these, 779 contain "down." A number of these citations seemed to refer to the demolition of the Berlin Wall, which started in 1989 and was a hugely symbolic event politically, often cited as a metonym for the reunification of Germany. In 406 of the 779 citations of *wall* + *COME* + *down*, the name *Berlin* occurs, usually in the string "Berlin Wall." As I wished to see whether "wall" could reference 'Berlin 1989' *without* explicit mention, I discounted these and analyzed the remaining 373 citations. Of these, I discounted a further 98 where "wall" either was not the grammatical subject of *COME* (15a) or was used with a different, metaphorical meaning (15b).

(15) a. I recall I looked above and saw an avalanche, nearly 200m width was coming down from the *wall*. (Rockclimbing.com articles 2004)
b. we saw a *wall* of raging water *coming down* on the car. (*American Morning*: News CNN transcripts 2008)

This left 275 citations, analyzed as shown in Table 11.5. Citations where "wall" references 'Berlin 1989' are much more frequent that the others. Further, these have a much stronger tendency to appear in the direct lexico-grammatical form *wall COME down*. Lexico-grammatical variants such as "wall had come crashing/tumbling down" are more likely to reference other meanings in these citations. Conversely, the bare form *wall COME down* almost invariably references 'Berlin 1989.'

Taylor's use of the expression "the wall is coming down" (sentence 60) can be analyzed as a mapping of STRUCTURE, or as noted above, if "wall" is taken to denote a kind of barrier, as a JOURNEY mapping. However, this analysis shows that it shares its lexico-grammatical form with established ways of referring to the demolition of the Berlin Wall, in fact, that this lexico-grammatical form is only very rarely used to talk about other kinds of walls. It seems possible therefore, that Taylor's utterance either deliberately or

Table 11.5 *Main senses of* wall + COME + down *in the Oxford English Corpus*

Reference	Examples	Freq
Accidental or deliberate demolition of a physical wall, unconnected with Berlin 1989	– When they tried to fix it, the outside *wall came crashing down.* (*Croydon Guardian*, 2003)	29
The demolition of the Berlin Wall	– After the *Wall came down*, East German teachers had to plan new curricula more in line with the schools in the West. (student history essay, 2005) – . . . two years before *the Wall came down* he [Reagan] was making that statement and everybody thought that this was pie in the sky at the time. (Insight program *Remembering Ronald Reagan* CNN transcript 2004)	215
Removal of other literal or psychological political barrier	– Protestant and Catholic communities come together only through a gate in the concrete "Peace line" wall that divides them, both sides expressed the same sentiments. No one is ready for *the wall to come down,* but neither do they want to go back to the 30 years of the Troubles. (*The Telegraph*, March 12, 2009) – Later that year, Congress passed, and President Lyndon Johnson signed, the voting rights act. All Americans could vote. Another *wall had come tumbling down.* (CNN News, March 5, 2000)	31
Total		**275**

subconsciously references 'Berlin 1989,' thereby apparently comparing the claimed divide between schools and universities with the division between the East and West parts of the city. Well-known facts about the Berlin Wall include the lack of communication of any kind between ordinary people on opposite sides of the wall, and the widespread jubilation when the wall came down, and friends and families who had been separated for decades could finally mix freely. The narrative scenario has evaluative components that make it ideal for putting a positive spin on dismantling an institutional barrier.

5 Conclusions

In the previous section, I described the analysis of four expressions from two speeches, using two complementary approaches. I claimed that the second approach, considering them in terms of scenarios, and more broadly the narratives they may reference, especially when compared with other examples from a reference corpus, gives additional insight into associations and evaluations. This is consistent with what Musolff (2006, 2007) found in his work on scenarios, using a range of text types. I also drew on Cameron and Deignan's (2006) work on metaphoremes, which – while similar in its broad approach – adds an informative emphasis on lexico-grammatical patterns.

Earlier in this chapter, I discussed three artifacts that seem to realize LIFE IS A JOURNEY largely following the previous work in the literature that has stressed correspondences. It may be that correspondences have been over-emphasized in discussions of this mapping. The people who produced or saw these three artifacts very readily produced and identified correspondences when prompted, but both the artifacts and people's reactions to them largely represent creative thinking and production. Creative and conventional thinking and discourse draw on the same resources (Lakoff 1993, 2008a) but may use them unevenly. In all metaphorical communication, especially the prosaic, the narrative element of metaphor seems to be important.

The relationship between the two in ongoing production and reception is interesting, and perhaps of different types. Sparkes and Smith (2005), authors of the study of disabled men's discussions of their lives, described "Quest" as the overarching narrative in these discourses; they write that "Quest" contains some JOURNEY metaphors. That is, in their model, narrative operates at a higher level than metaphors. It is possible that the relationship works the other way as well, that is, a JOURNEY mapping can unite a whole passage, with mini-narratives inside. This may be what happens in the two pictures; in the 13-year-old's drawing, a road – a metaphor – frames a number of narrative incidents along the way. Similarly, when students saw the photograph metaphorically depicting the Ph.D. process, they produced mini-narratives such as "getting lost in the woods." In the education speeches, a number of war-related expressions suggest a systematic mapping of the domain of WAR onto teaching in schools; within this there are narratives such as a soldier being "parachuted in" behind enemy lines.

For the linguistic examples, I have tried to show how the use of a reference corpus can help to show which narratives may be referenced, but this methodology is, obviously, much more difficult to pursue for multimodal artifacts.

My preliminary studies, presented here, and the work of scholars cited here, such as Musolff, Semino, Hanne, and Ritchie, seem to suggest that metaphors interact with narratives in several ways. In terms of nesting and levels, narratives may operate at both a higher and a lower level than metaphors. The relationship between them, in different kinds of texts and non-linguistic artifacts, remains to be fully explored.

Notes and Acknowledgments

1 Italics are used as in the original.
2 Figure 11.1 is reproduced with the kind permission of the student and his parents.
3 I thank my colleague for the permission to reproduce her photograph in Figure 11.2.
4 Elena Semino, "Metaphor and narrative in health communication." Keynote presentation at Modelling Narrative across Borders, European Narratology Network, University of Ghent, April 2015.
5 For technical details on conceptual blending/integration, see Fauconnier & Turner (2002).
6 Both speeches are available on the UK government website: www.gov.uk/government/speeches/ (last accessed June 3, 2016).
7 All inflected tokens of a lexeme form its "lemma." Lemmas are given here as capital letters in italics.

12 Contextual Activation of Story Simulation in Metaphor Comprehension

*L. David Ritchie**

Chapter Preview

Recent research has produced evidence that both embodied simulations and abstract lexical processes are involved in language comprehension, with the balance between embodied and lexical processes influenced by the abstractness of the language and the cultural, social, and linguistic context. The role of simulations in processing metaphorical language, however, is subject to continued debate, not least because it is influenced by a variety of factors. In previous work (Ritchie 2017), I have shown that stories are often used as metaphors (metaphorical stories), and metaphors often imply or activate stories (story metaphors). In this chapter I argue that story metaphors have the potential to activate a rich and extended context and induce and shape both lexical elaboration and perceptual simulation. I propose that Context-Limited Simulation Theory (Ritchie 2006) provides a framework which is compatible with the experimental evidence about embodied simulation, and that a focus on story metaphors and the role of stories in metaphor use and comprehension will support our understanding of metaphor as shaped by both cognitive and discourse/social factors.

1 Word Meanings vs. Concepts in Metaphor Comprehension

1.1 Traditional Approaches to Metaphor Comprehension

Until recently, metaphor theory was largely developed through discussion of nominative metaphors such as "Achilles is *a lion*" and "Lawyers are *sharks*" (e.g. Glucksberg et al. 1992), invented to illustrate a particular point and presented with little or no context. Language was considered a code, matching words and syntax with particular ideas, and language generation and comprehension were seen as simple encoding and decoding. Metaphor was regarded as semantic, and metaphor theory concerned with how metaphors create new semantic connections. The most common theories posited that attributes of the vehicle are transferred to the topic or that a metaphor vehicle creates an ad hoc category based on some attribute common to vehicle and topic (Glucksberg 2008; Wilson & Carston 2006).

In order to illustrate major points (on the basis of authentic and adequately contextualized examples), I will inspect two passages from the speech "A more perfect union," given by Barack Obama in 2008.[1]

(1) one of the tasks we *set forth* at the beginning of this campaign – to *continue the long march* of those who *came before us*, a march for a more just, more equal, more free, more caring and more prosperous America. I chose to *run* for the presidency at this moment in history because I believe deeply that we cannot solve the challenges of our time unless we solve them together – unless we perfect our union by understanding that we may have different stories, but we *hold* common hopes; that we may not look the same and we may not have come from the same place, but we all want to *move in the same direction – towards* a better future [...]

In this passage, each italicized phrase is a familiar metaphor, and the first sentence can be rephrased as something like 'one of the tasks we announced ... is to continue the processes of political change begun by earlier generations.' This paraphrase seems somewhat impoverished, for reasons discussed below.

(2) comments that have been *made* and the issues that have *surfaced* over the last few weeks *reflect* the complexities of race in this country that we've never really *worked through* – a *part* of our union that we have yet to perfect. And if we *walk away* now, if we simply *retreat into our respective corners*, we will never be able to *come together*

In the second passage "walk away" and "retreat" both imply something like 'ignore problems.' "Our respective corners" implies something like 'our own social groups' but could also mean something more like 'our own habits and beliefs.' "Come together" is a common metaphor for 'experience a harmonious relationship.' It all fits together only if the entire passage is taken as a "metaphorical story" (Ritchie 2017) that maps a vehicle story about physical separation, perhaps boxers in a ring or quarreling children in a play room, onto a topic story about something much more complex, which can be sorted out only within the larger context of the speech.

More fundamentally, the traditional approach to interpreting these metaphors requires the identification of some quality shared by vehicle and topic. But what does "setting forth (an object)" have in common with 'announcing a task'? What does 'a process of political change' have to do with a "long march"? It is fairly apparent what "come together" has in common with 'harmonious relationship,' since people in harmonious relationships tend to live close together and sit and stand close together, but what about "retreat into our respective corners"? In many examples the relevant qualities are themselves metaphors that need further interpretation (Ritchie 2003).

1.2 Conceptual Metaphor Theory

Lakoff and Johnson (1980) turned the traditional approaches to metaphor upside-down, arguing that metaphors are primarily cognitive, not linguistic, that they consist of relationships that map more concrete, bodily-experienced concepts (like OBJECT, or PHYSICAL PROXIMITY) onto more abstract concepts (like TASK, HOPE, or HARMONY). These underlying conceptual metaphors stem from the repeated co-experience of the vehicle and topic concepts and are often called "primary metaphors" (see Grady 1997a; Grady & Ascoli, *this volume*). Though they can be expressed in the traditional "X is Y" form (HOPE IS AN OBJECT, HARMONY IS PHYSICAL PROXIMITY), they are usually encountered in language structures that do not explicitly specify the metaphorical mapping but mix source- and target-related expressions (e.g. "*hold* common hopes," "tasks we *set forth*").

More complex "compound metaphors" are generated by blending several primary metaphors (Grady 1997b). To use an example from Grady, THEORIES ARE BUILDINGS (as in "*foundations* of a theory," "*demolish* a theory") blends two basic metaphors, ORGANIZATION IS PHYSICAL STRUCTURE and PERSISTING IS REMAINING ERECT. More than a hundred primary metaphors have been identified (cf. Grady 1997b: 281–299; see also Lakoff & Johnson 1999: 49–59).

An early criticism of Lakoff and Johnson's work was that they inferred conceptual metaphors intuitively by examining examples of metaphors (many of which they recalled from memory or invented for purposes of illustration, like many other metaphor theorists) and that their claims about the existence of conceptual metaphors were not precise enough to be empirically tested. In many cases, it is also unclear how to identify the conceptual metaphors reflected by actual discourse.

The beginning of passage (1), "continue *the long march* of those who *came before us*," is relatively straightforward: "Came before us" blends two standard metaphors, TIME IS SPACE and ACTION IS MOTION with two opposite realizations of a sequence metaphor THE FUTURE IS AHEAD – but also PREVIOUS GENERATIONS HAVE GONE AHEAD. These and other phrases in this passage fit a commonplace (i.e. conventional) complex conceptual metaphor POLITICAL ACTION IS A JOURNEY, itself a blend of TIME IS SPACE with ACTION IS MOTION.

On the other hand, some of the metaphors in passage (2) pose difficulties. "Walk away now" blends STATES ARE LOCATIONS with CHANGE IS MOTION, but what is the topic? The issue of race relations? Discussion of the race issue? "Retreat into" and "come together" also suggest MOTION metaphors, but "walk away" and "come together" additionally suggest DISTANCE metaphors, which could refer to either (DIS)HARMONY or CONFRONTATION – the primary metaphor associates FAMILIARITY with CLOSENESS. "Corners" suggests STRUCTURE as a source domain.

Only by considering the larger linguistic context as well as the overall political and cultural context of the speech, what Lakoff (2014) calls "frame knowledge," can these separate concepts be knit together into a reasonable interpretation. However, the cultural frames in themselves are insufficient: Both passages also imply complex vehicle stories that map onto topic stories about Obama's campaign and the Civil Rights movement, and these implied metaphorical stories are essential to understanding the passages.

In brief, primary metaphors provide important cognitive motivations for the choice of the vehicle, but their (combined) effect does not complete our understanding of these passages.

2 Metaphor Comprehension and Perceptual Simulation

Within a few years of the initial formulation of Conceptual Metaphor Theory, the computational model of cognition and the code model of language were challenged by a new set of theories of cognition as embodied. "Embodied" is usually taken to mean, at the least, that both thought and language make use of neural structures that primarily serve other functions such as perception and motor control. These ideas extend the claims of Conceptual Metaphor Theory in a way that is empirically testable and have been tested through long series of experiments.

Barsalou (2008b) proposes that much of cognition, including language comprehension, is conducted by perceptual symbols abstracted from neural activity associated with sensorimotor experience. He also notes that perceptual information is filtered and consolidated in a series of stages, leading to a "convergence zone" where perceptions of the same object or situation in various modes (vision, sound, tactile, etc.) are consolidated into a single mental representation. At the highest (i.e. most abstract and consolidated) level, perceptual experience is consolidated into complex concepts, for example of 'fire' or 'marching.'

Barsalou (ibid.) proposes that the *perceptual* nervous system is paralleled by a *conceptual* nervous system. Within the conceptual nervous system, "simulators" associated with each concept are capable of generating simulations of the neural patterns that would be activated by an actual encounter with the object or situation. Simulations are always partial and more or less abstract, including detailed perceptual features only if they are relevant to the cognitive context, e.g. processing a particular utterance. For example, most of us have a rich and complex concept of 'fire' that includes detailed information in every perceptual mode, visual, aural, tactile, and so on. Each of us, however, will have a somewhat unique concept, based on our own experiences with fire. When Obama, in his 2008 speech, characterized some of his friend Reverend Jeremiah Wright's controversial remarks as "incendiary," hearers may have activated simulations of heat and destruction associated with fire, but probably not the smell of smoke and the pain of a burn. On the other hand, when he referred, early in the speech, to a personal story that is "seared into my genetic makeup," the pain and smell of burning flesh may have been simulated.

Barsalou (ibid.) acknowledges that semantic associations (like those proposed by code models of language) play a role in language processing, particularly when deep processing is not required, but he argues that conceptual thought is accomplished by activating and manipulating "perceptual symbols" – simulators at a high level of abstraction. Even abstract concepts like 'equality' and 'fairness' can be understood by way of "interoception" (perception of our body's inner state) and "introspection" (perception of our own thoughts). "Gut feeling" is often used metaphorically but it also refers literally to an interoceptive awareness of constricted abdominal muscles that sometimes alerts a person about conflicting desires or potential hazards. 'Equality' can be understood in terms of a simulation of the cognitive awareness that two perceptions match. These and other simulations of interoceptions and introspections provide perceptual symbols that are sufficient for all abstract thought, even logic and philosophy. There is no need for a separate "language of the mind."

2.1 *Perceptual Simulation in Processing Literal Language*

Elements of language, including words and syntax (as well as gestures, facial expression, etc.) activate – and are activated by – the perceptual symbols that form our concepts. For familiar concepts, this activation is automatic: When a person sees a flame or a picture of a flame, the word "fire" is likely to come to mind, and upon hearing or reading the word, simulations of the shape, color, and movement associated with fire may also come to mind – in a level of detail that depends in part on the salience of the concept to a particular person at the moment when the image (or word) is encountered. This central claim – that familiar words are automatically associated with simulations of salient perceptual features – has been tested through hundreds of experiments, using a variety of methods (for a detailed survey, see Bergen 2012).

In a typical experiment, a sentence is presented, followed by an image, and participants are asked to decide whether the object depicted in the image was mentioned in the preceding sentence. Speed of recognition is increased when the orientation and shape of the image matches that which was implied by the sentence (Stanfield & Zwaan 2001), when the perspective of the implied viewer or the implicit quality of the image matches that which was implied by the sentence (Winter & Bergen 2012), and when a sequence of objects are either changed in size or displaced in the field of vision in a way that matches motion implied by the sentence (Bergen 2012).

2.2 *Lexical Processing*

What about new, unfamiliar, or abstract words? On first encountering words for which they have no experiential grounding, like "dragon," "synapse," or "paradigm," in a sentence, how do people understand them? Landauer and Dumais (1997) argue that most vocabulary (at least in a literate society) is initially acquired and understood through relationships of words with similar and related words and with the context in which they are initially encountered. Only a limited number of words are initially understood through direct experience (as when "hot" is encountered in the physical presence of a hot object), and definitions are often not provided when new words are encountered. They have developed a program based on relationships between words and linguistic contexts, Latent Semantic Analysis (LSA), which successfully simulates several aspects of human language performance, including vocabulary and general knowledge tests as well as grading student writing. For example, grades assigned to student essays by LSA correlate as strongly with those assigned by actual teachers as the teacher-assigned grades do with each other.

The ability of an algorithm to simulate the outcome of human language processing does not demonstrate that humans do it the same way. Moreover, approaches like LSA that rely purely on word-to-word connections cannot explain how word meanings can be grounded in experience with the actual world. However, we know from research on semantic priming (e.g. Lucas 2007) that words are directly connected in lexical memory and that encountering one word increases the salience of other, related words. The findings of research on LSA and other semantic connection algorithms as well as the long tradition of semantic priming research support the claim that links among words and phrases play some role in understanding language, including metaphorical language. Finally, pertinent to the present concerns, Kintsch (2008) has demonstrated that LSA can simulate human interpretation of simple metaphors like "Achilles is *a lion*" and "Lawyers are *sharks.*"

2.3 *Perceptual Simulation in Processing Metaphorical Language*

Over the past two decades, the predictions of Conceptual Metaphor Theory have been supported by an impressive body of experimental research focusing on non-linguistic behavioral effects (see Gibbs & Matlock 2008). In one series of experiments, Wilson and Gibbs (2007) found that sentences containing conventional metaphors like "grasp the concept" or "swallow your pride" were understood more quickly if participants had previously performed actions congruent with the source-domain actions implied by those metaphors (as opposed to their having performed an entirely unrelated action). Several experiments have shown that experiencing physical warmth or coldness affects people's social judgments and, conversely, that positive or negative social experiences affect people's assessment of physical temperature (e.g. Zhong & Leonardelli 2008). Other researchers have demonstrated similar relationships between moral feelings and physical cleanliness (Zhong & Liljenquist 2006) and between height and perceived social status (Schubert et al. 2008).

Matlock (2004b) showed that the length of a journey described in a story affected how long participants took to respond to a question about the story, suggesting that participants were simulating the journey. Gibbs (2006b) found that use of a metaphor based on A RELATIONSHIP IS A JOURNEY affected both the distance and the time people walked when blindfolded and asked to walk toward a distant object. Both series of experiments suggest that people simulate time as well as other perceptions implied by metaphor vehicles.

2.4 Evidence from Neurological Studies

Research using neural imaging techniques like fMRI has yielded more equivocal results. Casasanto and Gijssels (2015) review evidence from several neuro-imaging studies confirming the activation of modality-specific perceptual and motor-control neuron groups in the processing of *literal*, but not of *metaphorical* language. On the other hand, Bergen (2012) reviews evidence from several studies that perceptual simulations are sometimes activated by metaphorical language. Both Boulenger and colleagues (2009) and Desai and colleagues (2011) found that motor areas in the brain are activated by novel metaphorical language ("*kick* this meeting into overdrive") but weakly or not at all by familiar metaphors ("*bite* the bullet," "The public ... *grasped* the idea"). Taken together, these results are more consistent with a *weaker* version of "embodied cognition" in which metaphorical language activates more abstract multimodal simulations at the level of convergence zones, but not necessarily at the level of specific perceptual modalities.

3 Context, Elaboration, and Simulation

3.1 Depth of Processing

Zwaan (2014) identifies two distinct perspectives on cognition and language processing, "symbolic" cognition and "grounded" cognition. According to the symbolic-cognition perspective, cognitive processing is a matter of applying a small set of logical or computational rules to a set of arbitrary amodal symbols. Even familiar words are understood by means of definitions in the form of propositions stored in a kind of mental lexicon. Language is processed by assembling propositions associated with words and syntax into mental representations, sets of interrelated propositions. By contrast, grounded cognition assumes that cognition manipulates non-arbitrary and multimodal symbols that are grounded in neural systems of perception, action, and emotion.

Zwaan (2014, 2016) argues that both perspectives are required, because neither perspective can provide a complete account. On the one hand, the symbolic perspective cannot explain how abstract amodal symbols are able to refer to actual perception and action (the "grounding" problem). On the other hand, there is a need for abstract concepts such as 'property,' 'ownership,' 'economic payment systems,' and so on (the "scaling" problem). Although Barsalou (1999) demonstrated that abstract thought can in principle be accomplished through grounded perceptual systems alone, Zwaan argues that in practice abstract representation is necessary.

Zwaan criticizes research on psycholinguistics that has focused on individual words and sentences, with little attention to the broader context in which language is used. He points out that referents occur in a rich setting of agents, objects, events, etc., and that the words representing these referents likewise occur both in the context of other language and in the context of knowledge and beliefs about the broader context. To test people's understanding of phrases like Obama's "continue the long march" (ex 1) and "retreat into our respective corners" (ex 2) without providing the full context would be incomplete at best.

Not only does context contribute to assembling a mental representation from an utterance; it also mediates between symbolic and grounded representations, and these two systems are *both* active in most language processing. Zwaan focuses on the degree of "embeddedness," the extent to which the communication concerns objects, persons, and actions that are *particular* and *present* in the communicative situation. He argues that the use of grounded symbols will be directly related – and the use of abstract symbols inversely related – to the degree of embeddedness.

In sum, the balance between abstract and grounded symbols is a factor of the *depth of processing*: perceptual symbols, grounded in the brain's perceptual, motor, and emotional systems, are employed for deeper and more elaborate processing; abstract symbols for shallower and more cursory processing. Based on a review and synthesis of social psychological research on persuasion, Petty and Cacioppo (1981) proposed that depth of processing, the degree to which a hearer/reader processes and elaborates on a message, is a factor of both motivation and ability to process. *Motivation* includes personal relevance, but it is also affected by "need for cognition," the tendency to enjoy thinking about new concepts and ideas. Apart from situational factors like distraction or tiredness, *ability* includes knowledge of relevant cultural and situational factors – what Zwaan (2016) summarizes as "context."

3.2 Context-Limited Simulation Theory (CLST)

Consistent with Zwaan's claims about the balance between abstract and grounded symbols in cognition generally, Ritchie (2006) proposed that metaphor comprehension is accomplished through some combination of lexical connections and perceptual simulation; the balance between the two processes is influenced by various aspects of the communicative context. These ideas are partially supported by the more recent research reported in the previous sections, although the evidence for the weak/partial simulation of metaphor vehicles that are linguistically expressed suggests that we still need to work out and confirm the details of what is currently hypothesized to be multimodal simulations at the more abstract level of convergence zones. The role of metaphorical stories (and implicit story metaphors) in metaphor cognition (Ritchie 2010b, 2017) especially requires more detailed attention.

3.3 Deliberate Metaphor Use

Attributions about the speaker's intentions are also likely to influence the degree to which an individual thinks about a message. If we assume that hearers are motivated to cooperate in the communicative interaction, it follows that they are more likely to expend cognitive effort on central aspects of the message, aspects the speaker emphasizes, rather than on peripheral features that are not emphasized. Although he focuses on the message and the source/speaker, Steen's analysis of intentionality (Steen 2015, *this volume*) implies that hearers are more likely to process a metaphor more deeply if they perceive it as *deliberate*, rather than unintended.

Steen (2015: 67) defines "deliberate metaphor" use as "the intentional use of a metaphor *as* a metaphor," and then elaborates the idea of *intentional* as when a communicator ponders (deliberates) over the production of an utterance and chooses to employ a particular metaphor (implicitly rejecting alternative ways to express an idea). Although the definition emphasizes the intentions of the *source*, it is partially operationalized in terms of the *message*. A metaphor is deliberate when its structure signals the receiver (hearer or reader) to shift attention from the topic to the vehicle. Steen (ibid.) illustrates the concept with the following passage from a *TIME* magazine article about Alzheimer's disease:[2]

(3) Imagine your brain as a house filled with lights. Now imagine someone turning off the lights one by one. That's what Alzheimer's disease does. It turns off the lights so that the flow of ideas, emotions, and memories from one room to the next slows and eventually ceases. And sadly – as anyone who has ever watched a parent, a sibling, a spouse succumb to the spreading darkness knows – there is no way to stop the lights from turning off, no way to switch them back on once they've grown dim. At least not yet.

The passage is novel (not encountered routinely in ordinary discourse) and fits Steen's (ibid.: 69–70) definition of "extended metaphor" as "one where a cross-domain mapping is deliberately developed as a series of metaphorical utterances presenting a coherent cross-domain mapping" (for detailed discussions of metaphors elaborated over larger stretches of discourse, see *this volume*: Müller; Semino & Demjén). Steen does not comment on a salient additional feature of the passage, namely, that it tells a *story*.

Steen (2005: 68) acknowledges that "addressees do not always verbally pick up on such intentions of deliberate metaphor use," but he does not develop this important point, focusing instead on the intentions of the source and the features of the message. As such, then, his approach has something important to say about metaphor *use*, but it does not answer the questions it raises about metaphor *comprehension*. People who encounter metaphors in discourse have at their disposal much the same information that cognitive and linguistic researchers have: They can notice if a metaphor is novel or extended (along with other features of the metaphor) and make attributions on that basis about the intentions of the source, the speaker or writer. But they do not always notice these features or make the "correct" attributions about speaker's intentions, and sometimes they will *incorrectly* attribute deliberateness and "over-interpret" utterances. (To be sure, researchers also do this.) Conversely, even if deliberateness is correctly attributed, listeners will not always obey the "signal" and refocus their attention on the metaphor vehicle.

3.4 Context and Simulation Again

Observable attributes of the communicative context, the message, and the receiver (hearer or reader) are likely to influence how much the receiver elaborates the message, including relevant simulations of the metaphor vehicle. Attributes of the context that merit investigation include Zwaan's "embeddedness," relevant background cultural and social knowledge, the preceding co-text, and the nature of the interaction (as playful, formal, informal, etc.).

In an informal or playful interchange, messages may be elaborated simply because they are interesting; in a formal and serious interchange, elaboration may be restricted to what is necessary to make sense of a message and respond appropriately. Relevant attributes of the receiver include knowledge of relevant social and cultural information. A person who has never lived in a home with electricity would be unlikely to elaborate the Alzheimer's disease metaphor discussed by Steen and might not understand it at all. A person lacking knowledge of the long struggle for civil rights could understand "continue the long march" from Obama's speech (ex 1) on only the most cursory level.

Aspects of a metaphor that may induce cognitive elaboration and perceptual simulations include novelty and creativity, the use of language in the message that calls attention to the metaphor, and extended development of the metaphor. Especially if a metaphor either is presented as a story or implies a story, it may induce a listener to extend and complete the story. Storytelling is a universal feature of social interaction, typical conversations are sprinkled with stories (Norrick 2010), and stories are deeply implicated in knowledge and memory (Schank & Berman 2002). Stories and metaphors that imply stories are dynamic and likely to draw the reader or listener into the story so that they are "transported into the story world" (Gerrig 1993), which in turn increases the persuasiveness of a message (Green 2004).

4 Stories and Metaphors

Scholars and researchers have offered a variety of definitions for what constitutes a story. All of the definitions involve at least a sequence of causally related events; most require that the events include actions toward a goal. If "metaphor" is understood as the use of language from one domain of experience to express an idea from a totally different domain of experience, then a "metaphorical story" is a story about a sequence of events from one domain (the vehicle story) that expresses something about a sequence of events from another domain (the topic story). Following Snaevarr (2010), I will call a metaphor that refers to or implies a metaphorical story a "story metaphor."

4.1 Metaphorical Stories

There are many types of metaphorical stories; sometimes collectively referred to as "allegories." Gibbs (2015a: 265) casts the net even wider, defining allegory as "an extended metaphor in which the entire narrative introduces and elaborates upon a metaphorical source domain ... to evoke larger life themes." However, it is important to preserve the ability to distinguish among different types of metaphorical stories – and to distinguish metaphorical stories from other types of extended metaphor. Accordingly, I refer to a text like *Pilgrim's Progress* and *The Faerie Queene*, in which people, places, and events are mapped onto (and usually named for) spiritual or philosophical ideas or qualities, as allegory. Metaphorical stories are also familiar in the form of fables (*Sour Grapes*, *The Tortoise and the Hare*) and parables ("The Prodigal Son"). A fable typically maps some commonplace dilemma or personality quirk (disappointment or frustration) onto a fantasy situation (a fox unable to reach a bunch of ripe grapes). A parable maps some philosophical or religious principle onto a fictional situation, which may be literal or metaphorical (Ritchie 2017).

Unlike literary forms, metaphorical stories in ordinary discourse are often presented informally. Sometimes the metaphorical mapping is spelled out, sometimes it is left implicit. Sometimes the metaphor is adapted from popular culture, as in this example from Tony Blair's 2005 address to the Labour Party's annual conference (analyzed in detail in Ritchie 2008a):[3]

(4) all of a sudden there you are, the British people, thinking: you're not listening and I think: you're not hearing me. And before you know it you *raise your voice*. And *I raise mine*. Some of you *throw a bit of crockery*. And now you, the British people, have to *sit down* and decide whether you want *the relationship to continue.*

Here, a part of the target is provided by "you, the British people"; otherwise the listener is left to elaborate the mapping and draw the conclusions.

The situation is different with the above-quoted passage from *TIME* magazine, in which the mapping is made explicit at the beginning and at several points throughout the passage. This example also illustrates another common phenomenon, namely, the blending of stories. The main vehicle story, someone turning off the lights in a house with the inhabitants unable to stop them, maps onto the story of how dementia progresses. A related story, about watching a loved one with Alzheimer's, is part of the topic story, but not part of the vehicle story.

Often familiar metaphors are transformed into stories (Ritchie 2010b, 2017). In a public meeting about police–community relations (ex 5), one speaker transformed the commonplace metaphor "*blind* justice" into a metaphorical story to protest the D.A.'s failure to indict a police officer accused of shooting an unarmed citizen (Ritchie 2011: 83):

(5) Somebody said that "justice is *blind*," but we as Portland citizens, we need to know, or I need to know, that our elected and sworn officials are not *taking advantage of her* or us just *because she's blind*

In this example the speaker transformed the original metaphorical mapping of "blind" onto 'administered without regard for individuals' status or personal characteristics' into an alternative mapping onto a kind of justice that is 'visually handicapped and can't see what's obvious to anyone else.'

Metaphorical stories are sometimes quite short, leaving it up to the audience to elaborate both vehicle and topic stories. At the 1988 Democratic National Convention, Jim Hightower said that George Bush was "born on third base," but "he thought he had hit a triple." This passage combines and contrasts two abbreviated stories. The first metaphorical story describes Bush's *actual* family background (He was "born on third base"). This maps onto his family heritage as the descendant of wealthy and influential men. The second and contrasting metaphorical story maps onto Bush's oft-repeated claim to have built his fortune by his own hard work, as if his inherited wealth and connections had nothing to do with it. The two abbreviated metaphorical stories are combined into an implied story about Bush's campaign rhetoric that discredits his claim to be "an ordinary guy." This example illustrates the importance of context: In order to elaborate the stories enough to understand the metaphor, a person has to have a thorough knowledge of baseball (for example, what does it mean to "hit a triple") as well as of Bush's life story and his campaign rhetoric. It also illustrates how both motivation and processing ability might influence the amount of cognitive elaboration achieved: A person who is passionate about baseball and/or who has strong feelings about Bush would be more likely to entertain an elaborate simulation of the vehicle story than a person with neither of these characteristics.

4.2 Story Metaphors

It is often possible to understand a word or phrase as a simple metaphor, but activating a story indexed by the vehicle and blending it with a salient story about the topic leads to a much richer meaning. During the 2012 Republican Presidential primary debates, Governor Rick Perry referred to Mitt Romney as a "vulture capitalist." This could be understood as a simple nominal metaphor in which the vehicle is an ugly, ungainly, and bad-smelling bird, and these qualities are mapped onto the topic, Mitt Romney. Insults of this sort are common in politics; for example, Civil War General George McClellan repeatedly referred to Abraham Lincoln as "a gorilla," apparently intending no more than disparagement of Lincoln's physical appearance.

However, the context of Perry's remark suggests a more meaningful story metaphor – and subsequent remarks by Perry imply that he intended it as such. Moreover, the context of the remark (a series of political debates) is likely to have motivated a much deeper processing by informed members of the audience. Romney's claim to managerial competence was based on his career as a co-owner of Bain Capital, a venture capital/equity capital firm. The wordplay is based on the formal similarity between "venture" and "vulture," but the behavior implied by the story metaphor is associated with equity capital firms. (It is unlikely that this distinction was salient to many members of the audience.) Equity capital firms buy failing companies, usually companies with assets valued at more than the total value of outstanding shares of stock. They often burden the company with debt to repay themselves for the cost of the stock, and they frequently sell off part or all of the assets. Sometimes they restore the (now much smaller) company to profitability and sell it to other investors, but they often lay off the workers and close the company down.

In the context of the political debate over economic policy, interacting with common ideas about venture capitalism, the phrase "vulture capitalist" is likely to have activated a vehicle story about vultures for many listeners, which maps onto a topic story about venture capitalists. The vulture is fairly familiar in US popular culture, along with a popular story schema about its reputed behavior. Vultures appear, often as harbingers of death or doom, in cartoons and jokes and are frequently used as a metaphor for crude and/or greedy behavior (e.g. "He eats like a vulture"). Venture/equity capitalists are perhaps a little less common in popular culture, although movies like *Wall Street* have contributed to the cultivation of a popular story schema associated with them.

The story metaphor resulting from the activation of both stories will map the vulture's reputed behavior onto that of venture capitalists: Vultures circle around looking for dead or dying animals, and they are commonly reputed to begin feasting on a dying animal before it is completely dead. In parallel, venture capital firms watch for weak or failing firms, and they are commonly reputed to hasten the failure of firms they acquire by selling off productive assets. During the South Carolina primary debates, Perry described two South Carolina companies that Romney's firm, Bain Capital, had bought and closed down and elaborated the implied metaphorical story by claiming that Romney and his company had "picked their bones clean."

Many ordinary metaphors may require activation of a vehicle story to make sense. For example, a "bulldozer" (Wilson & Carston 2006) is a massive and heavy piece of construction equipment. As a metaphor for a demanding boss or obstinate negotiator, it only makes sense in terms of a story that can be blended with another story of the topic person's actions in a staff meeting or negotiation. Associated metaphorical expressions like "push people around" and "run over people" likewise require at least the partial activation of a vehicle story in order to make sense.

Story metaphors are often combined with other story metaphors, or with metaphorical stories, to create even more complex metaphorical stories. Obama's 2008 campaign speech quoted in (1) at the beginning of this chapter provides an example. The first phrase tells a literal story built around a metaphor: Obama's team literally announced (metaphorically "set forth") a list of tasks. "The long march" implies a story metaphor, referring to the centuries-long attempt to achieve full citizenship for African Americans. Listeners with a detailed knowledge of the Civil Rights movement will recognize that this struggle for civil rights included literal marches such as the one memorialized in the movie *Selma*. "Those who came before us" evokes another story metaphor, referring in the first place to the succession of generations but in the context of the Civil Rights movement to the succession of activists and leaders. The phrase combines these two story metaphors into a metaphorical story about Obama's plans to continue the civil rights struggle.

Passage (2) above combines two hypothetical metaphorical stories into a compound story and contrasts it with a metaphorical story implied by "come together": "Walk away" is a common metaphor for ignoring, rather than dealing with, a dispute or problem; "retreat into our separate corners" can be understood in terms of a vehicle story about the sport of boxing (or about a parent imposing a timeout on a couple of quarrelsome children). The entire phrase builds a vehicle story of two boxers (or children) walking away from a physical confrontation into separate corners of a boxing ring or playroom, which maps onto the topic story of two groups of people refusing or ceasing to discuss their disagreements. This complex metaphorical story requires detailed knowledge of the situation Obama described in the preceding part of his speech as well as of the more extended struggle for civil rights.

4.3 Transportation into the Story World and Simulation

Readers and listeners can become "transported into the story world" created by even fairly brief narratives, so that they experience the narrative as if it were really happening and they were part of it. This feeling of "transportation" contributes to the persuasiveness of a narrative message (Green 2004); it should thus be a prime candidate for research on embodied simulation.

To my knowledge, the relation between transportation and simulation has not been extensively researched, although transportation appears to involve multimodal perceptual, motor, and emotional simulation. Gibbs (2011a) has shown that two-thirds of college students can readily identify and interpret allegorical content in fiction and poetry, but he did not test for simulation or transportation into the story world. Research on the simulation of "ordinary" metaphors, presented as decontextualized words or short phrases, has been somewhat inconclusive (section 2.4). Similarly, the implications for perceptual simulation of Steen's (2015) arguments about deliberate metaphor have not yet been tested in detail.

4.4 Story Metaphors in Visual Communication

Forceville (2009b) argues that metaphors are also expressed in modes other than language, and a complete theory of conceptual metaphors must address metaphors in other media, including visual images. By their nature, images depict only a frozen moment. A series of images can depict a series of scenes that imply a story, or a single image can suggest or imply a story in various other ways, but it is up to the viewer to fill in the story line. A solitary visual image resembles a story metaphor in that it can imply but not tell a story.

Visual images can imply metaphors and metaphorical stories in various ways. The Statue of Liberty shows a woman clothed in a draping garment associated with other statues of Roman goddesses, bearing a tablet inscribed with the date of the American Declaration of Independence in one hand, an uplifted torch in the other, and a broken chain at her feet. The torch evokes the metaphor vehicle LIGHT implying both KNOWLEDGE IS LIGHT and FREEDOM IS LIGHT/SLAVERY IS DARKNESS. The torch also signifies a beacon and implies a metaphorical story based on MOTION in that it 'lights the way out of the darkness of slavery and into freedom.' The chains symbolize slavery; the broken chains activate a generic story of breaking chains that maps metaphorically onto the abolition of slavery.

A similar set of symbols is present in the famous statue of the goddess of Justice that stands in or in front of many courthouses. Typically, she is blindfolded and carries a scale in one hand and a sword in the other. Motivated by the primary metaphors KNOWING IS SEEING and CONSIDERING IS WEIGHING, the scales imply a story in which evidence is *weighed* by someone who is *blindfolded* so she cannot see the social status or other irrelevant personal attributes of those brought before her. (As in the example discussed in section 4.1, the metaphor "blind justice" lends itself readily to ironic transformation.) Based on the *weight* of the evidence, she administers justice with the sword.

Editorial cartoons use a visual image, sometimes alone but often in combination with language, to comment on some aspect of current life and politics. Because they need to appeal to a wide range of readers, they tend to draw on familiar cultural images: The statues of Liberty and Justice are staples of political cartoons. However, editorial cartoons also frequently draw on metaphors and metaphorical stories from other media which may not be as familiar to members of the audience. To comment on two US Supreme Court rulings that effectively eliminated controls on the political influence of wealthy individuals, Jamiol (Figure 12.1) drew on the allegorical novel *Animal Farm*. Orwell's (1946) novel tells a story about a revolution in which farm animals defeated the farmer and took over the farm, a thinly veiled reference to the Russian revolution. Eventually the pigs, led by Napoleon, coopt the revolution and, at a crucial point in the story, the original slogan "All animals are equal" is modified to "All animals are equal – but some animals are more equal than others." Jamiol's cartoon shows the Supreme Court justice who speaks the slogan as a pig, i.e. as one of the "more equal" animals. To understand the vehicle story in this cartoon requires detailed knowledge of both the novel and the controversy surrounding these two rulings.

In addition to a relatively high level of visual literacy – ability to read images and recognize symbols and references – political cartoons like these require extensive cultural knowledge, including the ability to recognize the metaphorical stories underlying phrases like blind justice (El Refaie 2009a). The importance

Figure 12.1 *SCOTUS/Animal Farm*, cartoon by Jamiol (2014)[4]

of detailed contextual knowledge raises a crucial question: How do readers who see editorial cartoons of this sort actually understand them?

El Refaie (2009a, 2009b) examined this question with two studies using cartoons from US politics and British politics. In each study El Refaie interviewed the cartoonists regarding their intended meanings. In the first study participants were well-educated people who claimed to be familiar with the newspapers in which the cartoons appeared; in the second study participants were young people age 16–19, including thirteen Muslims and six white native-born British. In each study she asked participants to give a detailed explanation and interpretation of the cartoons. Some participants found it difficult or frustrating to give any interpretation at all. Most participants were able to give *some* reasonable interpretation based on the elements of each cartoon, but only a few of the participants who did not speak English as a native language were able to arrive at an interpretation that resembled the cartoonists' stated intention. El Refaie concludes that understanding images like these requires both general visual literacy and highly specific cultural and political knowledge (related to both source and target domains).

5 Conclusions

The above survey of experimental research can be taken to suggest that metaphor processing involves grounded perceptual symbols. It is highly plausible that perceptual and motor information associated with metaphor vehicles is at least partially activated as *simulations* at the more abstract multimodal level of convergence zones, and that these simulations influence behavioral responses. Furthermore, there is evidence that the processing of both literal and metaphorical language, as well as images, also involves amodal abstract symbols and activation of semantic links to other words, phrases, categories, and lexical meanings. These findings confirm some of the claims made a decade ago by Context-Limited Simulation Theory (CLST).

It has been emphasized that the balance of abstract amodal and grounded symbols in language processing, including metaphor processing, is highly dependent on the immediate linguistic context as well as the extended social and cultural context. It is also influenced by receiver characteristics associated with cognitive and linguistic ability, distraction, and motivation. With respect to metaphors in particular, it is likely that the extent of elaboration and depth of processing is also influenced by whether receivers attribute *deliberateness* to speakers'/writers' use of metaphors. I have shown that, apart from a number of metaphor properties, such as uniqueness, unusual transformations, "tuning devices" (e.g. "so to speak," Cameron & Deignan 2003), and "extended metaphor" (i.e. a series of metaphors elaborating a common conceptual metaphor), metaphorical stories and story metaphors are also important clues that influence the attribution of deliberateness, and hence the depth of metaphor processing.

Stories are often told with metaphorical intent, and the persuasive effects are increased by elements that enhance "transportation into the story world." I have suggested that this can be taken as a dynamic form of embodied simulation. Until quite recently, most research on *metaphorical stories* focused on allegories and other metaphors in literary works. However, metaphorical stories often appear in ordinary conversations where they are sometimes used to illustrate a point, but sometimes employed just for their humor and entertainment value. These are often developed by elaborating idiomatic metaphors ("*blind* justice") or by transforming stories from common cultural knowledge ("be born on third base"). The spontaneous use of metaphorical stories, as well as their repetition in multiple conversations, merits closer examination in its own right – not least for what that might tell us about the intersection of cultural, social, and cognitive processes in language use and comprehension.

Story metaphors – ordinary metaphors with the potential to activate metaphorical stories – are more common, and arguably even more important as a topic for future research. Research might also usefully investigate the origins of story metaphors. Some story metaphors develop from puns and wordplay ("vulture capitalist"), but others may originate in a vivid mental image ("bull in a china shop").

Many familiar metaphors have at most a weak potential to activate stories (old standards like "Achilles is *a lion*" come to mind), but other metaphors, even idiomatic metaphors, almost require activation of a metaphorical story.

"Bulldozer" and "bull in a china shop" make very little sense without activating a story about the actions or behavior of the vehicle and mapping it onto a story about the topic. Metaphors range in a continuum between these extremes: The potential of some ordinary metaphors to activate metaphorical stories, the stories they activate, and the factors that influence the degree to which particular individuals experience these stories should be an integral part of any theory of metaphor use and comprehension.

It has also been emphasized that story metaphors – both in text and in visual images – are often embedded in specialized cultural knowledge. As a result, different members of an audience may process these metaphors in very different ways. Detailed research on the interaction of cultural knowledge with metaphorical stories can thus contribute both to our understanding of language and to our understanding of the discourse in which the metaphorical stories appear. This finding greatly expands the importance and enriches the meaning of "context" in Context-Limited Simulation Theory.

Finally, most of the experimental research on metaphor comprehension has been carried out with simple, usually idiomatic and decontextualized metaphors. The kind of novel and complex metaphorical expressions Steen calls "deliberate" metaphors, including metaphorical stories and story metaphors, may provide a much more fruitful (if also methodologically more challenging) area for future research. In this respect, the possible role of metaphorical stories and transportation into the story world in the comprehension of ordinary metaphors also bears examination.

It is doubtlessly the case that the role of context in limiting (or facilitating) simulations is more complex than it previously seemed and that it may work differently with different types of metaphors. Future research should thus examine the effects of different aspects of context on the comprehension of different types of metaphor.

Notes and Acknowledgments

* The author is deeply indebted to Beate Hampe for many useful suggestions, edits, and words of advice that have contributed greatly to the final form of this chapter. Mistakes and omissions are entirely the responsibility of the author.

1 Barack Obama, "A more perfect union." Speech given at the Constitution Center, Philadelphia, PA, March 18, 2008, passages from paragraphs 3 and 16. A recording of the speech is available from www.youtube.com/watch?v=pWe7wTVbLUU (uploaded March 18, 2008).

2 J. M. Nash, "The new science of Alzheimer's," TIME, July 17, 2000.

3 Tony Blair, "A fight we have to win." Address given to the annual conference of the Labour Party, Gateshead, UK, 2005.

4 The artist's cartoons are published online at: www.jamiolsworld.com/.

13 From Image Schema to Metaphor in Discourse: The FORCE Schemas in Animation Films

*Charles J. Forceville**

Chapter Preview

Moving toward a place and manipulating objects are probably the most important manifestations of goal-oriented actions. Both SELF-PROPELLED MOTION TOWARD A DESTINATION and MAKING AN OBJECT are thus profoundly embodied source domains for the metaphorical conceptualization of PURPOSIVE ACTIVITY. Of these metaphors, only the former – popularly known as LIFE IS A JOURNEY – has received a large amount of attention. Focusing especially on the role of the various FORCE schemas (Johnson 1987), this chapter investigates metaphors from both source domains in three short animation films. Animation provides a perfect medium to express these metaphors in a condensed, aesthetically appealing, and emotion-generating manner. In line with Conceptual Metaphor Theory, it is argued that viewers' understanding and appreciation of these metaphors critically depends on image schemas. Stressing that the body is the beginning but not the end of meaning-making, the chapter also shows that this understanding cannot be reduced to them and that cultural and contextual factors qualify and fine-tune embodied schemas.

1 Introduction

A key claim of Conceptual Metaphor Theory (CMT) is "the centrality of embodiment as *the* mechanism of meaningfulness" (Lakoff 2014: 12, emphasis in original). Conceptual metaphors draw on source domains consisting of schemas that fundamentally depend on the body's ways of negotiating the world. This crucially implies that such image schemas are not primarily propositional structures. Rather, they are patterns of bodily engagement, feeling, experience, and action. It is precisely because they are not reducible to propositions that image schemas help theorize how we understand a broad range of multimodal and non-linguistic discourses, such as cartoons, comics, advertisements, and films. In turn, studying non-verbal and multimodal instantiations of image schemas will alert us to dimensions of such schemas that may not be so prominently present – or even absent – in language.

To demonstrate how image schemas play a role in non-verbal and multimodal discourse, I will in this chapter examine FORCE schemas in three short animation films. This is an excellent way to study these schemas *in action*, and thus take seriously Mark Johnson's (2005: 28) warning that an exclusive focus on the *structural* dimensions of image schemas may prevent scholars from "captur[ing] fully the qualities that are the flesh and blood of our experience."

Forces play a central role in physical events and actions, and thus in movement. Moving toward a place and manipulating objects are among the essential bodily actions undertaken to achieve goals. Unsurprisingly, therefore, SELF-PROPELLED MOTION TOWARD A DESTINATION, and MAKING AN OBJECT, both of which involve the application of various forces, are often used as source domains that are metaphorically coupled with the target domain of achieving goals. Both LONG-TERM PURPOSEFUL ACTIVITY IS SELF-PROPELLED MOTION TOWARD A DESTINATION (popularly known as the JOURNEY metaphor) and LONG-TERM PURPOSEFUL ACTIVITY IS MAKING AN OBJECT are thus profoundly embodied and widespread metaphors.

While the MAKING AN OBJECT metaphor has to my knowledge hitherto not been systematically investigated within CMT, the JOURNEY metaphor has been studied not only in its verbal manifestations (e.g. Katz & Taylor 2008; Ritchie 2008b; see also Deignan, *this volume*) but also in live-action film (e.g. Forceville 2006b, 2011; Yu 2009). More recently, I have investigated this metaphor in animation film (e.g. Forceville 2013, 2016; Forceville & Jeulink 2011).[1] Short animation films are a perfect medium to express the JOURNEY metaphor in a condensed, aesthetically appealing, and affect-eliciting manner. That many such films make no or minimal use of language supports the claim that viewers' understanding and appreciation of them is first of all triggered by deep-rooted, embodied image schemas and metaphors. The goals of this chapter are to demonstrate

(i) how narrative animation films crucially depend on the various literal uses of FORCE schemas;
(ii) how the medium of animation can draw on FORCE schemas to present primary as well as complex metaphors;
(iii) that meaning-making requires complementing embodied cognition with many aspects of cultural knowledge;
(iv) that a better understanding of image schemas, and of "embodied cognition" more generally, can much benefit from researching the multimodal discourse medium of animation films.

2 Conventional Metaphors, Primary Metaphors, and Image Schemas

Grady (1997a,b) has argued that many of the structural, conventional metaphors analyzed by Lakoff and Johnson (1980) are in fact not as basic as they have been presented to be but constitute combinations of more fundamental metaphors, which he calls "primary metaphors." In Grady's model, the complex metaphor THEORIES ARE BUILDINGS can be further decomposed into the primary metaphors ORGANIZATION IS PHYSICAL STRUCTURE and PERSISTING IS REMAINING ERECT in order to account for the pertinent mappings. In primary metaphors, the distinction between target and source is not, as in "classic" CMT, one between abstraction or complexity versus concreteness; target and source in a primary metaphor are equally rooted in everyday basic experience. Evans and Green (2006: 305, emphasis in original) sum up the key distinction between target and source in Grady's theory as follows: "primary source concepts relate to sensory perceptual experience, while primary target concepts relate to subjective responses to sensory-perceptual experience." They go on to explain that since human beings have more immediate conscious access to sensory-perceptual experiences than to subjective (judgmental, evaluative) experiences, primary metaphors help human beings come to grips with the latter in terms of the former. In the specific situation in which they occur, the target and source in primary metaphors thus cannot be reversed. Although frequent co-occurrence of target and source may cause activity in the part of the brain associated with the source even upon being confronted with the target alone (Lakoff 2014: 8), the mapping of pertinent features and structures among features goes unidirectionally from source to target, in non-verbal metaphors no less than in verbal ones (e.g. Carroll 1996, for more discussion, see also Forceville 2002; for further discussion of this, see *this volume*: Grady & Ascoli; Shen & Porat).

Lakoff and Johnson (1999: 50–54) provide a non-exhaustive list of primary metaphors, including AFFECTION IS WARMTH, IMPORTANT IS BIG, HAPPY IS UP, DIFFICULTIES ARE BURDENS, CATEGORIES ARE CONTAINERS, SIMILARITY IS CLOSENESS, and STATES ARE LOCATIONS.[2] "Since they arise directly from experience – and in many cases, from the bodily experience of the world shared by all humans – [primary metaphors] are more likely to be universal than the more complex metaphors which are combinations of them" (Grady 1997b: 288). Grady's formulation is rightly cautious, though, since even primary metaphors are not necessarily culture-free. While the human body's natural tendency to move forward (essential in the JOURNEY metaphor) may seem universal and thus completely "natural," once we take *manner* of movement into account, we may become aware of cultural differences. For instance, a

Chinese woman whose feet have been bound to create "lotus feet" will definitely walk in a very different way from a barefoot Indian, or an Inuit in heavy boots slugging through snow (see also Ibarretxe-Antuñano 2013; *this volume*: Casasanto; Cuccio; Winter & Matlock).

Image schemas, such as PATH, BOUNDED REGION, UP/DOWN, NEAR/FAR, CONTACT, and the FORCE schemas, are directly meaningful, preconceptual structures rooted in the body's movement through space, perceptual interaction with the environment, and the handling of objects (Hampe 2005b; Evans & Green 2006). Image schemas occur as embodied source domains in primary metaphors, which in turn combine and thus help structure complex metaphors. It is at the level of these complex metaphors that the embodied part is complemented by accultured features, and it is particularly these latter that are "mapped" (Kövecses 2010b: 7) or "projected" (Black 1993: 28) from source onto target domain. This mapping/projecting process constitutes the interpretation of the metaphor. A metaphor, however, is an incredibly complex phenomenon. As Gibbs (2012: 353) points out, "no single linguistic, conceptual, or cultural fact shapes metaphor performance, and each of these factors should be studied collectively in terms of the interactive effects on the structure and use of metaphoric language and thought." Moreover, metaphors in turn interact with numerous other dimensions of cultural meaning to achieve their effects.

3 The FORCE Schemas according to Johnson (1987)

The FORCE schemas are central to the way human beings conceive of events – that is, to the "event structure metaphor" (Lakoff 1993). Basically, the event structure metaphor draws on the closely related primary metaphors CHANGE IS MOTION and CAUSES ARE FORCES. Since ACHIEVING GOALS and MAKING OBJECTS necessarily involve change from one state to another, the FORCE schemas unsurprisingly play a central role in the complex metaphors LONG-TERM PURPOSEFUL ACTIVITY IS SELF-PROPELLED MOTION TOWARD A DESTINATION and LONG-TERM PURPOSEFUL ACTIVITY IS MAKING AN OBJECT.

Johnson (1987: 42–48) draws attention to the rich potential of the FORCE schemas as source domains that help shape and structure abstract target domains. Johnson emphasizes the need to explore more concretely how forceful bodily experiences give rise to image-schematic structures that can be transformed, extended, and elaborated into domains of meaning that are not strictly tied to the body, such as social interactions, rational argument, and moral deliberation. Without claiming to be exhaustive, he points out the following "pre-conceptual gestalts" for FORCE: (i) we experience forces through interaction, since they affect us or something in our perceptual field;

(ii) they involve movement through space in a certain direction; (iii) a thing subject to a force tends to follow a specific path of motion; (iv) forces have origins and, when under the influence of agents, can be directed to certain targets; (v) forces have degrees of intensity; (vi) they make themselves felt according to a certain structure, or "sequence of causality." Johnson further outlines seven types of common FORCE schemas. While retaining their original labels, I provide a slightly broadened description here:

a. COMPULSION. An agent or entity is pushed into a certain direction by external forces that can be human as well as non-human.
b. BLOCKAGE. An agent or entity is prevented from moving along the envisaged path by an obstacle, which must be negotiated in one way or another, e.g. by passing round it, climbing over it, or destroying it.
c. COUNTERFORCE. An agent or entity meets with a force that exerts pressure on him/it, hindering movement into the planned direction.
d. DIVERSION. An agent or entity collides with a force that causes him/it to deviate from the intended course.
e. REMOVAL OF RESTRAINT. A (potential) barrier or blockage is eliminated, allowing for unhindered movement to an agent or entity.
f. ENABLEMENT. Some sort of internal or external force provides the means for the agent or entity to move into the desired direction.
g. ATTRACTION. An agent or entity is physically drawn toward an object or place.

Johnson (1987: 48) acknowledges that forces have yet other dimensions. "A more complete list, for example, would have to distinguish among schemata for IMPACT versus CONTINUOUS STEADY FORCE versus INTERMITTENT FORCE versus DIMINISHING FORCE and so on."

4 Literal FORCE in a Bugs Bunny Animation

In this section, I will discuss the various FORCE schemas as they occur *literally* – although in exaggerated form – in a mainstream US animation film (usually called a "cartoon").[3]

Summary of the story: Bugs Bunny is hunted by Elmer Fudd. When Bugs is trapped and about to be shot, Elmer suddenly gets a telegram telling him his Uncle Louie leaves him 3 million dollars – but only on the condition that he does not hurt any animals, "especially rabbits." Bugs subsequently takes advantage of the situation by taxing Elmer's hospitality.

Here are some examples of the forces identified by Johnson. At the start of the film, Bugs has to negotiate the obstacle of a bush and, barging through it in order to escape the hunting dogs that are pursuing him, is momentarily deflected from his track, losing his balance (Figure 13.1: DIVERSION).

Figure 13.1 DIVERSION. Bugs tumbles from screen left through a bush.

Figure 13.2 BLOCKAGE. Bugs is trapped in a "dead end."

Figure 13.3 ATTRACTION. Bugs jumps up and down, falling back to earth.

Figure 13.4 COMPULSION. Bugs is pinned against a tree by Elmer's gun.

Figure 13.5 REMOVAL OF RESTRAINT. Elmer opens a door.

Shortly afterwards he runs into a natural "dead end" (Figure 13.2: BLOCKAGE). Jumping up and down as if he himself were one of them to deceive Elmer's dogs, Bugs lands on the ground each time, being subject to the law of gravity (Figure 13.3: ATTRACTION).

Elmer, having caught up with the dogs, pins Bugs against a tree with his gun (Figure 13.4: COMPULSION). When Elmer enters his house, he opens the door (Figure 13.5: REMOVAL OF RESTRAINT).

Irritated by Bug's shameless behavior, Elmer forgets himself and sticks his gun through the bath curtains where Bugs is having a shower, against the latter's body. Bugs responds by plonking the bath plug in the barrel, causing Elmer to jump backwards (Figure 13.6: COUNTERFORCE). When Bugs simulates he is going to die after being chucked out of the house, Elmer gets nervous he may lose Uncle Louie's inheritance, and Bugs finds himself luxuriously carried back into the house by Elmer (Figure 13.7: ENABLEMENT).

Several more examples of the various forces identified by Johnson could have been given from this eight-minute cartoon. In fact, these forces are completely routine in numerous cartoons of the golden age of Hollywood short animation films with heroes such as Bugs Bunny, Daphne Duck, the Roadrunner, Woody Woodpecker, Tom and Jerry, Popeye, and many others.

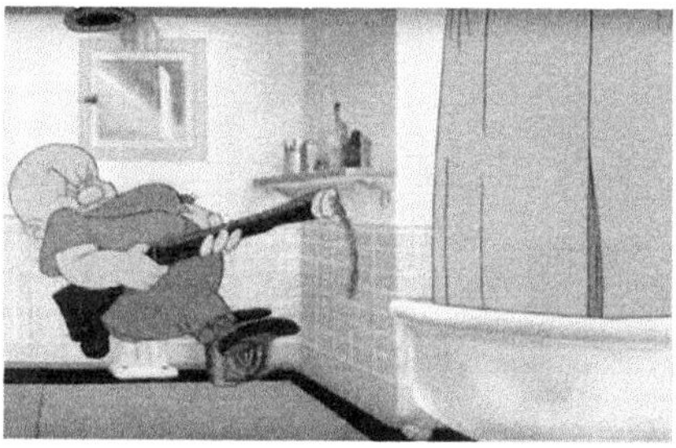

Figure 13.6 COUNTERFORCE. After Bugs (behind the curtains) has plonked a bath plug in Elmer's gun, Elmer falls backwards.

Figure 13.7 ENABLEMENT. Elmer carries Bugs back into the house.

Chasing, trying to get hold of a desired person or object, and trying to avoid an unpleasant person or object are standard ingredients in the visual gags, reinforced by sound effects, that dominate these shorts. My point is that the forces are here primarily *literal*, and viewing their various manifestations is intrinsically pleasurable and spectacular.

Of course, forces play a role in the characters' attempts to achieve goals, but inasmuch as they are to be understood metaphorically, they partake in primary metaphors rather than in complex ones: For one thing, the purpose is to be formulated as SHORT-TERM rather than as LONG-TERM. This claim is supported by the fact that the cartoon consists of a series of more or less independent scenes, whose order is, moreover, to some extent arbitrary. For another, the PURPOSEFUL ACTIVITY in each case exemplifies the "co-occurrence" (Gibbs 2014b: 170) or even "conflation" (Lakoff & Johnson 1999: 48) of target and source. That is, the FORCE schemas permit no, or only minimal, metaphorical mappings on the PURPOSEFUL ACTIVITY domain. It is presumably for this reason that this type of cartoon is so attractive for children: What you see is what you get.

5 Metaphorical FORCES in Art Animation: *Death and the Mother*

Let me now consider manifestations of the FORCE schemas in a much more complex animation film, Ruth Lingford's *Death and the Mother*, in black and white, with some red highlights, based on a fairy tale by Hans Christian Andersen.[4]

Summary of the story: Death approaches a house where a mother tends to her sickly daughter. He transforms himself into an old man and asks her for food. When the mother turns to her furnace, he steals the baby from its cradle. The mother is desperate and frantically tries to find Death to retrieve her

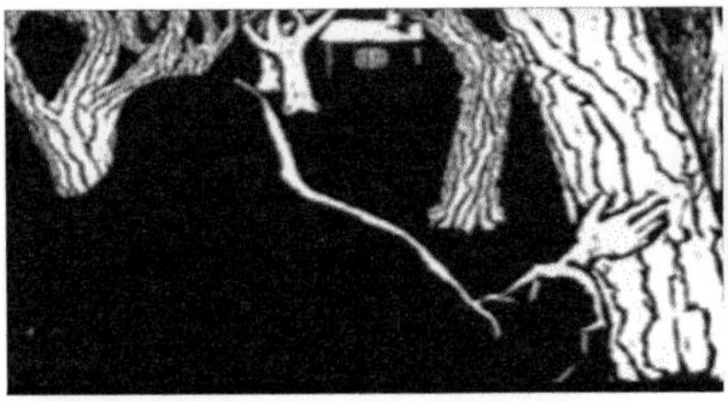

Figure 13.8 ENABLEMENT. Death walks (i.e. "self-propels") toward the house of the mother and child.

Figure 13.9 REMOVAL OF RESTRAINT. Death opens the door himself.

daughter from his clutches. She continually loses her way but is helped by various agents guiding her. Once she has found Death, she attempts to wrench her child from his arms. Then Death shows the mother, in a magic mirror, the unhappiness that lies in store for her daughter. The mother cries and, now definitively, surrenders her child to Death.

Here is an analysis of the way in which physical forces help propel the narrative both literally and metaphorically. Black-cloaked Death walks toward the house (Figure 13.8) where the mother nurses her child. His is "self-propelled motion" (ENABLEMENT by his own muscle power), but we know from myths and fairy tales that Death has a desire to take people with him, so we could also say that Death is here drawn to the sickly child, a candidate to be seized away from life by him (ATTRACTION). If we recruit this folk knowledge, we interpret FORCE not just literally but also as a source domain in a metaphor that would run something like DESIRE IS PHYSICAL ATTRACTION (or COMPULSION IS A COMPELLING FORCE, Grady 1997a: 287). Transformed into an old man, Death subsequently opens the door of the house (Figure 13.9: REMOVAL OF RESTRAINT). Tellingly, he obtains access to the house without knocking: Death is an uninvited guest. This could be construed metaphorically as DEATH INTENT ON FETCHING SOMEONE IS AN UNBLOCKABLE FORCE.

When the mother has gone out into the cold darkness outside, inasmuch as she uses her own muscle power to move forward, this is another instance of ENABLEMENT. However, she also meets several "agents" whose help she invokes. In most cases she needs to make a sacrifice to that agent before she is guided into the right direction. These sacrifices take the form of a forceful violation of her body. When the mother meets a thorny rose bush, she needs to allow the hand-like thorns to scratch her breasts (Figure 13.10), drawing blood to make the roses flower. When she arrives at a frozen lake, the ice is too thin to hold her (BLOCKAGE), exemplifying both literal obstruction and the primary metaphor DIFFICULTIES ARE IMPEDIMENTS TO MOTION.

Figure 13.10 The mother lets hand-like thorns of a rose bush scratch her breasts, drawing blood (the latter depicted in red in the original).

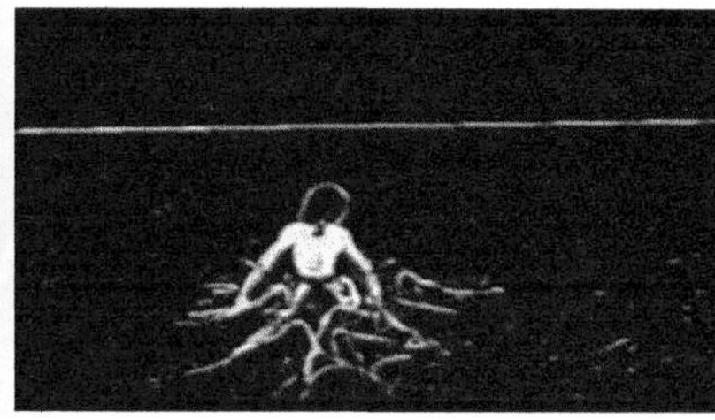

Figure 13.11 ENABLEMENT. The lake magically sweeps the mother across to the other side.

The lake demands her to tear out her eyes and surrender them in return for melting its ice and sweeping her across the waves to the other side (Figure 13.11: ENABLEMENT). There another sacrifice is required of her: The price for being told the way by an old hag is donating her long hair (Figure 13.12).

Of course, we can consider the three bodily violations to which the mother voluntarily submits as purely literal ones: blood-drawing scratches on her breast, tearing out of her eyes, removing of her hair. However, the context in which these forceful actions occur are non-realistic: The blood allows the bush to flourish into roses that outline the path the mother is to take; the waves of the water take her up and in a swift, magic, and sweeping movement transport her to the other side; and the hair, finally, is not cut with scissors but is drawn off the woman's head in one smooth moment, as if it were a wig. I propose that, based on a primary metaphor that can be formulated as PSYCHOLOGICAL PAIN IS PHYSICAL PAIN (Lakoff 2014: 7), these repeated instances of physical suffering – all forceful acts of violation – *in this specific story* give rise to a more complex metaphor that could be rendered as SELF-SACRIFICIAL LOVE IS FORCEFUL SELF-MUTILATION.

The hag takes the now blind mother by the hand and leads her toward Death (ENABLEMENT/ATTRACTION). When they arrive at a rocky porch, she pushes the mother through it (Figure 13.13: ENABLEMENT/COMPULSION). Again, this act of pushing triggers non-literal interpretations: The hag is willing to help the mother only so far; actually meeting Death is a dangerous enterprise that the mother will have to undertake alone. The blind mother feels her way through the dark and finds Death, who holds her child. They wrestle over the child (Figure 13.14: COUNTERFORCE). After Death has given the mother's eyes back to her and shown her the child´s tragic future, the mother gives her child back to Death and pushes him away (Figure 13.15: COMPULSION), thereby metaphorically showing that she now, finally, accepts her daughter´s life will end.

Figure 13.12 An old hag takes the mother's hair in return for giving her directions.

Figure 13.13 COMPULSION/ENABLEMENT. The hag pushes the mother through the rocky porch into the realm of death.

Figure 13.14 COUNTERFORCE. Death and the (blind) mother wrestle over the child.

Figure 13.15 COMPULSION. The mother has surrendered her daughter to Death and pushes him away.

6 Metaphorical FORCE in Art Animation: *The Hand/Ruka*

While *Death and the Mother* portrays a journey, *The Hand* takes place in one location.[5] This has consequences for the kinds of forces that propel its plot. In this section, I will consider both the physical and the metaphorical forces that can be identified in the story.

Summary of the story: A potter wants to make simple clay pots for his plants. However, an enigmatic giant Hand, whose owner is not visible on-screen, continually invades his room and changes the clay into an image of itself, a hand, indicating that it wants the potter to make a sculpture of the Hand instead of making pots. The potter refuses, but the Hand keeps raiding his room as well as haunting his thoughts. When the potter remains stubborn, the Hand locks him up in a cage and forces him to sculpt a hand. The potter gets depressed and dies. The Hand provides him with some sort of state burial, as if the potter had always voluntarily celebrated the Hand.

The transformation of clay into a pot, or a hand, requires the exercise of literal pressure on the clay (Figures 13.16, 13.19). We could categorize this exertion of

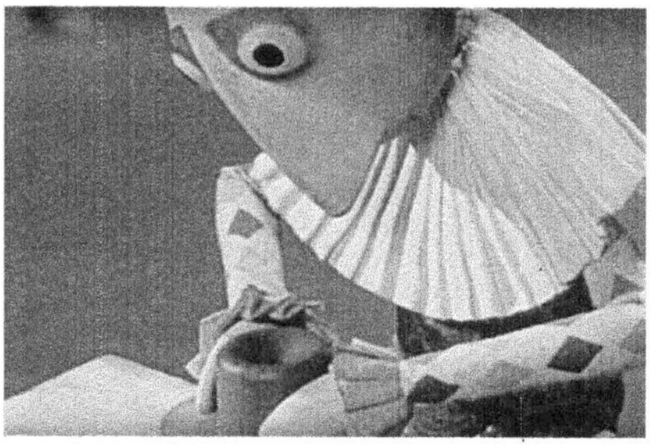

Figure 13.16 COMPULSION. The potter exerts pressure to make a clay pot.

Figure 13.17 COUNTERFORCE. The Hand is prevented from entering by the door (BLOCKAGE); the potter pushes against it to keep the Hand out (COUNTERFORCE).

Figure 13.18 REMOVAL OF RESTRAINT/ COMPULSION. The Hand pushes open one of the shutters, causing a potted plant to fall from the window ledge.

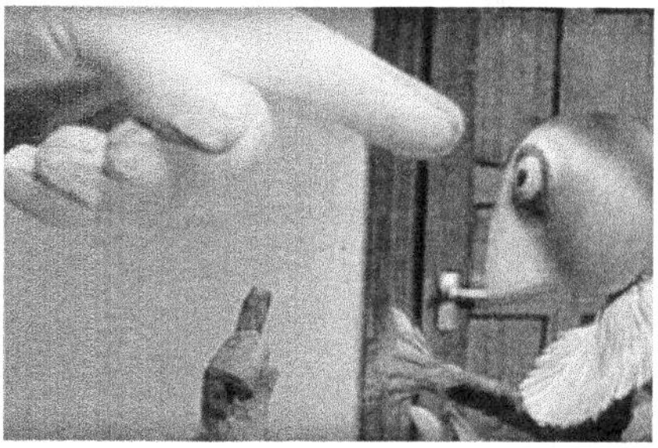

Figure 13.19 COMPULSION. The Hand shows the potter that he should create a hand.

physical force to transform the clay into a pot and a hand, respectively, as compulsion. When the Hand attempts to come in through the front door, the potter tries to push it closed (Figure 13.17: BLOCKAGE, COUNTERFORCE), but the Hand bursts open one of the shutters to gain entrance (Figure 13.18: REMOVAL OF RESTRAINT/COMPULSION). When its various seduction strategies have no effect on the potter, the Hand (now tellingly in a *dark* glove) sets him before his wheel and draws his hand toward the clay that is to be transformed into a hand (Figure 13.20: ATTRACTION). When even that does not help, the Hand fits the potter's hands into strings, effectively turning him into a marionette, puts him into a cage, and manipulates the craftsman's hands into sculpting a hand (Figure 13.21).

As in *Death and the Mother*, there are strong suggestions that we should interpret the various forces not just literally, but also metaphorically. It is vital

Figure 13.20 COMPULSION. The Hand draws the potter's hand toward the clay that he wants made into a hand.

Figure 13.21 The Hand has put strings on the potter's hands to manipulate him into making a hand sculpture (DIVERSION, COMPULSION) in a cage.

to emphasize that the time and place of production of this animation film favor a reading of the various FORCES in terms of the primary metaphors SOCIAL CONTROL IS PHYSICAL CONTROL, BEING IN CONTROL IS BEING ABOVE (Grady 1997a: 290), and especially Lakoff's (2014: 3) CONTROL IS CONTROL BY THE HANDS (for discussion of the distinction and interaction between metaphor and metonymy, see *this volume*: Littlemore; Mittelberg; Ruiz de Mendoza).

In terms of genre, *The Hand* is a high-culture art animation, aimed at adults, and the production context is Czechoslovakia in the 1960s. While to an uninformed contemporary viewer the Hand could be a metonym for *any* repressive agency, awareness of the historical context makes it difficult to see the Hand as anything else than the personification of the Communist regime of the period. Consequently, the various forces the Hand exercises on the potter are to be understood as metaphorically mapping onto the non-physical pressure that a totalitarian power inflicts on its people. Thus, the brute ways in which the Hand literally assaults the potter's house signify the manners in which it – and by extension the Communist authorities – violates the potter's privacy and freedom. Similarly, the literal pushing and dragging and marionetting of the potter by the Hand metaphorically cue the dogmatic rules that the potter is to obey in his creative work. If we take the potter to symbolize the artist, as we are undoubtedly invited to do, the metaphorical projections from the FORCE domain become even more focused.

7 Combining the FORCE Schemas with Other Concepts to Create Metaphorical Meaning

It is essential that, as theorists, we do not burden the various FORCE schemas – or any other image schemas, for that matter – too heavily with intrinsic meaning. Image schemas are profoundly embodied building blocks for meaning-making. They have minimal structure. *In a given context* the basic meanings they have can be, and usually are, enormously enriched, for instance by being deployed as source domains in complex metaphors. As Johnson (1987: 169) points out, "creativity is possible, in part, because imagination gives us image-schematic structures and metaphoric and metonymic patterns by which we can extend and elaborate those schemata." The precise meaning of metaphors, that is, is often dependent on a specific discourse context and can, moreover, develop within that context (Cameron et al. 2009; *this volume*: Deignan; Jensen; Müller; Semino & Demjén).

In my analyses of *Death and the Mother* and *The Hand*, I have suggested several ways in which forces can be interpreted metaphorically. But awareness of these FORCE metaphors alone is by no means sufficient to do justice to the (potential) meanings of these sophisticated art animation films. Indeed, it is because the various forces and the metaphors they trigger interact with other salient metaphorical and cultural information templates that we are invited to construe the FORCE schemas metaphorically in the first place. In the following, I will briefly discuss some of these kinds of information for the two art animations.

7.1 The JOURNEY and MAKING-AN-OBJECT Metaphors

In *Death and the Mother,* all the mother's relocations are motivated by her attempt to save her daughter from death and thus exemplify the metaphor LONG-TERM PURPOSEFUL ACTIVITY IS SELF-PROPELLED MOTION TOWARD A DESTINATION. Most of the non-literal meanings of the forces must be understood as part of this overarching, complex metaphor. The metaphor governs other events and objects as well. When the mother gets lost in the woods, we interpret this as her despair about not being able to achieve her goal, i.e. save her child. Similarly, the rocky porch (Figure 13.13) symbolically marks a liminal space, here a transition between the realms of life and death. In *The Hand*, many of the literal forces pertain, in one way or another, to the making of something, namely, a pot or a hand. This suggests the metaphor LONG-TERM PURPOSEFUL ACTIVITY IS MAKING AN OBJECT. It is within this metaphor that the distinction between the pots that the artist wants to make and the hands he is compelled to make obtains significance.

7.2 Personification

Personification is one of the most common forms of metaphor (e.g. Martínez et al. 2013). Personification can serve different purposes: It can turn abstract phenomena into embodied, live agents with the powers of choice and featuring specific attributes and typical behaviors. Moreover, in animations, personification is a highly useful tool to *visualize* plot events, since "persons" undertake (self-enabled) actions. In *Death and the Mother*, the pertinent personification is not just that of death, but also that of the rose bush and of the lake. In *The Hand*, the essential personification, via metonymy, is that of the disconnected hand into the Hand of the dictatorial Communist authorities.

7.3 Other Image Schemas, Feeding into Conventionalized Metaphors

Among the image schemas that play a role in *Death and the Mother* are the LIGHT/DARK schema, giving rise to the primary metaphor(s) BAD/UNKNOWN/DANGEROUS IS DARK (Forceville & Renckens 2013; Winter 2014, *this volume*), as in the mother's wandering in the wood, and the related KNOWING IS SEEING (Sweetser 1990), pertinent when the mother, by sacrificing her eyes, surrenders control to the personified lake – and later is given back her eyes by Death so that she can witness her daughter's fate in the magic mirror. The BALANCE schema is closely tied to the FORCE schemas: BEING IN CONTROL IS BEING IN PHYSICAL BALANCE – and when the lake swirls the mother around in transporting her to the other side, the mother has completely relinquished her balance. The UP/DOWN image schema pair is notable, too. When the hag takes the mother by the hand, they go up a rocky road, its rising orientation presumably connoting the difficulty of the journey (DIFFICULTIES ARE IMPEDIMENTS TO MOTION). By contrast, when the mother definitively relinquishes her daughter to Death, the latter descends a long flight of steps toward a river in the "underworld." It is noteworthy, incidentally, that these two instances, while both drawing on the UP/DOWN schema, cue *different* conceptual metaphors, namely EXPERIENCING DIFFICULTIES IS GOING UP versus DYING IS GOING DOWN. This is a healthy reminder that an image schema can be recruited to mean different things in different contexts (Hampe 2005d). A more culturally informed pertinent metaphor is A LIFETIME IS A YEAR, which equates death with winter.

In *The Hand* we probably understand the potter's/artist's house in terms of a CONTAINER that is continually invaded by the unwelcome Hand, recruiting the IN/OUT image schema pair. The CONTAINER schema plays a role in another way, too: The artist wants to make pots, which are containers that can accommodate, and facilitate the growth of, a variety of flowers, as a dream of the artist makes clear. In this respect they are completely unlike the hand sculptures, which are merely unimaginative copies of the relentless Hand. The pots thus acquire an ad hoc symbolical meaning: They literally help the growth of flowers, and metaphorically aid the flourishing of the artistic imagination. It is therefore all the more sad and telling that in his paranoia to keep out the

Hand, the artist nails wooden planks against his own cupboard – so that as a result of all this hammering, the potted plant that stands on top of it falls on his head, killing him and shattering to pieces. Ironically, the very act of fighting totalitarianism and censorship causes the artist to destroy his own art and actually leads to his death.

More generally, animation offers attractive opportunities for examining the "manner of motion" dimension of what Dodge and Lakoff (2005) propose to call the LOCOMOTION image schema. However many verbs a language may boast to convey this dimension (walk, run, jump, trudge, stroll, crawl . . .), it can be embodied in infinitely more ways in the medium of animated film.

7.4 Myths and Folk Knowledge

The two wordless art animation films (accompanied, however, by information in the musical and sonic modes) presuppose an enormous number of shared assumptions, myths, and beliefs to be recruited from what relevance theory (Sperber & Wilson 1995: 38) calls the "cognitive environment" of its envisaged audience, i.e. from background frames that are mostly accessed automatically and subconsciously. A few shared assumptions of this type that are relevant to *Death and the Mother* and *The Hand*, respectively, are listed in (1) and (2).

(1) "Personified death looks like a skeleton, often wearing a black cloak"; "It is rude to enter the house of somebody one does not know without knocking"; "Providing food for hungry strangers is a virtuous deed"; "Being out in the snow at night without warm clothing is lethally dangerous"; "There is no stronger love than the love of a mother for her child"; "Christ shed his blood to save the world"; "In medieval mythology, a pelican was believed to tear open its breast to feed blood to its young"; "*Red* symbolizes suffering"; "*Roses* symbolize love"; "Making sacrifices is often necessary to achieve one's goal"; "Fairy tales feature creatures with magical powers"; "Many women consider their hair as essential to their attractiveness"; "Dying is crossing the river Lethe" . . .

(2) "People making handstands and pirouettes tend to be in a happy mood"; "Plants need continual watering to grow"; "Bowing and taking off one's hat is a sign of respect"; "Hands are the body parts that we use *par excellence* to manipulate (Latin *manus*: 'hand') the world around us";[6] "People are afraid of agents that gain access to their homes via brutal force"; "Willfully destroying other people's creations is cruel and intimidating"; "Artistic freedom is incompatible with repression and political interference" . . .

Note that not all viewers will (be able to) access all of these assumptions, myths, and beliefs. Indeed, it is precisely because, by definition, cognitive environments among viewers vary that any discourse will yield minor or major divergences in interpretation by different recipients. After all, as relevance theory insists, relevance is always relevance to an individual (Sperber & Wilson 1995: 142–151).[7] That being said, a considerable number of these assumptions will nonetheless need to be drawn upon in conjunction with the FORCE schemas to lead to meaningful interpretations.

7.5 The Style of the Films

Although it is difficult to measure how exactly they affect the animations' interpretation, the stylistic choices made by their creators undoubtedly have an enormous impact on narratives and the metaphors used in them. Indeed, it is the style of a film (or any other type of narrative) that transforms what narratologists call the "fabula" – i.e. the chronological, cause-and-effect order of a plot, summarizable irrespective of medium – into a "story" or "syuzhet," the latter being the actual representation in a given medium (a novel, a film, a comics album, a dance performance, an opera, etc.) that the audience is presented with (Bal 2009; Bordwell & Thompson 2008).

The film scholar David Bordwell (1985: 53, emphasis in original) links the three dimensions as follows: "In the fiction film, narration is *the process whereby the film's syuzhet and style interact in the course of cueing and channeling the spectator's construction of the fabula.*" Without style, the audience of a story would be presented with only bare, propositional information. But, as Francisco Yus (2011: 147, emphasis added) rightly claims, "propositional *attitude* is essential in human communication." In short, style in films, and by extension in any metaphors that help structure them, is enormously influential in guiding audiences toward the presumably intended attitudinal and emotional responses toward fabula events. In film, stylistic choices pertain to camera angles, camera movements, framing, lighting, props, actors, and many others. In the animation films discussed, specific mention needs to be made of the technique: digital animation with a woodcut-engravings look for *Death and the Mother* and puppet animation for *The Hand* – rather than, for instance, claymation or sand animation or cut-out animation. This pertains, for instance, to the stark black-and-white contrasts in *Death* and to the colorful details of the artist's harlequin-like outfit, the flowers, and the Hand glove's change of color from white to black in *The Hand*; but also to the musical score and the sound effects as well as numerous other facets.

8 Concluding Remarks

In this chapter I have considered the FORCE schemas with reference to one mainstream and two art animation films. The schemas are expressed on a physical, literal level throughout all three. Johnson's (1987) seven various subtypes occur routinely.

In the Bugs Bunny cartoon, the FORCE schemas occur mainly as part of activities and events that pertain to survival, the fulfillment of ad hoc desires, and the avoidance of ad hoc unpleasant experiences. The FORCE schemas are used metaphorically only minimally, namely, in primary metaphors, if at all. By contrast, in the two art animations examined, viewers are emphatically invited to develop the FORCE schemas' straightforwardly literal meanings not just into primary metaphors but into complex metaphors. Specifically, the various forces identified eventually lead to the construal of the metaphors LONG-TERM PURPOSEFUL ACTIVITY IS SELF-PROPELLED MOTION TOWARD A DESTINATION (*Death and the Mother*) and LONG-TERM PURPOSEFUL ACTIVITY IS MAKING AN OBJECT (*The Hand*), respectively. Clearly, Johnson's claims about the metaphorical potential of the FORCE schemas in verbal expressions are no less valid for manifestations in the medium of animation – and these latter are commensurate with CMT's claim that "metaphor is primarily a matter of thought and action and only derivatively a matter of language" (Lakoff & Johnson 1980: 153).

The analyses of the two art animations have also made clear that conceptual metaphors can occur both as primary and as complex metaphors, which seamlessly interact with each other. From a dynamic systems perspective, Gibbs and Santa Cruz (2012: 305) formulate it like this: "A dynamical view of human performance is applicable to understanding the temporal unfolding of conceptual metaphor experience, in which conceptual metaphors act as multiple attractors that the system moves toward and away from given its past history and present circumstances ... No single conceptual metaphor has complete control over how an utterance is interpreted."

While the various primary and complex metaphors identified in the two art animations may provide the skeleton for understanding these profound films, their "flesh and blood" (Johnson 2005: 28) comes from the way these metaphors function in interaction, not only with each other but also with numerous facets of folk knowledge pertaining to social conventions, symbols, rituals, myths, symbols, customs, style, and daily practices. As I have argued, metaphorical construal *always* takes place in a highly specific context: in *this* discourse, in *this* genre, in *this* medium, at *this* moment, in *this* place, issued by *this* creator, to *this* audience. While a metaphor creator presumably has a more or less specific audience in mind, and thus can make a more or less precise assessment of that audience's cognitive environment, by definition the audience, whether an individual or a group of individuals, brings (or fails to bring) its own cognitive environment to the interpretation of the metaphors – and every other meaningful element, for that matter. Since much of an audience's cognitive environment is determined by culture, cultural knowledge, habits, and myths always affect and complement embodied knowledge (cf. Ibarretxe-Antuñano 2013).

Image schemas are the irreducible embodied building blocks of meaning-making, not least for providing the source domains of primary metaphors. These primary metaphors always occur together with other primary metaphors to form complex metaphors. Embedded in and supported by incredibly rich cultural contexts, these become the metaphors we actually live by.

Notes and Acknowledgments

* I am much indebted to Beate Hampe for alerting me to pertinent literature, for suggesting many useful improvements, as well as for meticulous editing. I also thank Thomas Wiben Jensen for a critical reading of an early draft. Finally, I have benefited from the comments of an anonymous reviewer, some of whose suggested formulations I gratefully use *verbatim* in the Introduction. Of course, I claim all mistakes and errors entirely for myself.

1 For other genres, see also Kromhout and Forceville (2013); Wietske Koelma, Iris Adriaansz, and Charles Forceville, "LIFE IS A JOURNEY: An animated metaphor" (5'28"). www.youtube.com/watch?v=MvocTKD5o5A (June 3, 2014).

2 For a comprehensive list of candidate primary metaphors, see Grady (1997a: 281–299).

3 Bugs Bunny Cartoon *The wabbit who came to supper* by "Friz" Freleng, USA 1942, 8'06", original in color. www.youtube.com/watch?v=aZSp0YQU9zM (last accessed: 12/3/2016).

4 UK 1997, 10'36". www.youtube.com/watch?v=hi4zdX-OG5Q (last accessed: 12/3/2016).

5 Jiří Trnka, Czechoslovakia, 1965, 18', original in color. www.youtube.com/watch?v=cS4Th36zN_g (last accessed 13/3/2016).

6 For detailed work on this latter point, see Yu (2003), Forceville (2009a), Abbott and Forceville (2011).

7 For a more detailed discussion, see Forceville (2014).

14 Doing Metaphor: An Ecological Perspective on Metaphoricity in Discourse

*Thomas W. Jensen**

Chapter Preview

This chapter adopts new theoretical insights from cognitive science and dynamic systems theory and employs the notion of "metaphoricity" to explore how metaphor in discourse can be understood more adequately. Relating the ecological turn in cognitive science to metaphor studies and insisting on a unified bio-social perspective, it argues that metaphoricity – if conceptualized within an ecological framework – can offer an alternative to viewing metaphor as primarily social or cognitive. In-depth analyses of two real-life examples analyze metaphoricity as the act of *doing metaphor* within an interpersonal ecology established by the ongoing and dynamic presence of other people, physical artifacts and sociocultural constraints. Rather than treated as a product of individual minds, metaphor is thus shown to emerge from the dynamics of human dialogue viewed as a complex living system. The chapter focuses especially on how metaphoricity works as a gradable, interactively negotiated phenomenon that is intertwined with affective behaviors and situational affordances.

1 Introduction

What is the key component in developing and experiencing metaphor in social interaction? In short, other people! Everything we say and do in the flux of social interaction is fundamentally addressed at and shaped by the constant, and constantly evolving, presence of other people. This co-presence constitutes an "inter-personal ecology" with distinct possibilities and constraints on the creation of metaphor. In writing, metaphors are ingrained in the linear architecture of sentences structurally nested in organized chunks of language allowing for more elaborate metaphoric images. Still, writing is – at least traditionally – a more solitary activity which lacks the principal "affordances" (Gibson 1979) of social interaction: The immediate inter-bodily dynamics and possibilities for impulsive action and thought enabled by the interactive environment in the here-and-now of *doing language*, or "languaging" (Thibault

2011), with other people. The explorative, other-oriented, and whole-bodied dynamics of human interaction can be seen as forming a complex "living system" in itself in which "metaphoricity" (Müller 2008a) plays a vital part by offering a potential "doubleness" in meaning (Jensen & Cuffari 2014).

Departing from real-life data, this chapter will examine how people *do metaphor* as part of their coordinated behaviors embedded in a larger discourse environment. In line with the goals of the present volume, it argues that the notion of metaphoricity, understood within an ecological framework, offers a useful, and intellectually stimulating, alternative to the dichotomous understandings of metaphor as *either* social, i.e. primarily belonging to language or social action, *or* cognitive, i.e. primarily belonging to (or originating from) the individual's conceptual system. In order to offer such an alternative in a more conclusive manner, the notion of metaphoricity needs to be adequately integrated in an ecological framework (Steffensen 2013; Thibault 2011) as well as further empirically supported and developed in terms of method and theory.

1.1 Metaphor and Metaphoricity

As part of the development of more dynamic views on metaphor proposed in recent years (Cameron 2010a; Gibbs 2012; Gibbs & Cameron 2008; Jensen & Cuffari 2014; Müller 2008a), the gradable notion of metaphoricity (Müller 2008a, 2011; Müller & Tag 2010) seems to be gaining ground:

> Degrees of activation are reconstructable through an account of foregrounding activities and strategies employed by participants in a conversation. Activating metaphoricity manifests itself as a dynamic and temporally orchestrated profiling of multimodal utterances ... Metaphor activation regarded in this way follows an interactively negotiated flow of attention; it has an interactive as much as a cognitive and an affective side. (Müller & Tag 2010: 93)

The shift from metaphor to metaphoricity is based on various studies indicating that, rather than solely the result of individual processes, "simple and complex behavior patterns – including metaphor performance in discourse – are higher-order, emergent products of self-organizing processes" (Gibbs & Cameron 2008). Psycholinguistic evidence confirms the assumption of gradability, suggesting that "most linguistic units fall somewhere between metaphoric and literal, so that metaphoricity is a scalar value which influences processing gradually."[1] Concerning the role of the body in metaphor performance, it occurs quite often that "the double meaning of certain verbal actions is as much in the behavior as in the words themselves" (Jensen & Cuffari 2014: 279).

Talking about metaphoricity thus entails a shift of focus from metaphor as a cognitive product (of a cross-domain mapping) and a well-defined linguistic entity to the *process* of creating and enacting some kind of metaphoric, i.e. double, meaning. This opens up the possibility of rejecting the idea of literal and/or figurative meanings as sharply distinguishable positions (Jensen & Cuffari 2014; Müller 2008a) and instead points to a perspective on words and utterances that entail meaning potentials which are to be explored and negotiated between members of a language community. On the one hand, the notion of meaning potentials implies a rejection of essential or fixed meanings of words and lexical items. On the other, it recognizes meaning potentials as being structured between core aspects and more peripheral ones (Linell 2009).

Furthermore, I will argue that we need to take the material aspects of language use more seriously. From an ecological perspective, language is deeply embedded in environmental factors which may indicate that the ways we do metaphor in discourse and writing are profoundly different. In naturally occurring social interaction (as opposed to more mediated or staged discourse, e.g. weather reports, talk shows, political debates, etc.), "full-fledged" metaphors with explicit source and target domains are relatively rare (Cameron 2007a; Steen 2008). The sheer notion of metaphor as a result/product of a source–target mapping may first of all be relevant to written language.[2] In relation to spoken discourse, however, this often turns out to be idealized and too complex. Instead, the complexity of metaphoricity in multimodal social interaction is to be found at other levels:

a. in the way instances of metaphoricity are distributed across stretches of discourse forming clusters and patterns in ways of expression (Cameron 2007a; Gibbs & Cameron 2008);
b. in the way metaphoricity varies over time and is – explicitly or implicitly – "turned up and down" in the ongoing interaction in accordance with various environmental factors (Müller 2008a);
c. in the way metaphoricity comes about, not just as a choice of words, but as integrated in inter-bodily dynamics and inter-affective behaviors in multimodal interaction (Jensen & Cuffari 2014; Müller & Tag 2010);
d. in the way metaphoricity functions as affordances for co-action and co-thinking (Jensen & Cuffari 2014); and
e. in the way metaphoricity is embedded in the dynamics of change within the ongoing talk, viewed as a dynamical living system offering a potential and shareable doubleness for the participants reorganizing the system (ibid.).

1.2 Metaphoricity in an Ecological Perspective

A core tenet of dynamic systems theory is that in a complex system there is no central control unit "delegating the tasks," and at the same time there are no autonomous entities operating entirely "on their own." Recent studies show that two or more people engaged in joint tasks come to adapt their behaviors through a trajectory of compensatory complementary behaviors, no matter whether these tasks are merely "social" or goal-oriented toward some kind of problem solving: "[T]hese behaviors influence one another locally and incrementally, making the whole conversational performance itself a kind of self-organizing synergy" (Dale et al. 2013: 56). Thus, a crucial difference in talking about dynamic systems, rather than, for instance, "communication," is that the latter still – to some extent – entails an idea of two separate interlocutors that send something (thoughts, ideas, feelings, directives, metaphors, etc.) back and forth in some manner, while the former emphasizes the adaptive, coordinated, and self-organizing nature of human interaction, viewing human dialogue as a *functional whole* (Dale et al. 2013; Fusaroli et al. 2014). Human behavior, including speaking, forms a living system that is divided into the separate entities of sender–receiver only as part of an analytical process of isolating and ascribing meaning to individuals.

The dynamic systems perspective thus clearly also "changes how we see metaphor: a metaphor is no longer a static, fixed mapping, but a temporary stability emerging from the activity of inter-connecting systems of socially situated language use and cognitive activity" (Cameron et al. 2009: 63). Metaphoric meanings can be examined as shared experiential processes that arise, develop, and fade out as part of the dynamics of the entire system. Following this line of thinking, the traditional linguistic object of study, i.e. our use of words and their representational value, can be reconceptualized as specific ways of managing interactive behavior within the system dynamics. In this respect, verbal actions do not stand alone, they must always be seen as part of a larger configuration of coordination, co-action, and even co-thinking and co-experiencing.

Thus, an ecologically valid option is to think of human dialogue as "a system of experience" (Jarvilehto 2000: 54) in which the experiences of participants are jointly shaped by the *constraints* and *affordances* (Gibson 1979) of the discourse environment. Metaphoricity brings forth a doubleness in meaning by which new experiences can be shared and developed within the interactional dynamics. A closer look at the finer details of human interaction in naturalistic data quickly makes apparent that a "single author" can only rarely be identified as solely responsible for the meaning of languaging acts. Following from this, I will argue that metaphoricity in spoken multimodal discourse often emerges as more than an individual achievement. Owing to the particular affordances of social interaction, metaphoricity emanates as a joint process and accomplishment embedded in the dynamics and constraints of living (dialogical) systems. It thus needs to be examined as a gradable and process-oriented phenomenon embedded in human action.

1.3 Rethinking Embodiment and Cognition

As implied in the introduction, the notion of metaphoricity can offer a consolidating perspective on the rift between social and cognitive approaches to metaphor. At the heart of this discussion is the notion of "embodiment" (Gibbs 2006a; Rohrer 2007).

The strong focus on embodiment in second-generation cognitive science meant a tremendous breakthrough in understanding the vital role of the body in virtually all aspects of our thinking, including language (Lakoff 1987; Lakoff & Johnson 1999; Talmy 2000), but it also came with a price: Since cognition is profoundly embodied, and since our bodies visibly have physical boundaries that separate us from the surrounding environment, cognition too must by definition be a *bounded* phenomenon tied to an individual body and reserved for processes in the head.[3] Even though the notion of embodiment was originally intended to *resolve* the mind–body dualism, the strong focus on embodied experience unwillingly came to refine and consolidate already established distinctions between individual/social, bodily/contextual, cognition/communication, thought/language, and so forth. Surely, it is vital to be able to make distinctions about the world in order to comprehend and navigate in it. However, these distinctions often appear as dichotomous and mutually exclusive:

> what is social is understood as that which by definition does not belong to nature or biology and the other way round. Likewise the cognitive is defined in virtue of its not being something "out there" in the world of communication. Furthermore, these dichotomies share the underlying premise that it is *the skin* that constitutes the principal boundary between the inner and the outer, and consequently the demarcation between what can be described and understood in *biological* or in *sociological* terms respectively. (Cuffari & Jensen 2014: 2019)

In recent years, a radically new notion of cognition has been put forward (Chemero 2011; Clark 2008; Cowley & Vallée-Tourangeau 2013; Jensen 2014). In this view cognition is not seen as skull-bound – and thereby tied to the individual – but rather as *skull- and body-transcending*. The basic argument is that even though cognition is clearly dependent on neural activation in the brain, it cannot be thoroughly understood as just an internal process. Instead, cognition "is something we do: we enact it, with the world's help, in our dynamic living activities. It is not something that happens inside us" (Noë 2009: 64). In this sense cognition is not (an internal) precondition for action; it is not (just) an inner mental architecture that defines the route by which we are able to navigate in the world. Rather cognition is part of the navigation itself. In other words, we do not have or possess cognition (or cognitive abilities), instead we *do* cognition in our active and explorative sense-making (Linell 2009;

Steffensen 2013; Cuccio, *this volume*). In this way cognition is reconceptualized as part of an "organism-environment-system" (Jarvilehto 2000; Steffensen 2013). In order to be developed further, metaphoricity needs to be conceptualized in the light of these new tendencies within cognitive science (Chemero 2011; Clark 2008; Cowley & Vallée-Tourangeau 2013; Stewart et al. 2010). An ecological perspective on metaphoricity transcends fixed and dichotomous categories between individual and the surrounding world.

2 Method and Data

When studying metaphoricity in discourse, we need to do more than just pick out potentially metaphoric expressions and then analyze them in isolation in terms of conceptual mappings as traditionally done in Conceptual Metaphor Theory (CMT). Such a decontextualizing maneuver can only be carried out by reifying metaphor as a kind of object demarcated from its surroundings and constituted by internal structures – be they cognitive, neural, or purely linguistic. In other words, a decontextualized analytical approach comes at the cost of losing sight of the distributed, dynamical, and fluctuating nature of metaphoricity. It is vital, however, to attempt to capture metaphoricity in its natural surroundings. How we enact and experience metaphoricity is bound up with the embodied, dialogical, sociocultural, and specific cognitive affordances of situated interactions. Consequentially, a focus on metaphoricity

a. redefines *the object of study* as more than isolated words or single utterances and requires that we look carefully at longer sequences of social interaction as well as the totality of multimodal expressions in order to investigate the entanglement of metaphoricity with the ongoing interaction;
b. regards metaphor as more than a solely individual achievement and views it as embedded in *supra-individual dynamics* arising from the constant change and reorganization of the system (of interaction) (Gibbs 2012; Gibbs & Cameron 2008);
c. demands the use of *naturalistic data*, e.g. naturally occurring spoken interaction or everyday products of communication (commercials, posters, designs, emails, etc.), or of experimental settings that simulate a "natural ecology" rather than test hypothetical or anecdotal examples.[4]

A more comprehensive understanding of how metaphoricity works requires an examination of the details of real-life data. The following examples are transcriptions of recordings of naturally occurring social interactions taking place in different institutional settings. In both cases the language spoken was Danish, but, due to space limitations, the transcriptions provide the English translations. The transcriptions follow a simplified version of the notation conventions within conversation analysis (Jefferson 2004, see Table 14.1).

Table 14.1 *Transcription conventions employed in the case studies*

(.)	speech pause, microseconds	°	soft voice
(1.0)	speech pause in seconds	°°	whisper
[...]	overlapping speech across turns	☺	smiley voice
::	prolonged sound	§	overly correct pronunciation
↑	rising intonation	→	gaze direction
...	emphasis	.h	audible in-breath
>..<	faster speech tempo	h.	audible out-breath
<..>	slower speech tempo	CAPS	high volume

3 Analysis

3.1 Case Study 1: Metaphoricity in the Affordances of a Staff Meeting

Example 1 is taken from a 55-minute audio recording of a staff meeting in a Danish municipality. This particular section of the municipality is the desk handling the many incoming phone calls from early in the morning. The topic of discussion concerns the work procedure in the morning, i.e. at what time members of staff need to be present before the phone calls begin in order to rearrange if anyone is absent. It is not the first time they are discussing this, and there is considerable disagreement as to what was agreed upon earlier. The words underlined twice are so called "vehicle terms" that contrast or stand out in relation to the ongoing topic, indicating a potential metaphoric meaning in and through "(1) the presence of lexical items from disparate (or incongruent) semantic fields and (2) the potential for extra meaning to be produced as a result of bringing these together" (Cameron 2007a: 116). The words with dashed underlining indirectly refer to the vehicle terms. The stretch of talk transcribed is fairly long in order to fully capture the distribution of metaphoricity.

Transcription of Example 1

Participants: M: Mary (team leader), W: Windy, T: Tracy, J: Jeanne; *Duration*: 1:53 minutes

W: so I have something to add >cause I'm sitting with Athena↑
and she wonders often about our workflow in relation to this
about Kate <being:: (.) is sick >then she says why don't you
sit down every morning and then figure out [wha-
M: [well actually we
agreed upon this Friday morning or at the Fri- at the last
Friday meeting we had (.) that is eh that every morning you
should talk together (0.5)

W: cause it is actually al [so
M: [you three were there then
T: but that requires that people are present in the morning
W: °I'm here°
J: when we open right °otherwise it is damn hard°↓
M: but [but
W: [but I'm thinking now when Kay isn't here when we sit down and say well is there something urgent (.) is there something we need to deal with or for instance Gil and her news [inquiry
M: [we have made a decision about that↑ (.) there is actually a decision made about (0.3)
W: °I [didn't know that°
M: [but it requi-] but IT LIKE DOES NOT MATTER that we make decisions if they are not enforced (1.5) and this is EVERYBODY'S equal responsibility it [has to be before the] phones starts ringing (.) it might - and if it's hard to do [it before half nine] (.) well try to
J: [when (.) when did]
M: listen when we make an agreement (.) we have a brainstorm and then you sit down in a room when I can at least the days I'm present do this (1.0) but but it is a shared responsibility (.) I can tell you to do it↑ but if you don't then it doesn't matter (1.0)
W: cause I'm thinking it can be a great annoyance (.) that eh things just lay there and then eh then there is one person the same person who always goes in eh and] deals with it and then it can be a nuisance for that same person why the hell [is there no one else↑]
M: [mhm mhm yes but but but]
W: who take over and then it steps [up hh
M: [why] don't you just do it then (0.2) we have decided upon it (1.5)
W: °°okay↓°°
M: well you have this one excuse that you weren't present at the meeting
J: you have been told
M: oh [so you have-
W: =no [I haven't goddammit↑
J: oh yes you have↓
M: oh my god
J: cause I told you when you arrived in the morning
W: told me what↑
J: that we had talked about it at that meeting
W: well not that we should sit down every morning goddammit

J: but (.) when eh we talked about collecting some cases that
we could use for Cindy
W: well yes but that is not that about every morning [we would
J: [then] we
talked about that we could sit down every morning and eh see
what there-
W: =well I have missed that↓ (.) I need it in writing otherwise
I don't believe it heh heh heh
M: well now you get it in writing and then I expect that you
actually do it

In the very first line Windy refers to a situation where she is "sitting with Athena." Apparently she refers to a mundane physical (the bodily posture of sitting) experience. Still, in the way Windy continues by saying "and she [Athena] wonders often about our workflow," it is clear that the social aspect of sitting together implies a conversational situation, too. Furthermore, in the following line a variant of the same implicit nature of sitting-as-talking is reused when Windy is referring to something Athena said: "why don't you sit down every morning and then figure out." Here "sit down" is coupled with "figure out" and thereby acquiring an additional meaning of 'talk' as well as 'confer' or 'plan.' This is confirmed later by Mary, the team leader, who insists that "every morning you should talk together" (line 7–8). Notice the reuse of "every morning," which tightly correlates "sit down" and "talk together." In this way the potential metaphoricity of "sit down" is upgraded, not only in the use of the phrase itself but also in the employment of other related expressions distributed throughout the conversation. Its metaphoric potential is primarily realized in-and-through its relation and embeddedness to the surrounding discourse environment.

Metaphoricity as Meaning Potential The highly conventionalized expression "to sit down" (in Danish, *at sætte sig ned*) literally refers to the physical condition of sitting down. But it is often used with an additional meaning of talking with each other, planning something or even sorting things out, as when you say "why don't you sit down together" to friends who have come to disagree on something. The tricky part is that they do not literally have to sit down in order to talks things through (they might want to go for a walk instead). Still in many cultures in the world (including the Western one), there is a strong tradition of actually sitting down if you have to seriously talk about or plan something. There is thus a double meaning potential in the expression, the metonymy PHYSICAL ACT FOR SOCIAL ACT creates a metaphoric potential (DISSOLVING SOCIAL CONFLICT IS SITTING DOWN TOGETHER). It is important to stress, however, that they are only "meaning potentials" which can be turned up or down depending on the discourse environment (Linell 2009).

Crucially, the metaphoric and metonymic potentials are often conflated, denoting the physical and the social act at the same time. As part of the coordination of the adaptive behaviors of the interlocutors, the "original" meaning of "sit down" is focused and specified as 'sit down while talking/planning,' which again is enhanced by the trajectory of the argument (see next section; for an in-depth discussion of metonymy, see Littlemore, *this volume*).

Furthermore, the use of metaphoricity in this example shows metaphoricity "to be more fundamental and more operative than metaphor when the target of analysis is languaging interactions (rather than texts)" (Jensen & Cuffari 2014: 283). When you study naturally occurring social interaction, this is often what you find: Relatively simple and only partially metaphoric and/or metonymic expressions which "show themselves only through the use of a vehicle term, with the other part of the metaphor (the Topic term) left implicit in the surrounding talk" (Gibbs & Cameron 2008: 69). In this case metaphoricity is turned up to only a moderately low level in the sense that it does not amount to a full-blown metaphor at any point and the literal and figurative meaning are conflated throughout the sequence in a way that blurs any sharp distinction between the literal and figurative.

Metaphoricity as Attractors in Arguing As illustrated in the transcription, the reuse and elaboration of variants of "sit down" is distributed throughout the sequence by all of the participants except Tracy (who speaks only once). The expression appears six times in total (direct use) in different variations during the sequence:

(1) a. I'm *sitting* with Athena (Wendy, line 1)
b. why don't you *sit down* every morning (Wendy, line 3–4)
c. when we *sit down* and say (Wendy, line 15–16)
d. and then you *sit down* in a room (Mary, line 28–29)
e. not that we should *sit down* every morning (Wendy, line 53)
f. that we could *sit down* every morning (Jeanne, line 58)

In addition, there is a distribution of different lexical items that in various ways refer to either the expression of sitting down or the idea of sitting down as a way of planning things, or both:

(2) a. well actually we agreed upon *this* Friday (Mary, lines 5–6)
b. we have made a decision about *that* (Mary, line 19)
c. we had talked about *it* (Jeanne, line 52)
d. well I have missed *that* (Wendy, line 60)

In total there are eleven lexical items spread across the sequence, which might be considered as (indirectly) referring to sitting-down expressions. Figure 14.1

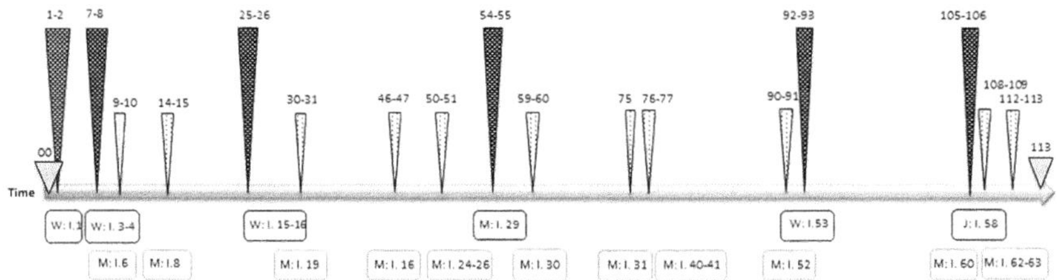

Figure 14.1 Trajectory of metaphoricity (Example 1)

captures the details of the temporal distribution and interactional trajectory of these patterns of metaphoricity.

While the sequence lasts 113 seconds, there are significant time-gaps in which the "sit down" phrase is not used, e.g. there are 28 seconds between the third and the fourth (direct) use, and likewise there are 37 seconds between the fourth and fifth (direct) instance. However, Figure 14.1 shows that these rather lengthy time laps are filled with other expressions that indirectly refer to the idea or practice of sitting down, e.g. between the third and fourth use, there are three instances of indirect uses and between the fourth and fifth (direct) use we can find another four indirect uses.

This indicates that the metaphoricity afforded by the notion of 'sitting down' is kept alive throughout the entire sequence even though there are considerable time stretches where the phrase itself is not used. In order to gain further insight into the impact of the distribution of this particular type of metaphoricity, we should consider it in terms of the notion of "attractors" within dynamic systems theory. An attractor can be described as a state that "the system occupies or approaches more often frequently than others" (Gibbs & Cameron 2008: 68), or "preferred modes of conversational behavior that the system tends to return to" (Larsen-Freeman 2008: 175). Furthermore, these modes are capable of exerting "a kind of pull on the system, bringing the system's behavior close to it" (Gibbs & Cameron 2008).

In the example, the repeated and frequent, yet uneven, use of metaphoricity comes to function as an attractor that exerts a pull on this stretch of this particular living dynamical system that is accelerating into an overt quarrel. The "sit down" expression enters the system in the beginning primarily as an event perception of a physical arrangement but quickly develops into a shared way of expressing a normative social configuration. By being reused and continuously kept alive throughout the sequence, this particular metaphoricity gains a powerful constraining effect and becomes a stabilizing factor that the trajectory of talk returns to in a manner which constrains the possible ways of understanding what they should do in the morning and what exactly they have agreed upon at an earlier meeting. The meaning potentiality of the "sit down" phrase can be seen as a coordinating feature in the flow of talk that creates a shareable as well as normative "system of experience" (Jarvilehto 2000: 59). In order to maintain the equilibrium of the system by endorsing the pull of the attractor, and as a way of ending the argument, Wendy has to acknowledge in the end that they had indeed talked about whether they "could sit down" (line 60), only she had missed it. In this manner her (verbal) behavior or way of framing the understanding of this particular situation has been modified by the coordinating dynamics in the creation of metaphoricity.

3.2 *Case Study 2: Metaphoricity in the Affordances of Couple's Therapy*

In the first example, we saw how the metaphoricity was distributed throughout a sequence of talk as a meaning potential that was neither "turned-up" to a high level at any point, nor extensively developed. In the second example, we will examine how metaphoricity, in a different setting with different affordances, has a different character. It is explicitly "foregrounded" (Müller & Tag 2010) and co-developed by the participants forming a coupled system of "inter-affectivity" (Horst et al. 2014) and metaphoricity.

This example is from a 58-minute video recording of a couple's therapy session involving a Danish couple, Mike and Ann, coming to the therapy for the second time. As a starting exercise, they are asked to say something positive about each other before they get to the problems in their relationship. The sequence begins with the therapist asking Mike to describe what it means to him when Ann is in a good mood. In his first turn and onwards, he tries to account for how he is positively affected by this; subsequently, Ann is mirroring his description. As before, the core vehicle terms are underlined twice, while other related vehicle terms are marked by dashed and dotted underlining.

Transcription of Example 2

Participants: K: Kelly (therapist), M: Mike, A: Ann; *Duration*: 1:15 minutes

1 **K:** °°what it means to me°°
2 **M:** what (.) yes what (.) what it means to me is that (.) eh:
3 like I sort of release some of my own resources (1.0) it's
4 like eh (0.5) that I (0.3) get a start >and now I can hear it's
5 getting too long< h heh it's like having the wind at one's
6 back from the start when you are running
7 **A:** hmm↑ (0.2) so what I hear you say is that you release (0.2)
8 some energy and that eh (0.5) it is like (.) running with the
9 wind at one's back right from the start without warming up

(0.2) is that correct (.) [is THAT]
M: [HEH HEH]
A: THAT what you are saying
M: ahr [what I mean]
A: [heh heh heh]
K: [yes↑ (0.1) yes]
M: now [try and listen] what I like (.) more like to be absolutely
precise what I mean is that (.) eh I get a starting point
that eh (.) I mean heh heh heh where I like eh:: (0.2) so
that (1.0) .h >we:ll I'm like moving fast >if you can put it
like that< like yeah exactly moving fast when you[start] the
race if you can put it like that (1.0) so eh (1.5) it just
runs °°that is how you explain it yes (0.2) and it gives you
something (.) that°° that's how it is [I think]
A: [yes .h] (0.1) so what
I (0.1) hear you say (.) is that eh (0.1) you simply feel
that you are running with the wind at one's back from the
start
M: .h↑
K: mhh↑
M: absolutely correct

The affective and metaphoric dimensions in this example are tightly coordinated and embedded in a shared meaning construction which accommodates the specific constraints and affordances of the couple's therapy as a particular interpersonal ecology. We thus need to see the metaphoricity in this sequence as a type of attunement to the specific affordances of this kind of "ecological niche," in this case the living practice of couple's therapy, in order to grasp its specific quality and appearance. According to Gibson (1979), an ecological niche is a set of affordances that offers the animal – or the person – different ways of life in the sense of different types of behavior. In this particular type of therapy, both physical and social affordances can be identified as playing a key role for a certain type of behavior. The physical arrangement of sitting closely, face-to-face, with the therapist in the middle clearly affords an interpersonal engagement and emotional coupling (see Figure 14.2). Equally important is the way the dialogue is structured around the practice of mirroring.

When the first speaker says something, the second speaker cannot reply freely with, for instance, counter-arguments, elaborations, questions, or just change the topic. Instead, the second speaker is obliged to mirror his/her conception of what has just been said beginning with the phrase "what I hear you say is . . ." The idea is to force the couples to listen and try to understand what each other are saying. This reduces the speed of the conversation

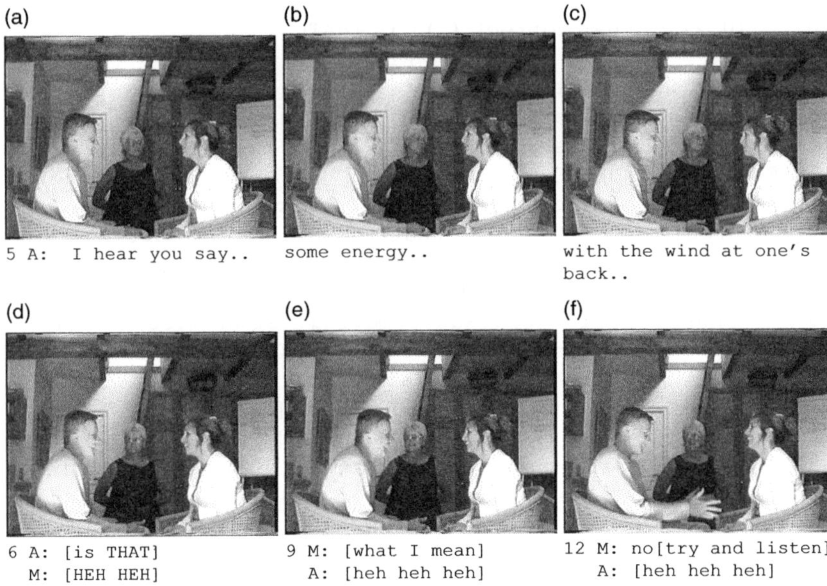

Figure 14.2 Affective dynamics in metaphoricity (Example 2)

considerably, and the topic of conversation is kept for a much longer time. These tight *social constraints* allow for more patience and in-depth understanding in the "inter-world" of dialogue (Linell 2009) while at the same time granting the therapist a governing and powerful role in that s/he can oversee and to some degree control the development of the dialogue. Regarding the development of metaphoricity, the low speed, repeated patterns, tendency to stay on the topic, and interpersonal focus of mirroring all afford a type of metaphoricity much more elaborated, negotiable, and fully developed than in the first example.

Patterns of Metaphoricity Throughout the sequence we can find a clear pattern of vehicle terms related to notions of running (and/or of moving fast) first introduced by Mike, and then reused and developed by Ann as adequate descriptions of how Mike feels when Ann is in a good mood. The image of running with the wind at one's back is repeated three times by both Mike and Ann and distributed throughout the sequence in the following way and includes Ann's elaboration "without warming up" (3b):

(3) Pattern 1

a. it's like *having the wind at one's back from the start* when you are running (Mike, lines 5–6)

b. it is like (.) *running with the wind at one's back right from the start without warming up* (Ann, lines 8–9)
c. you simply feel that *you are running with the wind at one's back from the start* (Ann, lines 26–27)

These ongoing conceptualizations draw on the physical experience of movement and propulsion as both troublesome and demanding, in the case of obstacles, or conversely, as easy and effortless if there is a helping factor like having the wind at one's back. Thus, we can identify a loosely structured pattern of vehicle terms that entails the metaphoric meaning potential: BEING POSITIVELY AFFECTED/FEELING GOOD IS RUNNING WITH THE WIND AT ONE'S BACK.

However, the metaphoricity in this example is by no means tied to a single type of vehicle term. Preceding the articulation of the image of running with the wind at one's back, Mike talks about "releasing my own resources" and "getting a start." Subsequently, these images are reused by Ann and also joined by other related expressions such as "moving fast," "start the race" (5d), and "it just runs" (5e):

(4) Pattern 2
a. like I sort of *release some of my own resources* (Mike, line 3)
b. *you release* (0.2) *some energy* (Ann, lines 7–8)

(5) Pattern 3
a. it's like eh that I (0.3) *get a start* (M, lines 3–4)
b. *I get a starting point* (Mike, line 17)
c. *I'm like moving fast* (Mike, line 19)
d. *moving fast when you [start] the race* (Mike, lines 20–21)
e. *it just runs* (Mike, lines 21–22)

It is important to stress that these three patterns of metaphoricity are entangled with each other both conceptually and on a pragmatic level. The notion of a 'start,' for instance, is prevalent in several instances of both patterns 1 and 3. As in the first example (section 3.1), these are highly conventionalized expressions with only little novel metaphoric value. Still, they can be combined with other expressions like "running," "moving," or "race." By stressing conceptualizations of various kinds of forward movement, a slightly higher level of metaphoricity is achieved. This structure is promoted and developed by both Mike and Ann; in this way the metaphoricity serves a function in building a shared way of understanding and highlighting certain aspects of how Mike feels when Ann is in a good mood.

Coupled Systems and Lexical Entrainment As in the previous example, the different patterns of metaphoricity can be viewed as "attractors" in the constantly evolving dynamical system. Here the three interrelated patterns of metaphoricity emerge, co-develop, and overlap as the sequence proceeds.

In her first attempt at mirroring in lines 7-10, Ann adds "without warming up" as a metaphoric elaboration to the idea of running with wind at one's back. In her second turn, this additional image is left out and instead the status of this condition as a feeling is emphasized (line 25: "you simply feel"). Thus, a considerable reduction in the variety of lexical terms has taken place. Not only is the warming-up metaphor omitted, but also, as described above, the most part of Mike's long second turn is not reflected in Ann's final, and successful, mirroring. In other words, the dynamical system has undergone a reduction in its diversity of relevant types of metaphoricity in the service of a "lexical entrainment": "the process by which people come to use the same terms in talk" in which "references are modified over repeated trials, becoming shorter and more efficient" (Larsen-Freeman & Cameron 2008: 183). Thus, both the trajectory and ultimately also the function and meaning of metaphoricity in this type of human interaction are co-created, and not a matter of individual minds generating independent ideas in the shape of linguistic form to be communicated to each other. There are prominent systemic and subpersonal features at stake that affect the process of metaphoricity as part of a living system: "When a system of many interacting components self-organizes, it undergoes a reduction *in its degree of freedom*" (Dale et al. 2013: 54, emphasis in original). Ann's final mirroring (lines 24–27) can be seen as a result of the ongoing coordination of the system that encapsulates features from patterns 1 and 3 ("running with the wind at one's back," "from the start") as well as the previous contributions from both Mike and Ann into a *single system* of metaphoricity. Thus, the ultimate result of the trajectory of emerging metaphoricity in this sequence is best conceived of as belonging to neither Mike nor Ann. Rather, it is the outcome of the process of co-creation, co-thinking – and even co-feeling – as will be discussed next.

The Coordination of Inter-Affectivity and Metaphoricity The trajectory of metaphoricity in this example suggests that, even though the two mirroring turns by Ann (lines 7–10 and 24–27) are quite similar, they receive almost opposing feedback in the dynamical system. The first one is more or less rejected by Mike (line 13: "ahr what I mean") and instead another elaborate account is offered as a correction or alternative explanation. The second one, on the other hand, receives an immediate non-verbal accept (line 28: .h↑) as well as an explicit verbal approval (line 30: "absolutely correct"). This is all the more noticeable since Ann's second last turn does not bear much resemblance to Mike's second long turn from lines 16–23, which it is supposed to mirror. In order to explain this discrepancy in responses, it is necessary to focus on how the inter-bodily dynamics influences the construction of metaphoricity as the sequence proceeds. We need to bear in mind that metaphoricity is not just about words but is deeply embedded in multimodal and expressive behaviors that are co-developed between the participants. Figure 14.2 shows two sets of images from different parts of interaction all in the first half of the sequence that leads up to a so-called *pivot point* which fundamentally changes the affective dynamics between Mike and Ann and thereby alters the coordination of metaphoricity.

Overall the two sets of pictures point to a clear development in the dynamics between Mike and Ann. The first set depicts Ann's first attempt at mirroring in lines 7–10. Ann and Mike are sitting still looking straight at each other, almost motionless; the only visible facial movements are related to Ann's talking. In other words, the level of inter-bodily dynamics (Thibault 2011) and inter-affective involvement is low. This stands in clear contrast to the second set of pictures. Ann is about to finish her mirroring when Mike starts to laugh. Ann smiles and immediately attunes her voice (volume and smiley voice) to Mike's loud laughter. Subsequently Mike starts talking with a smiley voice while leaning forward and smiling as Ann begins to laugh simultaneously. Interestingly this sudden increase in inter-bodily dynamics and inter-affectivity (Horst et al. 2014) happens when Mike is – on a verbal level – rejecting Ann's attempt at mirroring. Subsequently, he is trying to produce a new and better account of what he said in the beginning (lines 16–23). This account, however, is characterized by many pauses, hesitations, half-finished phrases, and meta-comments. Nevertheless, throughout this long turn the interpersonal alignment between Mike and Ann, established in the laughing sequence described above, is "kept alive" by the use of many head nods, smiles, and a general reciprocity of glance. In other words, an interpersonal synergy (Fusaroli et al. 2014) between Mike and Ann is sustained on the level of inter-bodily dynamics and affect.

In living dynamic systems, synergy comes about as "a functionally driven reduction of degrees of freedom, where components do not simply align, but also complement and compensate for each other" (ibid.: 54). Here the inter-bodily level complement and compensate for the discrepancy on the verbal level between Mike's long and somewhat messy turn and Ann's subsequent brief mirroring. In other words, the emergence and co-acceptance of the final metaphoric image is (also) affectively motivated. Affect in face-to-face interactions often "manifest itself as embodied inter-affectivity" suggesting that "affect is in fact a dynamical and shared 'in-between' phenomenon, jointly created by participating interlocutors" (Horst et al. 2014: 2116). Consequently, the co-creation of this metaphoric image is deeply embedded in adaptive and expressive behaviors and the coordination of the interactive flow of action.

In sum, this example illustrates how metaphoricity is not sufficiently captured as either an individual product of an underlying cognitive process, or a mere choice of words. Rather, metaphoricity is part of cognitive co-action that includes adaptive patterns as well as affective behaviors, both of which are a part of the inter-bodily dynamics. Metaphoricity needs to be understood as a doing in the world that is embedded in the environmental structures of the interpersonal ecology. In discourse we often think and feel together in and through our abilities to act in the present situation: "At the human level, cognition is action – we think in order to act, and we act as part of our thinking" (Johnson 2007: 126).

4 Deliberateness in an Ecological Perspective

This analysis of the shared nature of metaphoricity also has a bearing on the alleged "paradox of metaphor" as raised by Steen (2008, *this volume*) and critically discussed by a number of researchers (e.g. Gibbs 2011b; Müller 2011). From the present perspective, the sheer attempt to make a sharp and principal distinction between "deliberate" metaphors (where the speaker draws explicit attention to the source domain) and "non-deliberate" ones (which are entirely conventional uses, based on preestablished categorizations) seems to rest on a conception of the human mind as an autonomous self-navigating unity. However, such a conception of the human mind is not in line with recent tendencies within cognitive science, as described in section 1.3. In addition, the analyses presented here have shown that people engaged in dialogue with each other never act, experience, or feel entirely on their own.

The vocalizations and bodily movements of our interlocutors can be seen as affordances for different types of action, feeling, and thinking that, to a smaller or lesser degree, link the participants together. The employment of metaphoricity is embedded in the particular affordances of the discourse environment, be it staff meeting or a couple's therapy session, and they emerge as part of these environmental factors and the participants' efforts and abilities to make use of them. Taken together, this renders the question of whether these metaphoric expressions are used deliberately somewhat off target. As previously noted by Gibbs, "human cognition as a self-organizing system offers a way of thinking about mindful actions without placing 'deliberateness' as the single causal force in people's adaptive behavior" (Gibbs 2011b: 46). In continuation of this, I argue that even subjective experiences of participants engaged in interaction are jointly shaped by the constraints and dynamics arising between them: "subjective experience involves processes both in the organism and in the environment. This means that subjective experience is not absolutely subjective, but contains also elements which can be shared by other people" (Jarvilehto 2000: 54–55).

But where does this leave a principled distinction between deliberate or non-deliberate metaphor? It is important to acknowledge that Steen is right in claiming that metaphoric usage looks radically different in different usage situations, e.g. in written genres as opposed to more mundane discourse, and we need to take these differences seriously. As the analyses of the two examples demonstrated, there are often profound differences in the ways people engage in metaphoric action. Sometimes the metaphoricity is only partly activated, or turned up to a low level, as in the first example. At other times it is actively "foregrounded," explicitly negotiated, and thereby turned up high, as in the second example (see also Müller, *this volume*). However, this cannot fruitfully be described as a question of deliberate or non-deliberate metaphor use because the reasons are not solely to be found inside the minds of the interlocutors (as implied by the notion of "deliberateness"). Instead, we need to look more carefully at particular usage situations to see how different affordances offered by different types of discourse environments allow for different types of metaphoric language.

There is an exciting perspective in investigating more thoroughly the intricate connections between the degree and types of metaphoricity in relation to various affordances allowed by different physical as well as social settings. The present examples, for instance, clearly illustrate how different discourse environments afford different degrees of metaphoricity with distinct impacts and consequences for interpersonal action. Still, much more work in this direction is needed in order to substantiate the claim that different ecologies result in different types of metaphoricity.

5 Conclusions

As stated initially, a shift of focus from the fixed concept of metaphor to the more fluid notion of metaphoricity can offer a way forward that erases the need to distinguish between metaphor as either social or cognitive, i.e. as tied to discourse and communicative/normative functions only, or as tied to the psychology of the individual.

Metaphoricity is profoundly tied to use. In virtue of being part of our cognitive doings, it is deeply embedded in normative purposes and communicative functions. Metaphoricity is about both adapting to a specific interpersonal ecology and developing this ecology by engaging in it and exploiting its possibilities for action by enacting a possible double meaning for the participants to share (in one way or another). We need to include these dimensions of inter-bodily being and acting together when investigating the emergence of metaphoric meaning as an important part of human sense-making. Insisting on an ecological interpretation of cognition paves a middle-way that can aspire to lessen, and perhaps even dissolve, the dichotomies of biological/cultural, individual/social, inner/outer: "there is no inherent contradiction between seeing language as biogenic and as social, simply because sociality is our human way of being nature. This assumption … precludes [both] the bio-reductionism that ignores supra-individual (i.e. social or cultural) dynamics and the socio-reductionism that ignores the metabolic and ecological foundations of human existence" (Steffensen 2015: 114).

If metaphoricity is conceptualized as part of our ecology, the question is no longer whether metaphors can be designated as features of either the individual mind or the context. As living agents, we sometimes *do* metaphoricity co-evolving with the environment. This is never a completely solitary act and never dis-embodied.

Notes and Acknowledgments

* The data used for case study 1 were recorded by a student attending a course in interpersonal communication at the University of Southern Denmark and are presented here in anonymized form; all names are pseudonyms. I thank the municipality for the permission to use the audio-recorded material in my research. The data used for case study 2 were recorded as part of my Ph.D. project. I thank the participants for their consent to use the video data recorded for research purposes. Again, all names appearing are pseudonyms. Finally, heartfelt thanks to the editor, Beate Hampe, for her persistent and meticulous work on this chapter, which has improved it significantly.

1 Jonathan Dunn, "Measuring metaphoricity." Paper presented at the Proceedings of the 52nd annual meeting of the Association for Computational Linguistics, 2014, pp. 1–2.

2 I am indebted here to Per Linell's (2005) notion of the written language bias.

3 The idea that cognition or thinking take place in the head can be seen as a centuries-old and deeply rooted dualistic assumption in Western thinking right up to second-generation cognitive science, dating all the way back to René Descartes' (1596–1650) (in)famous distinction between *res cogitans* ('mental substance') and *res extensa* ('corporal substance').

4 Unfortunately, work on decontextualized or even invented examples has dominated the development of the CMT for a long time. For further discussion, see Gibbs (2011b).

Part IV

Salient Metaphor

15 Attention to Metaphor: Where Embodied Cognition and Social Interaction Can Meet, But May Not Often Do So

*Gerard J. Steen**

Chapter Preview

I will suggest that there is a fundamental difference between deliberate and non-deliberate metaphor use, which hinges on attention. Then I will address the most important implications of Deliberate Metaphor Theory (DMT) for research on Conceptual Metaphor Theory (CMT) and suggest that the experimental evidence in favor of CMT can be (a) reinterpreted as evidence for DMT and (b) given alternative explanations from the perspective of DMT. The CMT approach to metaphor may be less secure than is held by many, while its refinement and extension in DMT leads to new predictions about the diverging behavior of two groups of metaphor that were not distinguished in these terms before, deliberate versus non-deliberate metaphor.

1 Introduction

Since Lakoff and Johnson (1980), the study of metaphor in language use has concentrated on metaphor's cognitive underpinnings via presumably conventional metaphors in thought. Around the turn of the millennium, this approach was refined by the distinction advanced by Grady (1997a) between primary and complex metaphors, the former hypothesized to offer the true cognitive grounding of all metaphor in language and its use. The motivation of a lot of metaphor in language was then argued to depend on the embodied nature of sensorimotor experience, suggesting that complex metaphors such as LIFE IS A JOURNEY would be constrained and composed by distinct and specific configurations of primary metaphors like CHANGE IS MOTION, PURPOSES ARE DESTINATIONS, and so on (e.g. Lakoff & Johnson 1999: 49–59). Since then the argument for metaphor as a case of embodied cognition has steadily grown (Hampe 2005a; Gibbs 2006b).

It is an empirical question, however, how far this embodied view of metaphor reaches into the psychological processes of metaphor comprehension in language use (e.g. Gibbs 2007b; Zwaan 2016). On the one hand, there is evidence suggesting that metaphor comprehension indeed works by cross-domain mapping that typically starts out from sensorimotor domains (cf. Gibbs 2011c). On the other hand, however, there is evidence suggesting that metaphor comprehension does not work in just one way but includes comparison, categorization, and lexical disambiguation (Bowdle & Gentner 2005; Giora 2008; Glucksberg 2001; see also Ritchie, *this volume*). This issue has not been settled and requires a new model for metaphor that can accommodate all the evidence: For that purpose I have developed Deliberate Metaphor Theory (DMT) as another refinement as well as extension of Conceptual Metaphor Theory (CMT) (cf. Steen 2008, 2011a, 2011b, 2013, 2015).

I argue that we need to pay closer attention to one crucial level of discourse representation, the one of the "situation model" as first advanced by Van Dijk and Kintsch (1983) and as further developed within an embodied-simulation framework by, for example, Zwaan (2016). I hold that the difference between this level and the conceptual level of the "textbase" has been unjustly neglected in CMT and that most metaphor is not represented *as* metaphor in the situation model. This can explain why most people do not experience most metaphor identified in linguistics as indirect in their own language use (Steen 2011b, 2013). These regular metaphors may have other interesting properties, yet these properties do not necessarily lead to comprehension by cross-domain mapping, whether by retrieval or online construction and whether driven by embodied cognition or not – which is the basic CMT claim about the power of metaphor in thought that I challenge.

I will use the distinction between situation model and textbase to raise new questions about the need for cross-domain mappings in regular metaphor comprehension and suggest that most metaphor comprehension may be handled by lexical disambiguation, short-cutting genuine online conceptual use of the source domain. I hold that there is one crucial exception: My claim is that deliberate metaphor does require online cross-domain mapping, involving attention to the source domain as a conceptual and referential domain in its own right. Because of this attention to the source domain in the textbase and situation model, deliberate metaphor can also be experienced as a metaphor by ordinary language users. As a result, deliberate metaphor is where metaphor acquires a communicative function *as* metaphor between language users. This makes it a communicative tool for social interaction that can play a wide range of roles within and even between discourse events (Zinken 2007; Zinken et al. 2008).

My overall thesis, therefore, is that the representation of metaphor in situation models is the place where one can or cannot observe the effects of, on the one hand, embodied cognition and primary metaphor on metaphor in discourse, and on the other hand, the requirements of social interaction on metaphor as a tool for communication. I hold that a lot of metaphor does not get represented *as* metaphor in the situation model, that is, with distinct attention to the source domain as a separate referential aspect of the meaning of the utterance. Those metaphors do not have a social function as metaphor either: They are not shared between language users in a particular situation as a metaphorical model for some target domain referent simply because they are not available *as* a metaphor to the people interacting by means of it (for a close analysis of the social functions of a novel metaphor, see Semino & Demjén, *this volume*). This can only happen if speakers revitalize such a metaphor as a metaphor (cf. Müller, *this volume*), but this would involve deliberate metaphor use again, including attention to the source domain as a distinct domain of reference from which to (re)consider the target domain. It follows that attention to metaphor is the place where embodied cognition and social interaction can meet, but at the same time I predict that this is not likely to happen very often.

In the first half of this chapter I will present a brief description of DMT. I will suggest (a) that there is a fundamental difference between deliberate and non-deliberate metaphor use which hinges on attention and (b) that this difference interacts in crucial ways with embodied cognition and with social interaction. In the second half of the chapter, I will address the most important implications of DMT for research on CMT, answering to recent challenges by Gibbs (2015b,c, *this volume*) that DMT cannot deal with this evidence for CMT. I will suggest in particular that the experimental evidence in favor of CMT can (a) be reinterpreted as evidence for DMT and (b) be given alternative explanations from the perspective of DMT. This means that the CMT approach to metaphor may be less secure than is held by many, while its refinement and extension in DMT lead to new predictions about the diverging behavior of two groups of metaphor that were not distinguished in these terms in previous research, deliberate versus non-deliberate metaphor.

2 Deliberate Metaphor Theory (DMT)

2.1 Attention to Metaphor

Deliberate metaphor is the kind of metaphor use that requires separate representation of the source domain as part of the referential meaning of the utterance. Examples include explicit comparison (e.g. Shakespeare's 'Shall I compare thee to a summer's day?'), simile (e.g. Neil Young's 'You are like a hurricane'), novel *A is B* metaphor ('Science is a glacier'), and extended comparisons, parables, allegories, and so on (for further discussion, see Steen 2011a). Thus, for Shakespeare's famous first line of Sonnet 18, readers must build a meaning for the line which involves the following referents: the speaker, comparing, the addressee, and a summer's day. This meaning hence involves referents coming from two conceptual domains, that of a love relationship and that of summer's days.

Mandatory referential representation of source domains does not hold for non-deliberate metaphor. There people represent the meaning of an utterance in terms of referents from the target domain only. This holds for the bulk of metaphor as discussed in CMT, including, for instance, the following set of examples for THEORIES ARE BUILDINGS (Kövecses 2010b: 6):

(1) a. Is that the *foundation* for your theory?
b. The theory needs more *support.*
c. We need *to construct* a *strong* argument for that.
d. We need *to buttress* the theory with *solid* arguments.

The referential state of affairs that people must construct for (1b) would be something like 'The theory needs more help to prove something,' with all referents in this state of affairs belonging to the target domain of theories.

The referential meaning of an utterance is fundamentally different from the linguistic and the conceptual meanings of an utterance. These three kinds of utterance meaning have commonly been distinguished in linguistics and can be related to different mental models in discourse psychology (Van Dijk & Kintsch 1983; see also Macnamara & Magliano 2009): When people comprehend utterances, they integrate their meanings into a mental model of the surface text (linguistic meaning), of the textbase (conceptual meaning), and of the situation model (referential meaning). The situation model is a mental model that all language users must construct for any utterance. Situation models include representations of the referents that utterances are about and that language users attend to when they comprehend discourse. The content of the situation model is what the sentence is about, is part of working memory, and involves states of affairs that are open for introspection and can be reported in think-aloud studies.

These three types of utterance meaning as well as their relations to the three types of mental models in discourse processing have not, however, been adequately appreciated in metaphor studies: in CMT, in particular, conceptual and referential meaning have been conflated and are both subsumed under the rubric of 'thought.' Their differentiation is crucial for DMT. A brief illustration will show why.

For a non-deliberate metaphor like that in (1b), CMT says that there is one metaphor-related word, "support," presumably coming from the language about buildings. This then suggests that in this utterance there may be a cross-domain mapping between theories and buildings. And this is why the linguistic meaning of this utterance in the surface text involves metaphor.

Words activate concepts. The word "support" presumably activates the corresponding concept SUPPORT, which, still according to CMT, comes from the source domain of buildings. This means that the concept designates something that holds or bears weight. In the corresponding textbase the structure of the conceptual proposition corresponding to 'The theory needs more support' looks like this: (NEED THEORY MORE-SUPPORT). The proposition in the textbase is metaphorical for the same reason as the sentence in the surface text.

From a discourse point of view, this conceptual structure is incoherent. It is about the target domain of theories yet has one concept that is not about theories but about buildings. In order to construct a situation model for this utterance that is coherent and that captures the conventional referential meaning of the utterance, CMT says that people need to do a mapping across the two domains. This then leads to a referential meaning for the utterance that can be described as 'This theory needs more help to prove something.' This referential meaning is the state of affairs that is part of the situation model that addressees presumably construct for this utterance as the current part of the more encompassing discourse. It does not comprise referents from the source domain but only from the target domain.

According to CMT this is the product of an unconscious, automatic process. DMT adds that this is the reason why such metaphors are hard to recognize as metaphorical by language users: There is no trace in the situation model of the source-domain words (surface text) and source-domain concepts (textbase) – there are only target-domain referents. According to CMT interpreted as a processing model, these have been produced by a cross-domain mapping when resolving the conceptual incoherence problem (in the textbase) for constructing the referential state of affairs (in the situation model). Except for the differentiation between conceptual and referential mental representations for the textbase and the situation model, which are conflated to the conceptual level of thought in CMT, all of this is standard CMT analysis.

Contrast this to what happens in a deliberate metaphor like 'Shall I compare thee to a summer's day?' The *linguistic* meaning of this utterance also involves language coming from some other domain than that of the target: 'a summer's day.' The target domain concerns the relationship between two lovers. This is why in CMT the linguistic meaning of this utterance in the surface text is also related to metaphor. The *conceptual* meaning of this utterance is metaphorical by the same token. The words activate corresponding concepts and the resulting conceptual structure of the proposition may look like this: (COMPARE-TO SPEAKER ADDRESSEE SUMMER'S-DAY) (cf. Kintsch 1998). The concept of a SUMMER'S DAY derives from a different domain than the other concepts, which are part of the target domain. This makes the proposition as part of the textbase metaphorical, too.

As above, the presence of a concept from some different domain poses a threat to the coherence of the situation model. As above, since this is metaphor, this is supposed to be resolved by cross-domain mapping in CMT. However, what is different here is that this particular utterance includes an explicit instruction for the addressee to integrate the alien concept of summer's day into the encompassing frame of the rest of the utterance by comparison. As a result, all of these concepts must be represented as part of the referential meaning too, which reads something like this: 'Shall the speaker compare the addressee to a summer's day?' In other words, this utterance presents a state of affairs that explicitly concerns a comparison between a referent from the target domain, the addressee who is the lover, to a referent from some source domain, 'a summer's day.' This is a referentially mixed state of affairs in the developing situation model. The source-domain concept is represented as a distinct referent, belonging to a distinct domain that is to be compared to another referent, and this constitutes the referential meaning of the utterance. The cross-domain mapping involved in metaphor is here not something that presumably takes place between textbase and situation-model construction, as in our non-deliberate example; instead, it is something that the utterance explicitly puts on the referential agenda for the addressee who is instructed to represent a comparison between these referents.

This differentiation between these two scenarios for metaphor processing (non-deliberate versus deliberate) hinges on attending to elements of the source domain as part of the referential representation of the utterance. This is new and constitutes the cornerstone of DMT. (It is unclear, for instance, whether Müller, *this volume*, would accept these claims about attention and reference.) If we assume, from a broadly pragmatic starting point, that all language use is intentional, deliberate metaphor use involves the intentional use of the source domain as a distinct component in the referential meaning of the utterance. From a discourse-processing perspective, the latter is part of the developing situation model.

The inclusion of the source domain of the deliberate metaphor has a discourse function: It acts as the basis for a non-target perspective on the target referent from some 'alien' source referent. This means that some metaphors deliberately place source-domain elements within the window of attention of addressees so that they indeed experience understanding one thing in terms of something else, whereas most metaphors do not do this. In DMT, the former metaphors are identified as 'deliberate' metaphors and the latter as 'non-deliberate' metaphors. The fact that the source domains of some metaphors emerge in our attention (cf. Müller, *this volume*) can be modeled via the situation model. It makes them available for social interaction in terms of sharing, uptake, development, and criticism. However, this does not hold for the bulk of metaphor, which is non-deliberate. What looks like a metaphor in the structures of language and discourse, then, does not have to be used as a metaphor in psychological or social processes of discourse.

2.2 *Attention to Metaphor, Embodied Cognition, and Social Interaction*

According to CMT interpreted as a theory of processing, all metaphor, and therefore non-deliberate metaphor, too, requires resolution by a cross-domain mapping in the textbase before it ends up as a pure referential representation of the target domain in the situation model. However, an alternative is also possible: Most non-deliberate metaphor can cause regular activation of source-domain meanings during lexical access for surface text construction, spilling over into regular source-domain concept activation during textbase construction, but then lexical and conceptual disambiguation processes may kick in to suppress the role of the source-domain concepts so that target-domain meanings are the only remaining meanings used for reference (cf. Giora 2008). To illustrate, the word "support" in our example above might lead to activation of both a building and a theory sense; it might give access to both the corresponding concepts of 'building' and 'theory.' But then the irrelevant building concept might get suppressed and the already available theory concept might be retained to project the relevant theory referent in the situation model. What is crucial here is that these target-domain referents would not be the product of online cross-domain mapping, presumably caused by the activation of conventional conceptual metaphors. Instead, they would be the result of lexical disambiguation which capitalizes on already available target-domain meanings.

This alternative picture is compatible with research done by, for instance, Keysar and colleagues (2000), Bowdle and Gentner (2005), and Giora (2008). For non-deliberate metaphor in language use, it is hence not clear whether metaphor in fact needs online cross-domain mappings during referential meaning construction. Why would language users take the more elaborate route of doing a cross-domain mapping every time they come across an already conventional metaphor, for instance from concrete support in buildings to abstract support in arguments, if the intended product of such a mapping – abstract support in buildings – is already there, both in the language and in people's mental dictionaries? Even if some aspects of the activated source-domain concepts remain independently active as a result of prior automatic access (cf. Giora 2008), this does not give them the functional role attributed to them by classic CMT interpreted as a processing model, generating relevant cross-domain mappings for establishing the situation model that the utterance is about.

Taking this alternative scenario as a plausible starting point, DMT proposes a distinction between two roles for embodied cognition in metaphor. For non-deliberate metaphor, as in our "support" example (1b), sensorimotor knowledge would play an automatic role when a polysemous word and concept are accessed and activated, but that sensorimotor knowledge would then lose force and die down when the utterance is represented in the situation model. The stages of surface text and textbase construction might then give rise to source-domain-related feelings and the like, but these would remain fleeting and unconscious, not playing a functional role in the referential meaning of the utterance. The latter, however, is crucial for people's experience of the discourse as metaphorical. In other words, this alternative analysis of non-deliberate metaphor processing raises a question concerning the precise role such a process of embodied cognition might have to play in the construction and experience of any non-deliberate metaphor.

For deliberate metaphor, as in our Shakespeare example, sensorimotor knowledge would also play an automatic and unconscious role in lexical access and in concept activation but would then continue to be part of the dimension of meaning that is referential. What is more, since the source domain of the summer's day must be represented as a distinct referent, its basis in embodied cognition would remain alive and become part of people's experience of the utterance in attention (the situation model). This role has been predicated by CMT of all metaphor, but DMT argues that it is only deliberate metaphor which has such a meaning-constitutive role in discourse.[1]

I hence argue that, for deliberate metaphor, there is an effect of the cross-domain mapping on meaning in such a way that it becomes available for social interaction. Since for deliberate metaphor, the source domain and its basis in embodied cognition come up in the situation model, this can be attended to by both sender and receiver. Referential uptake of the source domain (which is typically not the same as the phenomena described by, e.g., Cameron 2007b) can then occur in various ways, for instance to appreciate the cross-domain mapping, to extend or constrain it, to play with it, or to criticize and resist it. This is when metaphor and its basis in embodied cognition can play a role in social interaction.

In non-deliberate metaphor, by contrast, there may be short-lived cognitive and affective effects of the brief activation of the source-domain senses and concepts, but these are at most associations. They do not feed into the construction of the referential representation of the utterance. Such associations, whether cognitive or affective, may of course be subliminally felt by sensitive language users, but they would not be the inevitable result of some cross-domain mapping that is constructed during processing, as has been suggested by CMT. The latter, I argue, only occurs with deliberate processing.

My overall thesis, therefore, is that the representation of metaphor as metaphor in situation models is the place where one can observe both the effects of embodied cognition on metaphor in discourse and the requirements of social interaction on metaphor as a tool for communication. However, since according to DMT most metaphor does not get represented as metaphor in the situation model, it does not have such a social function as metaphor very often.

As a result, attention to metaphor, and in particular to the source domain, in people's working memory may be a moment where embodied cognition and social interaction can meet, but at the same time I predict that this is not likely to happen very often either, since most metaphor use is non-deliberate. The moments when this does happen, in deliberate metaphor use, consequently become an interesting site for careful scrutiny.

3 Conceptual Metaphor Theory (CMT)

Perhaps the most important question about DMT and the way it sees the relation between metaphor in embodied cognition and social interaction is how it relates to CMT. Part of the urgency here is the claim that DMT "totally rejects" CMT (Gibbs, *this volume*). This is a misunderstanding. DMT is an extension of CMT that challenges some of the claims produced in CMT, but certainly not all of them (e.g. Steen 2011a, 2015). The central issue for this section is how DMT deals with the experimental evidence in favor of CMT (Gibbs 2015b,c, *this volume*).

There are two answers to this question. DMT first of all throws new light on experimental evidence for CMT and shows that some of it is in fact based on deliberate metaphor use. Second, other experimental evidence for CMT does not involve deliberate metaphor use but can be given an alternative explanation that is in line with DMT. Both of these issues will be elaborated below. Because of space limitations, I will focus on the experimental evidence used by Gibbs (2011c) for his positive evaluation of CMT, which he adduced as support for his own challenge to DMT in Gibbs (2015b,c). I will ask how the studies discussed by Gibbs (2011c) provide experimental evidence that conceptual metaphors *are* recruited during online processing, driving the comprehension of metaphorical utterances. This is the main claim that I have problems with in CMT.

Gibbs challenges DMT's skeptical view of the experimental evidence for CMT's central claim that metaphor processing in language always recruits cross-domain mappings. Section 3.1 provides a detailed discussion of the experimental evidence presented as support for CMT in Gibbs (ibid.).[2] It is followed by a reanalysis of that evidence from the standpoint of DMT in section 3.2.

3.1 Experimental Evidence for CMT as Evidence for DMT

I will now focus on the experimental studies argued to offer experimental evidence for the claim that conceptual metaphors drive the comprehension of metaphor in language use by means of online cross-domain mappings. Upon close scrutiny, many of these studies are in fact based on deliberate metaphor, i.e. they utilize metaphors that must be represented as metaphors in the situation model and give rise to attention to the source domain as a source domain, which then leads to online cross-domain mapping between source and target referents. I claim that it is this feature which explains their effect as metaphors upon comprehension.

The strongest line of research for CMT in Gibbs (2011c) involves online experiments with, for instance, reading-time measurements. Gibbs discusses two such studies that I argue involve deliberate metaphor. Pfaff and colleagues (1997) conducted six experiments to show that people's metaphorical conceptualization of a topic influences the appropriateness rating and processing times of conventional and novel euphemisms and dysphemisms, as in the following examples (ibid.: 62):

(2) Paragraph primes SEXUAL DESIRE IS A HUNTING ANIMAL

Dirk is a real wolf. He prowls the singles bars looking for unsuspecting young women to proposition. One night, he saw a particularly tasty-looking morsel in a mini-skirt and said to his friend,

"*I'm ready to pounce.*"

"*She's turning my crank.*"

(3) Paragraph primes SEXUAL DESIRE IS AN ACTIVATED MACHINE

Dirk is a real operator. He cruises the singles bars looking for young women to proposition. One night, he saw a particularly sleek-looking model with all the options and said to his friend,

"*I'm ready to pounce.*"

"*She's turning my crank.*"

For the first vignette, the paragraph should increase appropriateness ratings and processing speed of 'I'm ready to pounce' in comparison with 'She's turning my crank,' and this should work in the opposite direction for the second vignette. From the perspective of DMT, these preceding paragraphs depend on deliberate metaphor use: They exhibit a combination of an *A is B* construction in the first sentence with a continuation in at least one striking and novel metaphor in the next sentences. Novel metaphors, including novel *A is B* metaphors, are deliberate because they require online cross-domain mapping to project an unknown target-domain referent from a known source-domain referent. Conventional *A is B* metaphors can be deliberate because they are ambiguous between two readings: one in which the source-domain term is interpreted at target-domain level, which would make the cross-domain mapping unnecessary and would lead to categorization, and one in which the source-domain term is interpreted at source-domain level, which would draw attention to the source domain in the situation model (Glucksberg 2001). The latter reading would result in deliberate metaphor use.

The article by Pfaff and colleagues has an appendix with a list of conceptual domains, X-phemisms, and relevant conceptual metaphors in parentheses, but it does not show the experimental materials. This problem also holds for another online study, Gibbs and colleagues (1997), who conducted a priming experiment to test the role of conceptual metaphors in idiom comprehension. This precludes determining how representative the above text vignettes are of the stimuli used by Pfaff and colleagues, or examining how text vignettes were constructed in the 1997 study by Gibbs and colleagues. It is, hence, an open issue whether their findings are independent of the role of deliberate metaphor. If the illustrations are representative, they are not. In other words, the positive findings reported in both studies might be due to the fact that the linguistic realizations of the underlying conceptual metaphors used are deliberate and require a separate representation of the source domain as a distinct referential domain in the situation model.

The findings reported by Pfaff and colleagues (1997: 79) also invite careful scrutiny for another reason:

> One of the puzzling findings of our studies was the failure to replicate the consistency effect for familiar phrases across the different experiments. For instance, the participants in Experiments 3 through 5 found familiar, but inconsistent X-phemisms to be as appropriate and easy to understand as the familiar, consistent phrases. Even though Experiment 6 indicated (similar to Experiments 1 and 2) that familiar-consistent phrases took less time to process than familiar-inconsistent ones, it seems clear that the familiarity of an X-phemistic phrase may have greater impact on people's understanding than metaphoric consistency.

This is precisely what may be expected from a DMT perspective: Some of the story contexts may *not* have been deliberate, which is highly likely for familiar stimuli – in that case, the metaphorical endings may *not* work as metaphors in requiring cross-domain comparisons at the referential level. Then it would only be their coherent or incoherent target-domain ending of the story that may have an effect on the ratings and reading times, as reported by the authors. A careful analysis of the experimental materials might hence lead to new research where the distinction between deliberate and non-deliberate metaphorical paragraphs as well as endings is optimally controlled and manipulated. Until then the jury must remain out on whether this study presents evidence for CMT, DMT, or both.

Gong and Ahrens (2007) investigated whether conceptual metaphors were accessed during online processing by examining the effect of different tasks (judgments and reading time) and of different ways of presenting the materials (sentence by sentence or at the end of paragraphs). This study is in effect a combined re-run of Nayak and Gibbs (1990) and Glucksberg and colleagues (1993), which led to diverging findings. Gong and Ahrens (2007) do not find a sentence-by-sentence effect but do find a paragraph effect. The absence of a sentence-by-sentence effect would in fact be consistent with DMT if the metaphors in the stimulus materials are conventional but not deliberate.

However, the information in the article does not offer any information about metaphor conventionality or novelty (and obviously not about deliberateness). Yet the sample text and the intention of the overall argument suggest that the metaphors should be conventional and non-deliberate. This leads to my provisional conclusion that Gong and Ahrens' first finding is consistent with DMT but not with CMT.

The second finding, that there *is* a metaphor effect at paragraph level, is harder to understand: If the metaphors do not work as metaphors at a sentence-by-sentence level, how can an effect at the end of this set of sentences arise all the same? This finding may be comparable to the effect reported by Pfaff and colleagues (1997) discussed above: From the perspective of DMT, it raises the suspicion that there may be another factor at play through which the incongruent metaphor is perceived as less appropriate. One possibility is that it is not just metaphorically incongruent but also incoherent (content-wise) with the structure of the text. Consider the example text offered in translation in the article (ibid.: 317):

(4) When you write up a good research proposal, you first have to plan a complete design map. In addition, you have to clearly present the research points, including the literature review, the research questions, the motivation, etc. Then, you have to build up the correct research methods and steps. In this way, the model of your proposal will be complete.

Terminal targets

Congruent: So, it is not difficult to construct your own theory.

Incongruent: So, it is not difficult to promote your own theory.

The use of *promote* in contrast with *construct* is not just metaphorically incongruent but also makes less sense as a conclusion to the text: Theory *construction* follows naturally from the previous actions, whereas theory *promotion* is a new action that is relatively independent and, moreover, may be difficult in its own right. This could also explain a high incongruence rating. The study had thirty sets of materials like this, but they are not included in the article. It is, hence, unclear if the incongruent target sentence also always was structurally incoherent. The above example, however, suggests that this and other factors may have played a role. In conclusion, Gong and Ahrens offer support for one claim of DMT which goes against CMT, namely that non-deliberate conventional metaphor from one sentence to the next does not have an effect on reading, while the evidence is inconclusive about another claim of CMT, that the presence of conventional metaphor in a paragraph may have an effect on reading, which may possibly be explained by the presence of a confound.

Offline experimental research that may be shown to depend on deliberate metaphor includes work by Read and colleagues (1990) and by Robins and Mayer (2000) on how metaphor in text can affect people's reasoning and decision making after they have finished reading. Read and colleagues

(1990) studied metaphor in political rhetoric by examining the effect of four text-initiating metaphors and their associated passages on people's memory as well as on their attitudes. Here are the text-initiating metaphors (ibid.: 149):

(5) a. Giving loans to Zaire was like offering crates of whiskey to an alcoholic.
b. Passage of the tax bill was like feeding time for the hogs.
c. This investigation into government wrongdoing is run like the Salem Witch Trials.
d. My Congressional opponents are like spoiled children.

All of these metaphors set up explicit analogical cross-domain comparisons that must be represented as such in the situation model. The reader is deliberately instructed by the utterances to set up a cross-domain mapping including a separate role for the source domain as the referential meaning of the sentence in each case.

Along similar lines, Robins and Mayer (2000) investigated whether metaphors can have a framing effect in a series of six experiments. For Experiment 1, two vignettes about the international trade dilemma were created that comprised many metaphors which spell out a point-by-point explicit analogical comparison in an encompassing cross-domain mapping. Here is one example (ibid.: 58):

(6) Vignette with TRADE IS WAR metaphor frame

International trade is a war. Tariffs, or trade rules, are barricades that shield the vital interests of countries from harm. Victory is achieved when a country maintains its own safeguards but is able to penetrate the markets of its adversary. The trade deficit means that we are losing ground on the battlefield of the trade war. Tariffs would shield us from such loss and help us reclaim our trade territory.

The meaning of most of these sentences involves a cross-domain comparison between some referents of trade and some referents of war or traffic. These are deliberately constructed cross-domain mappings that the reader must represent as such in the situation model. The same holds for the materials in Experiment 2, where two vignettes on interpersonal relationships were created along the same lines.

For Experiment 3, three vignettes about company culture were developed. They ended with a sentence in three variations that comprise at least two deliberate metaphors (ibid.: 67):

(7) dedication and loyalty to the organization are most important. We expect our employees to be a family/good soldiers/good citizens

Saying that you expect your employees to be a family or good soldiers sets up an *A is B* structure that requires representation as a cross-domain comparison in the situation model (Bowdle & Gentner 2005), to the effect that the meaning of the utterance becomes 'employees must behave like a family does/good soldiers do,' with a separate referential domain or space in the utterance for 'family' and 'good soldiers.'

For Experiment 4 (Robins & Mayer 2000: 69), variations of two differently metaphorically structured texts were employed to study the occurrence of any framing effects, as illustrated in (8):

(8) Vignette with SAFETY NET metaphor frame and consistent information

John and Susan are getting married and are deciding whether or not to get the safety net of a prenuptial agreement. A prenuptial agreement is basically a document that explicitly states how a couple's resources would be divided in case of a divorce in the future, thus safeguarding against substantial loss. Because a marriage is risky and unpredictable, such a trapeze act requires having a safety net. John and Susan both think that it's probably a good idea to get a prenuptial agreement because it is difficult to foresee future events. The responsible thing, they argue, would be to have a safety net just in case something happens.

These frames are deliberately metaphorical, for the following reasons. They comprise the use of a coherent series of metaphors with some strikingly novel expressions (e.g. *trapeze act*, *safety net*). Moreover, some clauses are completely metaphorical ('such a trapeze act requires having a safety net'), requiring explicit representation in the situation model *as* a separate referential domain. And finally, the key phrase expressing the key referent from the source domain (*safety net*) is repeated no fewer than three times. Experiment 5 uses a similar textual set-up with another metaphorical frame, where academic teamwork is compared to football.

Experiment 6 used the following vignette, with more than one metaphorical expression per source domain, which itself is introduced by the signal for explicit comparison 'seeing X as Y.' (9) provides one example again:

(9) STRIKE IS A DANCE vignette

As you may know, many big company employees are currently on strike over some proposed decreases in health benefits. Some commentators see this as an inevitable dance that happens between management and the workers every once in a while, and are encouraged that workers are going through the steps.

These studies show comprehension and framing effects of deliberate metaphor. Whether they can also be seen as evidence for CMT depends on whether the related conceptual metaphors affect text processing for text versions without any deliberate metaphor.

Other offline experimental research also involves the use of deliberate metaphors, such as Allbritton and colleagues (1995), which has a recognition task of sentences and words from text. The stimulus texts, however, are heavily metaphorical in ways that are comparable to the materials discussed for Pfaff and colleagues (1997) above. Gibbs and Bogdonovich (1999) examine post-hoc reports of mental imagery for metaphor in poetry, but this genre has lots of deliberate metaphor. And McGlone (1996) presents an interpretation task that has numerous novel, and therefore deliberate, metaphors. It looks as if the findings of these studies are mainly due to deliberate metaphor use, supporting DMT.

In sum, both online and offline experimental research presumably offering evidence for CMT can be shown to depend on the presence of deliberate metaphor in the stimuli. The findings of these studies can therefore be taken as support for DMT. How these findings can be upheld as evidence for CMT in contradistinction from DMT is a challenge for advocates of that argument.

3.2 Experimental Evidence for CMT and Alternative DMT Interpretations

Most of the offline studies discussed by Gibbs (2011c) can be given another alternative interpretation from the perspective of DMT. In particular, it is quite possible, as Gibbs (ibid.) himself admits, that the conceptual metaphor (or even simply metaphor) affecting the outcomes of, for instance, a metaphor explanation task arises as a post-comprehension phenomenon of metaphor processing. This is entirely compatible with the DMT claim that conventional metaphors may give rise to representation by comparison again if they are revitalized by their deliberate use as a metaphor, which may happen when they need to be explained. This type of study therefore does not show that metaphor in discourse comprehension always requires online cross-domain mapping, as would be claimed by the strong version of CMT, but instead shows that metaphor effects can arise as the result of post-hoc deliberate metaphor processing, as is compatible with DMT.

In the following studies, the metaphors that might be non-deliberate in the materials may in fact have been revitalized as a metaphor by the task. This applies to Boers and Littlemore (2000), where participants have to explain conceptual metaphors; to Gibbs (1991), which collects verbal explanation of idioms by children; to Gibbs (1992), which also focuses on intuitions about and ratings of metaphorical idioms in five out of six studies; to Gibbs and colleagues (2006), which focuses on people's reported imaginations of impossible actions; to Gibbs and colleagues (2004), which is based on a questionnaire about people's knowledge about desire as hunger; to Gibbs and O'Brien (1990), which again examines reported images of idioms; to Nayak and Gibbs (1990), which collects offline appropriateness judgments (cf. the above discussion of Gong & Ahrens 2007); and to Siqueira and Gibbs (2007), who carried out a question-answering study about primary metaphors. In all of these cases, it may have been the task that has made the participants focus on the properties of the source domain, which then turns the understanding process of the metaphor into a case of deliberate metaphor use; alternatively, descriptive language use presumably related to some activated source domain may have been conventionalized metaphorical expression that does not in fact derive from online metaphorical mapping.

Related methodological problems play a role in some of the well-known studies discussed by Gibbs (2011c) that examine time as space (Boroditsky 2000, 2001; Boroditsky & Ramscar 2002; Gentner et al. 2002; McGlone & Harding 1998; Nunez et al. 2006; Santiago et al. 2007). In varying ways these studies suggest that the comprehension of language about time is comparable to the comprehension of language about space, which is then claimed to be the driving force behind the comprehension of time. This has been presented as one of the strongest cases for CMT. However, Boroditsky (2000: 1) draws a conclusion that would be entirely compatible with DMT: "with frequent use, mappings between space and time come to be stored in the domain of time and so thinking about time does not necessarily require access to spatial schemas." Other claims by Boroditsky (2001) elaborating this position in ways that are more positive for CMT are less solid and have been criticized by Chen (2007), who was unable to replicate the findings.

Results that at first glance support CMT are presented by McGlone and Harding (1998) and by Gentner and colleagues (2002). However, these authors also acknowledge that there are methodological problems that may compromise the validity of these studies. For instance, it is noted that the stimuli representing two different temporal perspectives are not just presumable reflections of different underlying conceptual metaphors but also differ regarding their lexico-grammatical structures (Gentner et al. 2002: 545) – this is a confound that might equally well explain the findings and has been taken by the same researchers as the motivation for conducting better studies. Another problem explicitly acknowledged by the authors is that both publications make use of a spatial timeline for participants to order events on: This may have revitalized the spatial dimension of the cognitive task presumably addressing temporal understanding alone, which may then be seen as another example of a task that elicits deliberate metaphor understanding. This is a problem that also besets the study by Matlock and colleagues (2005), who use a drawing task to capture people's understanding of fictive-motion sentences.

The solution to methodological complications like the above has been to restrict the linguistic scope of these experiments to an increasingly smaller set of materials: McGlone and Harding (1998), Boroditsky and Ramscar (2002), and Gentner and colleagues (2002) limit themselves to studying the effect of just a few fairly specific spatio-temporal words in English: *ahead*, *before*, *behind*, and *forward*. Apart from the limited representativeness of these terms, a new light has more recently been cast on the validity of these space-time studies by Nunez and colleagues (2006), who have presented a new, more complex theory of metaphorical models for the conceptualization of time. All this suggests that we need to go back to these previous studies and reanalyze the stimulus materials and the predictions that follow from them in order to be able to assess whether previous research can still be said to offer support for CMT-based predictions.

All in all, there are methodological properties of or problems with some of the evidence for CMT that can be given new interpretations from the perspective of DMT. The most important issues involve post-hoc revitalization of metaphors in, for instance, metaphor-explanation tasks or online revitalization of SPACE-TIME metaphors, for instance metaphor-comprehension tasks. Both of these problems can be accounted for as compatible with DMT in that they demonstrate how deliberate metaphor processing may affect metaphor comprehension and explanation. In how far these studies may be taken as evidence for CMT in contradistinction from DMT is a challenge for researchers advocating that argument.

4 Attention to Metaphor: Embodied Cognition and Social Interaction

Most metaphor may not be represented *as* metaphor in people's situation models of metaphor-related utterances. Instead, most metaphor may get naturalized to some target-domain representation at the level of referential utterance meaning. This is the new claim of Deliberate Metaphor Theory, which explains this phenomenon by pointing to the ways in which metaphor-related utterances in context do or do not instruct language users to represent the source domain as a distinct referential domain in the situation model. Since the situation model is the window of attention that language users employ when processing discourse, not many metaphors arise as cross-domain mappings in people's attention. They remain unconscious, as has been argued for more than three decades by Conceptual Metaphor Theory. What is now added to this account is the prediction that some metaphors do become available for attention, and that this happens when they are deliberately used as metaphors. As a result, DMT goes against some of the claims formulated by CMT but does not reject it completely – instead, it should be seen as a refinement of CMT, raising new questions about unconscious and conscious metaphor processing in relation to utterance structures and functions, intentionality, and attention.

In his challenge to DMT, Gibbs (2015b,c) argues that DMT cannot deal with the huge amount of experimental evidence for CMT. However, both online and offline experimental findings for CMT involve a lot of deliberate metaphor, some of it in the materials and some of it in the tasks. That such metaphorical representations may also be connected with postulated conceptual metaphors is self-evident and not denied by DMT – inasmuch as conceptual metaphors have been established independently in behavioral research and can also be reconstructed as local online reconstructions by language users. To show that these findings also, or still, support one of the strong versions of CMT in contradistinction from DMT requires experimental research which allows no role for deliberate metaphor, either in the materials or in the tasks.

I have, of course, not been able to discuss all possibly relevant details of all studies mentioned by Gibbs (2011c) in the limited space that is at my disposal here. With the exception of a handful of studies that were also discussed by Gibbs, I have included all of these studies in one way or another in the present argument to explain how DMT can deal with the extant evidence for CMT in a critical but constructive manner. I hope that this contribution will therefore assist in advancing the debate over metaphor from different theoretical perspectives.

For now, however, I believe that attention to metaphor is the key issue in the question about the relation between embodied cognition and social interaction. Attention to metaphor is elicited by deliberate metaphor use, and since deliberate metaphor is rather infrequent in most discourse contexts, I submit that this is the moment when embodied cognition and social interaction *can* meet.

Notes and Acknowledgments

* Many thanks to Christian Burgers, Valentina Cuccio, and Jean Wagemans for their helpful comments on an earlier version. I would also like to express my sincere gratitude to an anonymous reviewer as well as the editor of this volume, whose help has been invaluable in reducing this chapter to its current pitch.

1 Current research by Valentina Cuccio and Gerard Steen investigates how these two routes can be incorporated in an embodied-simulation framework ("Attention to metaphor: From neurons to representations". In preparation with John Benjamins, Amsterdam). For further discussion of metaphor from an embodied-simulation perspective, see also *this volume*: Cuccio; Ritchie.

2 Of the papers cited in Gibbs (2011c), I exclude from discussion: fourteen publications that are not experimental but present theory, methods, or other work; seventeen publications that do not concern metaphor in language processing; as well as twelve papers that do not presentexperimental evidence but other types of evidence for CMT in language processing.

16 Waking Metaphors: Embodied Cognition in Multimodal Discourse

*Cornelia Müller**

Chapter Preview

The consciousness of metaphoric meaning has traditionally been a controversial issue. Often only novel metaphors have been assumed to be vital, whereas conventional metaphors were characterized as dead. This chapter argues that the vitality of metaphoric meaning is a matter of language in use *and* of speakers' linguistic repertoires. As long as metaphoric expressions are transparent, metaphoricity can be vitalized and – by being foregrounded – become a focus of shared attention in an interaction. Metaphors may thus dynamically shift between "sleeping" and "waking," i.e. be more or less experienced and understood as metaphors. The source domain of a "waking" metaphor is active and in the foreground of shared attention. This dynamics of metaphoric meaning is particularly evident in the interplay of speech and gesture. Presenting a micro-analysis of multimodal interaction in a dance class, the chapter shows that issues of vitality are aspects of discourse dynamics and embodied meaning-making and that, consequentially, questions debating the consciousness and the processing of metaphoricity are answered by the participants in discourse themselves.

1 Introduction: Consciousness and Vitality of Metaphoric Meaning

Much of the contemporary discussion on whether the ubiquity of metaphorical expressions in discourse goes along with metaphoric thinking can be regarded as a revitalization of a long-standing controversy concerning the vitality of conventional metaphor in language use. From Aristotle's first formulation in his *Poetics* to contemporary research – no matter whether cognitively oriented or discourse oriented – issues of the consciousness and vitality of metaphoric meaning have been controversially discussed. Historically, consciousness of metaphoric meaning has been associated with novelty of metaphors. Novel metaphors have been assumed to be vital, whereas conventional metaphors were characterized as dead (e.g. Black 1993; Ricoeur 1986). This chapter takes the position that the vitality of metaphoric meaning is an issue of discourse and interaction, of language in use. As long as metaphoric expressions are transparent to their users, metaphoricity can be activated, vitalized, and – by being foregrounded – become a more or less salient focus of shared attention. Transparent metaphors may thus dynamically shift between "sleeping" and "waking," i.e. they may be more or less experienced and understood as metaphors, the only difference being the degree of attention they receive.

While many classic theories of metaphor have assumed that conventionalization of metaphor goes along with a loss of vitality of metaphoric meaning, Conceptual Metaphor Theory assumes that what is most entrenched is most vital, most active in the conceptual systems of language users (Lakoff & Johnson 1980, 1999).[1] Current theories of metaphor continue to address this controversy.

Cameron's (1999) distinction between "linguistic" and "process" metaphors as well as her treatment of "deliberate" and "conventional" metaphors in educational discourse (Cameron 2003: 100–119) distinguish different forms of consciousness of metaphors. Taking a discourse dynamics position, Cameron (2010b) argues that discourse analysts cannot be sure whether a given linguistic metaphor is actually processed metaphorically and therefore points out the *potentiality* of verbal metaphor in discourse.

Proposing that most metaphors in discourse are not processed metaphorically, Steen's notion of "deliberate" metaphor puts cognitive processing in terms of cognitive situation models center stage, suggesting that most metaphors in discourse are not processed metaphorically (e.g. Steen 2008, 2011d, 2015). Based on findings from experimental psychology, Gibbs counters this position and argues for an embodied understanding which grounds the conceptual activation of metaphoric meaning in actively experienced source domains (e.g. Gibbs 2006b, 2011b, 2014b, 2015b,c). This is also supported by research on "primary" metaphors (Grady 1997a; Matlock 2004a, 2010; Matlock et al. 2011).

The overall line of argument emerging from this discussion remains fairly dichotomous: Either metaphoric meaning is considered as conscious as well as experienced and processed metaphorically, or not. However, following Giora (2003), verbal metaphors might be conceived as being more or less salient depending on their frequency of use. Along similar lines, Cameron's discourse dynamics approach as well as Cameron's and Gibbs' dynamical systems view of metaphor advance an understanding of a dynamic metaphoric meaning that emerges from discourse processes (Cameron 2010b,c; Gibbs & Cameron 2008).

The concept of "waking" metaphors (Müller 2003, 2008a,b, 2011) approaches the consciousness of metaphoricity from a discourse *and* embodied-cognition point of view. It assumes that co-participants in an interaction display for each other whether metaphoricity is an active aspect of meaning at a particular moment in a discourse event: They do so by using different kinds of foregrounding strategies which operate upon a given metaphor. For instance, a verbal metaphoric expression, such as somebody talking about the "ups and downs" of a love relationship, can be interactively foregrounded by performing a big up–down gesture right in the center of a co-participant's visual attention – instead of being accompanied by a small up–down movement of a finger, or no movement at all. Such a gesture makes manifest that the verbal metaphoric expression is not sleeping but waking, i.e. that the metaphoric meaning is in the foreground of shared attention. But the gesture does more than that, it offers an embodied subjective experience of the metaphoric source domain, of how the "moving up and down and continuously further down" of a relationship actually *felt* (cf. Kappelhoff & Müller 2011; Kolter et al. 2012; Müller & Tag 2010). The gesture *is* an embodied experience, a "felt sensation" in Sheets-Johnstone's (1999) sense (see also Gibbs 2006a; Johnson 2007).

The concept of waking metaphors implies that a source domain is active and in the foreground of shared attention. Depending on the flow of interaction and the respective contexts of use, the same verbal metaphor can be sleeping at one point in discourse and waking at another. This potential for metaphor activation by discourse contexts disappears only when metaphors stop to be transparent to their users. Only if a historical metaphor cannot be activated by an average speaker – because the experiential source domain that inspired the metaphoric mapping is no longer part of a shared language and culture – can this metaphor be appropriately characterized as "dead."

Questions of both the consciousness and the processing of metaphoricity, including Steen's "paradox of metaphor," are thus answered by the co-participants in a discourse themselves.

2 A Dynamic View of Metaphoric Meaning: Sleeping and Waking Metaphors

The dynamic view offers a theoretically motivated and empirically grounded answer to the question of vitality or consciousness of metaphor. Merging an embodied-cognition position with a communicative-interaction perspective provides the grounds for empirically reconstructing degrees of activated "metaphoricity" (Müller 2008a). A descriptive methodological framework allows documenting the vitality of metaphors and shows that, far from being a static and fixed property of a word, a phrase, or a sentence, metaphoricity is in fact a dynamic, emergent, gradabale, shifting facet of meaning-making along primarily (but not exclusively) multimodal discourse contexts (ibid.).[2] In this view, metaphors are observed "in the wild," in their contexts of use. They go with a moving and shared flow of attention in discourse, and are dynamically fore- and backgrounded in a process of interactive meaning-making.

The dynamic view of metaphoric meaning-making starts out from four basic assumptions:[3]

1. Metaphoric meaning-making builds on a process of *seeing and feeling* one experiential domain in terms of another.
2. Metaphoric meaning-making is based on a *triadic relation*. The activation of metaphoricity depends on an intersubjectively shared focus of attention and mobilizes subjective experiences of language users. Mappings between domains are thus not dyadic but triadic, where the third node represents the mediating process – the *seeing-and-experiencing-in-terms-of*, which is at the core of metaphoric meaning-making.
3. Metaphoric meaning-making is *modality-independent*. Metaphors are expressed in different modalities, ranging from words and gestures, to music, pictorial advertisements, pieces of art, including films and audiovisual compositions more generally.
4. Metaphoric meaning-making is a *matter of use*, and hence a dynamic and intersubjective process. Metaphoric meaning is gradable and temporally orchestrated. Along a discourse, metaphoricity may shift dynamically between sleeping and waking.

Metaphoricity is activated dynamically in an interaction – over the course of a discourse event and to varying degrees. Metaphor activation is understood as an embodied process of putting metaphoric meaning into the foreground of attention. This involves presenting selected experiential qualities of the source domain; it involves feeling and understanding. When metaphoric meaning is foregrounded, metaphors are considered as "waking." When it is in the background and the metaphoric expression – be it verbal, pictorial, or audiovisual – is (potentially) transparent, it is considered "sleeping." Rather than adhering to rigid dichotomies of dead versus alive/vital, conventional versus novel, or deliberate versus non-deliberate, I use the term "metaphoricity" to stress that metaphoric meaning is dynamic and gradable. Documenting the orchestration of various forms of dynamic foregrounding allows the reconstruction of the path of a shifting and moving focus of attention and reveals different forms of graded metaphoricity.

Waking metaphors are a specific and highly salient way of using language. This is often realized by intertwining expressions from different modalities. Verbal metaphors may go along with gestures (Cienki & Müller 2008a,b), with pictorial advertisements or photographs in newspapers (Forceville 1996; Müller 2008a), and they may as well be part of audiovisual compositions in film and television (Fahlenbrach 2015; Forceville & Urios-Aparisi 2009; Kappelhoff & Müller 2011; Müller & Schmitt 2015). Activating transparent metaphors with foregrounding devices turns sleeping metaphors into prominent and salient embodied experiences (Müller & Tag 2010). Sleeping metaphors have a different level of consciousness; they are in the background of attention. Yet, as psychological studies have shown (Gibbs 2011b, 2014b; Gibbs & Matlock 2008; Matlock 2004b, 2010; Matlock et al. 2011), they may be experienced as metaphors on a subconscious level. The difference between sleeping and waking metaphors thus comes down to that between a low or high level of activated metaphoricity.

Microanalytic studies of metaphors show that different forms of foregrounding metaphoric meaning are a natural facet of meaning-making in speech and gesture. In an ongoing face-to-face conversation, metaphoric meaning appears anything but fixed to a lexical item: It may first show up in a gesture, then disappear in gesture and reappear in speech, and eventually merge into a verbo-gestural metaphoric expression (Kolter et al. 2012). This flexibility can be methodologically exploited to reconstruct metaphor activation.

In applied approaches to metaphor analysis, aspects of this have been discussed under the label of "tuning/activation devices" (Cameron 2003; Cameron & Deignan 2003; Goatly 1997; Stibbe 1996). Examples of verbal devices are given by repetition, diversification, modification, extension, mixing, compounding of metaphors, literalization, and overdescription.[4] These have the common effect of increasing the salience of metaphoric meaning, i.e. to foreground a metaphor as metaphor. Unsurprisingly, multimodal forms of communication show comparable ways of activating metaphoric meaning: as, for example, when a gesture highlights the "literal" meaning of a verbal metaphoric expression by enacting bodily movements related to the experiential source domain of the metaphor expressed in speech. By giving its experiential source domain a subjective take, the gesture activates metaphoricity of a lexical item. A gesture tracing the UPS and DOWNS of a long-standing relationship as an ephemeral PATH not only turns this metaphorical movement into a lived and felt sensation but also increases the prominence of the metaphor for attending partners in a conversation. With the gesture, the metaphoric meaning is moved into the communicative foreground and given more salience. In this manner, gestures may function as activation devices of verbal metaphoric expressions.

However, such multimodal activation devices are not limited to "revitalizing" conventional verbal metaphors (or activating sleeping ones); they may foreground gestural metaphors as well. Speakers employ different kinds of multimodal devices to draw the attention of conversational partners to their individual understanding of metaphoric meaning. Examples include the following: prosodic marking of a verbal metaphor, semantic oppositions, gaze to gesture, enlarging and extending gestures, repeating gestures, holding gestures, or moving gestures into the visual center of attention. These devices are salience markers for metaphoric meaning, and the ways in which they are used and combined reveals degrees of salient metaphoricity. Thus, the greater the communicative effort a speaker puts into making metaphoricity into a prominent and vital experience for addressees, the more salience markers will direct the addressee's attention to the metaphoric meaning.

Metaphorical meanings can be profiled by employing (a) *multiple instantiations* of an experiential source domain and (b) *salience markers*, operating upon and highlighting metaphoric expressions. The more frequently an experiential source domain is displayed or pointed to (for instance, an up and down movement depicting the UPS and DOWNS of a relationship, not only in gesture but also in head movement), the more this metaphoric experience of a love relation that moves over hilly ground is activated and becomes a vital, lived sensation for both speaker and recipient. This increases the degree of activated metaphoricity as well as the degree of interpersonal salience.

Profiling metaphoric meaning in this way can be accounted for in terms of the following *foregrounding techniques*: (i) iconicity, (ii) interactive attention, and (iii) the semantic and/or syntactic integration of gestures and other bodily expressions. The expression of metaphoricity in more than one modality foregrounds metaphoric meaning via the cognitive-semiotic principle of the iconicity of quantity: "More material is more meaning." The highlighting of metaphoric gestures by gazing at the gesture, by enlarging or extending the gesture, follows interactive logic, as interaction addresses meanings which receive the mutual attention of co-participants (Goodwin 1981; Streeck 1993). Semantic and/or syntactic principles, finally, target multimodal metaphoric expressions in which a body movement is either used to replace a verbal expression and/or simply adds a new facet of meaning, i.e. they govern the integration of a metaphoric gesture into a speech pause or a co-expressive gesture accompanying speech.

In the following section, this dynamic view of metaphoric meaning-making will be illustrated with microanalyses of waking metaphors in an Argentine Tango dance class. The material comes from a dance workshop on balance and posture. It was filmed with two cameras with a focus on the teacher.

3 From Waking Metaphors to a Salient Metaphoric Theme in a Tango Dance Class

The following microanalysis of the HEAVY LEG AS ANCHOR CHAIN example demonstrates how the dance teacher uses waking metaphoric expressions in speech, gesture, and whole-body movements to explain the core subject of his class: balance and posture. In a process of foregrounding metaphoricity, these metaphoric variations become a salient, interpersonally shared object of attention, eventually forming a *metaphoric theme*, which structures a large part of this Argentine Tango class. As confirmed in an interview after class, this metaphoric theme was neither planned in advance nor drawn from a repertoire. The teacher clearly did not deliberately use metaphors in speech and gesture, as they did not receive any meta-communicative awareness. It will be shown that, nevertheless, these metaphors must be described as waking and perceived, acted out and felt, because much communicative effort was put into foregrounding them. In fact, the HEAVY LEG AS ANCHOR CHAIN becomes a recurring metaphoric theme that changes in degrees of activation but remains salient throughout the class.

The lesson addressed two fundamental but quite challenging body techniques for novice tango dancers: namely, how to maintain balance and an upright posture while walking and turning. Tango dancers have to keep a very stable upper body, while doing a lot of subtle footwork. Even highly experienced dancers never stop working on their walking techniques because walking is at the core of Argentine Tango. Maintaining a smoothness of movement, as if gliding over water, even when standing or turning on one foot, is what characterizes this specific walking technique.

In the lesson, the teacher (Carlos) is working on the close connections between the tango style of walking and a stable balance. As he is doing this, a metaphoric theme emerges that characterizes his understanding of how balance connects with walking: KEEPING BALANCED IS FEELING STABLE LIKE A SHIP (in the middle of the ocean) WITH A HANGING ANCHOR CHAIN (that stabilizes the ship). One way in which this metaphoric theme plays out is the HEAVY LEG AS ANCHOR CHAIN metaphor expressed in body movements and speech. Figure 16.1 shows how, by talking about it and by pointing to it with his left hand, the teacher draws attention to the stretched heavy leg. Before becoming the target domain of a metaphor, the heavy leg is introduced as a sensorimotor experience which his students rehearse (see the woman depicted on the left-hand side of Figure 16.1). The heavy leg as a bodily experience is thus a salient topic in speech and in body movement as well, right from the beginning of the lesson.

Over the course of the dance workshop, students quite obviously struggle with the 'heavy-leg' idea of walking and repeatedly ask for further explanations. Carlos uses the metaphoric theme to work on the elegant, smooth walking style, which requires balance and an upright, stable posture. Figure 16.2 shows the moment in class when the teacher begins to use this metaphoric theme to help them understand and experience the 'heavy leg.'

Figure 16.2 shows snapshots of a moment in the class, in which the experiential source domain of the metaphoric theme is worked out in a close

Figure 16.1 Introducing the concept and the feeling of a 'heavy leg'

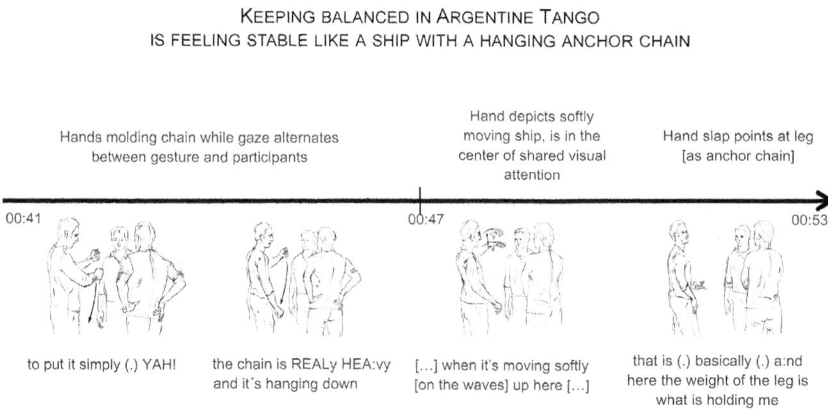

Figure 16.2 Explanation of the metaphoric theme: The 'heavy leg' becomes a stabilizing anchor chain.

conversation with two male dancers. Carlos describes the feeling of a heavy leg by developing a scenario of how a ship is stabilized by its hanging anchor chain. The idea is that, when shifting weight from the back leg to the front leg, the leg that is"left behind" is stretched out and moved heavily over the ground. Its weight is imagined to be the hanging anchor chain of a boat. The teacher explains, "It's just the heaviness of the chain that stabilizes the ship and prevents it from moving away. It is not the anchor actually touching ground." Patting his 'long' stretched back leg, he refers to it as "anchor chain" (ex 1):

(1) Teacher summarizing his idea of the 'heavy leg'

TEACHER: To put it simply(.)yeah (.) and the weight force of the chain simply (.) the chain is really heavy and it is hanging down (.) until you have pulled it away eventually
STUDENT: Yeah
TEACHER: You would need enormous strength well (.) when it's moving softly[on the waves, CM] up here (.) that is basically here (.) the weight of my leg is what´s holding me, right?

Not only does he treat *his* leg as an anchor chain, he does the same with the back leg of his two students: "until *you* have pulled *it* away." Emphasizing that an anchor chain stabilizes the boat through its weight, not by being hooked onto the ground, Carlos depicts the stabilizing effect of the long and heavy leg. The anchor chain metaphor also directly evokes the second important effect of the heavy leg: namely, a calm and well-balanced upper body. In fact, another waking metaphor emerges: UPPER BODY IS BOAT. The speaker establishes the metaphoric link between the boat and the upper body explicitly. First, he sets up a deictic reference to the source-domain scenario, namely the ship on small gentle waves ("when it's moving softly *up here*") and then, in an explanatory move, he specifies the target domain of the metaphor by indicating the upper body verbally and gesturally: "that is basically *here* (pointing to his upper body)."

This is one of many instances in the class when the metaphoric scenario is used to explain the sensorimotor experience of a heavy leg and its stabilizing effect on the dancer's balance. All these verbal and bodily expressions of the metaphoric theme must be considered as waking metaphors; they are foregrounded as a result of this instructive conversational setting. In fact, the metaphoric theme emerges from the sensorimotor experience of the teacher *and* as a consequence of his interaction with a group of dancers having difficulties understanding, feeling, and "doing" the heavy leg. However, once this theme is established and verbalized explicitly, it also feeds back into the interactive setting, thus triggering further metaphoric expressions in speech, gesture, and body movement. This is a kind of metaphor emergence cycle. Such metaphoric themes are related to but not identical with Cameron's notion of "systematic" metaphor (Cameron 2010b; Cameron et al. 2009). A systematic metaphor is a dynamic theme that is based on clusters of all verbal metaphors used in a discourse whose metaphoricity is *potentially* active. The metaphoric theme addressed here, however, emerges from the repeated use of *waking* metaphors. They certainly show different degrees of activation and thus also different degrees of consciousness. This includes "deliberate" uses of metaphors in Steen's sense, but those are just the tip of the iceberg of a dynamically graded metaphoricity. Waking metaphors might thus well be considered a subgroup of those metaphors in a discourse that Cameron would identify as potentially metaphoric.

In the examples reported here, the metaphoric theme KEEPING BALANCED IS FEELING STABLE LIKE A SHIP WITH A HANGING ANCHOR CHAIN is grounded in the sensorimotor experience of a heavy leg, and it is being formed over the course of a series of waking verbal metaphoric expressions. One of them has already been discussed: the HEAVY LEG AS ANCHOR CHAIN metaphor. Notably, this metaphor is "embodied" in two different ways: a body gesture and a hand gesture. While the body gesture directly enacts the felt experience of the heavy leg represented (the long leg represents a chain), the hand gesture depicts the anchor chain with a molding gesture, molding the shape of a big chain. Even though both gestures clearly enact some facet of the source domain, i.e. an anchor chain drifting in deep waters, its two versions involve different embodied experiences and include quite distinct perspectives on the subject matter. While the hand gesture underlines the weight of the chain and its slightly diagonal orientation, the body gesture addresses the location of the heavy feeling in the dancer's body.

Figure 16.3 illustrates those two gestures: The drawing on the left depicts Carlos describing the weight of the chain with reference to his own stretched leg. In this locational enactment of the body metaphor HEAVY LEG AS ANCHOR CHAIN, he steps sideward and stretches his leg, and then looks at it and talks about the weight of the chain, "It is the weight force of the chain (. . .)." In the speech-pause he finishes the sentence with a bodily performance of a heavy leg and a flat hand pointing that patches the leg. Continuing, with a further multimodal explanation, he underlines the heaviness and inertia of the chain: He now depicts the chain with a molding hand gesture, performed in the center of a shared visual attention, and expresses the properties of this object of reference verbally: "It is the heaviness and the inertia." With this verbo-gestural metaphor, the inertia of a slowly drifting chain is moved into the center of attention and thus becomes of core importance for teaching a sense of the 'heavy leg.' The change from body gesture to hand gesture thus involves a shift in perspective, a refocusing of attention, and a refocusing of embodied experience.

Through this interplay of verbal and bodily actions, the leg literally becomes a bodily metaphor, enacting the source domain of the verbal metaphor. The hand gesture comes up when Carlos describes how the chain (not the anchor hooked to the ground) stabilizes the ship. His hands mold a vertically oriented chain, which means that, now, the LEG AS ANCHOR CHAIN metaphor is gesturally conceptualized as a thick, vertically oriented object, where the molding gesture highlights the weight of the chain through its massive size. An iron chain of the size that Carlos' hands depict must be very heavy indeed. While this hand gesture is an enactment of the source-domain scenario, too, it highlights a very different aspect of it, namely its weight – not the location in the body, as the body gesture does. Moreover, the body gesture implies a different form of embodied experience from the hand gesture. The body gesture goes along with the actual sensorimotor experience of the HEAVY LEG, its goal is to evoke a very specific feeling in the legs, which *is* the target of the metaphoric explanation. The hand gesture in contrast depicts an aspect of the imaginary scenario, which describes 'weight' and 'heaviness' as such – as a gestural conceptualization – detached from the localized site of the body, where its heaviness is supposed to be experienced. In sum, bodily enactments of metaphoric meaning may present very distinct perspectives of experiential source domains. They each offer very specific kinds of embodied experiences; and it is not just because there is body movement that there is embodiment, too.[5]

The next two sections will illustrate two dimensions of the same overall dynamics of waking metaphors: The *grading of attention* and the *temporal flow of metaphoric meaning*.

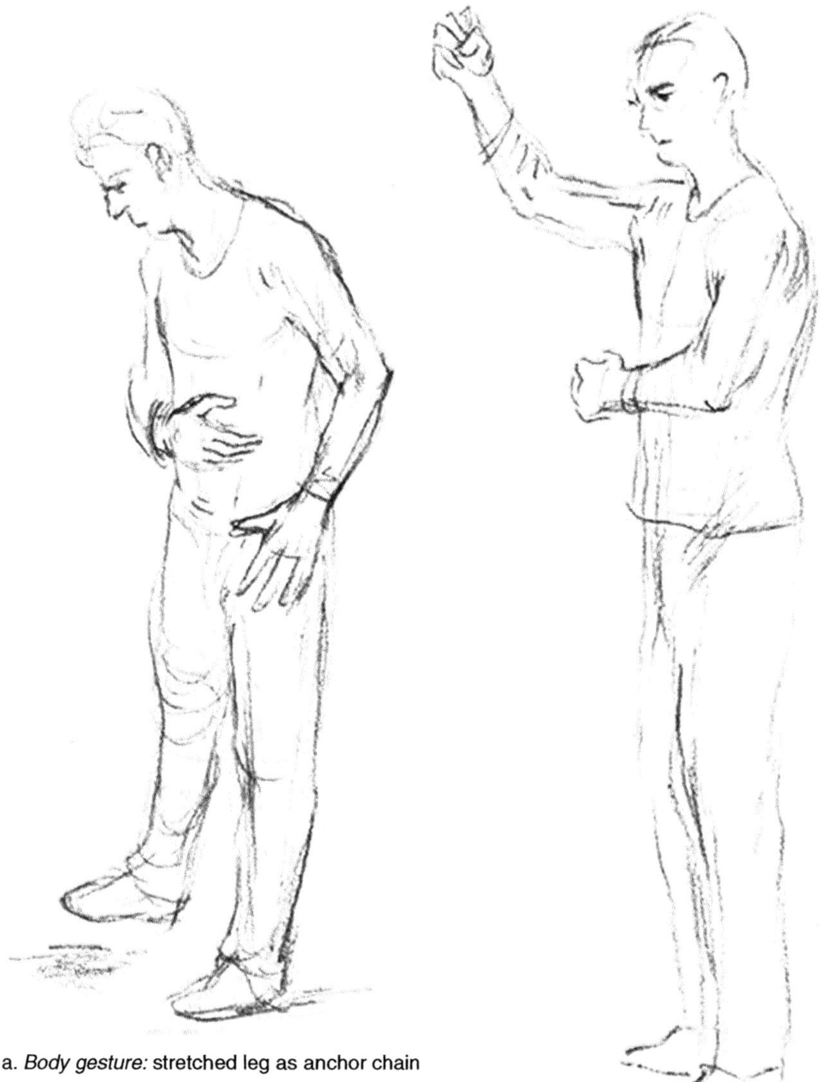

a. *Body gesture:* stretched leg as anchor chain

b. *Hand gesture:* hands molding anchor chain

Figure 16.3 Two different forms of embodying the experiential source domain

4 Grading of Waking Metaphors: Attention, Dynamic Foregrounding, and Salience

Looking at gestures in relation to spoken language opens up the possibility to literally see which aspects of metaphoric meaning are in the foreground of shared attention of the participants in a particular communicative situation. This is possible because gestures are embodied conceptualizations which interact with the semantics and pragmatics of verbal utterances. They are bodily forms of imagination and thought and embodied presentations of shared meanings. They have been characterized as forms of imagistic thought (McNeill 1992), as visible actions that become utterances (Kendon 2004), as forms of "thinking for gesturing" (Cienki & Müller 2008b), as "cepts" and as "ceiving" actions (Streeck 2009), and as expressive movements (Müller 2014).

Despite distinct theoretical positions, gesture scholars unanimously agree that gestures contribute significantly to verbal communication. This intertwining of gestures with spoken discourse opens up interesting venues to study the consciousness of metaphoric meaning – because a gesture can actually display experienced metaphoricity even if it is not in the focus of a deliberately employed linguistic metaphor. In Streeck's terms, this would be a ceiving type of gesture, a gesture that does not receive interactive attention (as displayed in gaze direction onto the gesture). When, however, the speaker and her conversational partner look at such a metaphoric gesture (for instance, because it is performed in the center of the shared visual attention space), then metaphoric meaning, displayed gesturally, becomes the focus of shared attention. The cognitive salience of metaphoric meaning is increased when over the course of an interaction a metaphoric gesture is foregrounded by activation devices (or salience markers). Sleeping metaphors are dynamically transformed into waking ones – by the co-participants in an interaction.

The methodological point is that micro-descriptions of such empirical cues allow reconstruction of the graded metaphoricity of waking metaphors. To document that, a descriptive methodology was developed, which combines metaphor foregrounding analysis with linguistic gesture analysis. *Metaphor Foregrounding Analysis* (MFA) identifies activation devices (salience markers) to determine the communicative effort put into the foregrounding of metaphoric meaning. The more foregrounding, the higher the degree of activated metaphoricity (in whatever mode of metaphoric expression, verbal, gestural, pictorial, audiovisual, etc.) (Müller 2008a,b; Müller & Tag 2010). Only metaphoric expressions that are foregrounded by such activation devices are considered as waking. All other transparent metaphors are considered sleeping, e.g. they show a lower degree of metaphor activation. The meaning of metaphoric gestures is accounted for by applying the *Method of linguistic Gesture Analysis* (MGA). This is a form-based two-step analysis of the semantics and pragmatics of gestures. Starting out from the meaning of the form, it describes how an underspecified form meaning is contextually specified (Müller 2010).

Both methods are considered descriptive and reconstructive forms of analyzing multimodal metaphoric meaning-making. They follow a cognitive-linguistic spirit of language use as a dynamic conceptualization and as organized according to principles of gestalt perception (Langacker 2008; Talmy 2000). At the same time, they are inspired by Chafe's notion of the flow of consciousness (Chafe 1994), the conversation-analytic understanding of attention as a joint activity of conversational partners and of interaction itself as an embodied and situated activity (Goodwin 2011a; Streek 2008, 2009). Concerning the identification of verbal metaphors, MFA differs from the word-by-word *Metaphor Identification Procedure* (MIP, Pragglejaz 2007) in two important respects: First, instead of using lemmas in dictionaries to 'identify' metaphor, it uses the communicative activities of speakers to decide whether, for these speakers, at that given moment in a communicative encounter, a metaphor was used and understood metaphorically. Second, metaphors are considered not as being bound to single lexical items, but as dynamic forms of meaning-making expanding over stretches of discourses. The latter position is backed by Cameron's discourse dynamics of metaphor (Cameron 2010b; Cameron et al. 2009; see also Deignan, *this volume*).

Over the course of the workshop, the anchor chain metaphors are repeated and moved into the foreground of attention in various ways. Different foregrounding principles and devices are employed to direct the attention of the workshop participants to this metaphoric theme (see also Müller & Tag 2010). As discussed in section 1, three foregrounding principles operate to dynamically grade metaphoricity: (i) iconicity, (ii) interactive attention, (iii) semantics and syntax.

In the ANCHOR CHAIN example, the iconicity of quantity is used to foreground metaphoric meaning all the time: A body and a hand gesture enact different aspects of the verbal metaphor's source domain. Carlos uses gestural and bodily expressions of the verbalized source domain of the metaphor in the example as a whole. To illustrate how, in combination, the three foregrounding principles lead to salient metaphoricity, the molding anchor chain gesture will be analyzed more closely.

When Carlos says, "To put it simply (.) yeah (.) the chain is really heavy and it's hanging down," his hands mold the shape of a big, vertically oriented object. Here the source domain is expressed twice, namely in two modalities at the same time, reflecting the iconicity of quantity. The fact that a verbalized metaphor is being bodily enacted, i.e. that the source-domain meaning stimulated those expressive gestural renditions, not only foregrounds metaphoric meaning but also indicates that the verbal metaphor receives at least some attention. Hence, the metaphoricity of this verbal metaphoric expression must be considered active – though the level of consciousness cannot be precisely determined by a descriptive analysis of discourse events.

With his hands and words, Carlos unfolds an experiential scenario. He is giving a bodily exposition of his experiential source domain, thus making clear that this source domain is accessible to him at that moment. With the molding chain gesture, the metaphor of the leg as heavy anchor chain turns into a lived experience, an embodied metaphoric meaning for the students, who quite desperately seek an understanding of this unfamiliar body concept. However, Carlos additionally employs other means to foreground the multimodal expression of the anchor chain metaphor. Following the interactive principle, gaze direction is quite commonly used to foreground metaphoricity. A speaker's gaze generally indicates an interactively relevant focus of attention (Goodwin 1981; Streeck 1993). Carlos repeatedly gazes at the anchor chain gesture and even puts the gesture right up into the center of visual attention, i.e. he puts a gestured version of a massive chain in front of his student's faces. They cannot *not* perceive the gesture, and with it the imagined experiential scenario which constitutes the source domain of Carlos' metaphoric theme for his dance lesson. In this way the anchor chain metaphor becomes an interactively shared object of attention (Figure 16.4).

In addition to foregrounding metaphoric meaning through iconic and interactive means, Carlos also forms multimodal utterances. He semantically integrates the anchor chain gesture into his verbal utterance. While saying, "To put it simply (.) yeah (.) the chain is really heavy [. . .] and it's hanging down," he is doing the anchor chain gesture which highlights the weight and the verticality of

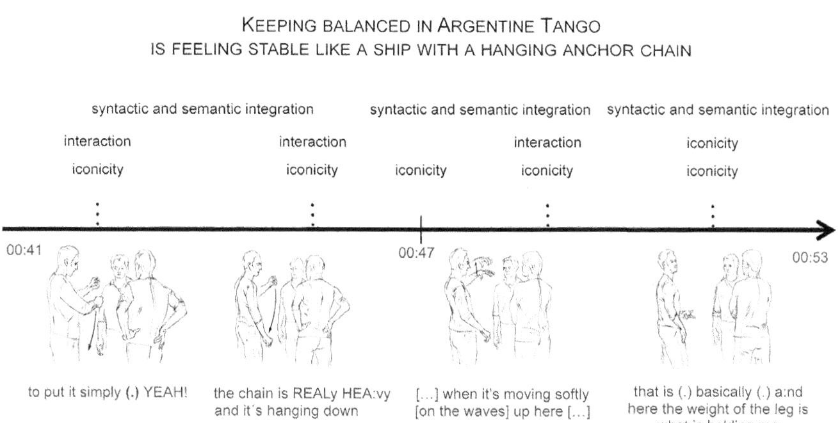

Figure 16.4 Foregrounding the anchor chain as metaphor for the heavy leg: iconicity, interaction, and semantics

the chain. Both concern core ideas for the heavy-leg prerequisite of the smooth foot- and legwork needed for the basic steps of tango. In this way, the semantic principle helps to foreground metaphoricity and to focus the addressee's attention to particular aspects of an experiential source domain (Figure 16.4).

A detailed description of the actual devices used to foreground the anchor chain metaphors in their various instantiations allows the researcher to empirically determine how metaphoric meaning is graded dynamically at any point of the ongoing discourse (Figure 16.5): Carlos uses a gesture depicting a verbal metaphor, he gazes at the gesture, he performs a big gesture in the center of the visual attention, and the gesture semantically elaborates the verbal metaphor. Taken together, this accumulation of foregrounding devices indicates that metaphoricity must be strongly activated, that it is embodied, experienced, attended to, and lived at that moment in the dance lesson.

Depending upon the number of foregrounding cues employed, metaphoric meaning is more or less moved into the foreground of an interactively shared attentional space. As a result, metaphoricity can vary between being in the background (for instance, with a random small gesture that is not further highlighted) and being highly salient in the foreground of attention. In both cases, metaphoricity can be considered as active, and as a vital and shared experience. In both cases, these metaphors are waking, but to different degrees. This is the kind of dynamics that characterizes the grading of waking metaphors. When, in cases of transparent metaphors, the metaphoric meaning

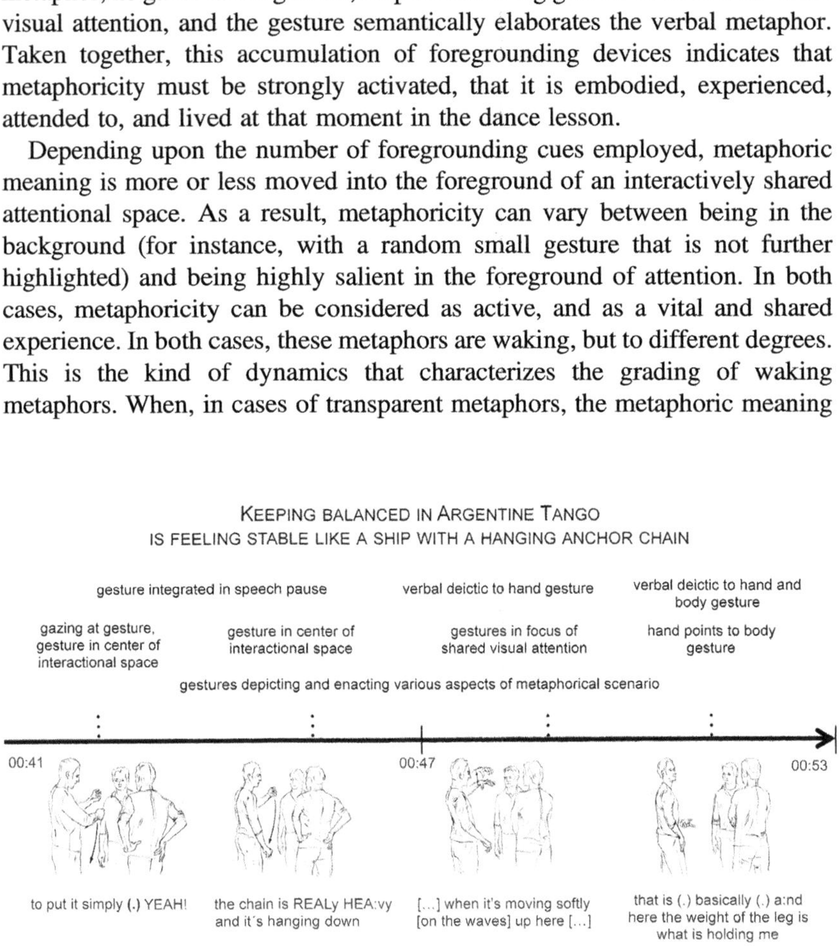

Figure 16.5 Accumulating foregrounding devices: metaphor in gesture, gaze to gesture, large gesture, performed in the center of visual attention, semantic specification

is not foregrounded at all, metaphoricity is sleeping, i.e. only a potential is there to be (or not to be) activated in that specific context of usage.

5 Flow of Attention as Salience Profile: The Temporal Dynamics of Waking Metaphors

Waking metaphors form part of two different yet intrinsically related forms of dynamics: the grading of metaphoricity (e.g. the shifting of salience through foregrounding) and a temporal salience profile. From the variable ways in which metaphors are being foregrounded over a discourse, a salience profile emerges. The sequentiality of metaphoric meaning-making, i.e. its embeddedness in interaction, constitutes the temporal dynamics of waking metaphors. Ongoing foregrounding activities display a shared flow of attention and create a dynamic temporal salience profile of waking metaphors.

This temporal orchestration can be documented employing *Keynote based Timeline Annotation* (KeaTA).[6] Presupposing a thorough Metaphor Foregrounding Analysis (MFA) and a gesture analysis (MGA), the annotation documents the repeated use of a particular metaphor (verbal, gestural) and its degrees of activation over time, thus providing a depiction of the grading of metaphoricity in the course of a discourse event: The timeline depicts the duration of the discourse and shows how a particular metaphor is distributed across the course of a discourse and across modalities (speech and gesture). In terms of foregrounding principles, iconicity and interaction are documented – albeit only in a rudimentary form, as the diagrams can quickly become too complex. However, there is no fixed rule as to how fine-grained the analysis depicted in the annotation should be. If necessary, all foregrounding devices can be documented in their temporal dynamics. In short, KeaTA visualizes foregrounded metaphors. The result is a graphic display of the flow of attention as an interactive salience profile of waking metaphors.

Figure 16.6 displays such a profile for the anchor chain metaphor as used by Carlos over the course of a 45-minutes tango lesson on balance and the walking technique of Argentine Tango. The timeline annotation shows when and how Carlos uses the anchor chain metaphor throughout the lesson. Below the time arrow, variable instances of bodily enactments of the anchor chain metaphor are shown. The gray bars above the arrow document the verbalization of the metaphor.

For basically two-thirds of the lesson, Carlos' focus is only on the target of the metaphor: the feeling of a heavy "long" leg. Only in the last 15 minutes does this feeling become the target of a multimodal waking metaphor. In response to his students' questions and obvious struggles, Carlos invents the anchor chain metaphor, which is then unfolded into an imaginary scenario of a

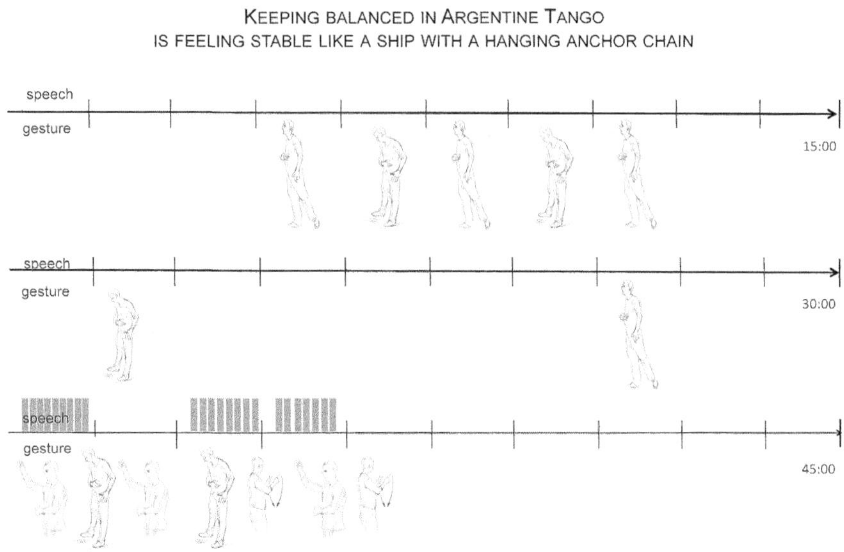

Figure 16.6 Salience profile of the tango teacher's waking metaphor HEAVY LEG AS ANCHOR CHAIN

ship on softly babbling waters in the middle of an ocean, being stabilized by the weight of a massive anchor chain reaching down into deep waters. As a result of this conversational interaction, the stable posture of a tango dancer is metaphorized as a gently moving, but stabilized, ship, and the gliding walking movements of the dancer become the anchor chain, stabilizing the ship through its weight.

From this temporal dynamics, a metaphoric salience profile emerges which displays a series of more or less waking metaphors expressed in body gestures, speech, and hand gestures. This salience profile also shows how a metaphorical theme may emerge from the repeated and variable use of waking metaphors that are inspired by the needs and dynamics of an interactive instructive setting. So far, however, we have documented this only for the teacher; what about his students? Figure 16.7 provides a glimpse of the interactive nature of the anchor chain metaphor. A thorough analysis of the sharing of attention to the anchor chain metaphor extends beyond the scope of this chapter. However, a first, coarse-grained analysis shows that the anchor chain metaphor is taken up by the students in the form of speech, hand, and body gestures. The interactive variants of the anchor chain metaphor underline once more that, for the participants in this workshop, metaphoricity was a lived experience and a vital embodied conceptualization.

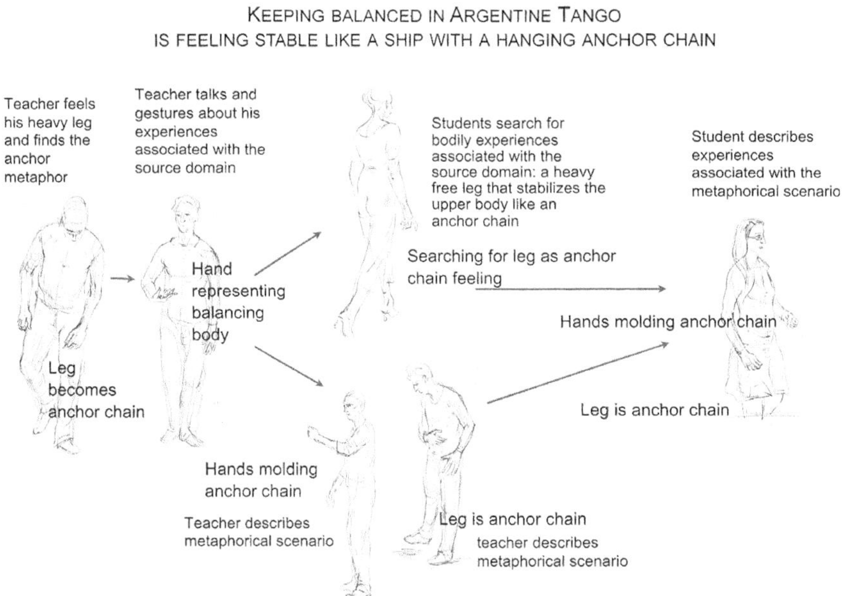

Figure 16.7 Working with anchor chain metaphors throughout the workshop

6 Conclusion

Taking multimodal language in use as a starting point for theorizing metaphor shows that there is not necessarily any opposition between an embodied-cognition and a discourse point of view. By studying closely how participants in a communicative encounter deal with metaphoric meaning as they talk and gesture, it is possible to document when metaphoricity is in the foreground of attention and thus *experienced* as such. It is possible, in fact, to see whether metaphoricity is activated, vital, lived – and sometimes also how it emerges. From this vantage point, metaphor becomes a matter of meaning-making – a process rather than a product. And as such it depends on interaction. I therefore suggest talking about establishing, creating, or activating metaphoricity as a process in which the subjective is a consequence of the intersubjective (see also Jensen & Cuffari 2014; Jensen, *this volume*).

In my view, metaphoric meaning is meaning-making and an embodied form of understanding. Its prerequisites are twofold: mappings between two domains of embodied experience and interactions between them. Metaphoric gestures may present those experiential domains from the perspective of the speaker. They are designed for an attending co-participant, i.e. embedded in a particular interactive moment. Metaphors are thus dynamic forms of embodied understanding.

Activating metaphoricity – as a dynamic form of meaning-making – characterizes all forms of multimodal communication, face-to-face communication as much as the watching of audiovisuals (Kappelhoff & Greifenstein 2015; Kappelhoff & Müller 2011; Müller & Schmitt 2015); it also applies to monomodal forms of metaphor usage, such as in written texts. It actually is the mode in which meaning is to be characterized. Meaning in whatever communicative format is first and foremost a matter of use, of somebody talking to somebody else, reading a newspaper or a book, watching movies or a news program, or passing by an advertisement billboard. Other, decontextualized forms of meaning, such as the lemmas we find in dictionaries, the formal analysis of propositional structures, or the pragmatic analysis of speech acts, take meaning out of its dynamic, temporal, and deeply intersubjective realm of being. Their units of analysis are sedimented abstractions over usage events. Studies of language change, of lexicalization and grammaticalization, of the emergence of signed languages all testify to the fact that language is primarily and *by its very nature* dynamic. Sedimentation and conventionalization only seemingly produce static units of meaning because all words exist only when applied in some kind of discourse. Metaphors are thus embodied cognition *in* discourse.

Notes and Acknowledgments

* Special thanks go to F. Boll and L. Hotze for working with me on the analysis. I'd also like to thank S. Greifenstein, D. Horst, S. Ladewig, S. Tag, B. Marienfeld, T. Scherer, and C. Schmitt for giving great support during the work on this chapter. I am extremely grateful to B. Hampe for her meticulous and lucid editing of this chapter. Thanks go also to the reviewers for highly valuable comments as well as to the artist Mathias Roloff for the drawings (www.mathiasroloff.de). A grant by the German Ministry of Education supported the research on dance workshops.

1 For more detail concerning the consciousness-novelty debate, see Müller (2008a, 2011).

2 For an overview of multimodal metaphor: Forceville and Urios-Aparisi (2009); for metaphor analysis in a discourse dynamics perspective: Cameron and Maslen (2010) and Cameron et al. (2009).

3 For a detailed discussion of the dynamic view, see Müller (2008a: 22–39).

4 For a survey, see Müller (2008a: 188–202).

5 Mittelberg's cognitive-semiotic explanation of the metonymical motivation of metaphoric gestures provides another relevant pathway to the experiential grounding of metaphoricity (Mittelberg & Waugh 2009; see also Mittelberg & Joue, *this volume*).

6 This annotation system was originally developed in the context of a research project on multimodal metaphor and expressive movement in conversation, film, and television (www.hermann-kappelhoff.de/node/24); see also: Kappelhoff & Greifenstein 2015; Müller & Ladewig 2013; Müller & Schmitt 2015).

Epilogue (A Personal View)

17 The Embodied and Discourse Views of Metaphor: Why These Are Not So Different and How They Can Be Brought Closer Together

Raymond W. Gibbs, Jr.

Chapter Preview

Metaphor scholars have long debated whether the possibility that metaphor is "conceptual" or possibly "embodied" ignores crucial social and linguistic facts about metaphor in discourse. Scholars adopting either of the "embodied" and "discourse" views of metaphor typically advance different theories on the origins, motivations, functions, and uses of metaphors in language and thought. These different theoretical perspectives are also generally studied by scholars from different academic disciplines that employ very different empirical methods (e.g. discourse analyses vs. experimental techniques). My aim in this chapter is to show how these different perspectives are closely related given (a) the embodied nature of metaphoric discourse and (b) the social context for all embodied action. Rather than arguing for the superiority of one approach over the other, my plea is for a better integration of these views to capture the complex realities of metaphoric experience.

1 Introduction

Metaphors are butterflies. I have long thought about metaphors in this particular metaphorical manner, which has afforded me various insights into how metaphors work and the different ways they can be studied. For example, some butterflies aficionados, called lepidopterists, closely examine individual dead butterflies while they are neatly arranged, and pinned down, under glass. Peering down at the butterflies may perhaps tell one about aspects of their biology, their exquisite color patterns, and differences between types of butterflies. I have no doubt that much can be learned from staring at butterflies in this way. Still, butterflies are beautiful living creatures, fluttering about in nature, interacting with plants, animals, people, and, of course, other butterflies. My personal preference is to see butterflies in the wild, even if this makes them more difficult to study compared to dead specimens in a laboratory. There may be huge benefits to this research as it allows one to explore how butterflies evolve and function in rich ecological contexts.

Metaphors are also living creatures, like butterflies, and they are most beautiful when seen in the context of persons interacting in the world, whether metaphors spill from our lips, pens, or fingers/hands/arms, as in the case of metaphorical gestures. Similar to the study of butterflies, metaphor enthusiasts have choices over how best to explore what metaphors are and how they function in nature. We can, of course, still examine metaphors "under glass," as when placed individually down on paper, to better understand their structure and possible meanings. However, we should never ignore the fundamental fact that metaphors are human actions. Divorcing metaphors from how people create metaphors, the bodies they have, the ways they use metaphor to coordinate with other persons, provides us with only a small glimmer of the roles that metaphors have in human life.

This preamble sets the stage for the discussion in this chapter on the choices scholars make when they adopt particular research strategies when studying metaphor. My primary argument will be that the philosophical and methodological approaches we embrace in studying metaphor have enormous implications for our respective theories of metaphor. I am especially concerned with the unfortunate tendency in metaphor scholarship to focus only on certain aspects of metaphor, and to adopt only certain methodological ways of doing so. These habits are prevalent in many academic disciplines, perhaps quite naturally. Yet looking at metaphors from singular points of view sometimes leads to inaccurate, misleading theories of metaphorical thought and language.

2 Levels of Analysis

How do we explain the processes and products of metaphor performance? I purposely talk about "metaphor performance" rather than "metaphor use" because "performance" gives proper attention to the fact that metaphors are enacted and not simply selected for use from a mental metaphor thesaurus. But trying to explain metaphor performance is a tricky business precisely because we can do so using a variety of different approaches. Consider some of the ways or perspectives in which scholars have studied metaphor performance.

- evolutionary
- historical
- sociocultural
- discourse

- linguistic
- cognitive
- psychological
- embodied
- neural

In each case, different scholars have claimed that metaphor can be most fruitfully examined almost exclusively in terms of specific levels of analysis. Metaphor may be characterized as emerging from evolutionary, or sociocultural, or cognitive, or neural activities, to name just a few of the relevant forces that possibly influence metaphorical structure and meanings. Yet once again, there is often the explicit or implicit claim that one's own preferred level of analysis argues against the relevance of other perspectives on metaphor performance. For example, with the emergence of Conceptual Metaphor Theory (CMT) in metaphor studies (Kövecses 2010b; Lakoff & Johnson 1980, 1999), various scholars have responded by suggesting that CMT ignores other important levels of analysis (e.g. cultural, linguistic) that may better describe the nature of metaphorical actions (Haser 2005; Quinn 1992; Rakova 2003). More recently, various metaphor scholars have explicitly suggested that neural and embodied levels of analysis are far less relevant than are sociocultural and discourse perspectives on metaphor (Zinken 2007). I am most interested in how these debates often limit our understanding of what metaphor is all about.

3 Different Methods

Accompanying arguments for the importance of certain levels of analysis in accounting for metaphorical thought and language is the embrace of particular research methods as being best suited for explaining metaphor performance. Consider some methods by which metaphors have been studied.

- Ethnographic studies
- Literary analyses of individual works or genres
- Philosophical (conceptual) analyses
- Linguistic analyses (intuitionist, corpus)
- Psychological analyses (experimental)
- Neuroscience (case studies, brain imaging)

Metaphor scholars will typically employ research methods appropriate to their own disciplinary backgrounds, such that anthropologists will use ethnographic methods, linguists will use different linguistic methods, psychologists will adopt experimental techniques, and neuroscientists will stick with case studies and experimental measures of brain activity.

However, the relations between levels of analysis and research methods do not always neatly match one another. Linguists, for example, will use various intuitionist and corpus methods to discern important facts about metaphor performance regarding levels of analysis ranging from the evolution of language to cultural perspectives on metaphor down to possible neural underpinnings of metaphorical thought and language. Discourse analysts, who often embrace different linguistic methods, frequently aim to describe something about forces motivating metaphor from the evolution of language down to cognitive and embodied levels of analysis. Psychologists sometimes use experimental methods to uncover insights about cultural factors down to embodied perspectives on metaphor.

Still, the important fact remains that scholars will often adopt specific research methods and create theories of metaphor performance which, in their minds, best explain the empirical findings when using their preferred methods. Scholars who adopt particular methods sometimes ignore, and write dismissively about, other empirical methods. Psychologists, for instance, who embrace experimental measures frequently do so explicitly because of a great distrust of intuitionist linguistic analyses of metaphor (e.g. McGlone 2007).

In general, part of the background in contemporary debates concerns which levels of analysis and which empirical methods are best capable of explaining the nature and functions of metaphor in thought and language. Metaphor, in all its guises, is clearly a complex phenomenon, and it is not surprising that so many scholars approach their studies in so many different ways. Let me now briefly review four concrete examples of metaphor in action to illustrate some of the debates over what may be the preferred level of analysis and empirical methods for studying and explaining metaphor performance.

4 Four Examples of Metaphor Performance

Kövecses (2015) has offered an explanation of where metaphors come from by considering a number of real-world linguistic examples. For instance, he observed the following metaphorical utterance with the term "capsized" (literally referring to an overturned boat in the water) in a news article about the famous, now elderly, rock 'n' roll musician Fats Domino, who lives in New Orleans, Louisiana. Back in 2005, Domino lived through the very destructive Hurricane Katrina in that part of the world. The article made the following observation about Domino (ibid.: 121):

(1) The 2005 hurricane *capsized* Domino's life, though he's loath to confess any inconvenience or misery outside of missing his social circle . . .

The use of "capsized" to refer to Domino's life, and not to a boat tipping over in water, is clearly metaphorical in context. Kövecses' main point was that this boating term was employed in a metaphorical way precisely because Hurricane Katrina gives rise to images of vast bodies of water and tremendous flooding in which many buildings, animals, and people did not survive. Thus, a term referring to a temporary overturning of a boat was conceptually salient given the context of talking about the impact that Katrina had on many people's lives, including Domino's. It simply makes sense and is contextually apt, then, to metaphorically speak of a temporary upheaval in life as being "capsized."

What level of analysis best explains this small bit of metaphorical creativity? What empirical research method is most appropriate for explaining how this particular metaphor performance arose and is understood by others? I wish to focus on two different possibilities, even though there are surely many others. One debate is whether metaphor is best explained purely as a discourse phenomenon as opposed to a cognitive and embodied one.

Under a classic CMT perspective, the use of "capsized" in the above context is motivated by a "primary" metaphor (Grady 1997b), namely that PERSISTENCE IS REMAINING ERECT. Under this view, the metaphorical use of "capsized" emerges from an enduring correlation in bodily experience. Thus, the existence of things in the world that persist is correlated to a significant, positive degree with things that are capable of remaining upright. For instance, people, animals, and plants exist in a generally upright form when alive but lose that upright stance when ill or dead. Similarly, buildings and other artifacts typically remain upright when they are still in working order yet will fall apart, over time, when no longer in use. These *correlations* are understood in deeply embodied ways, given our viewing of upright objects that are alive or persisting, and because we feel ourselves, our bodies, as being more capable of being upright when we are healthy than when ill. Once again, these correlations in our experiences are not perfect, yet they are strong enough in a positive direction to help serve as the concrete foundation in structuring certain abstract concepts, including those referring to different facets of our lives (e.g. our careers, marriages). Different linguistic expressions provide evidence for the reality of the PERSISTENCE IS REMAINING ERECT primary metaphor, such as "The relationship *fell* apart," and "I can no longer *stand* working with my boss."

As is well known within CMT, primary metaphors can motivate the existence of different conceptual metaphors such as THEORIES ARE BUILDINGS, which is why it makes sense to talk of "The theory *collapsed* under the weight of the new evidence" (Grady 1997b). Furthermore, the PERSISTENCE IS REMAINING ERECT primary metaphor interacts with another primary metaphor, PURPOSES ARE DESTINATIONS, to create the enduring conceptual metaphor LIFE IS A JOURNEY. When speaking of Domino's life being negatively affected by Hurricane Katrina, the combination of these two primary metaphors more specifically gives rise to the idea that LIFE IS A SEA JOURNEY. Not surprisingly, sea journeys are often taken in boats, which we all know are unable to proceed toward their destinations when they capsize.

This embodied conceptual metaphor perspective on metaphor performance suggests one reason why people talk in particular ways, and not others, when referring, for example, to success and failure in one's personal life story. In the context of a discussion about the impact that Hurricane Katrina had on Fats Domino's life in 2005 and beyond, it makes sense to think of his situation as a temporary inability to remain upright, which can be *creatively instantiated* with the highly salient idea of a boat capsizing. Even if the social and physical context of the "capsized" metaphor makes the use of this term more of a one-shot analogy, the motivation for this creative metaphorical word is still solidly grounded in the embodied primary metaphor.

A very different way of explaining how "capsized" came to be used when describing Domino's life suggests that the metaphor is best explained solely in discourse terms. Thus, the specific discourse situation, including talk of the devastation brought on by Hurricane Katrina, provides all the information needed to establish the novel, metaphorical use of "capsized." The discourse context prompted the one-shot analogy of a life temporally being upset is like a boat capsizing. For this reason, many scholars would maintain that the use of "capsized" when speaking of Domino's situation is an example of a "discourse metaphor."

A discourse metaphor is "a relatively stable metaphorical projection that functions as a key framing device within a particular discourse over a certain period of time" (Zinken et al. 2008: 363). Metaphorical language may be best explained in terms of the local interactions between the discourse participants, and not at the level of preexisting conceptual analogies or metaphors. Indeed, appealing to primary or conceptual metaphors in explaining the creation and meaning of metaphors, such as "capsized" in the Domino case, may only be "post-hoc artefact[s] of sorting utterances on the part of researcher[s]" (Zinken 2007: 461). This slap at researchers who engage in systematic analyses of both conventional and novel metaphorical expressions to infer conceptual metaphors is a direct attack on the relevance of the cognitive and embodied perspectives to explain real-world metaphor performance.

Consider now a different example of metaphor performance that has also been used to advance the relevance of the discourse perspective and downplay the role of conceptual metaphors. Quinn (1992) offered a strong argument in favor of a cultural view of metaphor in an analysis of how Americans talked about their marriages. Consider an excerpt from one of her interviews with a male participant who described how his marriage developed over time (ibid.: 73):

(2) Accepting the differences that were there and that were going to – you know, and that I would have to put up with some of the situations that I didn't like and continue to until we had worked it out. But that *however long and stony a road it was*, we had agreed to *set out on it* and *meet each small situation as it came*.

The "long and stony road" metaphor conveys something about the difficulty and lastingness of marriage. According to CMT, the chain of reasoning underlying the husband's narrative rests on the embodied conceptual metaphor ROMANTIC RELATIONSHIPS ARE JOURNEYS, which is more deeply rooted in the primary metaphors PURPOSES ARE DESTINATIONS and CHANGE/PROGRESS IS MOTION (for a discussion of primary metaphors motivating various JOURNEY metaphors, see also Winter & Matlock, *this volume*).

Under Quinn's view, however, journey metaphors are quite popular to talk about marriage because they are excellent "cultural exemplars of a protracted activity having an ultimate objective, beset with difficulties that require effort to overcome, and that can be undertaken with another person – a cluster of factors that also characterize marriage" (Quinn 1992: 75). Metaphors that can clarify many of the complexities of abstract concepts, such as marriage, will be most appealing and become widely shared among speakers. In this way, metaphor does not constitute how people grasp their marriages but is simply a rhetorical device they use when talking about what is essentially a non-metaphorical concept.

A participant in a different interview described the development of his marriage over time in the following manner (Quinn 1992: 84):

(3) But it could be that the situation when we got married, that it was such that we had lots of room to adjust. Because *we didn't have any idea what we were getting into*. That *gave us a lot of room to adjust*. And by the time we had been through the first year we realized, you know, there would *have to be adjustments made*. And a few years afterwards, when things really got serious we were – you know, when *the marriage was strong*, it was very strong because *it was made* as we went along – it was sort of *a do-it-yourself project*.

A conceptual metaphor analysis of this excerpt rests on an overlapping entailment of two metaphors – MARRIAGE IS A CONTAINER (e.g. "We didn't have any idea about what we were getting into") and MARRIAGE IS A MANUFACTURED PRODUCT (e.g. a "do-it-yourself project"). Although the speaker starts out using one metaphor to make his point (the container metaphor), he soon switches to another (the manufactured product metaphor) to complete his momentary thoughts about marriage. Both metaphors are grounded in embodiment as related to bodily experiences of containment and physically building something. The idea of a marriage being a building is partly motivated by an enduring primary metaphor – SOCIAL STRUCTURES (in this case social relationships) ARE PHYSICAL STRUCTURES.

Quinn rejects this embodied conceptual metaphor account and maintains that people's beliefs about their marriages emerge strictly from cultural knowledge, which is entirely non-metaphorical. Her argument focuses on the fact that people appear not to have a single, stable assemblage of ideas about marriage. Instead, people use verbal metaphors in discourse to momentarily illuminate different parts of the completely non-metaphorical concept for marriage.

The question, again, is whether the discourse or embodied approach to metaphor best explains speakers' uses of verbal metaphors, such as that seen in people talking about their marriages.

Another contrast between the discourse and embodied views of metaphor is revealed in research emerging from the "discourse dynamics approach" to metaphor (Cameron 2008a, 2010b; Cameron et al. 2009). Embracing this perspective entails that scholars work inductively from the what people say in discourse to reveal what their metaphors say about their attitudes and values. Metaphor performance is typically manifested through successive metaphor sources that shift and develop as people negotiate meaning, extend their ideas, or exploit potential opened up by the use of a source term in a particular discourse. Metaphorical talk is not simply the outward manifestation of static conceptual metaphors in the minds of individuals.

Consider, for example, the following short segment from an extended conversation among members of a focus group discussing terrorism (Cameron et al. 2009: 77). A speaker, Phil, describes his reactions to the events of 9/11:

(4) when that Twin – . . . Twin Tower er., .. happened, it, . . . (1.0) *put a flaw in the system* . . . someone's never done that before.

Although the exact topic of the "put a flaw in the system" is vague, it appears, partly based on earlier discourse, to refer to Phil's idea that society is a mechanical system. Thus, the discourse itself leads one to draw this inference that a larger metaphorical theme underlies Phil's metaphorical words. Cameron et al. (2009) explicitly argued that this metaphorical theme, called a "systematic metaphor," arises from within the discourse and is not, more simply, the retrieval of a previously entrenched metaphor in mind, or conceptual metaphor. One can postulate that Phil's comment reflects the idea of SOCIETY IS A MECHANICAL SYSTEM yet claim that this metaphorical thought emerged only within the discourse context. For this reason, conventional metaphors, such as "flaw in the system," do not have similar meanings in different contexts but are dynamically re-created depending on the specific histories of the participants at the very points in which their talk unfolds. There is never a neutral position to which the cognitive system retreats after each use of a metaphor source, because each word is spoken in an always changing dynamic context that constrains what words, and metaphors, will come next.

Cameron, more broadly, sees the discourse dynamics approach to metaphor as having many positives in revealing more about how people's metaphorical discourse reveals their in-the-moment thoughts as they emerge in interpersonal interaction. She criticizes CMT in the following way (Cameron 2016: 29):

> My basic objection to this claim of fixedness and invariance is that it leads to an impoverished, asocial view of metaphor that denies important realities of human noticing, reasoning and languaging, and that I find inadequate for describing and explaining what people do with metaphor and thus what metaphor "is."
>
> Furthermore, the scientific method of reduction(ism) that seems to underpin a cognitive linguistic drive to peel back, abstract away, and purify concepts in order to theorise can be inappropriate for studying human phenomena; at some point in the peeling back, the flesh is damaged, the object of study changes nature and construct validity disintegrates.

Cameron's approach does not necessarily reject embodiment as being relevant to the study of metaphor, even if she says little about it. Still one can again ask if a discourse level of analysis is superior to an embodied perspective on conceptual metaphor in explaining the details of verbal metaphorical language (for an extensive case study employing a discourse dynamics approach, see *this volume*: Semino & Demjen).

My final example of the contrast between the discourse and embodied views is seen in work on "deliberate" metaphor. Consider the following conversational exchange (Gibbs 2015b):

(5) Mark and Larry were old friends who had not seen each other for several years. Mark was telling Larry about his marriage.

Mark said, "We experienced many problems early on after we got married."

"My wife and I always seemed to argue about even the littlest thing."

Larry replied, "This must have been difficult for both of you."

"Have things improved over time?"

Mark replied, "We really *have come a long way since the wedding.*"

Most people readily understand Mark's final reply to express the idea that his marriage has improved over time, thus providing an implicit "yes" to Larry's question. One possibility is that people infer Mark's intended meaning through the recruitment of a relevant conceptual metaphor, in this case ROMANTIC RELATIONSHIPS ARE PHYSICAL JOURNEYS. Under this view, listeners tacitly recognize that "come a long way" in this context reflects metaphorical meaning because of the conceptual metaphor specifying a specific cross-domain mapping between marriages and physical journeys.

"Deliberate metaphor theory" (Steen 2008, 2011c) completely rejects the traditional CMT account. It maintains that only certain linguistic expressions are produced and understood as metaphors, namely those that are "deliberate," which can be identified by their novelty (e.g. "Juliet is the sun") or through various markers or signals of metaphors seen in conversation or texts. For instance, there may be cases in which a conventional expression such as "We really have come a long way since the wedding" can be seen as deliberate, and again when a speaker marks this as metaphorical through the use of "so to speak," "like," "metaphorical," or some other relevant marker. This perspective assumes, then, that metaphor is very much a discourse phenomenon, with its meanings and structure being best explained by reference to speakers' communicative purposes and not through the blind recruitment of embodied conceptual metaphors.

Does deliberate metaphor offer a better explanation of verbal metaphor use than does embodied Conceptual Metaphor Theory?

5 Some Misleading Distinctions

Part of the debate over what level of analysis best explains metaphor performance involves scholars' different opinions about the theoretical aim of their research studies. For example, one characterization of the world of metaphor scholarship maintains that there are three primary ways to conceive of metaphor – metaphor in language, thought, and communication (Steen 2008, 2011c). Some scholars are most interested in discovering the ways metaphor works within language, others study the way that metaphor shapes thought, and still others focus on how metaphor functions as a communicative device. Each of these topics demands its own research methods, which, more generally, align with thinking about metaphor as a *purely* linguistic (language), psychological (thought), or communicative (social) phenomenon.

One possibility is that each part of this tripartite division may constitute an autonomous theoretical explanation of the forms and functions of metaphor (Steen 2008). Even if it may eventually be possible to combine these perspectives in order to create a comprehensive theory of metaphor via principles such as "converging operations," scholars should continue to engage in "methodological solipsism" (Fodor 1975). Metaphor scholars should pursue their respective studies at the level of analysis and use the methodological tools that they believe are most appropriate for understanding what metaphor is all about. There is no need, however, to seek connections with research findings and theories that employ different methods or address different levels of analysis.

When debates between the embodied and discourse perspectives arise, they are often accompanied by related discussions about the goals of metaphor theory. For example, many discourse analysts, in particular, claim that their work is devoted toward understanding metaphor use at the supraindividual rather than the individual level of analysis. Although some advocates of CMT also suggest that their linguistic analysis likely best reflects the supra-individual level (Kövecses 2002), many conceptual embodiment scholars maintain that their findings are directly relevant to individual psychology. Indeed, there is a huge body of experimental research from psycholinguistics and cognitive neuroscience that is consistent with the claims that many aspects of verbal metaphor recruit *enduring* embodied conceptual metaphors (Gibbs 1994, 2006a, 2017b; Gibbs & Colston 2012). Simply put, people typically produce and interpret verbal metaphors partly in terms of their preexisting conceptual metaphorical knowledge and experience.

Metaphor scholars who embrace the discourse perspective are often dismissive of the cognitive linguistic findings of embodied metaphors because, as was mentioned earlier, these ideas may reflect the bias of individual metaphor scholars attempting to deal with systematicity among linguistic expressions (Steen 2008; Zinken 2007). Yet there are hardly any attempts by discourse scholars to address and explain the vast, complex experimental studies that offer support for embodied conceptual metaphors. From my point of view, this failure is astonishing. Even if discourse analysts are cautious about imputing metaphorical themes into people's individual minds within their own work, the existence of behavioral and cognitive neuroscience evidence supporting the embodied perspective must be properly considered within any theory of metaphor. To assume that individuals do not engage in embodied metaphorical thinking when using metaphors in discourse is downright misleading about what we really know about both individual and collective behavior.

One response to my severe criticism above is to suggest that what happens in the private minds of individuals in psycholinguistic experiments, for example, should not be extended to characterize what people do in social, discourse situations. Once again, drawing a distinction between metaphor in language, thought, and communication offers a theoretical scaffold for ignoring the relevance of both the linguistic evidence on CMT (i.e. metaphor in language) and experimental studies from psychology and neuroscience (i.e. metaphor in thought), leaving the discourse level of analysis alone and untouched by the two other parts of the tripartite distinction.

However, this kind of push back against the embodied conceptual perspective on metaphor performance misunderstands a key facet of the experimental research. Many psycholinguistic studies, in fact, clearly demonstrate not simply that individuals think in embodied metaphorical ways on certain occasions when they process verbal metaphors. Instead, the experimental data often show that people's interpretations of what others imply or communicate by their words are both quite metaphorical and shaped by enduring embodied metaphorical knowledge and experience. Thus, much of the psychological and neuroscience research directly addresses the effects of understanding verbal metaphor in discourse as a communicative process. Various studies from psychology also reveal how many aspects of private thought, including metaphorical thought, are always employed, either implicitly or explicitly at some future point, for social purposes (Gibbs 2013a). For these reasons, the tripartite distinction between metaphor in language, thought, and communication has little basis in human metaphor reality. Similarly, there is a tight, coupled relationship between what people do individually and their collective intelligence (i.e. supra-individual) such that it makes little sense to maintain a strict divide between these two levels of analysis within metaphor theory.

Finally, one difficulty in the wars over conceptual metaphor is that scholars on both sides of the debate often adopt rhetorical stances which make it seem as if they are completely resistant to other points of view when, in fact, they may accept that there are multiple reasons for why people think and express themselves in complex metaphorical ways (Gibbs 2017b). For example, conceptual metaphor theorists are often criticized for their failure to acknowledge the social and cultural foundations of verbal metaphor use. Yet there is ample work within cognitive linguistics, for instance, that explores the relevance of social and cultural forces in motivating specific ways in which people speak metaphorically (for a survey, see Gibbs, ibid.). Similarly, certain critics of Conceptual Metaphor Theory, such as those advocating discourse perspectives on metaphor, may reject CMT because of its insistence on the primary importance of embodiment in motivating the reasons for much metaphorical language and thought. However, these critics are not necessarily completely opposed to embodied influences on verbal metaphor use. The ways people interact in face-to-face discourse are surely shaped by many in-the-moment bodily actions. Scholars who advocate for a discourse perspective on metaphor may still see some role for embodiment in a theory of metaphor. Nonetheless, the wars over conceptual metaphor, and its embodied foundations, too often manifest themselves in strongly worded rhetorical ways that cover up scholars' more nuanced theoretical views. Is it possible, though, to move beyond the heated debates over whether metaphor is best understood as an embodied or discourse phenomenon?

6 Putting the Embodied and Discourse Views Together

My primary argument, once more, is that metaphor is fundamentally something that humans do and, therefore, a theory of metaphor performance should be consistent with what is known about how human beings work. Contemporary research within cognitive science, and originating in widely held approaches within the physical and biological sciences, suggests that both simple and complex behavioral phenomena generally involve multiple temporal and spatial scales (Bak 1997). A scale refers to the set of units typically used to characterize some behavior. For example, the temporal scale of neural activity tends to emphasize the milliseconds to seconds range. On the other hand, the temporal scale of geology tends to emphasize kiloannums-to-gigannums (thousands to billions of years).

Different academic disciplines also embrace different spatial scales. Neuroscience, for instance, works mainly in the nanometer-to-centimeter scale as researchers focus, to a significant extent, on activities in very small areas of the brain. Ecology, to take a different field, considers environments on the meter-to-kilometer scale. Of course, some academic disciplines consider multiple temporal and spatial scales. Physics considers everything from the smallest scales of particle physics to the largest scales of the cosmos.

A prime example of a complex, multi-scale cognitive and behavioral phenomenon is human language. Thus, linguistic entities, including phonemes, syllables, words, phrases, texts, and discourse, all exist at distinct scales. Each is studied at corresponding temporal and spatial scales (from raw acoustic energy patterns unfolding in the millisecond range up to larger structures encompassing minutes, hours, and even days). Language evolution occurs over timescales of years and centuries. But cognitive science research has demonstrated that these different linguistic phenomena are all interacting, such that the behaviors seen at one level are always influenced by the activities at other levels (Gibbs & Santa Cruz 2012; Spivey 2007).

All metaphor performance, including non-linguistic ones, are emergent from a constellation of factors, rather than being simply explained by one perspective or research method. Metaphorical actions always result from multiple, interacting kinds of causation. No single force drives the way people think and use metaphor. A dynamical perspective offers a major corrective to past debates by highlighting the ways metaphor emerges in the moment from the interaction of many factors via self-organizational processes (Gibbs 2012, 2017a,b; Jensen, *this volume*).

Consider some of the different forces that simultaneously constrain the production of the metaphorical use of "capsized" in the earlier discussed Fats Domino example. These are arranged from slowest-moving timescales to fastest-moving ones.

- *Evolutionary forces* to maintain survival and enhance cooperation to enhance individual and group welfare. Primary metaphors (e.g. PERSISTING IS REMAINING ERECT) emerge from both evolutionary and experiential forces.
- *Culturally specific ideas about different topics*, such as how best to deal with difficult life challenges.
- *Historical forces* related to the author's past experiences as a writer for the specific forum in which the Fats Domino profile was published.
- *Social forces* that enable speakers to negotiate specific meaning in particular contexts.

- *Linguistic factors* related to conventions about particular word and grammatical uses including, in this case, employing nautical terms to refer to human experiences.
- *Immediately salient contextual information* such as the presence of the aftereffects of Hurricane Katrina.
- *Immediate communicative motivations* to state something that is vivid, memorable, contextually relevant, and succinct regarding a rather complex abstract idea related to difficulties in one's life.
- *Previously stated words* that primed the author's use of certain boating and water terms which were related to earlier talk about the physical damage to buildings caused by Hurricane Katrina.
- *Bodily experiences* related to enduring concepts that are relevant for speaking about temporary set-backs in life, such as the idea of BEING UNABLE TO PERSIST IS NOT BEING ABLE TO REMAIN ERECT OR UPRIGHT.
- *Brain and neural activity* including that which emerges as brain systems become coupled during particular interaction between speakers and listeners or writers and readers.

These are some of the forces that lead to the emergence of "capsized" being used in a metaphorical manner in a specific discourse context. Each force operates along a different timescale, with some of these crawling along at very slow speeds, such as evolutionary and cultural forces, while others zip along at very fast speeds, such as immediate linguistic processes and the firing of neurons in human brains. The various timescales are not independent but are hierarchically organized and nested within one another so that different forces affecting language experience are coupled in complex, non-linear ways.

The writer's "choice" of "capsized" is by no means a conscious decision but emerged given his exact brain, body, and world contingencies at the very moment of writing about Domino. We can offer a model of how those possible contingencies arise, and interact, according to the principles of self-organization, to explain the writer's metaphorical behavior without postulating the existence of any specific component of mind, such as an embodied conceptual metaphor or deliberate metaphor mechanism, as the *sole* driving force in the metaphor production process.

A major advantage of a dynamical view of metaphor performance, one that separates it from all other theories, is its ability to account for the coordination between speakers and listeners or authors and readers. For example, in face-to-face speech situations people coordinate along many different linguistic and non-linguistic levels. Studies show that there are implicit "behavioral couplings" during interpersonal interaction in terms of people's gestures, eye movement, body postures, laughter, lexical choice, syntax, and prosody.

To take two examples, people tend to engage in synchronous bodily behaviors, along many dimensions, when they are discussing a topic in which both speakers agree, compared to cases in which they diverge in their opinions (Paxton & Dale 2013). Even people's brain activities become coordinated during talk (Stephens et al. 2010).

Many discourse studies have illustrated the ways that people tend to negotiate their use of metaphors, and what these expressions may mean in context (e.g. Cameron 2011). However, with the exception of important work on metaphorical speech and gesture (Müller & Cienki 2009; *this volume*: Mittelberg & Joue; Müller), metaphor theories have not explored how metaphorical language is integrated within the whole-body coordinated repertoires seen in interpersonal interactions. The coordination between two people using metaphorical language is an emergent product of self-organization. People do not produce or understand verbal metaphors because of some mental matching-up of their different conceptual metaphorical representations or simply via the recognition that some metaphor was stated deliberately. Metaphorical meanings, and even embodied metaphorical concepts, are not properties of individual minds but are higher-order products of the coupling among two or more individuals as they interact. Once again, multiple timescales shape both individual and joint metaphor performance.

7 Conclusion

Contemporary debates over what is the right level of analysis or best empirical method to adopt when studying metaphor have led to unproductive stalemates in which researchers glibly dismiss the general perspective or empirical findings offered by those working from different points of view. But arguments over whether an embodied or discourse perspective is best to study and explain metaphor, to take one example, is focused on the wrong question. The right question is how do different temporal and spatial scales operate and interact with one another to give rise to particular metaphorical actions? Answering this question demands that scholars do not assume that they can study some aspect of metaphor from their own autonomous point of view. They should also not assume that metaphor theories will eventually be able to add up the knowledge acquired from the study of metaphor at different levels of analysis or from using different research methods (e.g. those relevant to metaphor in language, thought, and communication). Instead, metaphor scholars must realize, and openly acknowledge, that metaphorical actions, of all sorts, always emerge from the interaction of a constellation of forces which, again, operate along different time and spatial scales. What happens at the level of culture is shaped by actions at the purely linguistic level. What happens at the social level is always influenced by embodied actions and experience. What happens at the cognitive level is partly determined by neural and evolutionary constraints. The discourse level is always partly embodied, and, indeed, bodily experience is itself shaped by cultural and discourse factors. Most generally, every level of analysis is always in interaction with every other, such that human metaphorical actions should be properly characterized as dynamical and not merely an assortment of isolated perspectives or properties of mind.

Embracing a dynamical perspective does not require that individual scholars study metaphor at multiple levels of analysis or use different research methods. Discerning linkages between different kinds of analyses, and using different empirical paradigms, within an individual set of studies is always welcome and appreciated. Conducting dynamical studies may become an important future direction for metaphor studies, similar to what has been occurring in other areas of the cognitive sciences. Nonetheless, most of us are trained to study metaphor in specific ways, which makes it challenging to simply pick up other methods and focus on other levels of analysis.

My main plea, though, is for metaphor scholars to open themselves up to ideas and research findings from disparate research enterprises; this volume offers a range of encouraging attempts to do so. Seeking convergences between one's own empirical results and those from the study of different levels of analysis will be critical to understanding the complexities of metaphorical action. These convergences are, once again, not simply additive across the existing level of description now seen in metaphor research. A dynamical view emphasizes that the various levels of analysis are interactive, such that what happens at one level always influences what is ongoing at other levels of analysis. Scholars will have to turn away from the automatic rejection of research from other levels, just because it offers explanations of metaphorical performance that differ from our own respective scholarly interests.

The single best thing to do as a first step is to read other people's research (e.g. discourse people need to read research from psycholinguistics on embodied conceptual metaphor use, and vice versa). Doing so is not that difficult these days, especially given that many scholarly journals in the world of metaphor publish articles looking at different levels of analysis, and using varying research methods, often within the same issue. There is admittedly a great deal to consider in the vast world of metaphor scholarship. But we should not continue to be like butterfly enthusiasts who insist that examining butterflies under glass or alternatively out in the wild of nature is the only way to understand butterflies. We may end many of the endless, unproductive debates about metaphor theory by appreciating that metaphor is always a multi-scaled full-bodied human performance. The imperative is to create theories of metaphorical action that take full account of what we know about how people really work in the real world.

References

Abbot, Michael, and Forceville, Charles J. (2011). LOSS OF CONTROL IS LOSS OF HANDS in Azumanga Daioh volume 4. *Language and Literature*, *20*(2), 91–112.

Abreu, Ana Maria, Macaluso, Emiliano, Azevedo, Ruben, Cesari, Paola, Urgesi, Cosimo, and Aglioti, Salvatore Maria (2012). Action anticipation beyond the action observation network: A functional magnetic resonance imaging study in expert basketball players. *European Journal of Neuroscience*, *35*(10), 1646–1654.

Adam, Hajo, and Galinsky, Adam (2012). Enclothed cognition. *Journal of Experimental Social Psychology*, *48*(4), 918–925.

Ahissar, Edud, Vaadia, Eilon, Ahissar, Merav, Bergman, Hagai, Arieli, Amos, and Abeles, Moshe (1992). Dependence of cortical plasticity on correlated activity of single neurons and on behavioral context. *Science*, *257*, 1412–1415.

Alibali, Martha W., Boncoddo, Rebecca, and Hostetter, Autumn (2014). Gesture in reasoning: An embodied perspective. In Shapiro (ed.), 150–159.

Allbritton, David W., McKoon, Gail, and Gerrig, Richard (1995). Metaphor-based schemas and text representations: Making connections through conceptual metaphors. *Journal of Experimental Psychology*, *21*(3), 612–625.

Allen, Chris, Vassilev, Ivaylo, Kennedy, Anne, and Rogers, Anne (2016). Long-term condition self-management support in online communities: A meta-synthesis of qualitative papers. *Journal of Medical Internet Research*, *18*(3), e61.

Alsmith, Adrian, and de Vignemont, Frédérique (2012). Embodying the mind and representing the body. *Review of Philosophy and Psychology. Special Issue*, *3*(1), 1–13.

Alverson, Hoyt (1994). *Semantics and Experience: Universal Metaphors of Time in English, Mandarin, Hindi, and Sesotho*. Baltimore: Johns Hopkins University Press.

Anderson, John (2010). *Cognitive Psychology and Its Implications*. New York: Worth Publishers.

Anderson, Michael C., Bjork, Elizabeth L., and Bjork, Robert A. (2000). Retrieval-induced forgetting: Evidence for a recall-specific mechanism. *Psychonomic Bulletin & Review*, *7*(3), 522–530.

Andrén, Mats (2010). *Children's Gestures from 18 to 30 Months*. Lund: Centre for Languages and Literatures.

Arend, Isabel, Henik, Avishai, and Okon-Singer, Hadas (2015). Dissociating emotion and attention functions in the pulvinar nucleus of the thalamus. *Neuropsychology*, *29*(2), 191–196.

Armstrong, Natalie, Koteyko, Nelya, and Powell, John (2012). Oh dear, should I really be saying that on here? Issues of identity and authority in an online diabetes community. *Health, 16*(4), 347–365.
Arnheim, Rudolf (1969). *Visual Thinking*. Berkeley, CA: University of California Press.
Attardo, Salvatore (1994). *Linguistic Theories of Humor*. Berlin/New York: Mouton de Gruyter.
(2000). Irony as relevant inappropriateness. *Journal of Pragmatics, 32*(6), 793–826.
Bak, Per (1997). *How Nature Works: The Science of Self-Organized Criticality*. Oxford: Oxford University Press.
Bal, Mieke (2009). *Narratology* (3rd edn.). Toronto: University of Toronto Press.
Barcelona, Antonio (ed.) (2000a). *Metaphor and Metonymy at the Crossroads: A Cognitive Perspective*. Berlin/New York: Mouton de Gruyter.
Barcelona, Antonio (2000b). On the plausibility of claiming a metonymic motivation for conceptual metaphor. In Barcelona (ed.), 31–58.
(2009). Motivation of construction meaning and form: The roles of metonymy and inference. In Panther, Thornburg & Barcelona (eds.), 363–401.
Bargh, John A., Chen, Mark, and Burrows, Lara (1996). Automaticity of social behavior: Direct effects of trait construct and stereotype activation on action. *Journal of Personality and Social Psychology, 71*(2), 230–244.
Barsalou, Lawrence W. (1999). Perceptual symbol systems. *Behavioral and Brain Sciences, 22*, 577–609.
(2008a). Grounded cognition. *Annual Review of Psychology, 59*, 617–645.
(2008b). Grounding symbolic operations in the brain's modal systems. In Semin & Smith (eds.), 9–42.
Barsalou, Lawrence W., Simmons, Kyle, Barbey, Aron K., and Wilson, Christine D. (2003). Grounding conceptual knowledge in modality-specific systems. *Trends in Cognitive Sciences, 7*(2), 84–91.
Barsalou, Lawrence W., and Wiemer-Hastings, Katja (2005). Situating abstract concepts. In Pecher & Zwaan (eds.), 129–163.
Barton, David (2007). *Literacy: An Introduction to the Ecology of Written Language* (2nd edn.). Oxford: Wiley-Blackwell.
Bavelas, Janet, Chovil, Nicole, Coates, Linda, and Roe, Lori (1995). Gestures specialized for dialogue. *Personality and Social Psychology Bulletin, 21*(4), 394–340.
Bednar, James A., and Wilson, Stuart P. (2015). Cortical maps. *The Neuroscientist*, 1–14, 10.1177/1073858415597645 [e-pub ahead of print]. Print edn. 2016, *22*(6), 604–617.
Bergen, Benjamin K. (2012). *Louder than Words: The New Science of How the Mind Makes Meaning*. New York: Basic Books.
(2015). Embodiment. In Ewa Dabrowska and Dagmar Divjak (eds.), *Handbook of Cognitive Linguistics* (pp. 10–30). Berlin/Boston: de Gruyter Mouton.
Bernárdez, Enrique (2013). Evidentiality and the epistemic use of the Icelandic verbs sjá and heyra: A cultural linguistic view. In Adam Gaz, David Danaher, and Przemysław Łozowski (eds.), *The Linguistic Worldview: Ethnolinguistics, Cognition, and Culture* (pp. 415–442). London: Versita.
Bierwiaczonek, Boguslaw (2013). *Metonymy in Language, Thought and Brain*. Sheffield: Equinox.

Bird, Chris M., Bisby, James A., and Burgess, Neil (2012). The hippocampus and spatial constraints on mental imagery. *Frontiers in Human Neuroscience*, *6*(142), 1–12. doi:10.3389/fnhum.2012.00142.

Bishop, Bill (2008). *The Big Sort: Why Clustering of Like-Minded America is Tearing Us Apart.* New York: Houghton-Mifflin.

Black, Max [1979] (1993). More about metaphor. In Ortony (ed.), 19–41.

Blanke, Olaf (2012). Multisensory brain mechanisms of bodily self-consciousness. *Nature Reviews Neuroscience*, *13*(8), 556–571.

Boers, Frank (1999). When a bodily source domain becomes prominent. In Gibbs, Jr. & Steen (eds.), 47–56.

Boers, Frank, and Littlemore, Jeannette (2000). Cognitive style variables in participants' explanations of conceptual metaphors. *Metaphor and Symbol*, *15*(3), 177–187.

(eds.) (2003). *Cross-Cultural Differences in Conceptual Metaphor: Applied Linguistics Perspectives.* Special issue of *Metaphor and Symbol*, *18*(4).

Bonnier, Pierre (1905). L'Aschématie. *Revue Neurologique (Paris)*, *13*, 605–609.

Boot, Inge, and Pecher, Diane (2010). Similarity is closeness: Metaphorical mapping in a conceptual task. *The Quarterly Journal of Experimental Psychology*, *63*(5), 942–954.

Bordwell, David (1985). *Narration in the Fiction Film.* London: Routledge.

Bordwell, David, and Thompson, Kirstin (2008). *Film Art: An Introduction* (8th edn.). Boston: McGraw-Hill.

Borkent, Mike, Dancygier, Barbara, and Hinnell, Jennifer (2013). *Language and the Creative Mind.* Stanford, CA: CSLI Publications.

Boroditsky, Lera (2000). Metaphoric structuring: Understanding time through spatial metaphors. *Cognition*, *75*(1), 1–28.

(2001). Does language shape thought? English and Mandarin speakers' conceptions of time. *Cognitive Psychology*, *43*(1), 1–22.

Boroditsky, Lera, and Ramscar, Michael (2002). The roles of body and mind in abstract thought. *Psychological Science*, *13*(2), 185–188.

Boulenger, Véronique, Hauk, Olaf, and Pulvermüller, Friedemann (2009). Grasping ideas with the motor system: Semantic somototopy in idiom comprehension. *Cerebral Cortex*, *19*(8), 1905–1914.

Bowdle, Brian F., and Gentner, Dedre (2005). The career of metaphor. *Psychological Review*, *112*(1), 193–216.

Bowes, Andrea, and Katz, Albert N. (2015). Metaphor creates intimacy and enhances one's ability to infer the internal states of others. *Memory & Cognition*, *43*(6), 953–963.

Breaux, Brooke O., and Feist, Michele I. (2008). The color of similarity. In B. C. Love, K. McRae, and V. M. Sloutsky (eds.), *Proceedings of the 30th Annual Conference of the Cognitive Science Society* (pp. 253–258). Austin, TX: Cognitive Science Conference.

Calbris, Geneviève (2011). *Elements of Meaning in Gesture.* Amsterdam/Philadelphia: John Benjamins.

Cameron, Lynne (1999). Identifying and describing metaphors in spoken discourse data. In Lynne Cameron and Graham Low (eds.), *Researching and Applying Metaphor* (pp. 105–132). Cambridge/New York: Cambridge University Press.

(2003). *Deliberate and Conventional Metaphors in Educational Discourse*. London: Continuum.
(2007a). Confrontation or complementarity? Metaphor in language use and cognitive metaphor theory. *Annual Review of Cognitive Linguistics*, *5*(1), 107–135.
(2007b). Patterns of metaphor use in reconciliation talk. *Discourse & Society*, *18*(2), 197–222.
(2008a). Metaphor and talk. In Gibbs, Jr. (ed.), 197–211.
(2008b). Metaphor shifting in the dynamics of talk. In Zanotto, Cameron & Cavalcanti (eds.), 45–62.
(2010a). The affective discourse dynamics of metaphor clustering. *Ilha do Desterro: A Journal of English Language, Literatures in English and Cultural Studies*, 41–62.
(2010b). The discourse dynamics framework for metaphor. In Cameron & Maslen (eds.), 77–94.
(2010c). Metaphors and discourse activity. In Cameron & Maslen (eds.), 77–94.
(2010d). What is metaphor and why does it matter? In Cameron & Maslen (eds.), 3–25.
(2011). *Metaphor and Reconciliation: The Discourse Dynamics of Empathy in Post-Conflict Conversations*. London/New York: Routledge.
(2016). Mixed metaphor from a discourse dynamics perspective: A non-issue? In Raymond W. Gibbs, Jr. (ed.), *Mixing Metaphor* (pp. 17–30). Amsterdam/ Philadelphia: John Benjamins.
Cameron, Lynne, and Deignan, Alice (2003). Combining large and small corpora to investigate tuning devices around metaphor in spoken discourse. *Metaphor and Symbol*, *18*(3), 149–160.
(2006). The emergence of metaphor in discourse *Applied Linguistics*, *27*(4), 671–690.
Cameron, Lynne, and Maslen, Robert (eds.) (2010). *Metaphor Analysis: Research Practice in Applied Linguistics, Social Sciences and the Humanities*. London: Equinox.
Cameron, Lynne, Maslen, Robert, and Low, Graham (2010). Finding systematicity in metaphor use. In Cameron & Maslen (eds.), 116–146.
Cameron, Lynne, Maslen, Robert, Todd, Zazie, Maule, John, Stratton, Peter, and Stanley, Neil (2009). The discourse dynamics approach to metaphor and metaphor-led discourse analysis. *Metaphor and Symbol*, *24*(2), 63–89.
Cang, Jianhua, and Feldheim, David A. (2013). Developmental mechanisms of topographic map formation and alignment. *Annual Reviews in Neuroscience*, *36*, 51–77.
Carroll, Noël (1996). A note on film metaphor. In Noël Carroll, *Theorizing the Moving Image* (pp. 212–223). Cambridge/New York: Cambridge University Press.
Caruana, Fausto, and Cuccio, Valentina (2015). Types of abduction in tool behavior. *Phenomenology and the Cognitive Science*. doi:10.1007/s11097-015-9450-y.
Casasanto, Daniel (2008a). Similarity and proximity: When does close in space mean close in mind? *Memory & Cognition*, *36*(6), 1047–1056.
(2008b). Who's afraid of the Big Bad Whorf? Cross-linguistic differences in temporal language and thought. *Language Learning*, *58*(177), 63–79.
(2009a). Embodiment of abstract concepts: Good and bad in right- and left-handers. *Journal of Experimental Psychology: General*, *138*(3), 351–367.

(2009b). When is a linguistic metaphor a conceptual metaphor? In Vyvyan Evans and Stéphanie Pourcel (eds.), *New Directions in Cognitive Linguistics* (pp. 127–146). Amsterdam/Philadelphia: John Benjamins.

(2010). Space for thinking. In Vyvyan Evans and Paul Chilton (eds.), *Language, Cognition and Space: State of the Art and New Directions* (pp. 453–478). London: Equinox Publishing.

(2011). Different bodies, different minds: The body-specificity of language and thought. *Current Directions in Psychological Science*, *20*(6), 378–383.

(2013). Development of metaphorical thinking: The role of language. In Borkent, Dancygier & Hinnell (eds.), 3–18.

(2014a). Bodily Relativity. In Shapiro (ed.), 108–117.

(2014b). Experiential origins of mental metaphors: Language, culture, and the body. In Landau, Robinson & Meier (eds.), 249–268.

Casasanto, Daniel, and Boroditsky, Lera (2008). Time in the mind: Using space to think about time. *Cognition*, *106*(2), 579–593.

Casasanto, Daniel, and Bottini, Roberto (2014a). Mirror reading can reverse the flow of time. *Journal of Experimental Psychology: General*, *143*(2), 473–479.

(2014b). Spatial language and abstract concepts. *WIREs Cognitive Science*, *5*(2), 139–149.

Casasanto, Daniel, and Chrysikou, Evangelia G. (2011). When left is “right”: Motor fluency shapes abstract concepts. *Psychological Science*, *22*(4), 419–422.

Casasanto, Daniel, and Gijssels, Tom (2015). What makes a metaphor an embodied metaphor? *Linguistics Vanguard*, *1*(1), 327–337.

Casasanto, Daniel, and Henetz, Tania (2012). Handedness shapes children’s abstract concepts. *Cognitive Science*, *36*(2), 359–372.

Casasanto, Daniel, and Jasmin, Kyle (2010). Good and bad in the hands of politicians: Spontaneous gestures during positive and negative speech. *Public Library of Science ONE*, *5*(7), e11805.

Chafe, Wallace (1994). *Discourse, Consciousness, and Time: The Flow and Displacement of Conscious Experience in Speaking and Writing*. Chicago/London: The University of Chicago Press.

Chapple, Alison, and Ziebland, Sue (2004). The role of humor for men with testicular cancer. *Qualitative Health Research*, *14*(8), 1123–1139.

Chemero, Anthony (2011). *Radical Embodied Cognitive Science*. Cambridge, MA: The MIT Press.

Chen, Jenn-Yeu (2007). Do Chinese and English speakers think about time differently? Failure of replicating Boroditsky (2001). *Cognition* *104*(2), 427–436.

Chiappe, Dan, Kennedy, John, and Smykowski, Tim (2003). Reversibility, aptness and the conventionality of metaphors and similes. *Metaphor and Symbol*, *18*(2), 85–106.

Ching, Marvin K. L. (1993). Games and play: Pervasive metaphors in American life. *Metaphor and Symbolic Activity*, *8*(1), 43–65.

Chklovskii, Dmitri B., and Koulakov, Alexei A. (2004). Maps in the brain: What can we learn from them? *Annual Reviews in Neuroscience*, *27*, 369–392.

Christakis, Nicholas A., and Fowler, James H. (2009). *Connected: The Surprising Power of Our Social Networks and How They Shape Our Lives*. New York: Little, Brown and Company.

Chui, Kawai (2011). Conceptual metaphors in gesture. *Cognitive Linguistics*, *22*(3), 437–458.
Cienki, Alan (1998). Metaphoric gestures and some of their relations to verbal metaphoric expressions. In Jean-Pierre Koenig (ed.), *Discourse and Cognition* (pp. 189–204). Stanford, CA: CSLI Publications.
(2005). Image schemas and gesture. In Hampe (ed.), 421–442.
(2010). Multimodal metaphor analysis. In Cameron & Maslen (eds.), 195–216.
(2013a). Cognitive Linguistics: Spoken language and gesture as expressions of conceptualization. In Müller, Cienki, Fricke, Ladewig, McNeill & Tessendorf (eds.), 182–201.
(2013b). Mimetic schemas and image schemas in cognitive linguistics and gesture studies. *Review of Cognitive Linguistics*, *11*(2), 417–432.
Cienki, Alan, and Müller, Cornelia (eds.) (2008a). *Metaphor and Gesture*. Amsterdam/Philadelphia: John Benjamins.
(2008b). Metaphor, gesture, and thought. In Gibbs, Jr. (ed.), 483–501.
Citron, Francesca, and Goldberg, Adele E. (2014). Social context modulates the effect of physical warmth on perceived interpersonal kindness: A study of embodied metaphors. *Language and Cognition*, *6*(1), 1–11.
Claridge, Claudia (2011). *Hyperbole in English: A Corpus-Based Study of Exaggeration*. Cambridge/New York: Cambridge University Press.
Clark, Andy (2008). *Supersizing the Mind: Embodiment, Action, and Cognitive Extension*. Oxford/New York: Oxford University Press.
Clark, Andrew, and Chalmers, David (1998). The extended mind. *Analysis*, *58*(1), 7–19.
Clark, Herbert H. (1973). Space, time, semantics and the child. In Timothy E. Moore (ed.), *Cognitive Development and the Acquisition of Language* (pp. 27–63). New York: Academic Press.
Clark, Herbert H., and Gerrig, Richard J. (1984). On the pretense theory of irony. *Journal of Experimental Psychology: General*, *113*(1), 121–126.
Coates, Jennifer (2007). Talk in a play frame: More on laughter and intimacy. *Journal of Pragmatics*, *39*(1), 29–49.
Coëgnarts, Martin, and Kravanja, Peter (2012). Embodied visual meaning: Image schemas in film. *Projections*, *6*(2), 84–101.
Cole, Jonathan (1995). *Pride and a Daily Marathon*. Cambridge, MA: The MIT Press.
Cole, Jonathan, and Paillard, Jacques (1995). Living without touch and information about body position and movement: Studies on deafferented subjects. In José Bermudez, Anthony Marcel, and Naomi Eilan (eds.), *The Body and the Self* (pp. 245–266). Cambridge, MA: The MIT Press.
Connor, Kathleen, and Kogan, Nathan (1980). Topic–vehicle relations in metaphor: The issue of asymmetry. In R. P. Honeck and R. R. Hoffman (eds.), *Cognition and Figurative Language* (pp. 283–310). Hillsdale, NJ: Lawrence Erlbaum.
Cook, Susan W., Duffy, Ryan G., and Fenn, Kimberly M. (2013). Consolidation and transfer of learning after observing hand gesture. *Child Development*, *84*(6), 1863–1871.
Corts, Daniel, and Meyers, Kristina (2002). Conceptual clusters in figurative language production. *Journal of Psycholinguistic Research*, *31*(4), 391–408.

Corts, Daniel, and Pollio, Howard (1999). Spontaneous production of figurative language and gesture in college lectures. *Metaphor and Symbol, 14*(2), 81–100.

Costantini, Marcello, Galati, Gaspare, Ferretti, Antonio, Caulo, Massimo, Tartaro, Armando, Romani, Gian Luca, et al. (2005). Neural systems underlying observation of humanly impossible movements: An FMRI study. *Cerebral Cortex, 15*(11), 1761–1767.

Coulson, Seana (2001). *Semantic Leaps: Frame-Shifting and Conceptual Blending in Meaning Construction*. Cambridge/New York: Cambridge University Press.

Cowley, Stephen J., and Vallée-Tourangeau, Frédéric (eds.) (2013). *Cognition beyond the Brain: Computation, Interactivity and Human Artifice*. London: Springer.

Croft, William (1993). The role of domains in the interpretation of metaphors and metonymies. *Cognitive Linguistics, 4*(4), 335–370.

Croft, William, and Cruse, Alan (2004). *Cognitive Linguistics*. Cambridge/New York: Cambridge University Press.

Cuccio, Valentina (2014). The notion of representation and the brain. *Phenomenology and Mind, 7*, 247–258.

(2015). Embodied Simulation and metaphors: Towards a direct role of the body in language comprehension. *Epistemologia, 37*, 97–112.

Cuffari, Elena, and Jensen, Thomas W. (2014). Living bodies: Co-enacting experience. In Müller, Cienki, Fricke, Ladewig, McNeill & Bressem (eds.), 2016–2025.

Cutting, James, Proffitt, Denis, and Kozlowski, Lynn (1978). A biochemical invariant for gait perception. *Journal of Experimental Psychology: Human Perception and Performance, 4*(3), 357–372.

Dale, Rick (2015). An Integrative Research Strategy for Exploring Synergies in Natural Language Performance. *Ecological Psychology, 27*(3), 190–201.

Dale, Rick, Fusaroli, Ricardo, Duran, Nicholas, and Richardson, Daniel C. (2013). The self-organization of human interaction. *Psychology of Learning and Motivation, 59*, 43–95.

Dancygier, Barbara, and Sweetser, Eve E. (2014). *Figurative Language*. New York: Cambridge University Press.

Dawson, Michael (2014). Embedded and situated cognition. In Shapiro (ed.), 59–68.

de Hevia, Maria D., Izard, Veronique, Coubart, Aurélie, Spelke, Elizabeth S., and Streri, Arlette (2014). Representations of space, time, and number in neonates. *Proceedings of the National Academy of Sciences, 111*(13), 4809–4813.

de Vignemont, Frédérique (2010). The body-schema and the body-image: Pros and cons. *Neuropsychologia, 48*(3), 669–680.

Deane, Paul D. (1992). *Grammar in Mind and Brain: Explorations in Cognitive Syntax*. Berlin/New York: Mouton de Gruyter.

Deignan, Alice (2003). Metaphorical expressions and culture: An indirect link. *Metaphor and Symbol, 18*(4), 255–271.

(2006a). The grammar of linguistic metaphors. In Stefanowitsch & Th. Gries (eds.), 106–122.

(2006b). *Metaphor in Corpus Linguistics*. Amsterdam/Philadelphia: John Benjamins.

(2008a). Corpus linguistic data and conceptual metaphor theory. In Zanotto, Cameron & Cavalcanti (eds.), 149–162.

(2008b). Corpus linguistics and metaphor. In Gibbs, Jr. (ed.), 280–294.
Deignan, Alice, Littlemore, Jeannette, and Semino, Elena (2013). *Figurative Language, Genre and Register*. Cambridge/New York: Cambridge University Press.
Deignan, Alice, and Semino, Elena (2010). Corpus techniques for metaphor analysis. In Cameron & Maslen (eds.), 161–179.
Demjén, Zsófia (2016). Laughing at cancer: Humour, empowerment, solidarity and coping online. *Journal of Pragmatics*, *101*, 18–30.
Dennet, Daniel (1969). *Content and Consciousness*. London: Routledge & Kegan Paul.
Denny-Brown, Derek, Meyer, John, and Horenstein, Simon (1952). The significance of perceptual rivalry resulting from from parietal lesion. *Brain*, *75*(4), 433–471.
Desai, Rutvik H., Binder, Jeffrey R., Conant, Lisa L., Mano, Quintino R., and Seidenberg, Mark S. (2011). The neural career of sensorimotor metaphors. *Journal of Cognitive Neuroscience*, *23*(9), 2376–2386.
di Pellegrino, Guiseppe, Fadiga, Luciano, Fogassi, Leonardo, Gallese, Vittorio, and Rizzolatti, Giacomo (1992). Understanding motor events: A neurophysiological study. *Experimental Brain Research*, *91*(1), 176–180.
Dijkerman, H. Chris, and de Haan, Edward H. F. (2007). Somatosensory processes subserving perception and action. *Behavioral and Brain Sciences*, *30*(2), 189–201.
Dirven, René, and Pörings, Ralf (eds.) (2002). *Metaphor and Metonymy in Comparison and Contrast*. Berlin/New York: Mouton de Gruyter.
Dodge, Ellen, and Lakoff, George (2005). Image schemas: From linguistic analysis to neural grounding. In Hampe (ed.), 57–91.
Dolscheid, Sarah, Hunnius, Sabine, Casasanto, Daniel, and Majid, Asifa (2014). Prelinguistic infants are sensitive to space-pitch associations found across cultures. *Psychological Science*, *25*(6), 1256–1261.
Dolscheid, Sarah, Shayan, Shakila, Majid, Asifa, and Casasanto, Daniel (2013). The thickness of musical pitch: Psychophysical evidence for linguistic relativity. *Psychological Science*, *24*(5), 613–621.
Dynel, Marta (2009). Creative metaphor is a birthday cake: Metaphor as the source of humour. *metaphorik.de*, *17*, 27–48.
(2011a). Joker in the pack: Towards determining the status of humorous framing in conversations. In Marta Dynel (ed.), *The Pragmatics of Humour across Discourse Domains* (pp. 217–242). Amsterdam/Philadelphia: John Benjamins.
(2011b). Pragmatics and Linguistic research into Humour. In Marta Dynel (ed.), *The Pragmatics of Humour across Discourse Domains* (pp. 1–12). Amsterdam/ Philadelphia: John Benjamins.
Eggertsson, Gunnar T., and Forceville, Charles J. (2009). Multimodal expressions of the HUMAN VICTIM IS ANIMAL metaphor in horror films. In Forceville & Urios-Aparisi (eds.), 429–449.
Eitan, Zohar, and Timmers, Renee (2010). Beethoven's last piano sonata and those who follow crocodiles: Cross-domain mappings of auditory pitch in a musical context. *Cognition*, *114*(3), 405–422.
El Refaie, Elisabeth (2009a). Metaphor in political cartoons: Exploring audience responses. In Forceville & Urios-Aparisi (eds.), 173–196.
(2009b). Multiliteracies: How readers interpret political cartoons. *Visual Communication*, *8*, 181–205.

(2014). Appearances and dis/dys-appearances: A dynamic view of embodiment in Conceptual Metaphor Theory. *Metaphor and the Social World*, *4*(1), 109–125.
(2017). Multi-modal metaphors. In Semino & Demjén (eds.), 148–161.
Evans, Nicholas, and Wilkins, David (2000). In the mind's ear: The semantic extensions of perception verbs in Australian languages. *Language*, *76*(3), 546–592.
Evans, Vyvyan, and Green, Melanie (2006). *Cognitive Linguistics: An Introduction*. Edinburgh: Edinburgh University Press.
Fahlenbrach, Kathrin (ed.) (2015). *Embodied Metaphors in Film, Television, and Video Games: Cognitive Approaches*. London/New York: Routledge.
Fauconnier, Gilles, and Turner, Mark (2002). *The Way We Think: Conceptual Blending and the Mind's Hidden Complexity*. New York: Basic Books.
(2008). Rethinking metaphor. In Gibbs, Jr. (ed.), 53–66.
Feldman, Jerome, and Narayanan, Srini (2004). Embodied meaning in a neural theory of language. *Brain and Language*, *89*(2), 385–392.
Fillmore, Charles J. (1977). Scenes-and-frames semantics. In Antonio Zampolli (ed.), *Linguistic Structures Processing 4* (pp. 55–81). Amsterdam: North-Holland Publishing Company.
(1982). Frame semantics. In Linguistic Society of Korea (ed.), *Linguistics in the Morning Calm* (pp. 111–137). Seoul: Hanshin.
(1985). Frames and the semantics of understanding. *Quarderni di Semantica*, *6*(2), 222–255.
Fillmore, Charles J., and Baker, Collin F. (2009). A frames approach to semantic analysis. In Bernd Heine and Heiko Narrog (eds.), *The Oxford Handbook of Linguistic Analysis* (pp. 313–340). Oxford: Oxford University Press.
Fischer, Martin H., Dewulf, Nele, and Hill, Robin L. (2005). Designing bar graphs: Orientation matters. *Applied Cognitive Psychology*, *19*(7), 953–962.
Fodor, Jerry A. (1975). *The Language of Thought*. Cambridge, MA: Harvard University Press.
Forceville, Charles J. (1996). *Pictorial Metaphor in Advertising*. London/New York: Routledge.
(2002). The identification of target and source in pictorial metaphors. *Journal of Pragmatics*, *34*(1), 1–14.
(2006a). Non-verbal and multimodal metaphor in a cognitivist framework: Agendas for research. In Gitte Kristiansen, Michel Achard, René Dirven, and Francisco Ruiz de Mendoza Ibañez (eds.), *Cognitive Linguistics: Current Applications and Future Perspectives* (pp. 379–402). Berlin/New York: Mouton de Gruyter.
(2006b). The source-path-goal schema in the autobiographical journey documentary: McElwee, Van der Keuken, Cole. *New Review of Film and Television Studies*, *4*(3), 241–261.
(2008). Metaphor in pictures and multimodal representations. In Gibbs, Jr. (ed.), 462–482.
(2009a). Metonymy in visual and audiovisual discourse. In Eija Ventola and Arsenio Jésus Moya Guijarro (eds.), *The World Told and the World Shown: Issues in Multisemiotics* (pp. 56–74). Basingstoke/New York: Palgrave MacMillan.
(2009b). The role of non-verbal sound and music in multimodal metaphor. In Forceville & Urios-Aparisi (eds.), 383–402.

(2011). The source-path-goal schema in Agnès Varda's Les Glaneurs et la Glaneuse and Deux Ans Après. In Monika Fludernik (ed.), *Beyond Cognitive Metaphor Theory: Perspectives on Literary Metaphor* (pp. 281–297). London: Routledge.

(2013). Metaphor and symbol: SEARCHING FOR ONE'S IDENTITY IS LOOKING FOR A HOME in animation film. *Review of Cognitive Linguistics*, *11*(2), 250–268.

(2014). Relevance Theory as model for analysing multimodal communication. In David Machin (ed.), *Visual Communication* (pp. 51–70). Berlin/Boston: de Gruyter Mouton.

(2016). The FORCE and BALANCE schemas in JOURNEY metaphor animations. In Carla Fernandes (ed.), *Multimodality and Performance* (pp. 8–22). Newcastle-upon-Tyne: Cambridge Scholar Press.

Forceville, Charles J., and Jeulink, Marloes (2011). The flesh and blood of embodied understanding: The source-path-goal schema in animation film. *Pragmatics & Cognition*, *19*(1), 37–59.

Forceville, Charles J., and Renckens, Thijs (2013). The GOOD IS LIGHT and BAD IS DARK metaphors in feature films. *Metaphor and the Social Word*, *3*(2), 160–179.

Forceville, Charles J., and Urios-Aparisi, Eduardo (eds.) (2009). *Multimodal Metaphor*. Berlin/New York: Mouton de Gruyter.

Frisson, Steven, and Pickering, Martin (1999). The processing of metonymy: Evidence from eye movements. *Journal of Experimental Psychology: Learning, Memory, and Cognition*, *25*(6), 1366–1383.

Fuhrman, Orly, and Boroditsky, Lera (2010). Cross-cultural differences in mental representations of time: Evidence from an implicit non-linguistic task. *Cognitive Science*, *34*(8), 1430–1451.

Fusaroli, Ricardo, Rączaszek-Leonardi, Joanna, and Tylén, Kristian (2014). Dialog as interpersonal synergy. *New Ideas in Psychology*, *32*, 147–157.

Gallagher, Shaun (1986). Body image and body schema: A conceptual clarification. *Journal of Mind and Behavior*, *7*, 541–554.

(2005). *How the Body Shapes the Mind*. Oxford/New York: Oxford University Press.

Gallagher, Shaun, and Cole, Jonathan (1995). Body image and body schema in a deafferented subject. *Journal of Mind and Behavior*, *16*(4), 369–389.

Gallagher, Shaun, and Zahavi, Dan (2008). *The Phenomenological Mind* (2nd edn.). London/New York: Routledge.

Gallese, Vittorio (2008). Mirror neurons and the social nature of language: The neural exploitation hypothesis. *Social Neuroscience*, *3*(3–4), 317–333.

(2009). Mirror neurons and the neural exploitation hypothesis: From embodied simulation to social cognition. In Jaime A. Pineda (ed.), *Mirror Neuron Systems* (pp. 163–190). New York: Humana Press.

Gallese, Vittorio, and Cuccio, Valentina (2016). The paradigmatic body: Embodied simulation, intersubjectivity, the bodily self and language. In Thomas Metzinger and Jennifer Windt (eds.), *Open MIND*. Cambridge, MA: The MIT Press.

Gallese, Vittorio, and Lakoff, George (2005). The Brain's concepts: The role of the sensory-motor system in conceptual knowledge. *Cognitive Neuropsychology*, *22*(3), 455–479.

Gallese, Vittorio, and Sinigaglia, Corrado (2011). What is so special about embodied simulation? *Trends in Cognitive Science*, *15*(11), 512–519.

Geeraerts, Dirk, and Cuyckens, Hubert (eds.) (2007). *The Oxford Handbook of Cognitive Linguistics*. Oxford/New York: Oxford University Press.

Geng, Joy J., and Vossel, Simone (2013). Re-evaluating the role of TPJ in attentional control: Contextual updating? *Neuroscience and Biobehavioral Reviews*, *37*(10–2), 2608–2620.

Gentner, Dedre, and Bowdle, Brian F. (2008). Metaphor as structure mapping. In Gibbs, Jr. (ed.), 3–13.

Gentner, Dedre, Imai, Mutsumi, and Boroditsky, Lera (2002). As time goes by: Evidence for two systems in processing space → time metaphors. *Language and Cognitive Processes*, *17*(5), 537–565.

Gernsbacher, Morton A., Keysar, Boaz, Robertson, Rachel R. W., and Werner, Necia K. (2001). The role of suppression in understanding metaphors. *Journal of Memory and Language*, *45*(3), 433–450.

Gerrig, Richard J. (1993). *Experiencing Narrative Worlds: On the Psychological Activities of Reading*. New Haven, CT: Yale University Press.

Gibbs, Raymond W., Jr. (1991). Semantic analyzability in children's understanding of idioms. *Journal of Speech and Hearing Research*, *34*(3), 613–620.

(1992). What do idioms really mean? *Journal of Memory and Language*, *31*, 485–506.

(1994). *The Poetics of Mind: Figurative Thought, Language, and Understanding*. Cambridge/New York: Cambridge University Press.

(1999). Taking metaphor out of our heads and putting it into the cultural world. In Gibbs, Jr. & Steen (eds.), pp. 145–166.

(2003). Embodied experience and linguistic meaning. *Brain and Language*, *84*(1), 1–15.

(2005a). Embodiment in Metaphorical Imagination. In Pecher & Zwaan (eds.), 65–92.

(2005b). The psychological status of image schemas. In Hampe (ed.), 113–135.

(2006a). *Embodiment and Cognitive Science*. Cambridge/New York: Cambridge University Press.

(2006b). Metaphor interpretation as embodied simulation. *Mind & Language*, *21*(3), 434–458.

(2007a). Idioms and formulaic language. In Geeraerts & Guyckens (eds.), 697–725.

(2007b). Why cognitive linguists should care more about empirical methods. In Gonzalez-Marquez, Mittelberg, Coulson & Spivey (eds.), 2–18.

(ed.) (2008). *The Cambridge Handbook of Metaphor and Thought*. Cambridge/New York: Cambridge University Press.

(2011a). The allegorical impulse. *Metaphor and Symbol*, *26*(2), 121–130.

(2011b). Are "deliberate" metaphors really deliberate? A question of human consciousness and action. *Metaphor and the Social World*, *1*(1), 26–52.

(2011c). Evaluating Conceptual Metaphor Theory. *Discourse Processes*, *48*(8), 529–562.

(2012). Metaphors, snowflakes, and termite nests: How nature creates such beautiful things. In MacArthur, Oncins-Martínez, Sanchez-García & Piquer-Píriz (eds.), 347–371.

(2013a). Metaphoric cognition as social activity: Dissolving the divide between metaphor in thought and communication. *Metaphor and the Social World*, *3*(1), 54–76.

(2013b). Walking the walk while thinking about the talk: Embodied interpretation of metaphorical narratives. *Journal of Psycholinguistic Research*, *42*(4), 363–378.
(2014a). Conceptual metaphor in thought and social action. In Landau, Robinson & Meier (eds.), 17–40.
(2014b). Embodied metaphor. In Littlemore & Taylor (eds.), 167–184.
(2015a). The allegorical character of political metaphors in discourse. *Metaphor and the Social World*, *5*(2), 264–282.
(2015b). Do pragmatic signals affect conventional metaphor understanding? A failed test of Deliberate Metaphor Theory. *Journal of Pragmatics*, *90*, 77–87.
(2015c). Does deliberate metaphor theory have a future? *Journal of Pragmatics*, *90*, 73–76.
(2015d). Metaphor. In Ewa Dabrowska and Dagmar Divjak (eds.), *Handbook of Cognitive Linguistics* (pp. 167–189). Berlin/Boston: de Gruyter Mouton.
(2017a). *Metaphor Wars: Conceptual Metaphor in Human Life*. New York: Cambridge University Press.
(2017b). Metaphor, language and dynamical systems. In Semino & Demjén (eds.), 56–69.
Gibbs, Raymond W., Jr., Bogdanovich, Josephine M., Sykes, Jeffrey R., and Barr, Dale J. (1997). Metaphor in idiom comprehension. *Journal of Memory and Language*, *37*(2), 141–154.
Gibbs, Raymond W., Jr., and Bogdonovich, Jody (1999). Mental imagery in interpreting poetic metaphor. *Metaphor and Symbol*, *14*(1), 37–44.
Gibbs, Raymond W., Jr., and Cameron, Lynne (2008). The social-cognitive dynamics of metaphor performance. *Journal of Cognitive Systems Research*, *9*(1–2), 64–75.
Gibbs, Raymond W., Jr., and Colston, Herbert L. (2012). *Interpreting Figurative Meaning*. New York: Cambridge University Press.
Gibbs, Raymond W., Jr., Gould, Jessica, and Andric, Michael (2006). Imagining metaphorical actions: Embodied simulations make the impossible plausible. *Imagination, Cognition, & Personality*, *25*(3), 221–238.
Gibbs, Raymond W., Jr., Lima, Paula L. C., and Francuzo, Edson (2004). Metaphor is grounded in embodied experience. *Journal of Pragmatics*, *36*(7), 1189–1210.
Gibbs, Raymond W., Jr., and Lonergan, Julia E. (2009). Studying metaphor in discourse: Some lessons, challenges and new data. In Musolff & Zinken (eds.), 251–261.
Gibbs, Raymond W., Jr., and Matlock, Teenie (2008). Metaphor, imagination, and simulation: Psycholinguistic evidence. In Gibbs, Jr. (ed.), 161–176.
Gibbs, Raymond W., Jr., and O'Brien, Jennifer (1990). Idioms and mental imagery: The metaphorical motivation for idiomatic meaning. *Cognition*, *36*(1), 35–68.
Gibbs, Raymond W., Jr., and Santa Cruz, Malaika J. (2012). Temporal unfolding of conceptual metaphor experience. *Metaphor and Symbol*, *27*(4), 299–311.
Gibbs, Raymond W., Jr., and Steen, Gerard J. (eds.) (1999). *Metaphor in Cognitive Linguistics*. Amsterdam/Philadelphia: John Benjamins.
Gibbs, Raymond W., Jr., and Tendahl, Markus (2008). Complementary perspectives on metaphor: Cognitive linguistics and relevance theory. *Journal of Pragmatics*, *40*(11), 1823–1864.
Gibbs, Raymond W., Jr., and Van Orden, Guy (2012). Pragmatic choice in conversation. *Topics in Cognitive Science*, *4*(1), 7–20.

Gibson, James J. (1979). *The Ecological Approach to Visual Perception*. Boston, MA: Houghton Mifflin.

Giora, Rachel (1997). Understanding figurative and literal language: The graded salience hypothesis. *Cognitive Linguistics*, *8*(3), 183–206.

(2003). *On Our Mind: Salience, Context, and Figurative Language*. Oxford/New York: Oxford University Press.

(2008). Is metaphor unique? In Gibbs, Jr. (ed.), 143–160.

Glenberg, Arthur M. (1999). Why mental models need to be embodied. In Gert Rickheit and Christopher Habel (eds.), *Mental Models in Discourse Processing* (pp. 77–90). Amsterdam: Elsevier.

Glenberg, Arthur M., and Robertson, David (2000). Symbol grounding and meaning: A comparison of high dimensional and embodied theories of meaning. *Journal of Memory and Language*, *43*(3), 379–401.

Glucksberg, Sam (2001). *Understanding Figurative Language: From Metaphors to Idioms*. New York: Oxford University Press.

(2008). How metaphors create categories – quickly. In Gibbs (ed.), 67–83.

Glucksberg, Sam, Brown, Mary, and McGlone, Matthew S. (1993). Conceptual metaphors are not automatically accessed during idiom comprehension. *Memory & Cognition*, *21*(5), 711–719.

Glucksberg, Sam, Gildea, Patricia, and Bookin, Howard B. (1982). On understanding nonliteral speech: Can people ignore metaphors? *Journal of Verbal Learning and Verbal Behavior*, *21*(1), 85–98.

Glucksberg, Sam, and Keysar, Boaz (1990). Understanding metaphorical comparisons: Beyond similarity. *Psychological Review*, *97*, 3–18.

Glucksberg, Sam, Keysar, Boaz, and McGlone, Matthew S. (1992). Metaphor understanding and accessing conceptual schema: Reply to Gibbs (1992). *Psychological Review*, *99*(3), 578–581.

Glucksberg, Sam, McGlone, Matthew S., and Manfredi, Deanna (1997). Property attribution in metaphor comprehension. *Journal of Memory and Language*, *36*(1), 50–67.

Goatly, Andrew (1997). *The Language of Metaphors*. London/New York: Routledge.

Goldberg, Adele E. (1995). *Constructions: A Construction Grammar Approach to Argument Structure*. Chicago/London: The University of Chicago Press.

Gong, Shu-Ping, and Ahrens, Kathleen (2007). Processing conceptual metaphors in ongoing discourse. *Metaphor and Symbol*, *22*(4), 313–330.

Gonzalez-Marquez, Monica, Mittelberg, Irene, Coulson, Seana, and Spivey, Michael J. (eds.) (2007). *Methods in Cognitive Linguistics*. Amsterdam/Philadelphia: John Benjamins.

Goodman, Nelson [1955] (1983). *Fact, Fiction, and Forecast*. Cambridge, MA: Harvard University Press.

Goodwin, Charles (1981). *Conversational Organization: Interaction between Speakers and Hearers*. New York: Academic Press.

(2011a). Building action in public environments with diverse semiotic resources. *Versus: quaderni di studi semiotici* (112–113), 169–182. Special issue: *The External Mind: Perspectives on Semiosis, Distribution and Situation in Cognition*, ed. Riccardo Fusaroli, Tommaso Granelli & Claudio Paolucci.

(2011b). Contextures of action. In Jürgen Streeck, Charles Goodwin, and Curtis LeBaron (eds.), *Embodied Interaction: Language and Body in the Material World* (pp. 182–193). Cambridge/New York: Cambridge University Press.

Goossens, Louis (1990). Metaphtonymy: The interaction of metaphor and metonymy in expressions for linguistic actions. *Cognitive Linguistics*, *1*(3), 323–340.

Grady, Joseph E. (1997a). Foundations of meaning: Primary metaphors and primary scenes. Ph.D. dissertation, Department of Linguistics, University of California at Berkeley.

(1997b). THEORIES ARE BUILDINGS re-visited. *Cognitive Linguistics*, *8*(4), 267–290.

(1998). The "Conduit Metaphor" revisited: A reassessment of metaphors for communication. In Jean-Pierre Koenig (ed.), *Discourse and Cognition: Bridging the Gap* (pp. 205–218). Stanford, CA: CSLI Publications.

(1999). A typology of motivation for conceptual metaphor: Correlation vs. resemblance. In Gibbs, Jr. & Steen (eds.), 79–100.

(2005a). Image schemas and perception: Refining a definition. In Hampe (ed.), 35–56.

(2005b). Primary metaphors as inputs to conceptual integration. *Journal of Pragmatics*, *37*(10), 1595–1614.

(2008). "Superschemas" and the grammar of metaphorical mappings. In Andrea Tyler, Yiyoung Kim, and Mari Takada (eds.), *Language in the Context of Use: Discourse and Cognitive Approaches to Language* (pp. 339–360). Berlin/New York: Mouton de Gruyter.

Grady, Joseph E., and Johnson, Christopher (2002). Converging evidence for the notions of "subscene" and "primary scene." In Dirven & Pörings (eds.), 533–554.

Grady, Joseph E., Oakley, Todd, and Coulson, Seana (1999). Blending and Metaphor. In Gibbs, Jr. & Steen (eds.), 101–124.

Grady, Joseph E., Taub, Sarah, and Morgan, Pamela S. (1996). Primitive and compound metaphors. In Adele E. Goldberg (ed.), *Conceptual Structure, Discourse and Language* (pp. 17–187). Stanford, CA: CSLI Publications.

Grandhi, Sukeshini A., Joue, Gina, and Mittelberg, Irene (2011). Understanding naturalness and intuitiveness in gesture production: Insights for touchless gestural interfaces *Proceedings of the ACM's 2011 Conference on Human Factors in Computing Systems (CHI), Vancouver, BC* (pp. 821–824). New York: ACM Press.

(2012). To move or to remove? A human-centric approach to understanding of gesture interpretation *Proceedings of the 10th ACM Conference on Designing Interactive Systems (DIS)* (pp. 582–591). Newcastle/New York: ACM Press.

Graziano, Michael S., and Aflalo, Tyson N. (2007). Mapping behavioral repertoire onto the cortex. *Neuron*, *56*(2), 239–251.

Green, Melanie C. (2004). Transportation into narrative worlds: The role of prior knowledge and perceived realism. *Discourse Processes*, *38*(2), 247–266.

Guerra, Ernesto, and Knoeferle, Pia (2012). Abstract language comprehension is incrementally modulated by non-referential spatial information: Evidence from eye-tracking. In Laura Carlson, Christoph Hölscher, and Thomas F. Shipley (eds.), *Proceedings of the 33rd Annual Conference of the Cognitive Science Society* (pp. 1620–1625). Austin, TX: Cognitive Science Society.

Halliday, Michael A. K. (1985). *An Introduction to Functional Grammar*. London: Edward Arnold.

Hampe, Beate (ed.) (2005a). *From Perception to Meaning: Image Schemas in Cognitive Linguistics*. Berlin/New York: Mouton de Gruyter.

(2005b). Image schemas in cognitive linguistics: Introduction. In Hampe (ed.), 1–12.

(2005c). On the role of iconic motivation in conceptual metaphor: Has metaphor theory come full circle? In Constantino Maeder, Olga Fischer, and William J. Herlofsky (eds.), *Outside-In – Inside-Out* (pp. 39–66). Amsterdam/Philadelphia: John Benjamins.

(2005d). When *down* is not bad and *up* not good enough: A usage-based assessment of the plus-minus parameter in image-schema theory. *Cognitive Linguistics*, *16*(1), 81–112.

Hampes, William P. (1992). Relation between intimacy and humour. *Psychological Reports*, *71*(1), 127–130.

Hanks, Patrick (2006). Metaphoricity is gradable. In Stefanowitsch & Th. Gries (eds.), 17–35.

Hanne, Michael (2015). An introduction to the Warring with Words project. In Michael Hanne, William D. Crano, and Jeffery Scott Mio (eds.), *Warring with Words: Narrative and Metaphor in Politics* (pp. 1–50). New York: Psychology Press.

Hartley, Tom, Lever, Colin, Burgess, Neil, and O'Keefe, John (2014). Space in the brain: How the hippocampal formation supports spatial cognition. *Philosophical Transactions of the Royal Society B: Biological Sciences, 369*(1635), 20120510.

Hartmann, Matthias, Gashaj, Verena, Stahnke, Antje, and Mast, Fred W. (2014). There is more than "more is up": Hand and foot responses reverse the vertical association of number magnitudes. *Journal of Experimental Psychology: Human Perception and Performance*, *40*(4), 1401.

Haser, Verena (2005). *Metaphor, Metonymy, and Experientialist Philosophy: Challenging Cognitive Semantics*. Berlin/New York: Mouton de Gruyter.

Hauk, Olaf, Johnsrude, Ingrid, and Pulvermüller, Friedemann (2004). Somatotopic representation of action words in human motor and premotor cortex. *Neuron*, *41*(2), 301–307.

Heath, Robin, and Blonder, Lee X. (2003). Conversational humour among stroke survivors. *Humor – International Journal of Humor Research*, *16*(1), 91–106.

Hebb, Donald O. (1949). *The Organization of Behavior: A Neuropsychological Theory*. New York: Wiley.

Held, Richard, and Hein, Alan (1963). Movement-produced stimulation in the development of visually guided behavior. *Journal of Comparative and Physiological Psychology*, *56*(5), 872–876.

Holmes, Kevin J., and Lourenco, Stella F. (2011). Horizontal trumps vertical in the spatial organization of numerical magnitude. In Laura Carlson, Christoph Hölscher, and Thomas F. Shipley (eds.), *Proceedings of the 33rd Annual Conference of the Cognitive Science Society* (pp. 2276–2281). Austin, TX: Cognitive Science Society.

Hopper, Paul J., and Thompson, Sandra A. (1980). Transitivity in grammar and discourse. *Language*, *56*(2), 251–299.

Horst, Dorothea, Boll, Franziska, Schmitt, Christina, and Müller, Cornelia (2014). Gesture as interactive expressive movement: Inter-affectivity in face-to-face communication. In Müller, Cienki, Fricke, Ladewig, McNeill & Bressem (eds.), 2112–2124.

Horton, William S. (2007). Metaphor and readers' attributions of intimacy. *Memory & Cognition*, *35*(1), 87–94.
(2013). Character intimacy influences the processing of metaphoric utterances during narrative comprehension. *Metaphor and Symbol*, *28*(3), 148–166.
Hostetter, Autumn, and Alibali, Martha (2008). Visible embodiment: Gestures as simulated action. *Psychonomic Bulletin & Review*, *15*(3), 495–514.
Hunston, Susan (2013). *Corpus Approaches to Evaluation: Phraseology and Evaluative Language*. London/New York: Routledge.
Hutchins, Edwin (1995). *Cognition in the Wild*. Cambridge, MA: The MIT Press.
(2005). Material anchors for conceptual blends. *Journal of Pragmatics*, *37*(10), 1555–1577.
(2010). Cognitive ecology. *Topics in Cognitive Science*, *2*(4), 705–715.
Ibarretxe-Antuñano, Iraide (2013). The relationship between conceptual metaphor and culture. *Intercultural Pragmatics*, *10*(2), 315–339.
IJzerman, Hans, and Koole, Sander (2011). From perceptual rags to metaphoric riches: Bodily, social, and cultural constraints on socio-cognitive metaphors. *Psychological Bulletin*, *137*(2), 355–361.
IJzerman, Hans, and Semin, Gün R. (2009). The thermometer of social relations mapping social proximity on temperature. *Psychological Science*, *20*(10), 1214–1220.
Ito, Yashuhiro, and Hatta, Takeshi (2004). Spatial structure of quantitative representation of numbers: Evidence from the SNARC effect. *Memory & Cognition*, *32*(4), 662–673.
Jakobson, Roman (1956). Two aspects of language and two types of aphasic disturbances. In Monique Monville-Burston and Linda Waugh (eds.), *Roman Jakobson: On Language* (pp. 115–133). Cambridge, MA: Harvard University Press.
(1960). Linguistics and poetics. In Krystyna Pomorska and Stephen Rudy (eds.), *Roman Jakobson: Language in Literature* (pp. 62–94). Cambridge, MA: Harvard University Press.
Jarvilehto, Timo (2000). Feeling as knowing – Part I: Emotion as reorganization of the organism-environment system. *Consciousness & Emotion*, *1*(2), 245–257.
Jefferson, Gail (2004). *Glossary of Transcript Symbols with an Introduction*. Amsterdam/Philadelphia: John Benjamins.
Jefferson, Gail, Sacks, Harvey, and Schegloff, Emanuel (1987). Notes on laughter in the pursuit of intimacy. In Graham Button and John R. E. Lee (eds.), *Talk and Social Organisation* (pp. 152–205). Clevedon: Multilingual Matters.
Jensen, Thomas W. (2014). New perspectives on language, cognition, and values. *Journal of Multicultural Discourses*, *9*(1), 71–78.
Jensen, Thomas W., and Cuffari, Elena (2014). Doubleness in experience: Toward a distributed enactive approach to metaphoricity. *Metaphor and Symbol*, *29*(4), 278–297.
Johnson, Mark (1987). *The Body in the Mind: The Bodily Basis of Meaning, Imagination, and Reason*. Chicago/London: The University of Chicago Press.
(2005). The philosophical significance of image schemas. In Hampe (ed.), 15–33.
(2007). *The Meaning of the Body: Aesthetics of Human Understanding*. Chicago/London: The University of Chicago Press.
Jostmann, Nils B., Lakens, Daniel, and Schubert, Thomas W. (2009). Weight as an embodiment of importance. *Psychological Science*, *20*(9), 1169 –1174.

Kanold, Patrick O., Nelken, Israel, and Polley, Daniel B. (2014). Local versus global scales of organization in auditory cortex. *Trends in Neuroscience*, *37*(9), 502–510.
Kappelhoff, Hermann, and Greifenstein, Sarah (2015). Audiovisual metaphors: Embodied meaning and fictionalization. In Kathrin Fahlenbach (ed.), *Embodied Metaphors in Film, Television, and Video Games: Cognitive Approaches* (pp. 183–201). London/New York: Routledge.
Kappelhoff, Hermann, and Müller, Cornelia (2011). Embodied meaning construction: Multimodal metaphor and expressive movement in speech, gesture, and in feature film. *Metaphor and the Social Word*, *1*(2), 121–153.
Kaschak, Michael P., Jones, John L., Carranza, Julie, and Fox, Melissa R. (2014). Embodiment and language comprehension. In Shapiro (ed.), 118–126.
Katz, Albert N., Cacciari, Cristina, Gibbs, Raymond W., Jr., and Turner, Mark (eds.) (1998). *Figurative Language and Thought*. Oxford/New York: Oxford University Press.
Katz, Albert N., and Taylor, Tamsen E. (2008). The journeys of life: Examining a conceptual metaphor with semantic and episodic memory recall. *Metaphor and Symbol*, *2*(3), 148–173.
Keil, Frank C. (1979). *Semantic and Conceptual Development: An Ontological Perspective*. Cambridge, MA: Harvard University Press.
Kendon, Adam (2004). *Gesture: Visual Action as Utterance*. Cambridge/New York: Cambridge University Press.
Keysar, Boaz, Shen, Yeshayahu, Glucksberg, Sam, and Horton, William S. (2000). Conventional language: How metaphorical is it? *Journal of Memory and Language*, *43*(4), 576–593.
Kintsch, Walter (1998). *Comprehension: A Paradigm for Cognition*. Cambridge/ New York: Cambridge University Press.
(2008). How the mind computes the meaning of metaphor: A simulation based on LSA. In Gibbs, Jr. (ed.), 129–142.
Kirkham, Natasha Z., Slemmer, Jonathan A., and Johnson, Scott P. (2002). Visual statistical learning in infancy: Evidence for a domain general learning mechanism. *Cognition*, *83*(2), B35–B42.
Kirsh, David (1995). The intelligent use of space. *Artificial Intelligence*, *73*(1), 31–68.
Kohler, Evelyne, Keysars, Christian, Umilta, M. Alessandra, Forgassi, Leonardo, Gallese, Vittorio, Rizzolatti, Giacomo (2002). Hearing sounds, understanding actions: Action representation in mirror neurons. *Science*, *297*, 846–848.
Koller, Veronika (2008). Brothers in arms: Contradictory metaphors in contemporary marketing discourse. In Zanotto, Cameron & Cavalcanti (eds.), 103–127.
Kolter, Astrid, Ladewig, Silvia H., Summa, Michaela, Koch, Sabine, Müller, Cornelia, and Fuchs, Thomas (2012). Body memory and the emergence of metaphor in movement and speech: An interdisciplinary case study. In Sabine Koch, Thomas Fuchs, Michaela Summa, and Cornelia Müller (eds.), *Body Memory, Metaphor and Movement* (pp. 201–226). Amsterdam/Philadelphia: John Benjamins.
Kotthoff, Helga (2006). Pragmatics of performance and the analysis of conversational humor. *Humor – International Journal of Humor Research*, *19*(3), 271–304.
Kounios, John, and Beeman, Mark (2014). The cognitive neuroscience of insight. *Annual Review of Psychology*, *65*, 71–93.
Kövecses, Zoltán (2002). *Metaphor: A Practical Introduction* (2nd edn.). Oxford/New York: Oxford University Press.

(2005). *Metaphor in Culture: Universality and Variation*. Cambridge/New York: Cambridge University Press.
(2009). Metaphor, culture, and discourse: The pressure of coherence. In Musolff & Zinken (eds.), 11–24.
(2010a). Metaphor and culture. *Acta Universitatis Sapientiae, Philologica*, *2*(2), 197–220.
(2010b). *Metaphor: A Practical Introduction* (2nd edn.). Oxford: Oxford University Press.
(2013). The metaphor–metonymy relationship: Correlation metaphors are based on metonymy. *Metaphor and Symbol*, *28*(2), 75–88.
(2015). *Where Metaphors Come From: Reconsidering Context in Metaphor*. Oxford/New York: Oxford University Press.
Kövecses, Zoltán, and Radden, Günter (1998). Metonymy: Developing a cognitive linguistic view. *Cognitive Linguistics*, *9*(1), 37–77.
Kromhout, Roelf, and Forceville, Charles (2013). LIFE IS A JOURNEY: The source-path-goal schema in the videogames "Half-Life 2," "Heavy Rain," and "Grim Fandango." *Metaphor and the Social World*, *3*(1), 100–116.
Ladewig, Silvia H. (2011). Putting a recurrent gesture on a cognitive basis. *CogniTextes*, *6*, http://cognitextes.revues.org/406.
Lakoff, George (1987). *Woman, Fire, and Dangerous Things*. Chicago: The University of Chicago Press.
(1990). The Invariance Hypothesis: Is abstract reason based on image-schemas? *Cognitive Linguistics*, *1*(1), 39–74.
(1993). The contemporary theory of metaphor. In Ortony (ed.), 202–251.
(2008a). The neural theory of metaphor. In Gibbs, Jr. (ed.), 17–38.
(2008b). *The Political Mind*. New York: Penguin.
(2012). Explaining embodied cognition results. *Topics in Cognitive Science*, *4*(1), 1–13.
(2014). Mapping the brain's metaphor circuitry: Metaphorical thought in everyday reason. *Frontiers in Human Neuroscience*, *8*, 1–14.
Lakoff, George, and Johnson, Mark (1980). *Metaphors We Live By*. Chicago/London: The University of Chicago Press.
(1999). *Philosophy in the Flesh: The Embodied Mind and Its Challenge to Western Thought*. New York: Basic Books.
(2003). *Afterword*. In *Metaphors We live By* (pp. 243–276). Chicago/London: The University of Chicago Press.
Lakoff, George, and Núñez, Rafael (2000). *Where Mathematics Comes From: How the Embodied Mind Brings Mathematics Into Being*. New York: Basic Books.
Lakoff, George, and Turner, Mark (1989). *More than Cool Reason: A Field Guide to Poetic Metaphor*. Chicago/London: The University of Chicago Press.
Landau, Barbara, and Lakusta, Laura (2009). Spatial representation across species: Geometry, language, and maps. *Current Opinions in Neurobiology*, *19*(1), 12–19.
Landau, Mark J., Meier, Brian P., and Keefer, Lukas A. (2010). A metaphor-enriched social cognition. *Psychological Bulletin*, *136*(6), 1045–1067.
Landau, Mark J., Robinson, Michael D., and Meier, Brian P. (2014a). Introduction. In Landau, Robinson & Meier (eds.), 3–16.

Landau, Mark J., Robinson, Michael D., and Meier, Brian P. (eds.) (2014b). *The Power of Metaphor: Examining Its Influence on Social Life*. Washington, DC: American Psychological Association.

Landauer, Thomas K., and Dumais, Susan T. (1997). A solution to Plato's problem: The latent semantic analysis theory of acquisition induction, and representation of knowledge. *Psychological Review*, *104*(2), 211–240.

Langacker, Ronald W. (1987). *Foundations of Cognitive Grammar*. Vol. I: *Theoretical Prerequisites*. Stanford, CA: Stanford University Press.

(1991). *Foundations of Cognitive Grammar*. Vol. II: *Descriptive Application*. Stanford, CA: Stanford University Press.

(2000). A dynamic usage-based model. In Michael Barlow and Suzanne Kemmer (eds.), *Usage-Based Models of Language* (pp. 1–63). Stanford, CA: CSLI Publications.

(2008). *Cognitive Grammar: A Basic Introduction*. Oxford/New York: Oxford University Press.

Larsen-Freeman, Diane, and Cameron, Lynne (2008). *Complex Systems and Applied Linguistics*. Oxford/New York: Oxford University Press.

Lee, Spike W. S., and Schwarz, Norbert (2012). Bidirectionality, mediation, and moderation of metaphorical effects: The embodiment of social suspicion and fishy smells. *Journal of Personality and Social Psychology*, *103*(5), 737–749.

Levin, Magnus (2008). "Hitting the back of the net just before the final whistle": High-frequency phrase in football reporting. In Eva Lavric and Gerhard Pisek (eds.), *The Linguistics of Football* (pp. 143–155). Tübingen: Gunter Narr.

Linell, Per (2005). *The Written Language Bias in Linguistics: Its Nature, Origins, and Transformations*. New York: Routledge.

(2009). *Rethinking Language, Mind, and World Dialogically: Interactional and Contextual Theories of Human Sense-Making*. Charlotte, NC: Information Age Publications.

Littlemore, Jeannette (2015). *Metonymy: Hidden Shortcuts in Language, Thought and Communication*. Cambridge/New York: Cambridge University Press.

Littlemore, Jeannette, and Taylor, John R. (eds.) (2014), *The Bloomsbury Companion to Cognitive Lingustics*. London: Blooomsbury.

Loetscher, Tobias, Bockisch, Christopher, Nicholls, Michael E. R., and Brugger, Peter (2010). Eye position predicts what number you have in mind. *Current Biology*, *20*(6), R264–265.

Lourenco, Stella F., and Longo, Matthew R. (2011). Origins and the development of generalized magnitude representation. In Stanislas Dehaene and Elizabeth M. Brannon (eds.), *Space, Time, and Number in the Brain: Searching for the Foundations of Mathematical Thought* (pp. 225–244). London: Academic Press, Elsevier.

Low, Graham, Littlemore, Jeanette, and Koester, Almut (2008). The use of metaphor in three university lectures. *Applied Linguistics*, *29*(3), 428–455.

Lucas, Margery (2007). Semantic priming without association: A meta-analytic review. *Psychonomic Bulletin & Review*, *7*(4), 618–630.

Lupyan, Gary (2012). What do words do? Toward a theory of language-augmented thought. *The Psychology of Learning and Motivation*, *57*, 255–297.

Lupyan, Gary, Rakison, David H., and McClelland, James L. (2007). Language is not just for talking: Redundant labels facilitate learning of novel categories. *Psychological Science*, *18*(2), 1077–1083.

MacArthur, Fiona, and Oncins-Martínez, José Luis (2012). Introduction: Metaphor in use. In MacArthur, Oncins-Martínez, Sanchez-García & Piquer-Píriz (eds.), 1–17.

MacArthur, Fiona, Oncins-Martínez, José Luis, Sanchez-García, Manuel, and Piquer-Píriz, Ana María (eds.) (2012). *Metaphor in Use: Context, Culture, and Communication* (Vol. 38). Amsterdam/Philadelphia: John Benjamins.

Macnamara, Diana S., and Magliano, Joe (2009). Toward a comprehensive model of comprehension. *The Psychology of Learning and Motivation*, *51*, 297–384.

Mahlberg, Michaela (2013). *Corpus Stylistics and Dickens's Fiction*. London: Routledge.

Mandler, Jean, and Pagán Cánovas, Cristóbal (2014). On defining image schemas. *Language and Cognition*, *0*, 1–23.

Marghetis, Tyler (2015). Every number in its place: The spatial foundations of calculation and conceptualization. Ph.D. dissertation, University of California, San Diego.

Marghetis, Tyler, and Youngstrom, Kendall (2014). Pierced by the number-line: Integers are associated with back-to-front sagittal space. In Paul Bello, Marcello Guarini, Marjorie McShane, and Brian Scassellati (eds.), *Proceedings of the 36th Annual Conference of the Cognitive Science Society* (pp. 946–951). Austin, TX: Cognitive Science Society.

Martin, Rod A. (2007). *The Psychology of Humor: An Integrative Approach.* Burlington, MA/London: Elsevier Academic Press.

Martínez, María-Ángelez, Kraljevic Mujic, Blanca, and Hidalgo-Downing, Laura (2013). Multimodal narrativity in TV ads. In Barry Pennock-Speck and María M. del Saz-Rubio (eds.), *The Multimodal Analysis of Television Commercials* (pp. 91–111). València: PUV Universitat de València.

Mashal, Nira, Shen, Yeshayahu, Jospe, Karine, and Gil, David (2014). Language effects on the conceptualization of hybrids. *Language and Cognition*, *6*(2), 217–241.

Maslen, Robert (2017). Systematic metaphors. In Semino & Demjén (eds.), 88–101.

Matlock, Teenie (2004a). The conceptual motivation of fictive motion. In Günter Radden and René Dirven (eds.), *Motivation in Grammar*. Amsterdam/ Philadelphia: John Benjamins.

(2004b). Fictive motion as cognitive simulation. *Memory & Cognition*, *32*(8), 1389–1400.

(2010). Abstract motion is no longer abstract. *Language and Cognition*, *2*(2), 243–260.

Matlock, Teenie, Holmes, Kevin J., Srinivasan, Mahesh, and Ramscar, Michael (2011). Even abstract motion influences the understanding of time. *Metaphor and Symbol*, *26*(4), 260–271.

Matlock, Teenie, Ramscar, Michael, and Boroditsky, Lera (2005). The experiential link between spatial and temporal language. *Cognitive Science*, *29*(4), 655–664.

Matthews, Justin L., and Matlock, Teenie (2011). Understanding the link between spatial distance and social distance. *Social Psychology*, *42*(3), 185–192.

McCreaddie, May, and Wiggins, Sally (2008). The purpose and function of humour in health, health care and nursing: A narrative review. *Journal of Advanced Nursing*, *61*(6), 584–595.
McGlone, Matthew S. (1996). Conceptual metaphors and figurative language interpretation: Food for thought? *Journal of Memory and Language*, *35*(4), 544–565.
(2007). What is the explanatory value of a conceptual metaphor? *Language & Communication*, *27*(2), 109–126.
McGlone, Matthew S., and Harding, Jennifer (1998). Back (or forward?) to the future: The role of perspective in temporal language comprehension. *Journal of Experimental Psychology: Learning, Memory, & Cognition*, *24*(5), 1211–1223.
McNaughton, Bruce L., Barnes, Carol A., Gerrard, Jason L., Gothard, Katalin, Jung, Min W., Knierim, James J., et al. (1996). Deciphering the hippocampal polyglot: The hippocampus as a path integration system. *Journal of Experimental Biology*, *199*(1), 173–185.
McNeill, David (1992). *Hand and Mind: What Gestures Reveal about Thought*. Chicago/London: The University of Chicago Press.
(2005). *Gesture and Thought*. Chicago/London: The University of Chicago Press.
Meltzoff, Andrew N., and Moore, M. Keith (1977). Imitation of facial and manual gestures by human neonates. *Science*, *198*(4312), 75–78.
(1989). Imitation in newborn infants: Exploring the range of gestures imitated and the underlying mechanisms. *Developmental Psychology*, *25*(6), 954–962.
Merlau-Ponty, Maurice (1945). *Phénoménologie de la Perception*. Paris: Gallimard.
Merritt, Dustin J., Casasanto, Daniel, and Brannon, Elizabeth M. (2010). Do monkeys think in metaphors? Representations of space and time in monkeys and humans. *Cognition*, *117*(2), 191–202.
Miall, Chris, and Wolpert, Daniel (1996). Forward models for physiological motor control. *Neural Networks*, *9*, 1265–1279.
Michotte, Albert (1963). *The Perception of Causality*. New York: Basic Books.
Miller, John H., and Page, Scott E. (2007). *Complex Adaptive Systems: An Introduction to Computational Models of Social Life*. Princeton: Princeton University Press.
Mitchell, Derek G., and Greening, Steven G. (2012). Conscious perception of emotional stimuli: Brain mechanisms. *Neuroscientist*, *18*(4), 386–398.
Mittelberg, Irene (2006). *Metaphor and Metonymy in Language and Gesture: Discourse Evidence for Multimodal Models of Grammar*. Ann Arbor, MI: UMI.
(2008). Peircean semiotics meets conceptual metaphor: Iconic modes in gestural representations of grammar. In Alan Cienki and Cornelia Müller (eds.), *Metaphor and Gesture* (pp. 115–154). Amsterdam/Philadelphia: John Benjamins.
(2010). Geometric and image-schematic patterns in gesture space. In Vyvyan Evans and Paul Chilton (eds.), *Language, Cognition and Space: The State of the Art and New Directions* (pp. 351–385). London: Equinox.
(2013a). Balancing acts: Image schemas and force dynamics as experiential essence in pictures by Paul Klee and their gestural enactments. In Borkent, Dancygier & Hinnell (eds.), 325–346.

(2013b). The exbodied mind: Cognitive-semiotic principles as motivating forces in gesture. In Müller, Cienki, Fricke, Ladewig, McNeill & Tessendorf (eds.), 750–779.
(2014). Gestures and iconicity. In Müller, Cienki, Fricke, Ladewig, McNeill & Bressem (eds.), 1712–1732.
(2017). Embodied frames, metonymy and pragmatic inferencing in gesture. *Gesture*, *16*(2).
Mittelberg, Irene, and Waugh, Linda (2009). Metonymy first, metaphor second: A cognitive semiotic approach to multimodal figures of thought in co-speech gesture. In Forceville & Urios-Aparisi (eds.), 330–356.
(2014). Gestures and metonymy. In Müller, Cienki, Fricke, Ladewig, McNeill & Bressem (eds.), 1747–1766.
Müller, Cornelia (1998). *Redebegleitende Gesten: Kulturgeschichte – Theorie – Sprachvergleich*. Berlin: Spitz Verlag.
(2003). Gestik als Lebenszeichen 'toter Metaphern': Tote, schlafende und wache Metaphern. *Zeitschrift für Semiotik*, *1*(2), 61–72.
(2004). The Palm-Up-Open-Hand: A case of a gesture family? In Cornelia Müller and Roland Posner (eds.), *The Semantics and Pragmatics of Everyday Gestures* (pp. 233–256). Berlin: Weidler.
(2008a). *Metaphors Dead and Alive, Sleeping and Waking: A Dynamic View*. Chicago/London: The University of Chicago Press.
(2008b). What gestures reveal about the nature of metaphor. In Alan Cienki and Cornelia Müller (eds.), *Metaphor and Gesture* (pp. 219–245). Amsterdam/ Philadelphia: John Benjamins.
(2010). Wie Gesten bedeuten: Eine kognitiv-linguistische und sequenzanalytische Perspektive. *Sprache und Literatur*, *41*(1), 37–68.
(2011). Are "deliberate" metaphors really deliberate? A question of human consciousness and action. *Metaphor in the Social World*, *1*(1), 61–66.
(2014). Gestures as "deliberate expressive movement." In Mandana Seyfeddinipur and Marianne Gullberg (eds.), *From Gesture in Conversation to Visible Action as Utterance* (pp. 127–152). Amsterdam/Philadelphia: Benjamins.
Müller, Cornelia, and Cienki, Alan (2009). Metaphor, gestures, and beyond: Forms of multimodal metaphor in the use of spoken language. In Forceville & Urios-Aparisi (eds.), 293–321.
Müller, Cornelia, and Ladewig, Silvia H. (2013). Metaphors for sensorimotor experiences: Gestures as embodied and dynamic conceptualizations of balance in dance lessons. In Borkent, Dancygier & Hinnell (eds.), 295–324.
Müller, Cornelia, and Schmitt, Christina (2015). Audio-visual metaphors of the financial crisis: Meaning making and the flow of experience. *Revista Brasileira de Linguistica Aplicada (RBLA), Belo Horizonte*, *15*(2), 311–341.
Müller, Cornelia, and Tag, Susanne (2010). The dynamics of metaphor: Foregrounding and activating metaphoricity in conversational interaction. *Cognitive Semiotics*, *10*(6), 85–120.
Müller, Cornelia, Cienki, Alan, Fricke, Ellen, Ladewig, Silvia H., McNeill, David, and Bressem, Jana (eds.) (2014). *Handbook: Body – Language – Communication: An International Handbook on Multimodality in Human Interaction* (Vol. 2). Berlin/ Boston: de Gruyter Mouton.

Müller, Cornelia, Cienki, Alan, Fricke, Ellen, Ladewig, Silvia H., McNeill, David, and Tessendorf, Sedinha (eds.) (2013). *Body – Language – Communication: An International Handbook on Multimodality in Human Interaction* (Vol. 1). Berlin/ Boston: de Gruyter Mouton.
Müller, Dana, and Schwarz, Wolf (2007). Is there an internal association of numbers to hands? The task set influences the nature of the SNARC effect. *Memory & Cognition*, *35*(5), 1151–1161.
Murphy, Gregory L. (1996). On metaphoric representation. *Cognition*, *60*(2), 173–204.
Musolff, Andreas (2000). Political imagery of Europe: A house without exit doors? *Journal of Multilingual and Multicultural Development*, *21*(3), 216–229.
(2004). *Metaphor and Political Discourse: Analogical Reasoning in Debates about Europe*. Basingstoke/New York: Macmillan.
(2006). Metaphor scenarios in public discourse. *Metaphor and Symbol*, *21*(1), 23–38.
(2007). Popular science concepts and their use in creative metaphors in media discourse. *metaphorik.de*, *13*, 67–86.
Musolff, Andreas, and Zinken, Jörg (eds.) (2009). *Metaphor and Discourse*. Basingstoke/New York: Palgrave Macmillan.
Nayak, Nandini, and Gibbs, Raymond W., Jr. (1990). Conceptual knowledge in the interpretation of idioms. *Journal of Experimental Psychology*, *119*(3), 315–330.
Nieder, Andreas (2005). Counting on neurons: The neurobiology of numerical competence. *Nature Reviews Neuroscience*, *6*(3), 177–190.
Noë, Alva (2004). *Action in Perception*. Cambridge, MA/London: The MIT Press.
(2009). *Out of Our Heads: Why You Are Not Your Brain, and Other Lessons from the Biology of Consciousness*. New York: Hill and Wang.
Norrick, Neal R. (2003). Issues in conversational joking. *Journal of Pragmatics*, *35*(9), 1333–1359.
(2010). *Conversational Narrative: Storytelling in Everyday Talk*. Amsterdam/ Philadelphia: John Benjamins.
Núñez, Rafael, Motz, Benjamin, and Teuscher, Ursina (2006). Time after time: The psychological reality of the ego- and time-reference-point distinction in metaphorical contruals of time. *Metaphor and Symbol*, *21*(3), 133–146.
Ortiz, Maria J. (2011). Primary metaphors and monomodal visual metaphors. *Journal of Pragmatics*, *43*, 1568–1580.
Ortony, Andrew (1979). Beyond literal similarity. *Psychological Review*, *86*(3), 161–180.
(ed.) [1979] (1993). *Metaphor and Thought* (2nd edn.). Cambridge/New York: Cambridge University Press.
Ortony, Andrew, Vondruska, Richard J., Foss, Mark A., and Jones, Lawrence (1985). Salience, similes, and the asymmetry of similarity. *Journal of memory and language*, *24*(5), 569–594.
Ouellet, Mark, Santiago, Julio, Israeli, Ziv, and Gabay, Shai (2010). Is the future the right time? *Experimental Psychology*, *57*, 308–314.
Panther, Klaus-Uwe, and Thornburg, Linda (2003). *Metonymy and Pragmatic Inferencing*. Amsterdam/Philadelphia: John Benjamins.
(2012). Antonymy in language structure and use. In Mario Brdar, Ida Raffaelli, and Milena Žic Fuchs (eds.), *Cognitive Linguistics between Universality and Variation* (pp. 161–188). Newcastle-upon-Tyne: Cambridge Scholars Publishing.

Panther, Klaus-Uwe, Thornburg, Linda, and Barcelona, Antonio (eds.) (2009). *Metonymy and Metaphor in Grammar*. Amsterdam/Philadelphia: John Benjamins.

Parise, Cesare V., Knorre, Katharina, and Ernst, Marc O. (2014). Natural auditory scene statistics shapes human spatial hearing. *Proceedings of the National Academy of Sciences*, *111*(16), 6104–6108.

Parrill, Fey, and Sweetser, Eve E. (2004). What we mean by meaning: *Conceptual integration in gesture analysis and transcription.* Gesture, *4*(2), 197–219.

Pashler, Harold, Coburn, Noriko, and Harris, Christine R. (2012). Priming of social distance? Failure to replicate effects on social and food judgments. *Public Library of Science ONE*, *7*(8), e42510.

Pauen, Michael (2012). The second person perspective. *Inquiry*, *55*(1), 33–49.

Paxton, Alexandra, and Dale, Rick (2013). Arguments disrupt interpersonal synchrony. *Quarterly Journal of Experimental Psychology*, *66*(11), 2092–2102.

Pecher, Diane, and Zwaan, Rolf A. (eds.) (2005). *Grounding Cognition: The Role of Perception and Action in Memory, Language, and Thinking*. Cambridge/New York: Cambridge University Press.

Peña, Sandra (2008). Dependency systems for image-schematic patterns in a usage-based approach to language. *Journal of Pragmatics*, *40*(6), 1041–1066.

Peña, Sandra, and Ruiz de Mendoza Ibañez, Francisco (2009). Metonymic and metaphoric bases of two image-schema transformations. In Panther, Thornburg & Barcelona (eds.), 339–361.

Petty, Richard E., and Cacioppo, John T. (1981). *Attitudes and Persuasion: Classic and Contemporary Approaches*. Dubuque, IA: W. C. Brown Co.

Pfaff, Kerry, Gibbs, Raymond W., Jr., and Johnson, Michael (1997). Metaphor in using and understanding euphemism and dysphemism. *Applied Psycholinguistics*, *18*, 59–83.

Piaget, Jean (1967). *Biologie et connaissance: Essai sur les relations entre les régulations organiques et les processus cognitifs*. Paris: Gallimard.

Ping, Raedy, Dhillon, Sonica, and Beilock, Sian Leah (2009). Reach for what you like: The body's role in shaping preferences. *Emotion Review*, *1*(2), 140–150.

Piquer-Píriz, Ana María (2005). Young EFL learners' understanding of some semantic extensions of the lexemes "hand," "mouth" and "head." Ph.D. dissertation, University of Extremadura, Spain.

Pragglejaz-Group (2007). MIP: A method for identifying metaphorically used words in discourse. *Metaphor and Symbol*, *22*(1), 1–39.

Pratt, Carol C. (1930). The spatial character of high and low tones. *Journal of Experimental Psychology*, *13*(3), 278–285.

Prestin, Abby, and Chou, Wen-ying Sylvia (2014). Web 2.0 and the changing health communication environment. In Heidi E. Hamilton and Wen-ying Silvia Chou (eds.), *The Routledge Handbook of Language and Health Communication* (pp. 184–197). Abingdon/New York: Routledge.

Quinn, Naomi (1992). The cultural basis of metaphor. In J. Fernandes (ed.), *Beyond Metaphor: The Theory of Tropes in Anthropology* (pp. 56–93). Stanford, CA: Stanford University Press.

Radden, Günter (2000). How metonymic are metaphors? In Barcelona (ed.), 93–108.

Radden, Günter, and Kövecses, Zoltán (1999). Towards a theory of metonymy. In Klaus-Uwe Panther and Gunter Radden (eds.), *Metonymy in Language and Thought* (pp. 17–59). Amsterdam/Philadelphia: John Benjamins.

Rakova, Marina (2003). *The Extent of the Literal: Metaphor, Polysemy, and Theories of Concepts*. New York: Palgrave Macmillan.
Read, Stephen, Cesa, Ian, Jones, David, and Collins, Nancy (1990). When is the federal budget like a baby? Metaphor in political rhetoric. *Metaphor and Symbol*, *5*(3), 125–149.
Rennig, Johannes, Bilali'c, Merim, Huberle, Elisabeth, Karnath, Hans-Otto, and Himmelbach, Marc (2013). The temporo-parietal junction contributes to global gestalt perception: Evidence from studies in chess experts. *Frontiers in Human Neuroscience*, *7*(513), 1–11.
Riceur, Paul (1986). *Die lebendige Metapher*. Munich: Wilhelm Fink.
Richardson, Michael J., and Chemero, Anthony (2014). Complex dynamical systems and embodiment. In Shapiro (ed.), 39–50.
Ritchie, L. David (2003). Categories and similarities: A note on circularity. *Metaphor and Symbol*, *18*(1), 49–53.
(2006). *Context and Connection in Metaphor*. Basingstoke/New York: Palgrave Macmillan.
(2008a). Gateshead revisited: Perceptual simulators and fields of meaning in the analysis of metaphors. *Metaphor and Symbol*, *23*(1), 24–49.
(2008b). X is a journey: Embodied simulation in metaphor interpretation. *Metaphor and Symbol*, *23*(3), 174–199.
(2009). Relevance and simulation in metaphor. *Metaphor and Symbol*, *24*(4), 249–262.
(2010a). Between mind and language: "A journey worth taking." In Cameron & Maslen (eds.), 57–94.
(2010b). "Everybody goes down": Metaphors, stories, and simulations in conversations. *Metaphor and Symbol*, *25*(3), 123–143.
(2011). "*Justice is blind*": A model for analyzing metaphor transformations and narratives in actual discourse. *Metaphor and the Social World*, *1*(1), 70–89.
(2013). *Metaphor*. Cambridge/New York: Cambridge University Press.
(2017). *Metaphorical Stories in Discourse*. Cambridge/New York: Cambridge University Press.
Rizzolatti, Giacomo, Sinigaglia, Corrado, and Anderson, Frances (2008). *Mirrors in the Brain: How Our Minds Share Actions and Emotions*. Oxford: Oxford University Press.
Robin, Shani, and Mayer, Richard (2000). The metaphor framing effect: Metaphorical reasoning about text-based dilemmas. *Discourse Processes*, *30*(1), 57–86.
Robinson, Peter, and Ellis, Nick C. (eds.) (2008). *Handbook of Cognitive Linguistics and Second Language Acquisition*. Mahwah, NJ: Lawrence Erlbaum.
Roffler, Suzanne K., and Butler, Robert A. (1968). Localization of tonal stimuli in the vertical plane. *Journal of the Acoustical Society of America*, *43*(6), 1260–1265.
Rohrer, Tim (2007). Embodiment and experientialism. In Cuyckens & Geeraerts (eds.), 25–47.
Rosca, Andrea (2012). *Bases for the Development of Ontological Semantics within the Conceptual Domains of Change and Possession: Implementations and Implications for the Lexico-Syntactic-Cognition Interface and the Development of Intelligent Agents*. La Rioja, Spain: University of La Rioja.

Ruiz de Mendoza Ibañez, Francisco J. (2011). Metonymy and cognitive operations. In Reka Benczes, Antonio Barcelona, and Francisco Ruiz de Mendoza Ibañez (eds.), *Defining Metonymy in Cognitive Linguistics: Towards a Consensus View* (pp. 103–123). Amsterdam/Philadelphia: John Benjamins.

(2014). On the nature and scope of metonymy in linguistic description and explanation: Towards settling some controversies. In Littlemore & Taylor (eds.), 143–166.

Ruiz de Mendoza Ibañez, Francisco J., and Diez Velasco, Olga (2002). Patterns of conceptual interaction. In Dirven & Pörings (eds.), 489–532.

Ruiz de Mendoza Ibañez, Francisco, and Galera, Alicia (2014). *Cognitive Modeling: A Linguistic Perspective*. Amsterdam/Philadelphia: John Benjamins.

Ruiz de Mendoza Ibáñez, Francisco J., and Pérez Hernández, Lorena (2011). The contemporary theory of metaphor: Myths, developments and challenges. *Metaphor and Symbol*, *26*(3), 161–185.

Rundblad, Gabriela, and Annaz, Dagmara (2010). Metaphor and metonymy comprehension: Receptive vocabulary and conceptual knowledge. *British Journal of Developmental Psychology*, *28*(3), 547–563.

Saffran, Jenny R., Aslin, Richard N., and Newport, Elissa L. (1996). Statistical learning by 8-month-old infants. *Science*, *274*, 1926–1928.

Saffran, Jenny R., Johnson, E. K., Aslin, Richard N., and Newport, Elissa L. (1999). Statistical learning of tone sequences by human infants and adults. *Cognition*, *70*, 27–52.

Santiago, Julio, Lupiáñez, Juan, Pérez, Elvira, and Funes, María Jesús (2007). Time (also) flies from left to right. *Psychonomic Bulletin & Review*, *14*(3), 512–516.

Santiago, Julio, Ouellet, Mark, Román, Antonio, and Valenzuela, Javier (2012). Attentional factors in conceptual congruency. *Cognitive Science*, *36*(6), 1051–1077.

Schank, Roger C., and Berman, Tamara R. (2002). The pervasive role of stories in knowledge and action. In Melanie C. Green, Jeffrey J. Strange, and Timothy C. Brock (eds.), *Narrative Impact: Social and Cognitive Foundations* (pp. 287–314). Mahwah, NJ: Lawrence Erlbaum.

Schelling, Thomas (1971). Dynamic models of segregation. *Journal of Mathematical Sociology*, *1*(2), 143–186.

Schnall, Simone (2014). Are there basic metaphors? In Landau, Robinson & Meier (eds.), 225–248.

Schneider, Iris K., Rutjens, Bastiaan T., Jostmann, Nils B., and Lakens, Daniel (2011). Weighty matters: Importance literally feels heavy. *Social Psychological and Personality Science*, *2*(5), 474–478.

Schön, Donald A. ([1979] 1993). Generative metaphor: A perspective on problem solving in social policy. In Ortony (ed.), 137–163.

Schubert, Thomas W., Waldzus, Sven, and Seibt, Beate (2008). The embodiment of power and communalism in space and bodily contact. In Semin & Smith (eds.), 160–183.

Semin, Gün R., and Cacioppo, John T. (2008). Grounding social cognition: Synchronization, coordination, and co-regulation. In Semin & Smith (eds.), 119–147.

Semin, Gün R., and Smith, Eliot R. (eds.) (2008). *Embodied Grounding: Social, Cognitive, Affective, and Neuroscientific Approaches*. Cambridge/New York: Cambridge University Press.

Semino, Elena (2006). A corpus-based study of metaphors for speech activity in British English. In Stefanowitsch & Th. Gries (eds.), 36–62.

(2008). *Metaphor in Discourse*. Cambridge/New York: Cambridge University Press.
(2010). Descriptions of pain, metaphor, and embodied simulation. *Metaphor and Symbol, 25*(4), 205–226.
Semino, Elena, Deignan, Alice, and Littlemore, Jeannette (2013). Metaphor, genre, and recontextualization. *Metaphor and Symbol, 28*(1), 41–59.
Semino, Elena, and Demjén, Zsófia (eds.) (2017). *The Routledge Handbook of Metaphor and Language*. Abingdon: Routledge.
Shapiro, Lawrence (ed.) (2014). *The Routledge Handbook of Embodied Cognition*. Abingdon/New York: Routledge.
Shayan, Shakila, Ozturk, Ozge, and Sicoli, Mark A. (2011). The thickness of pitch: Crossmodal metaphors in Farsi, Turkish, and Zapotec. *The Senses and Society, 6*(1), 96–105.
Sheets-Johnstone, Maxine (1999). *The Primacy of Movement*. Amsterdam/ Philadelphia: John Benjamins.
Shen, Yeshayahu (2008). Metaphor and poetic figures. In Gibbs, Jr. (ed.), 295–307.
Shen, Yeshayahu, and Gil, David, (2017). How language influences the way we categorize hybrids. In Henri Cohen and Claire Lefebvre (eds.), *Handbook of Categorization in Cognitive Science* (2nd edn.) (pp. 580–601). Amsterdam: Elsevier.
Shipp, Stewart (2004). The brain circuitry of attention. *Trends in Cognitive Science, 8*(5), 223–230.
Silver, Michael A., and Kastner, Sabine (2009). Topographic maps in human frontal and parietal cortex. *Trends in Cognitive Science, 13*(11), 488–495.
Siquera, Maity, and Gibbs, Raymond W., Jr. (2007). Children's acquisition of primary metaphors: A cross-linguistic study. *Organon, 21*(43), 161–179.
Slobin, Dan I. (1985). Crosslinguistic evidence for the language-making capacity. In Slobin (ed.), *The Crosslinguistic Study of Language Acquisition*. Vol. II: *Theoretical Issues* (pp. 1157–1256). Hillsdale, NJ: Lawrence Erlbaum.
(1996). From "thought and language" to "thinking for speaking." In John J. Gumperz and Stephen C. Levinson (eds.), *Rethinking Linguistic Relativity* (pp. 70–96). Cambridge/New York: Cambridge University Press.
Snaevarr, Stefan (2010). *Metaphors, Narratives, Emotions: Their Interplay and Impact*. Amsterdam: Rodopi.
Soliman, Tamer, and Glenberg, Arthur M. (2014). The embodiment of culture. In Shapiro (ed.), 207–219.
Sparkes, Andrew C., and Smith, Brett (2005). When narratives matter: Men, sport and spinal injury. *Journal of Medical Ethics: Medical Humanities, 31*(2), 81–88.
Sperber, Dan, and Wilson, Deirdre (1995). *Relevance Theory* (2nd edn.). Oxford: Blackwell.
Spivey, Michael J. (2007). *The Continuity of Mind*. Oxford/New York: Oxford University Press.
Srinivasan, Mahesh, and Carey, Susan (2010). The long and the short of it: On the nature and origin of functional overlap between representations of space and time. *Cognition, 116*(2), 217–241.
Stanfield, Robert A., and Zwaan, Rolf A. (2001). The effect of implied orientation derived from verbal context on picture recognition. *Psychological Science, 12*(2), 153–156.
Steen, Gerard J. (2008). The paradox of metaphor: Why we need a three-dimensional model of metaphor. *Metaphor and Symbol, 23*(4), 213–241.

(2011a). The contemporary theory of metaphor – now new and improved! *Review of Cognitive Linguistics*, *9*(1), 26–64.

(2011b). From three dimensions to five steps: The value of deliberate metaphor. *metaphorik.de 21*, 83–110.

(2011c). Issues in collecting converging evidence: Is metaphor always a matter of thought? In Doris Schönefeld (ed.), *Converging Evidence: Methodological and Theoretical Issues for Linguistic Research* (pp. 33–55). Amsterdam/Philadelphia: John Benjamins.

(2011d). What does "really deliberate" really mean? More thoughts on metaphor and consciousness. *Metaphor and the Social World*, *1*(1), 53–56.

(2013). Deliberate metaphor affords conscious metaphorical thought. *Cognitive Semiotics*, *5*(1–2), 179–197.

(2015). Developing, testing and interpreting Deliberate Metaphor Theory. *Journal of Pragmatics*, *90*, 67–72.

Stefanowitsch, Anatol (2004). HAPPINESS in English and German: A metaphorical-pattern analysis. In Michel Archard and Suzanne Kemmer (eds.), *Language, Culture, and Mind* (pp. 137–149). Stanford; CA: CSLI Publications.

(2006). Words and their metaphors: A Corpus-based approach. In Stefanowitsch & Th. Gries (eds.), 63–106.

Stefanowitsch, Anatol, and Gries, Stefan Th. (eds.) (2006). *Corpus-Based Approaches to Metaphor and Metonymy*. Berlin/New York: Mouton de Gruyter.

Steffensen, Sune V. (2013). Human interactivity: Problem-solving, solution-probing and verbal patterns in the wild. In Stephen J. Cowley and Frédéric Vallée-Tourangeau (eds.), *Cognition beyond the Brain: Computation, Interactivity and Human Artifice* (pp. 195–221). London: Springer.

(2015). Distributed language and dialogism: Notes on non-locality, sense-making and interactivity. *Language Sciences*, *50*, 105–119.

Stephens, Greg, Gilbert, Lauren, and Hasson, Uri (2010). Speaker-listener neural coupling underlies successful communication. *PNAS: Proceedings of the National Academy of Sciences of the United States*, *107*, 144425–144430.

Steward, John R., Gapenne, Oliver, and Di Paolo, Ezequiel A. (2010). *Enaction: Toward a New Paradigm for Cognitive Science*. Cambridge, MA: The MIT Press.

Stibbe, Astrid (1996). *Metaphor and Alternative Conceptions of Illness*. Lancaster: Lancaster University.

Straube, Benjamin, Green, Antonia, Bromberger, Bianca, and Kircher, Tilo (2011). The differentiation of iconic and metaphoric gestures: Common and unique integration processes. *Human Brain Mapping*, *32*(4), 520–533.

Streeck, Jürgen (1993). Gesture as communication I: Its coordination with gaze and speech. *Communication Monographs*, *60*(4), 275–299.

(2008). Laborious intersubjectivity: Attentional struggle and embodied communication in an auto-shop. In Ipke Wachsmuth, Manuela Lenzen, and Günther Knoblich (eds.), *Embodied Communication in Humans and Machines* (pp. 202–228). Oxford/New York: Oxford University Press.

(2009). *Gesturecraft: The Manu-Facture of Meaning*. Amsterdam/Philadelphia: John Benjamins.

Streeck, Jürgen, Goodwin, Charles, and LeBaron, Curtis (2011). *Embodied Interaction: Language and Body in the Material World*. Cambridge/New York: Cambridge University Press.

Stubbs, Michael (2003). Two quantitative methods of studying phraseology in English. *International Journal of Corpus Linguistics*, *7*(2), 215–244.

Sullivan, Karen S. (2007). *Grammar in Metaphor: A Construction Grammar Account of Metaphoric Language*. Berkeley, CA: University of California at Berkeley.

(2013). *Frames and Constructions in Metaphoric Language*. Amsterdam/ Philadelphia: John Benjamins.

Swales, John (1990). *Genre Analysis*. Cambridge/New York: Cambridge University Press.

Sweetser, Eve E. (1990). *From Etymology to Pragmatics: Metaphorical and Cultural Aspects of Semantic Structure*. Cambridge/New York: Cambridge University Press.

(1998). *Regular Metaphoricity in Gesture: Bodily-Based Models of Speech Interaction*. In *Actes du 16e Congrès International des Linguistes* (CD-ROM). Oxford: Elsevier.

(2007). Looking at space to study mental spaces: Co-speech gesture as a crucial data source in cognitive linguistics. In Gonzalez-Marquez, Mittelberg, Coulson & Spivey (eds.), 201–224.

Talmy, Leonard (1988). Force dynamics in language and cognition. *Cognitive Science*, *12*, 49–100.

(2000). *Toward a Cognitive Semantics*. Vol. I: *Concept Structuring System*. Cambridge, MA: The MIT Press.

Taub, Sarah (2001). *Language from the Body: Iconicity and Metaphor in American Sign Language*. Cambridge/New York: Cambridge University Press.

Theiner, Georg (2014). Varieties of group cognition. In Shapiro (ed.), 347–358.

Thibault, Paul (2011). First-order languaging dynamics and second-order language: The distributed language view. *Ecological Psychology*, *23*(3), 210–245.

Tiemersma, Douwe (1989). *Body Schema and Body Image: An Interdisciplinary and Philosophical Study*. Amsterdam: Swets & Zeitlinger.

Turner, Mark, and Fauconnier, Gilles (2009). Conceptual integration and formal expression. *Metaphor and Symbol*, *10*(3), 183–204.

Tversky, Barbara (2011). Visualizing thought. *Topics in Cognitive Science*, *3*(3), 499–535.

Tversky, Barbara, Kugelmass, Sol, and Winter, Atalia (1991). Cross-cultural and developmental trends in graphic productions. *Cognitive Psychology*, *23*(4), 515–557.

Urena, José Manuel, and Faber, Pamela (2010). Reviewing imagery in resemblance and non-resemblance metaphors. *Cognitive Linguistics*, *21*(1), 123–149.

Van Dijk, Teun A., and Kintsch, Walter (1983). *Strategies of Discourse Comprehension*. New York: Academic Press.

Walker, Esther, and Cooperrider, Kensy (2015). The continuity of metaphor: Evidence from temporal gestures. *Cognitive Science*, *40*(2), 481–495.

Walker, Peter, Bremner, J. Gavin, Mason, Uschi, Spring, Jo, Mattock, Karen, Slater, Alan, et al. (2010). Preverbal infants' sensitivity to synaesthetic cross-modality correspondences. *Psychological Science*, *21*(1), 21–25.

Wang, Xiaoqin, Merzenich, Michael M., Sameshima, Koichi, and Jenkins, William M. (1995). Remodelling of hand representation in adult cortex determined by timing of tactile stimulation. *Nature*, *378*, 71–75.

Waterworth, John A., Lund, Andreas, and Modjeska, David (2003). Experiential Design of Shared Information Spaces. In Alan Munro, Kristina Höök, and David Benyon (eds.), *Designing Information Spaces: The Social Navigation Approach* (pp. 125–150). London: Springer.

Watson, Wilfred (1986). *Classical Hebrew Poetry: A Guide to Its Techniques* (2nd edn.). Sheffield: JSOT Press.

Wertheimer, Max (1938). Laws of organization in perceptual forms In W. D. Ellis (ed.), *A Source Book of Gestalt Psychology* (pp. 71–88). New York: Harcourt Brace.

Whorf, Benjamin L. (1956). *Language, Thought, and Reality: Selected Writings of Benjamin Lee Whorf*. Ed. John B. Carroll. Cambridge, MA: The MIT Press.

Williams, Lawrence E., and Bargh, John A. (2008a). Experiencing physical warmth promotes interpersonal warmth. *Science*, *322*, 606–607.

(2008b). Keeping one's distance: The influence of spatial distance cues on affect and evaluation. *Psychological Science*, *19*(3), 302–308.

Williams, Lawrence E., Huang, Julie Y., and Bargh, John A. (2009). The scaffolded mind: Higher mental processes are grounded in early experience of the physical world. *European Journal of Social Psychology*, *39*(7), 1257–1267.

Wilson, Deirdre, and Carston, Robyn (2006). Metaphor, relevance and the "emergent property" issue. *Mind & Language*, *21*(3), 404–433.

Wilson, Deirdre, and Sperber, Dan (2012). Explaining irony. In Deirdre Wilson and Dan Sperber (eds.), *Meaning and Relevance* (pp. 123–145). Cambridge/New York: Cambridge University Press.

Wilson, Nicole L., and Gibbs, Raymond W., Jr. (2007). Real and imagined body movement primes metaphor comprehension. *Cognitive Science*, *31*(4), 721–731.

Winawer, Jonathan, Witthoft, Nathan, Frank, Michael C., Wu, Lisa, Wade, Alex R., Boroditsky, Lera (2007). Russian blues reveal effects of language on color discrimination. *Proceedings of the National Academy of Sciences*, *104*(19), 7780–7785.

Winner, Ellen (1988). *The Point of Words: Children's Understanding of Metaphor and Irony*. Cambridge, MA: Harvard University Press.

Winter, Bodo (2014). Horror movies and the cognitive ecology of primary metaphors. *Metaphor and Symbol*, *29*(3), 151–170.

Winter, Bodo, and Bergen, Benjamin (2012). Language comprehenders represent object distance both visually and auditorily. *Language and Cognition*, *4*(1), 1–16.

Winter, Bodo, and Matlock, Teenie (2013). More is up ... and right: Random number generation along two axes. In M. Knauff, M. Pauen, N. Sebanz, and I. Wachsmuth (eds.), *Proceedings of the 35th Annual Conference of the Cognitive Science Society* (pp. 3789–3974). Austin, TX: Cognitive Science Society.

Winter, Bodo, Matlock, Teenie, Shaki, Samuel, and Fischer, Martin H. (2015). Mental number space in three dimensions. *Neuroscience and Biobehavioral Reviews*, *57*, 209–219.

Winter, Bodo, Perlman, Markus, and Matlock, Teenie (2013). Using space and gesture to talk about numbers: Evidence from the TV News Archive. *Gesture*, *13*, 377–408.

Wiseman, Rob (2014). Social distance in hunter-gather settlement sites: A conceptual metaphor in material culture. *Metaphor and Symbol*, *29*(2), 129–143.

Wolff, Philip, and Gentner, Dedre (2011). Structure-mapping in metaphor comprehension. *Cognitive Science*, *35*(8), 1456–1488.

Wolff, Philip, and Holmes, Kevin J. (2011). Linguistic relativity. *Wiley Interdisciplinary Reviews: Cognitive Science*, *2*(3), 253–265.

Yu, Ning (2003). The bodily dimension of meaning in Chinese: What do we do and mean with "hands." In Eugene H. Casad and Gerry B. Palmer (eds.), *Cognitive*

Linguistics and Non-Indo-European Languages (pp. 337–362). Berlin/New York: Mouton de Gruyter.
(2008). Metaphor from body and culture. In Gibbs, Jr. (ed.), 247–261.
(2009). Nonverbal and multimodal manifestations of metaphors and metonymies: A case study. In Forceville & Urios-Aparisi (eds.), 119–146.
Yus, Francisco (2011). *Cyberpragmatics: Internet-Mediated Communication in Context.* Amsterdam/Philadelphia: John Benjamins.
Zaborszky, Laszlo (2002). The modular organization of brain systems. Basal forebrain: The last frontier. *Progress in Brain Research, 136*, 359–372.
Zanotto, Mara Sophia, Cameron, Lynne, and Cavalcanti, Marilda C. (eds.) (2008). *Confronting Metaphor in Use: An Applied-Linguistic Approach.* Amsterdam/ Philadelphia: John Benjamins.
Zhang, Jiajie, and Patel, Vimla (2006). Distributed cognition, representation, and affordance. *Pragmatics & Cognition, 14*(2), 333–341.
Zhong, Chen-Bo, and Leonardelli, Geoffrey J. (2008). Cold and lonely: Does social exclusion literally feel cold? *Psychological Science, 19*(9), 838–842.
Zhong, Chen-Bo, and Liljenquist, Katie (2006). Washing away your sins: Threatened morality and physical cleansing. *Science, 313*, 1451–1452.
Ziem, Alexander (2014). *Frames of Understanding in Text and Discourse.* Amsterdam/ Philadelphia: John Benjamins.
Zinken, Jörg (2007). Discourse metaphors: The link between figurative language and habitual analogies. *Cognitive Linguistics, 18*(3), 445–466.
Zinken, Jörg, Hellsten, Iina, and Nerlich, Brigitte (2008). Discourse metaphors. In Roslyn M. Frank, René Dirven, Tom Ziemke, and Enrique Bernárdez (eds.), *Body, Language, and Mind.* Vol. II: *Sociocultural Situatedness* (pp. 363–385). Berlin/ New York: Mouton de Gruyter.
Zinken, Jörg, and Musolff, Andreas (2009). A discourse-centred perspective on metaphorical meaning and understanding. In Musolff & Zinken (eds.), 1–8.
Zlatev, Jordan (2005). What's in a schema? Bodily mimesis and the grounding of language. In Hampe (ed.), 313–342.
Zwaan, Rolf A. (2014). Embodiment and language comprehension: Reframing the discussion. *Trends in Cognitive Science, 18*(5), 229–234.
(2016). Situation models, mental simulations, and abstract concepts in discourse comprehension. *Psychonomic Bulletin & Review, 23*(4), 1028–1034.
Zwaan, Rolf A., and Madden, Carol J. (2005). Embodied sentence comprehension. In Pecher & Zwaan (eds.), 224–245.
Zwaan, Rolf A., Taylor, Lawrence J., and de Boer, Mirte (2010). Motor resonance as a function of narrative time: Further tests of the linguistic focus hypothesis. *Brain & Language, 112*(3), 143–149.

Person Index

Subject Index